GORDON

The Man Behind the Legend

John Pollock

A LION BOOK

First published by **Constable and Company Limited**
This paperback edition published by
Lion Publishing plc
Sandy Lane West, Oxford, England
ISBN 0 7459 2698 3
Albatross Books Pty Ltd .
PO Box 320, Sutherland, NSW 2232, Australia
ISBN 0 7324 1286 2

10 9 8 7 6 5 4 3 2 1 0

A catalogue record for this book is available
from the British Library

Printed and bound in Great Britain
by Cox & Wyman Ltd, Reading

To
The Corps of Royal Engineers

and for
Mary Hammond Raitt

Contents

Part Three: THE PILLAR OF CLOUD, 1880–1883

Part Four: TOO LATE, 1884–1885

Acknowledgements

This book is based mainly on the great deposit of Gordon's letters and related material in the Manuscript Department of the British Library. I am most grateful to the joint copyright holders, Mr David Gordon and Mr John Bell for their generous permission to quote freely from this and other deposits of Gordon letters in public archives or private possession. I would like also to thank the officials of the British Library, especially Mrs Kathryn Johnson, Dr Frances Wood and Mr J. Conway for their courtesy and guidance.

I wish to acknowledge the gracious permission of Her Majesty the Queen to quote from the Journal of Queen Victoria and other manuscripts in the Royal Archives. I am grateful to Mr Oliver Everett, C.V.O., Librarian at Windsor Castle and Assistant Keeper of the Royal Archives, and Lady de Bellaigue, M.V.O., the Registrar, and her staff for their kindness which made research delightful.

I am very grateful to members of the Gordon family for their encouragement and loan of papers and photographs, especially Miss Elizabeth Blunt, Gordon's great-niece and her mother, the late Mrs Gordon Blunt; Mrs Henry Blunt; and Mrs Sonia Donaldson.

My greatest debt of gratitude is to Miss Mary H. Raitt of Washington, D.C. When I had nearly completed the main research in the British Library, Public Record Office, etc., Elizabeth Blunt introduced me to Mary Raitt and her sister Mildred. In 1969–70 Mary Raitt had researched Gordon very fully, accumulating photostats and microfilms of many letters and documents and contemporary printed sources, many books and photographs. All this she most generously gave me. Her collection includes photostats of more than a hundred of Gordon's letters to his great friend Charles Harvey which were then in private hands and later dispersed by sale.

There is also correspondence with experts no longer living.

What is more, Miss Raitt very kindly volunteered to be honorary research assistant in the Library of Congress and elsewhere, greatly enriching my book. All I have written is of course my own responsibility alone but I am deeply grateful to Miss Raitt. The entire research material, Miss Raitt's and my own, has been given to the Archives of the Royal Engineers at Chatham.

The Royal Engineers have been wonderfully helpful, and I especially thank Colonel G. W. A. Napier, formerly Secretary of the Institution of Royal Engineers and Director of the Museum, and Colonel J. E. Nowers, his successor; Miss Caroline Reed, Archivist, Major J. T. Hancock, Librarian, and Mrs M. Magnuson, Assistant Librarian. I would like to thank General Sir Hugh Beach, G.B.E., K.C.B., M.C., grandson of the Army chaplain who was so kind to the young Gordon in China; Brigadier W. I. C. Dobbie, Colonel G. R. Owens, C.B.E. and Colonel J. R. de G. Pilkington, O.B.E.

I am very grateful to Mr Anthony Larkin, secretary of the Gravesend Historical Society, and Mr Edward Williams, who showed me round and provided me with helpful material and gave me great encouragement.

For help in translating documents I thank Baroness Anna-Carla Taxis, Mr and Mrs Michael Muir-Brown, Miss Mary H. Raitt, and Mr Bruce Taylor with Mr David Morgan and Mr Matthew Doat. For advice concerning Gordon's medical history I am grateful to Lord Richardson, L.V.O., F.R.C.P., and on his theological ideas to the Reverend Dr Alister McGrath.

And a special word of thanks to Mrs J. E. Williams of Bideford, North Devon, who once again has skilfully typed my often messy manuscript. We have now worked together on seventeen books.

I thank the following people and institutions for permission to use copyright material and for help in research: General Sir Victor FitzGeorge-Balfour, K.C.B., C.B.E., D.S.O., M.C. (Journal of the Duke of Cambridge) and Lady FitzGeorge Balfour; Birmingham University Library (CMS Papers) and Miss C. L. Penney, Archivist; the Bodleian Library, Oxford; Boston, Mass., Public Library (Barnes, Jenkins and other Papers); Mr John Brinton (Olangier Papers); Cambridge University Library; Cape Town University (Miss Botha, Head Archivist, Mrs Meyer and Mrs Van Rynvest); the Earl of Derby (Diaries of 15th Earl) and Liverpool Record Office; Duke University, Manuscript Department of Williams R. Perkins Library (Ms Linda McCurdy, Assistant Curator); Durham University, Sudan Archive (Brocklehurst Papers, Wingate MSS, Stewart Journal, and other items, with thanks to Mrs Jane Hogan, Sudan Archivist, and to Miss Judith Prendergast who very kindly loaned me her manuscript of Colonel Hammill-Stewart's Journal; East Sussex, Hove Reference Library (Wolseley Papers) and Mrs M. Foley; Viscount Esher (Esher Papers) and Churchill College, Cambridge; Exeter University, Centre for Arab Studies; the Garden Tomb Association (Cowell Papers) and the Rev. N. L. White; Gordon School, Woking, (Mr Edward Firth, Headmaster); Mrs Edward Macken (Freese Papers) and Mr John N. Ross and Mr Connally Ross; Jardine Matheson and Co. (Parkes Papers) and Mr Allan Reid, Honorary Archivist; National Army Museum (Graham and Nugent Papers, and general advice); the National Library of Scotland (Elliot, Grant and Mackinnon Papers); the National Library of Wales; Overseas Missionary Fellowship and Dr A. J. Broomhall; the Public Record Office (Cromer Papers, Foreign Office Papers); the Public Record Office of Northern Ireland (Dufferin Papers, McKean Papers); Queen's University, Belfast (Hart Diaries); the Royal Geographical Society and Mrs C. Kelly, Archivist; Rhodes House, Oxford (Waller Papers) and Mr Allan Lodge, Assistant Librarian; Royal Botanic Gardens, Kew, and Mr L. E. Thompson, Assistant Librarian; St Antony's Oxford, Middle East Centre; the Marquess of Salisbury (Papers of 3rd Marquess) and Mr R. H. Harcourt-Williams, Librarian and Archivist at Hatfield; Mrs Brigette Spiro of New York, who very kindly gave me photostats of her collection of Gordon and related letters; Trinity College, Parkeville, Victoria (Rusden Papers); University of Texas at Austin (Scarth Papers); the Verona Fathers (Comboni Papers); West Sussex Record Office (Wilfred Blunt Papers); Williams College, Williamstown, Mass. (Birkbeck Hill Papers).

Many others have helped in one way or another, and I give warm thanks to: Lieutenant-Colonel G. P. Badham; Baring Brothers and Dr M. J. Orbell, Archivist; Mrs George Bell; Mr David Brown; Charterhouse School Library and Mrs Ann Wheeler, Librarian; Lord Cubbold; Miss M. G. L. Cranage and Miss C. Vines; Mr J. Davy, Lord Elton, Major Charles Enderby; Mr Peter Everington; Dr Noble Frankland, C.B., C.B.E., D.F.C.; Patrick Gordon-Duff-Pennington, M.B.E., and Mrs June Jones; Gravesend Public Library; Mr Robert Heasman of the Shaftesbury Society; the late Mr R. Joscelyne and Mr A. O. Blishen, O.B.E., the Rev. Prebendary Captain R. C. Lucas, Hon. Mrs Ian Macpherson; the Nova Scotia Manuscripts Archivist, Mr J. B. Cahill, Mrs E. B. Maund; Mr James Lees-Milnes; the National Register of Archives; Mr Martin Pollock; Mr Michael Robbins,

C.B.E.; Captain John Sedgwick, Lance-Sergeant L. Pearce and the Archives of the Coldstream Guards; the Somerset County Archivist (Mr Robin Bush); Southampton Public Libraries; Major-General Timothy Streatfeild, C.B.; Mr B. M. Thompson, proprietor of Gordon House, Heavitree, Exeter; Colonel John Walker; Dr Joanna Waley-Cohen; the Wellcome Institute for the History of Medicine; Mr Harry Welchman.

Finally, a special word of thanks to my publisher Mr Benjamin Glazebrook for his advice and help, and his patience, and to his team.

JOHN POLLOCK
Rose Ash,
Devonshire

Note on
Chinese and Arabic Names

The manuscript and printed sources of Gordon's time show no consistency in the transliteration of Chinese characters into Western script. I have therefore edited names to conform to postal use adopted in the later 19th century (*e.g.* Peking, not Pekin; Shanghai, not Shanghae). I have not used the recently adopted Pinyin forms (*e.g.* Beijing for Peking) as they tend to confuse Western readers.

For Arabic, I have used the form familiar in the West for famous names (*e.g.* Tel-el-Kebir; Ismail). For others I have tried to follow Richard Hill's *A Biographical Dictionary of the Sudan* (2nd edition, 1967) except for accents. With so much variety of transliteration in the sources I must confess to inconsistency which Arabic speakers will forgive. Zubair Pasha is spelt in three or four different ways in the manuscript letters and printed works of the period.

The word *and* is generally shown by a squiggle by Gordon and others writing at speed. I have usually spelt it out since the conventional printer's sign does not look like the squiggle and disrupts rather than eases the flow.

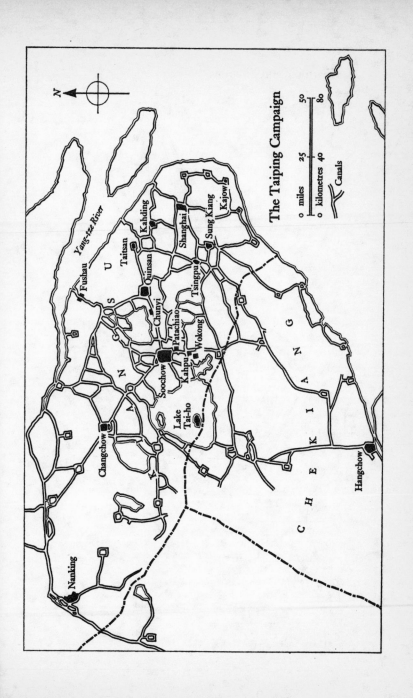

The Taiping Campaign

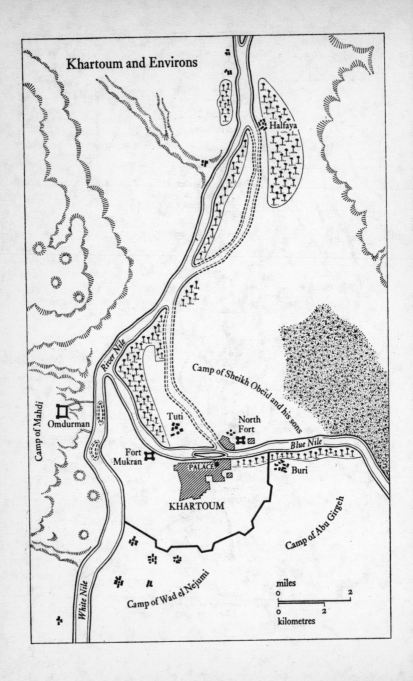

Khartoum and Environs

Halfaya

River Nile

Camp of Sheikh Obeid and his sons

Camp of Mahdi

Omdurman

Tuti

North Fort

Blue Nile

Fort Mukran

PALACE

Buri

KHARTOUM

Camp of Abu Girgeh

White Nile

Camp of Wad el Nejumi

miles
0   2

0   2
kilometres

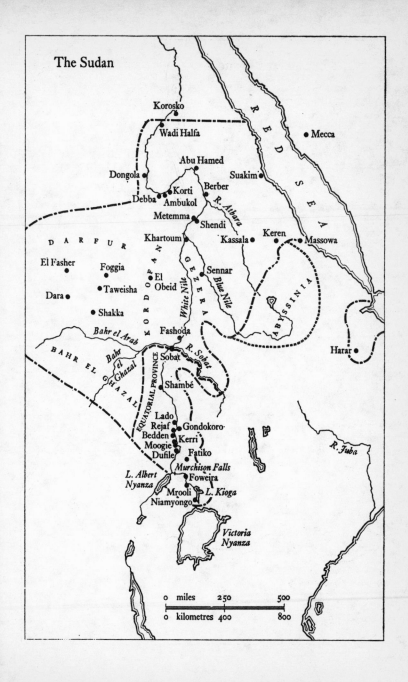

Prologue: 'Too Late'

About seven-thirty on the morning of Wednesday 28 January 1885 the armed paddle-steamer *Bordein* passed below a steep hill on the west bank of the Nile without needing to fire her guns.

Crammed with Sudanese and Egyptian soldiers and sailors, and ten men of the Sussex Regiment in guardsmen's tunics to proclaim that the British were coming, she was racing upriver to reach Khartoum before it fell to the Mahdi's armies. Behind her, with more Sudanese and another ten Sussex men, steamed her slightly longer sister ship the *Tel el Howein*. They were no larger than Thames pleasure boats or 'penny steamers.'

As the hill and an empty village fell astern Colonel Sir Charles Wilson, standing in the *Bordein's* armoured turret, lifted his field telescope. He could see in the far distance the buildings of Khartoum beyond the palm trees of Tuti island. Since 12 March, 322 days before, his friend and brother officer of the Royal Engineers, Charlie Gordon ('Chinese' Gordon to the world) had been besieged. At first the Liberal Government in England had refused to recognize his danger. When Gladstone had at last agreed to a relief expedition General Wolseley's cautious strategy caused further delays. Gordon held on. Cut off from the outside world except for occasional spies, he became the most famous person on earth as the public in all countries waited and hoped and prayed, knowing that most of his garrison and the cosmopolitan population would be put to the sword if Khartoum fell.

Sir Charles Wilson had never expected to lead the rescue. One officer more senior had been killed in the great battle at the wells of Abu Klea as the relief column crossed the desert, cutting across a great loop of the Nile; another senior officer lay fatally wounded. Wilson, an expert in survey and intelligence who had never commanded in a campaign, had delayed four days after reaching Gordon's steamers at Gubat; Wilson had good tactical

1

reasons but could be blamed for not risking a dash against all the odds when he had read Gordon's warning, in a letter dated five weeks earlier, that unless the expeditionary force arrived in ten days 'the town may fall.'

Gordon still held out when Wilson had started at last on 24 January. The steamers' four day race up the Nile had been slowed by mishaps. Wilson knew he could not raise the siege; like Havelock at Lucknow he could only bring supplies, more gun power, and the moral support which would enable the garrison to hold on until the main relief arrived. By this morning of 28 January, Gordon's fifty-second birthday, Wilson was within ten miles of success.

On the *Tel el Howein* Captain Edward Stuart-Wortley of the 60th was trying to attract Gordon's attention by flashing the heliograph. Then a Sudanese on the shore, of the friendly Shaggiah tribe, shouted to the men on the steamer that Khartoum had fallen two days before and Gordon was dead. They refused to believe it. Soon the *Bordein* came under heavy fire from both banks of the Nile, and Wilson's black riflemen and gunners fired back: the gunners, naked except for loin cloths, looked to Wilson 'more like demons than men in the thick smoke: and one huge giant was the very incarnation of savagery drunk with war.'[1]

The *Bordein* emerged unscathed into wider waters and now Wilson could see Gordon's Palace in the distance, its flat roof higher than surrounding buildings. Old Khashm el Mus, Gordon's friend and ally, the Melik or chief of the Shaggiahs, who was squatting below the parapet, urged Wilson to turn his telescope on the Palace flag pole. Wilson could see no flag. Khashm became anxious, saying that Gordon always kept the Egyptian flag flying: the place must be in the Mahdi's hands. Wilson would not believe it: 'at any rate we could not stop now until we were certain all was over.'

By the time they reached the sandspit at the junction of the two Niles, which gave Khartoum its name, 'Elephant's trunk,' the intense gun fire and rifle fire, and the hordes of the Mahdi's men waiting under their banners to oppose a landing, left no doubt. Wilson wrote later to Sir Henry Gordon, who never blamed him, 'It was a cruel disappointment to reach Khartoum on your brother's birthday and find I was too late. I went on as far as I could to the S. W. corner of Tuti Island: we were then under a cross fire of artillery from Omdurman and Tuti and I felt that if we turned the corner we should never have got back – I do not know how we escaped for the "penny steamers" as your brother calls them in his Journal had for nearly 4 miles to run the gauntlet of mountain guns, Krupps, Mitrailleuses and rifles.'[2]

When both steamers had begun their escape the black soldiers collapsed in grief, not only for their homes and families in Khartoum but even more for Gordon. In the words of Stuart-Wortley: 'They threw themselves down and sobbed ... They said, "We have lost our families, our properties and everything belonging to us, that is the fortune of war: but Gordon is dead, by the will of God, all is finished," and they gave themselves up to despondency and it was all we could do to get them to even manage the steamers.' Stuart-Wortley saw 'the spontaneous outburst of grief on the part of the black troops as the greatest proof of the extraordinary affection in which General Gordon was held by those who had experienced, and had learnt to value his great qualities.'[3]

At 7 pm one week later, on 4 February, General Lord Wolseley, with his limp and his glass eye and other scars of war, was going to dinner in the base camp of the Relief Expedition at Korti on the Nile, 280 miles from Khartoum, when two letters, one enclosing the other, were brought to him from Gubat across the desert: 'I was certainly knocked out of tune by the dreadful intelligence that *Khartoum* was taken by Mahdi's troops on 26 January and that Gordon's fate was uncertain but he was said to have been killed. I earnestly pray he may have been killed,' he wrote in his Journal, 'for to him death was always looked forward to as the beginning of a glorious and new life, whereas captivity would have been unbearable.'[4]

They had been friends since the Crimean trenches. Wolseley's persuasions had sent Gordon back to the Sudan; and Wolseley had begged for a relief expedition long before Gladstone saw the need.

'At one time I could almost feel Charlie Gordon's hand in mine: his relief seemed almost humanly speaking a certainty,' Wolseley told Sir Henry later;[5] and he described the 'sorrow and rage' of the troops at the news of the Fall: 'Sorrow for the gallant soul we had striven with might and main to save and rage at the Minister whose folly had prevented the effort to reach Khartoum from being undertaken earlier.

'Well, he is gone from amongst us and I shall never know his like again. Indeed many generations may come and go without producing a Charlie Gordon. His example will be one that fathers will hold up to their sons in England, and as long as any faith in God remains to us as a Nation, and that we continue to be manly enough to revere the highest form of courage and devotion to duty, so long will your brother be quoted and referred to as the

3

human embodiment of all manly and Christian virtues . . . I never knew but two heroes; one has been dead many years, and your brother was the other.'[6]

That same night, early in the small hours of 5 February 1885 in London, a clerk in the War Office in Pall Mall began to decipher a long telegram from Wolseley; and sent the first sentences at once to waken the Permanent Secretary, who immediately took a cab to Tilney Street in Mayfair and knocked up Reginald Brett, M.P., Private Secretary to the Secretary of State for War, the Marquess of Hartington. Gordon had been frequently at Tilney Street: Brett, as he dressed, could recall the last visit, when Gordon had walked up and down discussing the Sudan, cradling the infant Brett son and heir in his arms.

Brett jumped into the cab and they trotted through the ill-lit empty streets to collect the whole wire and then to Number Ten Downing Street. 'The blackest day since the horrible Phoenix Park murders*,' wrote the Prime Minister's Private Secretary, Edward Hamilton, in his Diary. 'The news of the fall of Khartoum was brought to me by R. Brett at 2.30 this morning while I was peacefully sleeping.'[7]

Gladstone was in the North. He and Hartington were staying with Lord Hartington's father, the Duke of Devonshire, at Holker Hall in Cartmel, south of the Lake District. 'After 11 am I heard the sad news of the fall or betrayal of Khartoum,' wrote Gladstone in his Diary. 'The circumstances are sad and trying: it is one of the least points about them, that they may put an end to this Govt.'[8] The Gladstones and Hartington left for London by the first train.

At Osborne House in the Isle of Wight Queen Victoria woke to 'a fine morning, my cold somewhat better. Dreadful news after breakfast. Khartoum fallen, Gordon's fate uncertain! All greatly distressed. Sent for Sir H. Ponsonby, who was horrified. It is too fearful. The Govt is alone to blame, by refusing to send the expedition till it was too late.'[9] She then despatched her famous telegrams *en clair* to Gladstone, Hartington and the Foreign Secretary, Lord Granville: 'These news from Khartoum are frightful, and to think that all this might have been prevented and many precious lives saved by earlier action is too frightful.'[10] The Queen's displeasure was read by several telegraphists as they forwarded the wires from place to place.

*On 6 May 1882 Lord Frederick Cavendish, Chief Secretary of Ireland, and his Under-Secretary T. H. Burke, were knifed to death by Fenians (Irish Republicans) as they walked in Phoenix Park.

Across the Solent, at 5 Rockstone Place, Southampton, Gordon's sister Augusta, eleven years the older but his closest friend and correspondent, opened a telegram at about 11 am from W. T. Stead, editor of the London evening paper, *Pall Mall Gazette*. He gave her the bad news, not yet public, to spare her the shock of placards or shouting newsboys. One year before, Stead had sat in her drawing room interviewing Gordon as the man who knew more about the Sudan than any other Englishman. The published interview and Stead's leading article had helped to force the Government's hand.

A few minutes later the parlour-maid brought another wire from Stead, and soon yet another, as Stead sent Augusta every fresh rumour, meaning to be kind: but when she read, 'Have just heard authentic news Mahdi informed Sir Charles Wilson that your brother is alive wearing Mahdi's uniform,'[11] she knew it must be false: Charlie would never convert to Islam.

At 1.41 pm a telegram reached Southampton from General Sir John Cowell, Gordon's brother officer in the Royal Engineers and fellow-enthusiast for the Holy Land, who was Comptroller of the Royal Household: 'I am on my way with my wife to see you from the Queen.'[12]

Back in London the Commander-in-Chief, H.R.H. the Duke of Cambridge, the Queen's first cousin, had heard 'the overwhelming news' immediately after breakfast. Early in the afternoon the placards of the first evening editions were all over London. 'It has produced a profound impression and is certainly a most overwhelming blow to the honour and interests of this country,' the Duke wrote in his Journal.[13] Cambridge could remember Gordon as a child, had sometimes been annoyed by him as a man yet admired him; and Gordon had written to a fellow general a few months before: 'After such a lot of insubordinate behaviour I feel H.R.H. was exceedingly kind. He has always had my earnest prayers.'[14]

The Duke worked at the War Office all day on fresh plans for the crisis, then called on his mother at St. James's Palace. The Duchess and her lady in waiting, Lady Geraldine Somerset, had already seen the placards on their afternoon drive. 'Dark day of deep tribulation!' wrote Lady Geraldine in her Journal. 'One of the darkest, in *shame* and pain, of all England's history ... Tea 6¼, 6½ came the Duke! As distressed and depressed as was to be expected!'[15]

As the Duke wrote next day, 'Nothing can equal the intense interest and excitement raised by this grave event since the period of the Crimean War and the Indian Mutiny.'[16] The Cabinet met for three hours and authorized

Wolseley to release Gordon if still alive or 'to smash up the Mahdi should he have fallen.'[17] The suspense made strangers stop in the street to ask each other for news. Wolseley still could not telegraph any certainties; and as General Sir Gerald Graham, V.C., one of Gordon's closest friends, who had been with him on the Nile for the first part of his journey to Khartoum, wrote to Sir Henry Gordon: 'I do not lose faith in your brother's wonderful resource and power over his followers even in the face of this terrible news. He may yet be holding out in the citadel or be a prisoner in the Mahdi's hands.'[18]

All Europe was anxious, wrote another friend of Sir Henry's, 'for if there be one man especially revered of all ages and conditions, that man is your heroic brother, when so much is dark around us, it is refreshing to discover one gleam of light – universal respect and affection for a noble saint-like soldier.'[19]

At last, on 10 February, Wolseley wired his conviction that Gordon was dead. Gladstone was due to dine with Lord Dalhousie, followed by a play at the Criterion theatre. 'I told Mr G in the morning it was foolish,' wrote Edward Hamilton, 'and I ought to have written to Lady Dalhousie to give up the idea of the theatre under the circumstances, but it was thought it would fuss Mr G.'[20] Mr G. found *The Candidate* 'capitally acted'; but in Hamilton's words 'the gloom and rage of London knows no bounds' for Britain had gone into unofficial mourning of extraordinary intensity: long obituaries and leading articles, memorial services at Westminster Abbey and in churches all over the country, plans drawn up for the national memorial which became the Gordon Home for Boys. The Princesses and Peeresses of Britain sent Augusta an address of condolence; town councils and organizations of every kind passed resolutions of condolence and admiration, while in Gravesend, although fourteen years had passed since Gordon had lived there, a journalist found that 'he has left, especially among the poor, so passionate a clinging to his memory, that his loss is to them a reality which cannot be observed without sharing the pain.'[21]

Tributes poured in to the family. 'My admiration for your brother was unbounded,' wrote Major Herbert Kitchener, the future field marshal who was to avenge Gordon's death and bring nearly sixty years of peace to the Sudan, 'and the regret unceasing that more could not have been done for him.'[22]

'I knew him well,' wrote General Sir John Stokes, the Royal Engineers' chief at the War Office, 'and appreciated at their full value his constant and exalted Faith, his noble courage, his single minded devotion to duty – his unfailing unselfishness and open-handed generosity. His was a Nature too grand for this sordid prosaic generation. He was worthy to rank with the best and bravest of Elizabeth's heros (*sic*). The whole Corps, the whole of England, aye the whole civilized world mourn for him – a victim to indecision and half heartedness.'[23]

'Could he,' asked another Sapper, his grief for a close friend spilling into purple prose, 'have left behind him a more glorious memory – a larger example for our small selfish age? – or a better ringing record of great sacrifice and chivalry for the Christian and Mahomedan world that have heard the sweet song of his life – from the basso booming of cannon and drums of his large brave deeds to the treble sweetness of his kindly nature to children and weak women and those who were in distress, but I am very sad ... '[24]

Thus the first legend was born, of the Bayard '*sans peur et sans reproche*,' built up by sermons and books. And as W. T. Stead wrote to Augusta on the last day of 1885, 'Your brother's death has done more to make Christ real to people than if he had civilized a hundred Congos and smashed a thousand Mahdis.'[25]

Lord Cromer, whom Gordon knew as Sir Evelyn Baring, British Agent and Consul General in Egypt, deleted from the printed version of his memoirs (1908) a comment which highlights both Gordon and his age: 'During this stage of national hysteria,' he wrote, any critic of Gordon 'would have been regarded with a dislike somewhat akin to that which is felt for any one who is heard talking flippantly in public of the truths of the Christian religion.'[26]

Cromer did not know Gordon well. They had quarrelled in Cairo in 1878 over the finances of Egypt, which Gordon wished to reform for the benefit of the Egyptians and Sudanese while Baring, as was his duty, put first the demands of England and other debtors. Five years later, after Baring had agreed reluctantly to Gordon's mission, they were together again in Cairo for three days, and in touch by telegraph for a further seven weeks before the line was cut.

The Fall of Khartoum was Cromer's one failure. As the years passed he transferred his bitterness from the Liberal Cabinet of 1884–5 which had

7

included a cousin and several friends, to Gordon himself. The young Winston Churchill in 1900 found Cromer 'very bitter' about Gordon 'and begged me not to pander to the popular belief on the subject. Of course there is no doubt that Gordon as a political figure was absolutely hopeless. He was so erratic, capricious, utterly unreliable, his mood changed so often, his temper was abominable, he was frequently drunk, and yet with all he had a tremendous sense of honour and great abilities, and a still greater obstinacy.'[27]

Cromer spread the rumour privately that Gordon drank. It reached Lieut-Colonel Louis Gordon, Sir Henry's son, in India. Concerned and puzzled, for he had known his uncle well and proudly displayed the 'magic wand' of 'Chinese Gordon's' victories, he wrote to Cromer. The reply is lost but it set Louis Gordon's mind at rest. Nevertheless Cromer wrote to Lord Knutsford in 1912: 'that Gordon was mad or semi-mad there is not the smallest doubt; also there is not in reality the least doubt that he drank deeply.'[28]

In 1918 Lytton Strachey published in *Eminent Victorians*, his brilliant though flawed essay on Gordon. Surviving relatives and brother officers were outraged by what they considered a barely recognizable literary caricature; yet despite later scholarly biographies, using some of the family papers, Strachey's tarnished Gordon remains lodged in the public mind. Authors, film producers, radio and television programme makers have tended to exaggerate a few facets of Gordon's character or build up an interpretation based on selective use of the printed versions of his vast correspondence, often taken out of context and supported by fiction. Thus the second legend replaced the first.

The real Gordon can now be recovered.

In 1963 his nephew Colonel Frederick Moffitt left to the British Museum the huge collection of Gordon's letters to his sister Augusta and the papers he had put in her care. Later that year two descendants of Sir Henry Gordon, the late Mrs Rose Bell and Mr David Gordon, gave the Museum Sir Henry's equally large collection of manuscript material, including much private and official correspondence. The Moffitt and Bell collections total forty-five volumes. Together with manuscripts already in the Museum a great deposit of Gordon Papers, running to many thousands of items and many millions of words became available in what is now the British Library.

This has been consulted or part-researched by some biographers and ignored by others. The present book may fairly claim to be the first to research the entire collection. I have also used many other collections in Britain, Ireland and America, including some which are now dispersed.

The result, I contend, is a fresh and believable story of a highly original man. The true Gordon has been smothered by layers of interpretation and assessment: I therefore tell the story straight, in the context of the times, leaving the reader to form his or her conclusions.

Gordon's relatives had long formed theirs. 'I think,' wrote his niece Margaret in 1885, 'everyone who ever saw Uncle Charlie loved him and when he talked to you, you could feel how much he loved God and was looking out for an opportunity to serve him.'[29]

PART ONE

YELLOW JACKET

1833–1864

CHAPTER ONE

The Powder Keg

Lieutenant-Colonel Henry William Gordon, Royal Artillery, felt he was 'sitting on a powder barrel' when his three youngest sons, William, Charlie and Freddie were home for the holidays at Woolwich.

As Charlie wrote laughingly many years later from the Sudan, to a nineteen year old niece whose own childhood had been at Woolwich among numerous brothers and sisters: 'You never, any of you, made a proper use of the Arsenal workmen, as we did. They used to neglect their work for our orders, and turned out some splendid squirts, articles which could wet you through in a moment.

'As for the cross bows, they were grand with screws; one Sunday afternoon 27 panes of glass in those large stores were found to have been perforated with a small hole (ventilation), and Capt. Loady nearly escaped a premature death, a screw passed his head, and was as if it had been screwed into the wall.

'Shot thrown against window panes, which made people think every pane was broken. Servants kept at the doors with continual bell ringings, your uncle Freddy put inside houses, and the door held, to prevent his escape, those were the days for the Arsenal.'[1]

Their father, the lieutenant-colonel, had come back to Woolwich in 1845 after commanding the guns in the Ionian Islands, a British protectorate. Born in Exeter in 1786 he was a future lieutenant-general and the fourth generation of his family to serve the Crown; with mysterious origins, his branch of Gordons looked on themselves as English of Scottish origin, rather than as Scots.* He had passed from the Royal Military Academy into the Artillery and fought at the battle of Maida in southern Italy but that was

*See Appendix: Gordon's Ancestry.

his last taste of glory. While other Gunners won renown in the Peninsular War and Waterloo, Captain H. W. Gordon was an adjutant at Woolwich for nineteen years, perhaps because he resisted stupid orders and 'was less fitted to obey than to command.'[2]

In 1817, aged nearly thirty-two, he married Elizabeth Enderby, nearly twenty-four, eldest daughter of a prosperous shipowner who lived near Woolwich. And if the Gordon ancestry brought a touch of the distant Highlands and a tradition of service to the Crown, the Enderbys brought a pioneering spirit.

Enderby ships had led the New England trade, bringing back whale oil and taking out tea: an Enderby vessel was the victim at the Boston Tea Party. Elizabeth's grandfather, Samuel, sent ships to the little known South Pacific, to harpoon whales and extract the oil; and they carried the first convicts to Botany Bay. Samuel died in 1797. His sons, rich and rising in the social scale, moved to large houses in Kent: his eldest son, Samuel, Elizabeth's father, settled at Crooms Hill in Charlton.[3]

The Enderbys were of Dissenter stock. Elizabeth's grandfather had belonged to the Walters' Hall meeting, which became Unitarian: he left money both to the meeting and to its pastor, Hugh Worthington. The next generation conformed to the Church of England. Neither Elizabeth's father nor her mother, born Mary Goodwyn in Norfolk, had philanthropic interests but an aunt by marriage founded and maintained a girls' orphanage in Blackheath.

While Enderby ships continued to sail the Pacific in an increasingly competitive trade, Elizabeth Gordon was bringing up her family at Woolwich. The Gordons' eldest child, the future Sir Henry, was born in 1818. When her husband was appointed to Halifax, Nova Scotia they had two boys and three girls and 'in an evil hour' he took the family to Dawlish in Devon to await their delayed embarkation and they sickened in the enervating air. He hurried them back to Kent, with a new baby, Emily. Another captain volunteered, and yet another baby arrived, Wilhelmina Harriet ('Mina'), before Captain Gordon sailed alone to Halifax on the last day of April 1829.

Elizabeth Gordon was even-tempered and always cheerful under the most trying circumstances, as a relative wrote, and was always thoughtful of others, a good wife for a soldier.

In May 1830 her husband was back at Woolwich and in 1831 their third son, William, was born. Captain Gordon took a house on the Common, 'which proved so small and uncomfortable a tenement that I quitted it, after a residence of eighteen months, for a new erected one at the corner of Jackson's Lane, which, although larger, was so badly built as to render its safety doubtful.'[4]

It was called Number One Kempt's Terrace, a street named after the Captain's old commandeer at the battle of Maida. And here, on 28 January 1833, Charles George Gordon was born. Although his father was nearly forty-seven and his mother nearly thirty-nine, another brother, Frederick and another sister, Helen, were to follow, making a family of five boys and six girls.

When Charlie[5] was three his father was posted for two years to Ireland and then to command the artillery in Scotland. Charlie's earliest memory[6] was of Leith Fort near Edinburgh, where all the family came briefly together before Henry, fourteen and a half years older than Charlie, went as a young infantry officer to Malta. In 1840 Colonel Gordon was ordered to the Ionian Islands, which had been under British protection since the end of the Napoleonic wars, before Greece had won independence from Turkey.

Charlie had the excitement of going with the family by sea from Leith to Greenwich, where he saw his eldest sister married to a future general; then by the newly opened 'railroad' to Southampton, and by the paddle wheel steamship *Oriental* by short stages to Malta. They transferred to *HMS Megaera* for the three day voyage to Corfu, where Henry was already stationed.[7] The Corfu years were happy. A schoolboy essay by the youngest brother, Freddie (which has been wrongly attributed to Charlie) describes the beautiful views from the ramparts of the moated citadel where the British troops and officials lived; and the delicious fruit and ices, the scenery and the colourful processions of the Greek Orthodox Church.[8]

The Gordons were a close knit family, for the Colonel, a most professional soldier, was no martinet at home unless a child neglected a duty or told a lie; he was 'firm yet genial,' in the words of his eldest sister's grandson, Egmont Hake, who was not old enough to know him in his prime but had talked with many who had: 'Those who knew him can never forget his lively and expressive face; his great round head – bald, and surrounded by short curly hair, black in his best days; his robust playfulness of manner; and above all the twinkle of fun in his clear blue eyes. In his company it was not possible to be dull; he had a look which diffused cheerfulness, and an inexhaustible fund of humour.'[9]

His cheerful wife was never remote from her offspring, now ranging in age (in 1842) from twenty-four to four years old. The Gordon nursery had long been ruled by their nurse, Cooper, in the finest tradition of British nannies, though according to Helen she 'loved the boys and merely tolerated the girls.' Charlie had been promoted to the parlour but would come back for supper when Cooper would tell stories, some of them ghoulish. Charlie lunched with the grown-ups but one day came rushing into the nursery, his rather prominent light blue eyes twinkling with mischief, as Cooper served midday dinner. He sniffed, and said: 'Goat!' Freddie and Helen refused their meat. Cooper reproved Master Charlie and ordered him never to say 'Goat!' again, so next day he arrived at the same time, sniffed and said, 'Capricona!' at which the children again refused.[10]

Charlie's education in Corfu was in the hands of Miss Rogers, the family governess, aided by his eldest unmarried sisters. Augusta was twenty in 1842 and Henrietta (Etta) eighteen months younger; but Charlie was devoted most to the next sister, Emily, who at sixteen had come out of the schoolroom but was near enough in age to be a special friend. Emily suffered from weak lungs and the heat and air of Corfu did not suit her.

In 1843 the Gordons had a royal neighbour when young Prince George, the future Duke of Cambridge and Commander-in-Chief of the British Army, arrived in Corfu as a colonel to command the infantry. After Gordon's death the Duke in his letter of condolence recalled knowing him as a child, 'for your good parents lived next to me at Corfu now forty two years ago, and I always valued them and took an interest in their children.' To his mother he was rather dismissive of the Colonel: 'a dull heavy common looking Scotchman' – Gordon must have picked up a Scots accent in Leith. As to Charlie, 'Nobody thought there was anything very remarkable about him.'[11]

By 1843 Charlie was ten and must return to England for school. Henry was now with his regiment in the West Indies; Enderby, the next brother, a cadet at Woolwich and William at a school in England, which was not doing him good. William was already a scamp. 'Poor William,' Gordon would write twenty-one years later when William died in New Zealand, where he had been sent in disgrace. 'He was a most good natured brother and was gifted with greater talent than any of us.'[12]

The Gordons, like many families of the day, regarded the great public schools as sinks of iniquity and had sent their sons to private schools. Miss Rogers now drew their attention to a small one near Taunton in Somerset, founded and run by her brother George; it already had a high reputation, and George Rogers, like the Colonel, had been born in Devon.

On 22 July 1843, Mrs Gordon, with Emily and Charles, embarked in *H.M.S. Acheron* for Malta, from where they returned to England in the same steamship *Oriental* in which they had come out three years before.[13] During the voyage Charles grew even closer to Emily, whose health was declining despite the sea air and the prospect of specialist doctors in England.

They all stayed with their Enderby grandmother at Crooms Hill House, Blackheath. Mrs Gordon then took Charlie down to Taunton to enter the Reverend George Rogers's school at Folland's House, out in the country a mile or two south-east. Her sister Caroline, married to a half-pay naval officer, 'Captain' Dow, lived in the neighbourhood with their four girls: the Dows could keep an eye on Charlie.

Rogers had started his small school for the sons of local gentry and merchants with such success that in 1840 he was able to move to the larger premises of Folland's, a small country estate with trees and grounds and a Regency mansion which for a few years had been let to a lunatic asylum until its proprietor, one Duck, had fled to America with the cash of a late patient. It stood empty until Rogers bought the lease (and later the property) and renovated the house, re-opening his school three years before Charles Gordon entered it at the age of ten years and eight months.[14] Folland's House had no connection with the moribund grammar school, while the town's more famous institutions were not yet founded: Taunton School (1847) and King's College (1880). Folland's had an ancient cedar tree and a view of the Quantocks. The twenty boarders were taught by Rogers and one assistant, Caleb Short. But hardly had Gordon settled down when he received calamitous news: his beloved sister Emily had died on 18 November 1843.

Gordon was devastated. Forty years later, in a letter from Palestine to his great friend Prebendary R. H. Barnes, who happened to have mentioned Taunton, Gordon replied with fond remembrance of the town and its church and the school and then wrote: 'I remember a deep bitterness there, never can I forget it though I was only 10 or 12 years then. Humanly speaking it changed my life, it was never the same since.'

Barnes and Gordon had been discussing a Hebrew word, *perets*, meaning a breach or breaking through, used in the Old Testament both literally, of rushing water, and metaphorically, of God breaking in on a nation or a person through a calamity; and Gordon told Barnes: 'It was a perets I feel sure and was good. I never had a sorrow like it, in all my life. Therefore I love children so very much, to know where they can rest their little souls when a perets happens.'[15]

After Emily's death Mrs Gordon returned to Corfu. Charlie's school holidays must have been spent with Freddy* at their grandmother's in Blackheath, where they would have been the special charge of their spinster aunt Amy, then in her mid-thirties, who was Charlie's godmother and gave him the Bible which eventually was presented to the Queen after his death. A family friend told the Queen's private secretary that Miss Enderby was, by then, 'a little old woman who had more to do in forming his character than anyone else, I believe, her own character being not unlike his.'[16] Aunt Amy certainly was a little eccentric, had a great sense of humour and cared nothing for money.

The boys would have often visited their uncle and aunt the Charles Enderbys, at their fine house on the river at Greenwich, next door to the Enderby rope and canvas factory. Charles Enderby was a founder member of the Royal Geographical Society and also celebrated for his intelligent light carriage horse, Artaxerxes, but not for efficiency. The shipping and whaling business ran into difficulties. Several voyages to the South seas had returned at a loss, uncompensated by the discovery and naming of part of the Antarctic continent as Enderby Land. Then, in March 1845, the rope and canvas factory, and their house, were burned down in a spectacular fire, throwing 250 men out of work.

In October 1845 Charlie's parents, his sisters and Freddy, with Cooper and an Albanian manservant, Palasco, returned from Corfu, overland by Venice, Switzerland, Germany and Belgium. The Colonel took up his next appointment, at Woolwich Barracks, and after the Christmas holidays Charlie took Freddy with him to Taunton, where 'all the best cream and butter come from', in Freddy's words. The two boys were put into lodgings at 42 Upper High Street, walking to Folland's each day.[17]

'Freddy gets on pretty well,' wrote Charlie to his mother in February 1846 with rather poor spelling, 'except sometimes he gets a little teazed but I always stop it before it is to late.' The two Gordon boys played each other up:

*The manuscript letters spell Freddy or Freddie, Charley or Charlie indiscriminately.

they were remembered as being 'rather "difficult" young gentlemen,'[18] but the school seemed a happy place. 'We had a half holiday yesterday,' Charlie wrote home, 'and went up to a hill called Pickeradge [Pickeridge, in the nearby Blackdown Hills]. We had a very fine day for it and we caught donkeys and nearly all the boys had tumbles.'[19] Charlie took up fencing and probably cricket, since the school field became Somerset County's earliest ground.

He told his mother that 'I hope to be much improved by midsummer';[20] he also bought a French translation of the Book of Common Prayer in order to learn French faster, the method used by the Duke of Wellington to learn Spanish; but Charlie's academic progress was not enough to assure him a place at the Royal Military Academy, 'The Shop' as it was called in the Army. His parents therefore removed him at the end of the summer term of 1846, not yet fourteen, to begin a year with a crammer, Mr Jefferies, on Shooters Hill, a short distance from Woolwich; Charlie probably slept at home, riding up and back each day.

The Gordons now lived in officers' quarters, having briefly had lodgings with a landlady who made excellent ground-rice puddings. Charlie had scrapped with her son and when, years later, he met him again, a stalwart sergeant in the Engineers, he would say delightedly, 'I knocked that fellow down!' Charlie, though small for his age, enjoyed fighting the town and Arsenal lads, though Helen in old age remembered that he was 'much frightened of the guns.'[21]

Woolwich was a great place for an adventurous boy, with the naval dockyard and the Royal Arsenal, the Gunner barracks and The Shop; and it was now, at weekends and especially when William and Freddy came home for holidays, that their father felt himself sitting on the powder barrel. With their screws and crossbows the boys once peppered the windows and frightened the senior cadets of The Shop during a lecture at the Arsenal, and escaped their wrath by superior knowledge of every alley and passage: had they been caught they would have had no mercy from the seniors' belts. When, in January 1847 Colonel Gordon was appointed to be Inspector of the Royal gun carriage factory[22] and they moved into the Inspector's house they found it over-run with mice. The boys, with Helen, trapped them and mischievously released mice after dark into the Commandant's House next door. The easy-going Gordon parents were unruffled by the escapades of their brood.

At this time the Enderby's business failed. The uncles lost almost all their money (when they called to discuss the collapse of Mrs Gordon's investment, and left their top hats in the hall, the boys took revenge by solemnly spitting into each.)[23] The Enderbys reorganized the firm into the Southern Whale Fishery Company but it petered out and they were left with no reminders of past glories except an ancient four-poster bed which they believed, wrongly, to date from Henry VIII, and a model of an Enderby sailing ship.

The Gordons now had little except a full colonel's pay. Helen's education was taken over by Augusta, who lacked Miss Rogers's skill. The Albanian manservant, Palasco, went back to Corfu, followed by notes dictated by the illiterate Cooper to Helen, warning him to beware of women. Cooper had a heart of gold beneath a rough exterior, and when William was dismissed from his post as a clerk in the War Office for putting oil on the chief clerk's pens and other misdeeds, and found himself in a debtors' prison, she took all her savings and bailed him out.[24]

Meanwhile another influence had come into the lives of the Gordons – the Reverend Capel Molyneaux. Molyneaux was in his early forties and was minister (perpetual curate) of Holy Trinity, Woolwich, a newly-built church which the Gordons attended. He had been an army officer after going down from Christ's College, Cambridge, and had then taken Holy Orders. He was well connected – first cousin of a baronet and married to the daughter of an admiral – and always well turned out. For relaxation he used the new railway on its eight mile run to London and rode in fashionable Rotten Row, for which young Charlie Gordon despised him. But Molyneaux had a special gift for making Christianity alive and compelling for officers and others who had looked on churchgoing as little more than a component of their gentility. And in later years he was much in demand at the theatre services organized by Lord Shaftesbury and others to reach the London poor.

Until they sat under Molyneaux the Gordons had not been particularly religious. They had attended Presbyterian services occasionally but, like most other army officers' families, did their duty by the Church of England. Capel Molyneaux's preaching impressed twenty-five year old Augusta. She became a woman of prayer, of earnest if somewhat labouring faith, and hoped to bring all her family into devotion to Christ, with Molyneaux's aid. He was overheard saying 'Etta is saved and Mina is saved and we have hopes of the little one.'[25]

Charlie was bored by sermons and laughed at his sisters. The only clue to inward stirrings at this time is a remark in a letter nearly forty years later: 'I wished I were an eunuch at fourteen,.'[26] The context, a discussion of the conflict between the flesh and the spirit, suggests that he had been troubled by puberty.

Early in 1848, at about the time of his fifteenth birthday, Gordon entered the Royal Military Academy as a gentleman cadet.

CHAPTER TWO

Young Sapper

The precise date of Gordon's entry to the RMA cannot be known because the records of the period were lost in the disastrous fire twenty-five years later: 'Everything went except one large book from 1832 giving names.'[1] At fifteen he was slightly older than the average age of entrants.

The Royal Military Academy, 'the Shop' as it was always known, trained officers for the Royal Regiment of Artillery and the Corps of the Royal Engineers; and at that time was a cross between a public school and a training barracks, rather than a military university which it later became. Bullying was rife, and Gordon, like other *neux*, would have had to stand still while older cadets lashed him with their belts in unofficial punishment, or roasted him before a hot fire or, in winter, made him cling to the window gratings, wearing little or nothing, to 'look out for squalls.' With drills, riding school, lectures and exercises on the Common, hours were long, except at week-ends, and the food sparse and unappetizing, eked out by private supplies. Conditions were spartan: for their morning bath the cadets stood under the pump.

Gordon took it in his stride and was soon known to have a mind of his own. Being rather short, his place on parade was in the rear rank, and when an officer, one morning in early winter, announced that the cadets, by doctor's orders, were not to use the open-air swimming pond across the Common, behind the horse hospital, Gordon muttered, with his slight lisp, 'Damned nonthence, coddling young soldiers. Let's bathe all winter and prove it's wholesome and the doctor a fool.' The front rank grinned, 'and got an extra drill for unsteadiness,' recalled one of the squad, Tom Bland Strange. 'Gordon stepped to the front, took the blame upon himself, and also got a drill for his pains. Next morning, after "oxters," (extras) as the defaulters' drill was called, they doubled over to the cadets' pond and bathed, continuing to do so all winter, though they had sometimes to break the ice.'[2]

'Long Tom' Strange and Gordon 'were sworn friends,' remembered another cadet, F. G. Ravenhill. 'Tom Strange used to get a rise out of Charley once a week, regularly, when they went out for a walk, by striding a bit long, with his long legs, and Charley could not keep up with him, this annoyed C. G. beyond everything.'[3]

On these walks they used to plan their lives, and Strange recalled that Gordon 'had always a hankering after Africa. They were to volunteer for service at the Cape, get long leave, not difficult in those days – equip a waggon, trek north, shoot elephants, and with the proceeds of the ivory carry on further explorations.'[4]

Among the other boys were two who would be Gordon's close friends throughout their lives, however much parted by the demands of the service. Charles Elwyn Harvey, son of a clergyman who was chaplain to the Duke of Cambridge and a canon of Bristol, had been born one day before Gordon and had gone to the new public school at Marlborough with the first batch at the age of ten, before entering the Shop at fifteen. His progress was rapid, which may explain Gordon's quip to Harvey's bride, twenty-one years later: 'He used to bully me at school but I forgive him.'[5]

The other, Gerald Graham, son of a doctor, was eighteen months older than Gordon but had spent some years of education at Dresden. Growing to six feet four he was right hand marker on parade, and was soon ahead of Gordon and would be commissioned two years earlier, so that their intimacy did not really begin until the Crimea. Graham would be with Gordon for the first part of his last journey up the Nile and later could have saved Gordon's life had the British government allowed. Gordon was already showing signs of some later characteristics. Not only would he refuse to join in cadet 'frivolities,' as Strange recalled, but sometimes, would 'without apparent reason withdraw himself from his friends, not speaking for days, then he would come up as if nothing had happened, and say: "Come for a walk, old fellow."'[6]

Strange did not think his 'impulsive little comrade was to be a great soldier ... "More likely me than him"'; but Gordon was long remembered for one incident at the Shop. The cadets having been told not to rush from the dining hall but to leave in an orderly manner, senior under-officer Harrison stood at the top of the narrow staircase, with outstretched arms, to stop a stampede. Gordon's hot temper flared at the order. He ran at Harrison with head down, butting him in the stomach, down the stairs and through the swing door at the bottom. Harrison picked himself up unhurt. Gordon was placed under close arrest. The Captain of cadets (later known as Adjutant), a thirty-six year old Gunner, Captain Frederick Eardley-Wilmot, nearly recommended his dismissal but in awarding punishment remarked, 'You'll never make an officer.' At this, Gordon pulled off the corporal's swabs from his shoulders and flung them at Eardley-Wilmot's feet.

The Captain was nicknamed Eardley the Upright or Ramrod, but he was a hero to the cadets because he secured them a wider range of games and athletics. Years later Gordon told his brother Enderby: 'I know no one who I ever felt more respect for and think few cadets could muster up courage to tell him a lie. Boys have very sharp eyes and I do not think one cadet, however much they feared him, would have wished him ill. He raised the whole morale of the Academy . . .'[7]

Charlie recalled being up before the Lieutenant Governor, an irritable veteran of Waterloo where he had lost a leg; and even facing the wrath of the Master-general of the Ordnance himself, the famous Waterloo veteran 'One Leg', the Marquess of Anglesey; and how Eardley-Wilmot had said, 'If I had been the Governor I would have put you in the Black Hole.'

Academically Gordon was slow but thorough. He showed weakness in Mathematics and French but won a prize for Fortification (a text book written in French) and had particular aptitude for pen and ink drawing, of plans, maps and sketches. He became a senior corporal and a strict disciplinarian, 'eccentric in his modes of punishment, as in all else,' according to Strange, who himself was once reduced to the ranks for rapping a slow cadet on the head with the edge of a ruler. Gordon rapped with a clothes brush. The authorities were having another attempt to put down bullying and Gordon was put on a charge. His eldest brother, Henry, who was serving abroad at the time always believed that for this 'slight offence' Gordon was put back two terms and lost the opportunity of following his father, and Enderby, into the Gunners; this story became part of the Gordon legend. But his classmate F. G. Ravenhill was certain that Gordon was not rusticated as a punishment but at his own request: he passed up the Gunners and worked hard for the Sappers: 'he purposely would not go out in the Arty (I remember it well) as he would have RE.*'[8]

---

*In the Sudan, some twenty years later, he joked as he wrote his official letters in French that had the RMA French professor not 'plagued' him he would have been a gunner.

As all records were lost in the fire of 1873 no contemporary evidence survives, except in the memories of fellow cadets. E. R. James, who would be a boundary commissioner in south-east Europe and Armenia with Gordon, recalled how Gordon had not been remarkable as a student, or intellectually interested, but had set his mind to gain a commission in the Royal Engineers to please his father. 'We, who knew Charlie so well, soon learnt to recognize in his character, in the firmness of purpose he displayed in conquering this first obstacle, an earnest of his indomitable will in all he undertook; and we felt certain that he only needed opportunities to gain a brilliant reputation. But we could not help seeing that there was no little danger that he might mar his fortune by the obstinacy of his strong will.'[9]

At last he was able to pass the interviews, take the examinations, which terrified him, and survive scrutiny of his reports. On 23 June 1852, aged nineteen and nearly five months, Gordon received Queen Victoria's personally signed commission as a second-lieutenant in the Corps of the Royal Engineers.

After leave Charlie Gordon reported to the Sapper depot at Brompton near Chatham, to the spacious barracks built by French prisoners during the Napoleonic Wars, and the grounds where his own statue, mounted on a camel, would one day stand. For the first time he ate in the magnificent officers' mess where his portrait in the robes of a Chinese mandarin would later hang in a place of honour.

The Corps of the Royal Engineers at that time was a corps of officers only: the men they commanded belonged to the Corps of Sappers and Miners, though officers were also known colloquially as Sappers. They looked on themselves as an élite, the most professional body in the Army, and cared not at all that the cavalry and the Brigade of Guards despised them for ungentlemanly zeal.

Gordon went through the normal training for young officers, in RE procedures and in leadership of Sappers. He also met great kindness from an older man who was not a Royal Engineer. Lieutenant Colonel Richard Jenkins[10] came from Monmouthshire and had served in Welsh regiments before becoming Staff officer of the Chatham Pensioners. He was a keen shot and on 1 September 1852, the opening day of the partridge shooting season, he invited Gordon to join his shoot. 'Do you remember the thistle field now over 20 years ago,' wrote Gordon to Jenkins from Central Africa on 1

September 1874, 'how hot we were, and the water out of cart ruts (I have drank worse water out here) and the rows over who should carry the hares.'[11] Mrs Jenkins had him to dine afterwards at their home in Brompton, 5 Mansion Row; but Jenkins was ill from plums and the cart-rut water, and a little light in the head, as Gordon naughtily reminded him in another letter.[12]

Gordon looked back on it as a red letter day. He wrote to Jenkins annually on 1 September and regarded him as 'the oldest of my friends.'

In October 1853 Charlie's parents left England, taking Augusta, Nina, Freddy and Helen: the colonel had command of the guns at Gibraltar and was promoted Major-General next year. Charlie now had no home, but the Jenkins made him free of theirs. Over the New Year of 1853-4 Gordon was briefly in southern Ireland with a Captain Inglis, later killed in the great storm of the next November,[13] and on 17 February 1854 was promoted lieutenant and took up his first appointment, as assistant garrison engineer at Pembroke Dock in South Wales. And there he experienced the first great crisis of his life.

Pembroke Dock, near the head of Milford Haven and close to the ancient town of Pembroke with its great castle, had been built as a naval base and dockyard forty years earlier. In 1854 the government decided to build more forts to protect it, although France, the only likely invader, became an ally against Russia a few weeks after Gordon's arrival: war was declared on 30 March 1854 though the Allies did not land in the Crimea until September.

Gordon was soon working on plans. At first he disliked the mild climate of Pembroke, the cornfields and the somewhat desolate pastures crowded with jet-black Castlemartin cattle, but 'I am very comfortable here,' he wrote to his mother. 'Our colonel is a very nice man and very kind.' The garrison families had their faults. 'This place would never suit you or our family. It is the most gossiping place in Europe I do believe: most of the people are at loggerheads, and all have some story against the other.'[14] One young couple, the Drews, became his friends, and before long he had accepted from them what he had spurned from Augusta and Molyneaux.

Captain Francis Barry Drew of the 11th Foot (which became the Devonshire Regiment) was twenty-nine years old: He had been born at Castle Drew, near Limerick in Ireland, to a landed family of the Protestant Ascendancy, while his wife Anne was a Cator from Norfolk, wealthy bankers who earlier had been Quakers. She had auburn hair and Gordon thought her 'very stylish.' Both the Drews were convinced Christians, eager to persuade others. The details of their influence on Gordon do not emerge from the manuscripts but fourteen years later Gordon told a friend: 'Ever since I remember I had a belief that Jesus was the son of God, and used to have feelings of deep depression on account of my faults.' From the time of the Crimean War, he continued, 'I knew Jesus to be my Saviour and had assurance,'[15] which to his correspondent would have implied an evangelical conversion: that at this time Gordon had repented, and believed with his heart and will, not only with his mind, that his sins had been laid on the Son of God on the Cross, and were forgiven; in response, Gordon had given himself to the living Jesus who had risen from the dead.

A one page tract, newly published in Birmingham and called *A Priceless Diamond*, may have helped: Drew displayed a copy on his mantelpiece, and Gordon had already seen it when Augusta sent another; but this tract has disappeared: the copy in the British Museum was destroyed in the second World War and none other exists. Whatever the course of his conversion Gordon now counted himself as 'serious', which did not mean, when the word was used in this context at that period, to be gloomy or solemn (many of the early Puritans were hilarious) but to take seriously the issues of life and death, of heaven and hell, and the Christian's care for his fellow beings on earth.

Gordon began to study the vast eighteenth century Commentary on the Bible by Thomas Scott, which he had laughed at when Augusta had acquired a new edition in monthly numbers at Woolwich. He seems to have been specially impressed by Scott's teaching on St. Paul's words: 'To me to live is Christ, and to die is gain.' The apostle, wrote Scott, 'had no other business, interest, honour, or pleasure for which to live, but Christ and his glory, service and favour: and therefore he knew that to die would be his greatest gain; as he should then be enabled more perfectly to know, love, serve, and enjoy the favour of his gracious Lord; and have done with sin, temptation, and suffering for ever.' From that time Gordon had no fear of death; it would be the best that could happen, to be welcomed with joy.

For Gordon longed to be 'done with' sin and temptation. 'I have turned over a new leaf,' he told Augusta in a letter which cannot be dated as the manuscript is lost. 'I feel much happier and more contented than I used to do. I did not like Pembroke but now I would not wish for a prettier place'; yet he was grateful that he had much time to himself and was not subject to the temptations of a crowded officers' mess because 'I am such a miserable wretch that I should be sure to be led away.'[16] He was aware of his hot temper, his ambition, and his love of praise, and was determined to be dead to them. This brought him a struggle against himself, and especially a disgust for his body. He was probably still virgin as he had not engaged in the frivolities of fellow cadets at Woolwich who had experimented with local prostitutes; to judge by his later comments he determined to reckon himself dead, in St. Paul's phrase, to the 'lusts of our flesh' and solemnly if informally dedicated himself to be celibate and chaste, although he could still admire a beautiful girl.

When the Drews went on leave he urged them to hear Molyneaux, now minister of the Lock Chapel in the Harrow Road, which on a Sunday morning would be thronged with the carriages of families hurrying to sit at his feet. Barry Drew came back 'highly pleased' and his wife 'an ardent admirer of Molyneaux.'[17] Gordon bought a horse and gig and when off duty he and Drew drove 'all about the country,'[18] but one day Gordon was thrown out 'and broke my knee.'[19] He hated two-wheelers ever after. The knee healed quickly and he longed to reach the Crimea with its opportunities of action and promotion: otherwise he would have to 'crawl up a list of ninety-two names.' He was not concerned with the political issues behind one of the most unnecessary wars in history: he wanted to see action.

The battles of the Alma (in which Enderby Gordon had distinguished himself) and Balaclava (the Charge of the Light Brigade) and Inkerman had already taken place when on November 29 Gordon received orders. To his annoyance he was ordered to Corfu, not the Crimea.

He supposed his parents had used influence at the War Office to keep him out of danger: 'it is a great shame of you; however I must not grumble as I am lucky not being sent to the W. Indies, or New Zealand.'[20] Gordon immediately addressed a plea to a family friend who was the head engineer of the Army, Sir John Burgoyne. Burgoyne was already in the Crimea but the sudden desperate need for huts to be erected in the Crimea, to relieve the sufferings of the men who were still in tents after the onset of winter, caused his staff at the War Office to smile on young Gordon's plea. His orders were changed: he should take out huts (each to hold 24 men, or two captains, or one general.)

As for New Zealand it was the feckless William who was about to go. Henry was settling William's affairs, paying his debts and refunding to Nanny Cooper the savings by which she had bailed him from a debtor's prison. 'William looks infinitely better than ever I saw him' wrote Charlie. 'He is getting quite fat ... I am extremely lucky in going by Marseilles, as I am such a bad sailor. Henry has been extremely kind, getting my outfit, which I was unable to do as I had no time in London.'[21]

Gordon had left Pembroke on 4 December 1854. The Drews drop out of his story; they may have corresponded, but Gordon preserved very few letters and the Drew Papers are lost.* Barry Drew served in India, distinguished himself in the second Afghan War and rose to be a major-general. Anne Drew died young and he married again. Between them the Drews had helped to make Gordon a different young man.

---

*It has emerged that General Drew's Papers were destroyed with other family papers by his granddaughter about 1980. Surviving papers show that in fact it was Drew's second wife, Henrietta née Hunter, whom Gordon knew, Anne having died before Gordon met Captain Drew (information kindly supplied by his great-grandson, Mr Timothy Pallister).

CHAPTER THREE

The Crimea

When Gordon landed at Balaclava, the small port below the plateau, on 2 January 1855, the Crimean campaign had settled into the slow siege of Sevastapol, hindered by the severe winter for which the British were not equipped. Gordon heard of officers frozen to death, or killed by charcoal poisoning as they crouched over braziers in airless quarters. 'The street of this village is quite a sight,' he wrote home on 8 January, 'What with 600 or 700 Zouaves carrying shell to our batteries, Turks mending roads and other drudgeries, the swell English cavalry and H. Artillery carrying rations, officers in every conceivable costume foraging for eatables ...' Ten days later he saw Sevastapol for the first time from one of the hills, 'and do not think I ever saw a prettier city, it looks quite open, and a Russian steamer was cruising about inside the harbour. Two of their steamers came out the other day and bombarded the French lines for two hours.'[1]

'We have every comfort,' he told Henry who was still in England, 'and I like it extremely. There are really no hardships for the officers. The men are the sufferers and that partly is their own fault, as they are like children thinking everything is to be done for them, the French soldier looks out for himself, and fares much better.'[2] He noted, however, that the men hated their French allies more than they hated the Russian enemy.

By mid-February Gordon had erected his huts and was free for more dangerous work in the trenches. The thaw had begun and he was told to extend the British line to link with the French. The slackness of infantry officers nearly cost him his life. They had not cleared some caves he must enter and Russians might be inside, rifles at the ready. 'I went on, however, and though I did not like it, explored the caves almost alone.' As he emerged, the infantrymen whom he had placed as sentries thought he was a Russian and fired. They missed, but his working party 'bolted, and were stopped with great difficulty.'[3]

A few days later some Russians 'as near as possible did for me, the bullet was fired not 180 yards off and passed an inch about my nut into a bank I was passing. They are very good marksmen.'[4] The 'large and pointed' bullet must have ricocheted, for in his diary he noted what he kept out of his letters home: 'Struck by a spent ball.'[5]

The coming of Spring allowed serious campaigning. Gordon was put to his favourite duty of drawing exact plans of the British defences and sketching enemy works in detail: photography being still in its infancy, with cumbersome equipment and slow exposures, the traditional arts of reconnaissance were much needed as staff officers planned for defence or assault.

He frequently came under fire. When Henry's brother-in-law, Charles Staveley, returned from sick leave to command part of the trenches known as the Left Attack, Gordon drew him exact plans and took him that night from trench to trench. 'He explained every nook and cranny,' recalled Staveley to Henry years later, 'and took me along outside our most advanced trench, the bouquets and other missiles flying about us in, to me, a very unpleasant manner, he taking the matter remarkably calmly.'[6]

Staveley was one of several Crimea friends who were to influence Gordon's career, but the most significant friendship in the trenches began when a young Irish infantry officer, who had distinguished himself in action in Burma, was appointed assistant engineer of the Left Attack. Garnet Wolseley, the future field-marshal, walked with a limp, caused by the serious wound which had sent him home from Burma. Like Gordon he was small, energetic, humorous and good company, impatient with the incompetence of seniors, and full of ideas for the efficiency and welfare of the men; and he was fond of sketching and surveying. They soon 'were friends, drawn together,' said Wolseley 'by ties never formulated in words.' Wolseley described the Gordon of 1855 as 'a good-looking curly-headed young man of my own age, both of us then being in our twenty-second year. His full, clear and bright blue eyes seemed to court scrutiny, whilst at the same time they searched into your inner soul.'[7]

Wolseley noted Gordon's 'indifference to danger of all sorts, or I should rather say, an apparent unconsciousness of it.' He wondered whether Gordon actually lacked the sixth sense that warns a man of danger, but when Gordon had approached that uncleared cave which might be full of armed Russians he had not liked it; he was aware of danger and dismissed it. Years later Gordon told his friend Prebendary Barnes that he had gone 'to the Crimea hoping, without having a hand in it, to be killed.'[8] Death was the gate to everlasting, life; when he revisited Pembroke in 1880, he wrote: 'I had a time of it here and I can well remember, when I was ordered to the Crimea my sincere hope that I should be killed there. It is odd to think what one has gone through since then and still to retain the wish for the other world.'[9]

Wolseley had a lively, if fatalistic, Christian faith, but he was humbled by Gordon's Christianity. Because Gordon seldom mentioned matters of faith in his Crimea Diary or his letters home, and was inclined in retrospect to belittle the state of his Crimean soul, he has sometimes been described as if little more than a nominal Christian at the time. Wolseley saw differently. Though his autobiography was inevitably coloured by memory of Gordon's last years, the two men were together in the Crimea more than at any other period, since their service in opposite parts of the world prevented more than occasional meetings after 1855, apart from a few weeks in China in 1860; Wolseley's comments, therefore, derive mainly from the months together in the trenches until he lost an eye in the assault on the Quarries on August 9.

Gordon 'absolutely ignored self in all he did,' wrote Wolseley eighteen years after Gordon's death, 'and only took in hand what he conceived to be God's work. Life was to him but a Pilgrim's Progress between the years of early manhood and the Heaven he now dwells in, the Home he always longed for.'

Between actions and duties Gordon would study his Bible and especially the Gospels. 'The character of Christ as therein depicted,' wrote Wolseley, 'was always uppermost in Gordon's mind. When in any difficulty his first thought was, "What would my Master do were He now in my place?" It was this constant reliance upon his Maker, this spiritual communing with his Saviour upon every daily occurrence in life, that enabled him absolutely to ignore self and take no heed for what the morrow might bring forth ... His absolute simplemindedness of purpose startled me at times, for it made me feel how inferior I was to him in all my aims in life to his.'

Wolseley was aware of Gordon's faults: 'he was mortal and not therefore perfect;' but looked up to him as a Christian hero.[10]

The Crimea had become quite a family affair. Charlie saw his brother Enderby, the Gunner, quite often and was serving with Mina's Sapper fiancé, Willie Anderson. In March Henry, nearly thirty-seven years old, arrived to reorganize the British Army's stores and clothing.

Henry Gordon was one of the unsung heroes of the Crimea and indeed of Army history, for he brought order into the haphazard system of supply. He found matters 'in sad confusion – a superabundance of stores in one department and a deficiency of similar articles in another: one regiment with five suits of warm clothing, another with none.' He came armed with strong authority from the Secretary of State for War and 'I had everything my own way.'[11] His proposals were accepted by government. He then sold his commission and became a permanent officer in the Ordnance Department, rising eventually to be Commisary General of the Ordnance and a Knight Commander of the Bath.

Meanwhile Enderby and Charlie kept Henry informed of impending operations, so that he witnessed the assaults and main actions, and Charlie at last became intimate with him. The three brothers met whenever they could, smoking as they talked. Officers smoked cigars, like most gentlemen of England: their social inferiors smoked pipes. Smoking was not identified as a hazard to health. Even when, in the eighteen-seventies, Jenner and a few others began to warn against tobacco they were ignored by the rest of the medical profession for another eighty years, for lung cancer was almost unknown. Charlie Gordon was unusual in that he took to smoking Turkish cigarettes as well as cigars, and became almost a chain-smoker.

Cigarettes had been unknown in England before the Crimean War. British troops were given them by Turkish soldiers and also learned the trick of screwing pipe tobacco into paper spills. Gordon may have picked up cigarette smoking from an interpreter, Romolo Gessi, who was part-Italian, part-Armenian, born on a British ship, and now a link between the Sardinian and the British contingents: Gessi and Gordon became friends and would work closely together nearly twenty years later.

Gordon wrote home frequently, though not enough to please his mother, and eagerly awaited letters back. 'Augusta has not written to me for a long time. Shabby I think. Have you heard from William lately, let me know if you have, and my love to him, and I must now wind up a very stupid letter,' with love to each member of the family by name.[12] In early May he described a ride over the valley and hills where the battle of Balaclava had been fought six months before: he saw skeletons of horses, including one which was still saddled, with a bit in its teeth. 'The plain is covered with wild thyme,' he told Augusta, 'which when marched on by the troops gives out a delicious smell. It is a beautiful country and a great change from the bare ground and rocky soil of our encampment.' He also lamented to her the lack of faithful chaplains. 'We have a great deal to regret in the way of good working clergymen, there being none here that I know of who interest themselves about the men.'[13]

By now the army longed to assault the strong fortifications and finish the siege. In the hot exchange of fire on 7 June Gordon in a forward trench 'was struck slightly with a stone from a round shot and stunned for a second, which old Jones has persisted in returning as wounded. However, I am all right; so do not think otherwise. Our fire was continued all night, and the next day until four o'clock, when we opened with new batteries much nearer, and our fire then became truly terrific. Fancy 1000 guns (which is the number of ourselves, the French, and Russians combined) firing at once shells in every direction.'[14] The French reached a fortification named the Mamelon, but were driven back, then they advanced again and held it.

Four days later Gordon wrote confidently: 'I am in great hopes that ten days will finish this siege. We had an armistice to bury the dead on the 10th, when the *Rus* appeared very downhearted.'[15] At 10 p.m. on 17 June he scrawled a note to Henry: 'You hear by this time that we open fire tomorrow (Sunday) morning and assault on Monday. I am told off for the assaulting column with Bent. In the event of my not seeing you before that, would you look after my traps etc and if I should happen to be taken away, would you manage my affairs. My debts are only to you and perhaps a few pounds to Cox. I leave another note to you in my sabretasche which you will get afterwards.

'Believe me my dear Henry, your ever affectionate Brother, C. G. Gordon.'[16]

The dreadful 18 June which followed, forty-one years after Waterloo, would be the subject of endless reminiscence over port and cigars wherever veterans met in the decades to come: the hot fire from both sides; the feats of gallantry by the ladder parties of sappers and bluejackets running up to the walls of the Redan; the poor leadership of the half-trained infantry who had been sent out to replace the losses of earlier battles, and were allowed to dribble out of the trenches 'and as soon as they appeared,' Gordon saw, 'they were cleared away' by Russian gunfire.

Gordon's commanding officer, Lieutenant-Colonel Tylden, held him in reserve. They saw one of the R. E. lieutenants rush out with the Riflemen skirmishers, he in a red jacket and they in green. The Russians picked him

34

off and he was carried back within minutes, his arm shattered. Tylden told Gordon to see to him. Gordon bound the arm with a tourniquet which he had in his pocket and called for stretcher-bearers, then ran forward to rejoin Tylden, only to see him fall, his legs shattered by grape shot.

Gerald Graham, with his height and great strength, plunged his sword into the ground, picked up the colonel and carried him off the field under a murderous fire. Graham then returned, pulled out his sword and continued. He was to be one of the first awarded the Victoria Cross (and deserved another at the parade in Hyde Park the next year when Queen Victoria, leaning down from her horse, drove the pin into his chest.)

The assault on the Redan had failed. The French having also failed, Raglan decided against a second attempt. Kinglake, the historian of the war, had a story that in the pause which followed, Gordon ran up to Graham and demanded to be assigned a command in the next attack since other officers were wounded; and that Graham replied that he thought the affair was over and there was nothing for Gordon to do. 'Gordon was so angry and disappointed that hot words ensued which caused for a short time a little estrangement between the friends.'[17]

The story, though in character, is suspect: Kingslake was writing long after the event because he composed his *History* so slowly; Gordon and Graham were not yet close friends; and Gordon in his letters implies that he fully approved the decision not to renew the attack. He believed the repulse to have been caused by failure to mine the Russian defences before the bombardment.

The Allied Army had to stay for another six weeks of gruelling high summer; Gordon had thirty-four consecutive twenty-four hour periods in the trenches ('a bit tedious.') He had 'already gained a reputation in our Corps for his extraordinary energy,' recalled another officer. 'There was not a day on which he did not go to the trenches – as an amateur, if he could not do so in the course of his duty. As a young man his constitution was of iron, and although he had exposed himself recklessly from first to last, his health had not suffered in the smallest degree.'[18]

Whenever a Russian shell dislodged or destroyed the baskets of earth which protected a trench, Gordon and his men must repair or replace them, often under fire. And he became well known for crawling forward beyond the trenches, again and again, to sketch any new Russian work. The military historian, Colonel Chesney (who was not in the Crimea himself) heard that Gordon developed 'a personal knowledge of the enemy's movements such as no other officer attained,'[19] or as another witness put it: 'If you want to know what the Russians are up to, send for Charlie Gordon.' He had his share of escapes. At last, after days of bombarding the Russian positions, orders were given for assault; the French would seize the Malakoff tower on the right at midday on 8 September 1855; the British would then attack the Redan on the left, so that the French could seize the Central Bastion.

The morning 'was windy and dusty,' wrote Gordon,'and at 10 o'clock began one of the most tremendous bombardments ever seen. We had kept up a tolerable fire for the last 4 days, quite warm enough, but for two hours this tremendous fire extending six miles was kept up, and at twelve the French rushed at the Malakoff, took it with ease having caught the defenders in their bomb-proof houses, where they had gone to escape from the shells, etc.'

Gordon saw the tricolour raised on the Malakoff and watched the British advance, for he was not with other sappers in the ladder parties, but held in reserve to run forward to captured works, where he would sketch and draw plans of the next objective.

'Our men went forward well, losing apparently few, put the ladders in the ditch and mounted on the salient of the Redan, but though they stayed there five minutes or more, they did not advance and tremendous reserves coming up drove them out. They retired well, and without disorder, losing in all 150 officers, 2400 men killed and wounded. We should have carried everything before us if the men had only advanced, but they did not behave as they ought, as the number of officers killed shows.' By the end of the day, only the Malakoff was in Allied hands.

The Highlanders were to assault the Redan again next morning. That night Gordon was detailed to the trenches. As he walked forward in the darkness he heard 'terrible explosions' and on reaching the trenches at 4 a.m. 'I saw a splendid sight, the whole town in flames, and every now and then a terrific explosion, which the rising sun shining had a beautiful effect (*sic*), the last of the Russians were leaving the town over the bridge, all the three-deckers etc., were sunk, the steamers alone remaining. Tons and tons of powder must have been blown up.'[20]

The Russians had withdrawn without waiting for the Highlanders: the Malakoff had been the key to the fortress. At 8 o'clock Gordon was ordered to start making a plan of the captured works and went up into the Redan 'where a dreadful sight was presented' – a mass burial of hundreds of British and Russian bodies, laid out in the ditch where the fiercest fighting had occurred. The Reverend Harry Wright, the principal chaplain, who had buried hundreds after the Battle of the Alma and had worked selflessly throughout the winter battles and the siege, with almost no other chaplain, was reading the Burial Service.

'We are at last in possession of the vile place,' Gordon wrote home exultantly from inside Sevastapol. 'The Russians set fire to it and evacuated it on Saturday at midnight after having repulsed the English in the Redan and the French in the central bastion. However the French took the Malakoff and the Russians fearing for their communications, cut. They have left a great many guns, etc. Anderson is all right, and Henry and Enderby also. We share in the guns, etc., halves with the French. The *Rus* sank all their ships etc. Is it not glorious? I am making a plan of the works with two other REs . . . The conflagration and explosions were terrible, their strong masonry forts blown to atoms. We are in great spirits.'[21]

The Russians left nothing 'except rubbish and fleas,' and the icons in the churches and three thousand wounded in the hospital, deserted without medical care and food for thirty-six hours when discovered: later the Russians sent in a party under a white flag to evacuate those still alive.

The war was not over. Gordon soon found himself in the Allied force sent by sea to capture the Fort of Kinburn at the mouth of the Dnieper river, the first operation undertaken by the Navy's new ironclads; but both Russia and the Allies were now seeking a way to extricate themselves from the war. The expedition returned to the Crimea in time for Christmas. Gordon found several of his company in hospital, with wounds or sickness, and paid for each man who could eat it to have a Christmas dinner of roast beef and plum pudding. A Sergeant Wheeler, wounded by a shell splinter, asked his help in sending £7 to his wife at home. Gordon said that was easy as he was sending some money himself. Next year, when Wheeler reached home he asked his wife whether she had received £7. 'No,' she said. 'I received £10.'[22]

Gordon next helped prepare shafts and galleries to blow up the Sevastapol dockyard. Gerald Graham, who now knew that he had been awarded the new Victoria Cross, was with him. 'Our intimacy began,' wrote Graham thirty years later, 'when we were thrown together in mining the docks at Sevastapol during the winter of 1855–6, a period Gordon always delighted in referring to whenever we met, by calling up old scenes and even our old jokes.'[23] The demolition was not well carried out. 'What a mess we made of that dock,' commented Gordon to Graham from the Sudan in 1877; and he wrote to another officer at the same time that nothing could exceed their ignorance of mining in the Crimea. 'Miserable is the only term which could be applied to our Dock demolition.'[24]

The war petered out. Gordon was stationed on the plateau, fifteen weeks at one place with little action. He seized the opportunity to explore the battlefields and even rode fifty miles there and back to visit the site of the Battle of the Alma. The opposing armies signed a truce, 'which may be broken off at any time,' while far away the statesmen were debating the terms of the Treaty of Paris to end the war, which the officers in the Crimea considered to be only half won. 'We do not generally speaking like the thoughts of peace until after another campaign,' wrote Gordon to his mother on 9 March 1856.

He added: 'I shall not go to England, but expect I shall remain abroad for three or four years, which, *individually*, I would sooner spend in war than peace. There is something indescribably exciting in the former.'[25] (Many years later he would recall this attitude with some disgust.) By late April, with peace signed and the regiments embarking from the Crimea, the Sappers had heard 'nothing of our future destinations. However I think I shall remain abroad as there is not much allurement in the home duties of our people, and I should not go on the survey, *even* if I had the offer.'[26] He knew that Colonel Edward Stanton, R. E., would represent Britain on an international Commission to survey and delineate the Treaty's new frontier between the Russian and Ottoman empires, designed to keep Russia away from the Danube.

A few days later he received his orders – to go on the survey with Stanton. The twenty-three year old Gordon, newly decorated with the French Legion d'honneur but neither receiving nor expecting one of the few British decorations awarded to subalterns (apart from his mention in despatches) had been given no choice: the survey was not an offer but an order.

CHAPTER FOUR

River and Mountains

On 23 May 1856 Gordon landed with Colonel Stanton, Lieutenant Edward Renouard James, R. E., and some Sappers, at Galatz, ninety miles up river from one of the mouths of the Danube, a town of narrow winding streets, old houses, synagogues and Orthodox churches, set on a hill between a marshy shallow lake and the left bank. Gordon found it 'very dusty and not at all a desirable residence';[1] it would be his headquarters fifteen years later.

For the next nine months the Boundary Commission surveyed and settled the frontier. The three Englishmen formed a well-knit team. Edward James, of Huguenot descent, had served in the trenches with Gordon but had been captured, finishing the War as an honoured prisoner. Six months younger, but slightly senior, he wrote of Gordon in his memoirs that 'we had been intimate friends at Woolwich and ever since. With his absolute sincerity and bright winning way, no one who knew him as well as I did could help loving him.'[2] Stanton, the handsome, charming and able British Commissioner, would later command Gordon at Chatham, and as consul-general help him greatly in the Sudan. Gordon wrote home that 'Stanton makes a capital commissioner, and is very much liked by the others.'

The French commissioner, Colonel Besson, had risen from the ranks, and was 'a splendid old soldier' to James, and 'very lively, and preferable to the generality of Frenchmen,' to Gordon. But whereas James recalled in old age that the English held the Austrian commissioner, Count Kalik and his assistant in 'highest respect,' Gordon at the time wrote that the Austrian general 'is cordially disliked by all.' There was an indolent Turk and a French-born Russian, General Fanton de Verrayon, always smart and courteous but 'a very wily old chap, and full of lawyers' tricks.' Stanton invited the French Colonel Besson to join their Mess as he had no assistant: his soldier servant acted as waiter, their Greek cook 'raised pies worthy of the luncheon table of the Rag' (the Army and Navy Club) and as Besson could not speak English they all improved their French; the work of the commission was carried on in French. They were always provided with 'excellent quarters' in houses and seldom needed to sleep in tents, though they had a marquee for the Mess and office.

Gordon described to his parents a kaleidoscope of experiences: in the Russian territory of Bessarabia he found that 'the Russians are uncommonly civil. It would have made you laugh to see the way the people crowd about, almost as if you were a wild beast.' Some of them belonged to a Christian sect which had left the Orthodox church and had curious habits and beliefs which Gordon studied with interest; the Imperial government had exiled the sect to the Danubian marshland. He met some Sevastapol Russian officers: 'they were also very civil;' but the local officials pocketed the money sent from St. Petersburg for the Commission's supplies and entertainment, so that life was hard and dull, while 'You cannot conceive the way in which the Russian merchants pillage you ... They are a nation of thieves.'[3]

When Stanton sent him with despatches to be forwarded by the British consul in the autonomous Ottoman territory of Moldavia, then occupied by Austrian troops, he travelled through a rolling country of vast corn fields, 'in post cars, a species of low-wheeled truck without springs, very light and quite open, which bump along the roads at a good rate with 4 horses. Through the rain, I was in a precious mess. I got on pretty well, not knowing one word of the language. I lost a wheel once.' At Jassy, which he liked, the gentry were eagerly discussing their hope of independence from Turkey: Moldavia and Wallachia, with the parts of Bessarabia ceded by Russia, would later form the Kingdom of Romania under a Hohenzollern. Gordon was presented to the local Hospodar, Prince Ghika: 'The prince keeps up a great state, and I was introduced in great state. The English uniform produces a sensation.'[4]

In the autumn the commissioners and their officers were able to go shooting, including a wolf hunt in the forest. In two days they shot only two wolves but numerous hares and foxes. 'It is not bad fun, but rather butchery as the hares, wolves, etc. try and break the line and run the gauntlet of all the guns until killed ... I have killed about 100 head of game of different sorts this year.'[5] Once the snow had come they could travel by sleigh, under a blue sky in cold air without wind, making duty delightful.

Much of Gordon's time was spent drawing plans, until by the spring thaw of 1857 he had made more than a hundred: 'For my part, I have had enough of them for my whole life.'[6] Then the Austrian general at Jassy invited James and Gordon to attend the spring manoeuvres and they drove together in mild weather through a pleasant wooded countryside. 'In descending the steep hill down to the Pruth,' recalled James, they needed to attach to one of the wheels the iron shoe which acted as brake. At the bottom Gordon 'got out to remove it, and not remembering that it must have become nearly red hot, he handled it incautiously, and burnt his hand so badly that I imagine he must have been scarred for life. With his usual insouciance he made very little of the circumstance, though I am certain he suffered terrible pain, and the wound was not cured for some time.'[7]

The Commission completed its work and Gordon hoped to go home on leave, although he had no wish to serve in England; but the Foreign Secretary ordered Stanton to hand over Gordon, James and their men to another R. E. Colonel, Lintorn Simmons, who was waiting at Constantinople to survey the new frontier between Russia and Turkey in Armenia. Gordon protested to the War Office. A telegram came back: '*Lieutenant Gordon must go.*'[8]

The second survey was much more adventurous, in rugged country little known to Western Europeans. The party sailed along the Anatolian coast of the Black Sea aboard a Turkish steamer 'in a beastly state of dirt, the deck being crowded with Turks and Armenians returning from different pilgrimages, some from Mecca and others from Jerusalem.'[9] Gordon liked his new chief. At the age of thirty-six Lintorn Simmons, who would rise to field-marshal, was a legend to young Sappers. After constructing defences against the Americans on the remote and disputed north-east frontier of Canada, and six years as Inspector of Railways in Britain at a time of great expansion, Simmons had unexpectedly found himself leading Turks against Russians, first in the Danubian provinces and then in the Crimea, where he covered himself with glory in saving the newly arrived Turkish contingent from defeat by a much larger Russian force. Later, at the severe battle on the River Ingur in the Caucasus he led a column across the river to take the Russians in the rear, compelling them to retreat.[10]

Gordon found Simmons not only heroic but 'very well read and amusing.' After a slow voyage watching higher mountains than Gordon had ever seen they landed at Trebizond. The Commissioners and their assistants, with three interpreters, three cooks 'and innumerable servants of every description,' set off into the roadless highlands in a vast caravan of ninety-nine horses, 'all in our service,' commanded by a magnificent head muleteer in a gold braided jacket, and a turban, who smoked a long-stemmed pipe. An old horse without a load, who had travelled the route many times, walked at the head of the train to trace the path; the string of laden horses behind him, roped from tail to head, would put their hooves in his marks when they plodded through the snow of the dreaded Zigana Pass.

The French Commissioner, Pelissier, soon fell ill and travelled, wrote Gordon, 'in a cage which is supported between two mules. He is much too old to be sent on an expedition like this.' The Turkish Commissioner provided an early insight into Turkish methods which Gordon was to deplore in the Sudan. As the Turk 'could get no money from the government for his journey, he was directed to take any horses he could lay his hands on, the consequence being that he stopped caravans on their way to Constantinople from Persia, on the road, threw off their goods, put his own on the animals, and made them carry them. This is not the fault of the Commissioner, but the government who would not give him money.'[11]

The British enjoyed each other's company. With Simmons, James and Gordon came a fourth Sapper officer, Helsham-Jones, and a man from the Foreign Office, de Norman, who three years later in China would be tortured to death. The expedition also included Assistant-Surgeon Woodfull, an excellent doctor and a great character: 'I can never forget,' recalled James, 'the way he brightened many a fatiguing march with his endless repertory of song and anecdote. He was never so tired that he could not sing at the top of his voice, and he seemed to know the music and words of every opera and every popular song.'[12]

They worked laboriously through mountains, hills and valleys, settling the precise line of the frontier between Russian and Turkish Armenia. 'What was extraordinary,' wrote Gordon rather ungrammatically, 'were the account (*sic* ?amount?) of perfectly deserted villages, which the inhabitants had left when Paskievitch* first entered the country in 1829. He then persuaded upwards of 60,000 inhabitants to emigrate to Russia, and the gap has never been filled up. All these villages have a square tower with loopholes etc. to protect their families against any sudden inroad of the Kurds or other wandering tribes who wanted their families for slaves etc., they are dotted all

*Field Marshal Ivan Fedorovich Paskeivich (1782–1856) who conquered these mountain territories for Russia during a war with Turkey, 1829–30. In 1831 he suppressed the Polish revolt and was made Prince of Warsaw. Tolstoy wrote about him.

over the country. We saw Ararat for the first time on June 18, it is a very fine mountain, rising alone in the plain, and covered as it is at present with snow. Mount Alagos, its rival, is also in view, but has not the fine appearance as Ararat.'[13]

The British officers had fanned out across the region to complete the survey quicker, and when Gordon reached the foot of Mount Ararat he determined to climb it, though his letters make no mention of the tradition that this Armenian mountain of nearly 17,000 feet was the Ararat where Noah's Ark had rested: an indentification which Gordon later disputed.

The night brought 'very bad rain and thunder which was a bad look out.' He set off at 4 a.m. with his interpreter, two Sappers and a corporal, all of whom had given up before the snow line except for Corporal Fisher and himself.

'The whole of this time there was a thick fog, only now and then clearing a little so as to enable us to get a splendid view of the country, spread out as a map beneath us, with cumuli clouds floating about. The snow which I mounted was at a very steep slope, and quite hard, nearly ice on the surface. It was so steep that you could not sit down without holding on to your poles. Corporal Fisher was about half a mile to my left, and had a better ascent, not quite so steep. About two o'clock I began to get very tired, not able to get up more than two yards without resting. This was caused by the rarification of the air. The mist cleared just at this time for a minute, and I was enabled to see the summit about 1000 feet above me with a very steep ascent, and Little Ararat 3000 feet below me. It began to snow soon after this, and was intensely cold. This settled me and although very reluctant I turned round and sitting down, slid over in a very few minutes the distance which had taken me so many hours to get up. I got back about five o'clock, rather tired. Corporal Fisher managed to get up to the top, and describes the crater to be very shallow, although the top is very large. I expect it was filled with snow.'[14] Gordon was sure he would have reached the summit had the weather been better.

The success of his slide down Mount Ararat nearly caused his death on Mount Aragos a few weeks later. On 9 August, having camped at its foot, James, Gordon and Doctor Woodfull, with a few Russian officers and some Cossacks, climbed the 13,500 foot mountain 'and were rewarded,' wrote James, 'by a magnificent view of Mount Ararat, 60 miles from us, and of the Araxes, looking like a thread of silver, extending as far as the eye could see.

'Our descent of the mountain was most exciting, as Gordon had a very narrow escape from losing his life. Exhibiting his characteristic impatience at the slowness with which we were descending, he seated himself on a snow slope, there being a good deal of snow on the mountain still, and commenced sliding down before we could prevent him from performing such a very rash act. We held our breath in awe while he sped down to a point which seemed a thousand feet below, and when, at length, we saw him turn over helplessly and disappear beyond a hump of snow, we lost all hope of seeing him again alive. The climb down to the spot at which we saw him last was tedious; and I can never forget our anxiety, or the joy we experienced, when Gordon met us smiling, looking as if nothing unusual had happened. After turning the somersault we had witnessed, his further descent had been providentially arrested by his tumbling on to a smooth rising surface of soft snow, and, beyond being slightly bruised, he was little the worse for the adventure.'[15]

Gordon had now been used to rough living for two and a half years. He was in excellent health and did not mind when the weather was hot by day and cool at night and the 'mosquitoes most venomous,' biting men and horses alike 'in a most atrocious way.' He found also that he enjoyed meeting comparatively primitive peoples. When his party fell in with Kurds, living in stone-walled villages in the mountain pastures for the summer months, 'I paid the chief of a tribe of 2000 a visit. He paid the English a great number of compliments.' Kurds were fanatical Moslems and not illiterate: 'although in such a deserted spot they read the Turkish papers.' They stole the Russian interpreter's horse but 'I should not mind trusting them at all, for the Bey would not allow them to take our horses, etc.; it was I expect only from hatred to the Russians.'[16]

Some weeks later he saw the immediate effects of slave trading for the first time when James and he went, with an escort of forty Turkish infantry, into Lazitan, through the country of the fierce Lazes. 'This tribe and the Kabouletians supply the Constantinople Turks with slaves, which they kidnap from the Gourelians, who are on the Russian side. These Gourelians are beautiful; in fact, generally speaking, I never saw so many handsome men and women as the peasants among them. The Adjars are most daring, and even proposed to us to bring any person we might choose out to Batoum for £40 to £120. In consequence of these kidnappings, etc., a deadly enmity exists between the two peoples, and whenever they get a chance they kill one another.'[17]

Gordon made no comment on slavery or The Slave Trade in his letters, nor does contemporary evidence suggest that he drew the attention of the Anti-Slavery Society to this remote frontier. His letters home were travelogues; apart from an occasional comment on family matters when the haphazard postal arrangements delivered mail from England, he gave no indication of feelings or sentiments, religious or secular, except once when they had passed through Kars, scene of the recent long and famous siege, ending in honourable surrender by the British general in command of the Turkish garrison. Gordon concluded that the defence had not been quite so heroic as England believed; a criticism which the editor of the letters, nearly thirty years later, discreetly omitted.[18]

By late September they were all back in Constantinople, their work completed in less than five months instead of the two years which Gordon had been warned to expect. He would have left for leave at once had not Simmons and three of the others fallen ill: 'My surveying duties have been usurped by those of sick nurse, etc.'[19] As soon as they were better he took ship for England. Colonel Simmons, the future field-marshal, like Colonel Stanton on the Danube, the future diplomat, became a strong friend: both would be warm supporters through all the vicissitudes of Gordon's later life.

Gordon spent Christmas 1857 with his parents, and Augusta and Helen, who was now twenty, in Southampton which the general had chosen for his retirement; Freddy, twenty-two and working in the War Office, was probably there too but no contemporary evidence illuminates this leave, except that Charlie had brought home his Russian servant, Ivan, whom Gordon may only have engaged in Constantinople a few weeks earlier, for it was not until they were in Armenia again that he found out that Ivan 'is a Lutheran and reads his Bible regularly';[20] he was probably a 'Stundist', one of the Russian converts of German settlers in the Ukraine, where an evangelical revival had begun in the eighteen fifties. Ivan was a favourite in the servants' hall.

After nearly four months, based mostly at the Royal Military College, Sandhurst,[21] Gordon was ordered back to Armenia, where problems of demarcation still troubled the chancellories of Europe. Colonel Simmons having been posted to Warsaw as consul-general, the Foreign Secretary addressed a joint letter on 17 April 1858 to Lieutenants James and Gordon, both in their twenties, appointing them at the request of the Russian and Turkish Commissioners, to 'act as absolute umpires between the topographical officers to be employed in marking the frontier line between Russia and Turkey in Asia Minor.'[22]

Gordon, Ivan and Doctor Woodfull, that 'capital energetic companion,'[23] went out by a steamer so slow that Gordon wished he had gone overland through Italy like James. Gordon reached Constantinople the same day as James, and the two young lieutenants held a solemn discussion with the Russian ambassador and the Turkish foreign minister, and agreed to separate: Gordon would umpire the northern section of the frontier, and James the southern, each travelling with a Russian and a Turkish officer. Gordon took a steamer which called at Sevastapol. 'The place is still an utter ruin, scarcely anything has been done to restore it.'[24] And so back to Armenia, where old acquaintances hurried to call. 'My camp here is on the sea-shore, in a capital position. The mountains of the Caucasus, covered with snow, extend to the north for some distance, and are superb, the whole country is beautifully wooded, and only requires draining to be a delightful residence, as there is scarcely any winter, and the heat is not unbearable in summer.'

Once in the mountains ('You can hardly conceive the magnificent views there are about the Caucasus') Gordon found the work 'most fatiguing' because the terrain prevented riding. With an escort of soldiers, and Ivan in attendance, and Duke the dog at his heels he spent his days checking and replacing damaged or stolen frontier marks, settling disputes between the Russian and Turkish Commissioners 'and in general keeping the two from squabbling.' With his own quick temper Gordon did not feel himself a natural peacemaker.[25]

Lighter moments were not lacking and at one town they watched 'some very pretty ladies' dance their national dances 'capitally. They dance alone and all the gentlemen beat time with their hands.' As he wrote to Helen the same day: 'The ladies are very pretty, but have not very cleanly habits in general, they prefer their nails tipped, and do not hesitate at taking a bone and gnawing it. They live in extremely dirty houses, or rather huts. They are generally all princesses, and the men all princes, who however do not hesitate to accept small donations. I am always in fear and trembling unless they should give me anything, as it is necessary to give in return (Freddy's notion; as I told him, he has several Eastern habits). I unfortunately happened to notice a certain glass letter-weight with the Queen on it, it was like H. Majesty; was given it on the spot, and with deep regret parted with my soda-water machine the next day. I admire nothing now you may be sure.'[26]

As summer gave way to autumn he found the work 'very monotonous,' made worse by the absence of home mail which he suspected was wandering around South Russia, but by 10 September he could write: 'If the roads are not impassable by the snow, you may expect us about December. I am quite in the dark as to how my mission has been fulfilled, but it is really immaterial to me, for I do not accept another place in such an anomalous position.'

At last, on 24 September 1858 Gordon and his northern section neared the rendezvous at Alexandropol, and saw James and his companions riding out to meet them. Gordon's Cossack escort performed feats of horsemanship 'of a circus nature' and as the whole party rode into the town the Cossacks sang in chorus.

Gordon and James had much to tell each other, and at the *vin d'honneur* James heard what the Russian and the Turk of the northern section thought about Gordon: 'I think the greatest grievance on the north side was the extraordinary energy displayed by Gordon, which had been often complained of by his colleagues, but was good-humouredly alluded to now that the work was over. They declared he used to keep them in the field for such long hours, that they became so tired as to be scarcely able to sit on their horses. They said they had never known such a man, for when they reached camp, and lay down from sheer exhaustion, he would take his gun, and stay out in search of game until dusk. They added that Gordon's horses were as fatigued as they were, and that, one day, one of them actually fell down and died on a mountain side as the section was at work ... I can readily conceive that a complaint might with more reason have been made by Gordon of the laziness of his easy-going comrades.'[27]

Gordon and Woodfull made an expedition to Tiflis, the ancient capital of the former Kingdom of Georgia. Then the Englishmen and their servants took a hair-raising route home by boat down a dangerous river, through scenery which Gordon thought was 'the finest I ever saw.' A tough voyage on the Black Sea brought them to Constantinople on 16 November 1858.[28]

Gordon wrote to his parents the next day: 'I do not feel at all inclined to settle in England and be employed in any sedentary way, and shall try and get employed here if it is possible, intending however to return to England first. Do you see how I am creeping up the list of lieutenants.'[29]

A possibility opened at once. He met Colonel Michael Biddulph, who was engaged in extending the telegraph line (which had reached Constantinople during the war) across Anatolia to Baghdad. Biddulph sent a telegram to the War Office. On 13 December Gordon's father in Southampton received a letter from the Deputy Adjutant General, 'My dear General, your son Charles' reputation as a good officer is so spread abroad that everybody wants to have him.

'He reached Constantinople but whilst there he was seized on by Col. Biddulph, R. A., and he is now ordered to assist in his telegraphic operation.

'I am afraid he will not turn up to eat his Christmas dinner with you. Though he will be absent you will have the satisfaction of knowing that his absence is the result of his meritorious conduct.'[30]

But the War Office forgot to confirm the order to Charlie in Constantinople, or the telegram went astray. He had decided to forgo the home leave to which he was entitled ('I do not like when I accept an appointment that the first thing they hear of you is an application for leave') and was prepared to wait a fortnight for a telegram. None came. 'I cannot explain it,' he told Biddulph, 'except under the idea that they think I am on my way home.' On the following Monday he wrote that he must leave on Wednesday, 'having had no answer to the Telegraph. This, and the fact of my having arranged my affairs with the Foreign Office will oblige me to return to England unless an answer comes before the mail leaves.'[31]

Charlie ate his Christmas dinner at home after all. For reasons unknown the orders to join Biddulph were withdrawn: the Deputy Adjutant General, Colonel (afterwards Lieutenant-General Sir) William Gordon (no relation) had been much impressed by his young namesake in the Crimea, where William Gordon had been nicknamed 'Old Fireworks' because his great height and his contempt for danger had brought down Russian fire whenever he walked about in the forward trenches. When Charlie unexpectedly arrived in England the Colonel may have decided that a spell at Chatham would do more for the future of a brilliant youngster than erecting telegraph poles in Turkey. Gordon was therefore named as the next second adjutant of the Corps of Royal Engineers and adjutant of the depot, a post which marked an officer as likely to reach high rank.

Had he disappeared to Anatolia he would probably never have gone to China and thus on to immortal fame.

CHAPTER FIVE

China Prelude

Stanton, Gordon's chief on the Danube, was commanding officer. Gordon's ideal for an adjutant was to be 'mild, firm, and *no favourites*.' On his horse Pompey he may not have impressed like an adjutant of the Brigade of Guards because of his lack of height but he was efficient. Like all adjutants he grumbled at reading 'a lot of useless trash' before the half-yearly inspection, and took a close interest in the activities and characters of the young officers, who would claim in after years that even then they 'realised his unusualness and his strength of character.'[1]

Gordon exchanged gossip by post with his friend of Woolwich days, Charles Harvey, who had left for Portland soon after Gordon had arrived: 'How is Nugent? He is very remiss in writing to me, he owes me a letter. I hear that he was Steward to some ball. What an honor! If I had only known of it in time. Old Sandham has just come back from five days leave (shooting.) Archie Ross has been shooting pheasants, and been rather troublesome the last two days. He has got Sgt. Pickles in arrest, and he only escapes a court martial by retreating into Hospital. Whether Sandham will try him I do not know, it is a humbugging case, about a mistatement, and Archie showed characteristic obstinacy.'[2]

Gordon had a house in the barracks, looked after by an excellent couple, Edward Bishop and his wife, 'most respectable people . . . honest and clean.' Sometimes Gordon slipped up to London to attend a soirée at the Royal Geographical Society, having been elected a Fellow the previous year, for his services to geographical knowledge in Armenia; or to meet friends like Harvey. ('I *am* disgusted! You wrote me word that you would meet me on Tuesday in London and you did not do so. I wandered about looking for you but it was a waste of time . . .')[3] His visits home to Southampton are not recorded and neither his mother nor Augusta kept any letters of this time.

Gordon had no desire to stay at Chatham. As his year drew to a close the Third China War broke out, to enforce Chinese ratification of the Treaty of Tientsin which had ended the Second War in 1859. A Franco-British force was about to land in Northern China, intending to march on Peking. Gordon volunteered. 'Old Fireworks' at the War Office approved his application and appointed Charles Harvey his successor.

Gordon bombarded Harvey in Portland with advice about Chatham duties, furniture, even the cost of his weekly washing. 'You will want a few tablecloths, sheets, blankets etc., which you can get down here. You must get', he joked, 'at least 18 pairs of spurs, as you require them on all occasions – sleeping in them is rather a nuisance at first for yourself; but you soon get used to them. Steel chain straps are the correct thing, they clank as one walks.'[4] As Harvey was a bachelor and moral, the – in the bed must have been a lighthearted hint that it was time Harvey married.

Gordon left for China in July 1860 by the overland route through France. In Paris he met his old acquaintance the French commissioner on the Danube, who took him to Versailles and St. Cloud where they saw the Empress Eugenie drive out. 'She is very pretty and seemed in high spirits. We were quite close to her.'[5]

At Hong Kong in September he learned that 'I am just too late for the fighting,'[6] for the Taku Forts which had barred the way to Peking had been taken; the Chinese Imperial government promised to ratify the Treaty. On 3 October 1860, in the British camp near Tientsin, Major Gerald Graham, V. C., wrote in his diary: 'Charlie Gordon arrived. He is still brimful of energy, but has sobered down into a more reflective character. He is really a remarkably fine fellow.'[7]

He was given command of an R. E. company vacant through illness, and as the Chinese had seized the diplomatic negotiators the war continued. Gordon served in the siege train which prepared to storm the walls of Peking before the Chinese surrendered, opened the gates and released the surviving prisoners. The Allies decided to punish the Emperor for the torture and death of the others by burning his Summer Palace with its pavilions and main residence, its stables and pagodas, set in gardens and park, and lakes with willow-pattern bridges.

'You could scarcely conceive the magnificence of this residence or the tremendous devastation the French have committed,' Gordon had written after its capture unopposed except by angry Pekinese dogs. 'The Throne room was lined with ebony carved in a marvellous way. There were huge mirrors of all kinds, clocks, watches, musical boxes with puppets on them, magnificent china of every description, heaps and heaps of silk of all colours . . . any amount of treasure etc., and the French have smashed everything in the most wanton way.' The British looting was more organized. Gordon bought 'heaps of things . . . for nearly nothing,'[8] but deplored the demoralizing effect ('Everybody was wild for plunder') and would never permit looting when he came to independent command. He was second-in-command of the Sappers who were ordered to commit the act of vandalism which disquieted western contemporaries and appalled posterity, though it may have shortened the war.

The Allies retained 3000 men at Tientsin until the Chinese should pay the whole agreed indemnity, and Gordon was appointed Commander Royal Engineers of the British brigade.

Gordon and his Sappers, with 350 Chinese labourers, prepared winter quarters. They made chimneys and fireplaces in requisitioned Chinese buildings, erected temporary barracks and stables and adapted places for hospitals. 'We, i.e. the Company, are getting on well together. I have scarcely any prisoners, and I believe there is little drinking.' His two subalterns 'as companions, are fine fellows but do not care about doing more than they can help, whereas Gordon never minded getting 'knocked about at all sorts of work,' with dirty hands 'which one would be vexed at in a servant.' His tendency to do everything must have tempted the others to shirk.[9]

He was unwittingly preparing for a future unforeseen: organizing large numbers of Chinese; learning how to administer and finance great quantities of stores. 'I like this place immensely,' he wrote to 'Old Fireworks,' from Tientsin, 'and do not care how long we may remain.' His position was 'far superior to any I could hold in England . . . I consider my coming out here a most happy event in every way.'[10] He told Augusta that he was 'not at all inclined to return to Great Britain' but she must keep that private as 'I do not want my mother or father to fret about it . . . I like the country, work, and independence: in England we are nondescripts, but in China we hold a good position and the climate is not so bad as it is made out to be.'[11]

His only regret was the surrounding poverty. He took on management of a relief fund (possibly his own idea) but the mandarins refused to organize a controlled distribution for the most deserving, so the British appointed a day for this purpose; 3000 of the poor arrived 'and in the crush seven women and one boy were killed.'[12]

Gordon's energy seemed inexhaustible. As the British and French had retained the Taku Forts and his duties included regular visits, he would ride the nearly forty miles down the banks of the Peiho river in the morning, often at a canter, and ride back to the Tientsin camp the same evening. In the winter of 1861–2 he and an infantry officer were sent on surveys up-country and he spent three weeks' leave exploring along part of the Great Wall, including areas not previously penetrated by Europeans.

The contingent's commander was Brigadier-General Charles Staveley, whose sister Rose was married to Henry Gordon, so Gordon had known him for years; nor had Staveley forgotten the day when Charlie had shown him round the trenches in the Crimea under fire. 'The Brigadier and myself hit it off very well,' wrote Gordon to Harvey. 'He is not popular but I think he is a very good chief worth fifty' of his predecessor. 'He is a fine soldierlike fellow and very sharp and selfish to a degree, but very clear headed.' And to Augusta, Charlie remarked: 'For such an essentially selfish man I like him well enough.' They had 'occasional skirmishes but are generally good friends'[13] Staveley liked Gordon well enough too, and noted his skill and resource with growing appreciation.

Early in 1862 Gordon fell ill. 'I have had a slight attack of smallpox,' he wrote to Augusta on 15 March from the Taku Forts, urging her not to tell their parents, 'which has passed off without marking me and has left me better than before.' In Staveley's opinion the illness was less virulent than smallpox but it led to a renewal of faith. 'I am glad to say,' Gordon continued to Augusta, 'that this disease has brought me back to my Saviour, and I trust in future to be a better Christian than I have been hitherto. I have had a capital friend in the chaplain, Mr. Beach, a very worthy man and who has been excessively kind.'*[14]

Years later Gordon wrote that his spiritual life in the decade after the Crimean War 'swung as a pendulum in broad sweeps.' He had survived the war, 'never fearing death, but not wanting to be too closely acquainted with God nor yet to leave Him.'[15]

The pendulum had swung back at a critical time. For the great Taiping rebellion was threatening the Treaty Port of Shanghai.

---

*The Reverend (later Canon) William Roberts Beach, born 1827. Originally a Wesleyan Missionary in Hong Kong he was ordained by the Bishop in 1855 and commissioned as an army chaplain in 1859. He was later chaplain at Sandhurst and senior chaplain at Aldershot, then rector of North Farmbridge, Essex. His grandson is General Sir Hugh Beach, Chief Royal Engineer 1982–87.

CHAPTER SIX

Taiping

The Taiping[1] rebellion had begun in South China eleven years earlier. Hung Hsiu-chuan, a farmer's son, had turned his self-made religious movement, based on a garbled understanding of Christianity, into a military crusade against the Imperial government of the Manchu (Ching) dynasty, the foreigners whose ancestors had invaded China from beyond the Great Wall in the seventeenth century and seized the throne from the Mings.

Famine, flood and high taxation had made South China ripe for rebellion, and on Hung's thirty-sixth birthday, 11 January 1851, he had proclaimed a new era: Taiping Tien-kuo, or Heavenly Kingdom of Great Peace, with himself as the Heavenly King. Hung immediately attracted support for a genuinely nationalist movement, well symbolized by the Taiping refusal to shave the front of their heads and wear pigtails, the sign of submission which the Manchus had imposed on the Chinese: the Taipings wore their hair long, wrapped round their heads like a turban, so that they became known as 'the Long Hairs.'

The Taiping armies expanded and swept northward. With ardent beliefs, strong discipline and able strategy, helped by the weakness and tactical mistakes of the Imperialists, they took city after walled city until on 19 March 1853 they captured Nanking on the Yangtze river; they slaughtered some 30,000 Manchus and their supporters, and made it their capital.

The Heavenly King had developed beliefs which mixed what he knew of the Old and the New Testaments with Chinese religion derived from Buddhism, the Tao and Confucius. Taiping soldiers learned the Ten Commandments, kept the Sabbath (not Sunday), said prayers, sung hymns and smashed Buddhist idols; but Hung taught that Jesus was his Elder Brother and that he himself ranked next in the sight of God.

Because of the stories filtering out of China and the impression gained by

British officers who went briefly to Nanking, several Western missionaries, forbidden by the Imperial government to evangelize inland from the Treaty Ports, were convinced that a great indigenous Christian movement had begun. The first Bishop of Victoria, Hong Kong, George Smith, whose diocese theoretically covered all China, wrote to the Archbishop of Canterbury in May 1853; 'The rebel chiefs profess to believe in Protestant Christianity; declare that they are commissioned by the Almighty to spread the knowledge of the one true God; have everywhere shown a determination to destroy idolatry of every kind; and now profess to await a further revelation of the divine will, ere they advance upon the northern capital Peking.'[2] A strong 'Taiping lobby' arose in England, convinced that China was about to become a Christian nation. The Gordon family itself was sympathetic until Charlie discovered what had really happened.

The attempt on Peking failed. The Imperial government raised better armies under a more able general. What might have been a swift campaign and a change of dynasty became a long-drawn out Rebellion which brought misery and devastation to millions. The Taipings quarrelled among themselves: the Heavenly King executed several of his leading generals, whom he had called Wangs (Kings) and their successors ravaged the countryside and conscripted its men; as an Anglican missionary exclaimed in 1861: 'Call the Rebels "the national party!" Why, the people loathe them, the very land abhors them.'[3]

Inevitably, in the next century, the Communists would hail the Taiping Kingdom as their forerunner, so that any who had opposed it would be regarded as lackeys and running dogs of the Imperialists but by 1862 the Taipings had indeed lost popular support, especially in the province of Kiangsu between Nanking and Shanghai, a rich area devastated by their invasions.

Once before they had nearly captured Shanghai. When the Taipings again moved towards the Treaty Port the western merchants and Chinese bankers raised money to recruit a force of Chinese led by foreign officers. The Chinese gave it the name of Ever Victorious Army; the Western officials called it the Disciplined Chinese or the Disciplined Force. An American adventurer aged twenty-nine, Frederick Townsend Ward,[4] took command. His European officers were recruited from the saloons of Shanghai, including unemployed mates from merchant ships, army deserters, clerks bored with office work. As General Staveley complained, most of them were 'totally ignorant of military organization or tactics; many, moreover, are addicted to drinking.'[5]

Ward's Ever Victorious Army, clad in green and blue uniforms designed by himself, had won battles, but not the war, by April 1862, when Charles Staveley left Tientsin to take command at Shanghai of a small British force defending the International Settlement.

Hardly had Staveley arrived when he received orders to drive the Taipings beyond a thirty miles radius from the city. He began operations at once, meanwhile sending for a thousand more troops from Tientsin and for Gordon, to be his Commander, Royal Engineers in preference to Colonel Moody, commanding the Engineers in Shanghai and North China and nominally Gordon's superior: Gordon later considered that Moody 'is perfectly unfit in every point of view for this command, and has caused more ill feeling towards us than I can describe.'[6] On 3 May 1862 Gordon landed at Shanghai and joined Staveley in the field.

Staveley was reducing walled cities held by the Taipings. 'Your brother was in these operations of the greatest possible use to me,' wrote Staveley to Sir Henry many years later, 'especially in reconnoitring the enemy's defences, and in arranging for ladder-parties crossing the moats, and escalading. He was also a source of much anxiety to me from the daring manner he approached the enemy's works to acquire information.

'Previous to the attack on a place called Tsingpu, and when with me in a boat reconnoitring the place he begged to be put ashore the better to see the nature of the defences. Presently to my dismay I saw him gradually going nearer and nearer, by rushes from cover to cover, until he got behind a small outlying pagoda within a hundred yards of the walls and here he was quietly making a sketch and taking notes. I in the meantime was shouting myself hoarse in trying to get him back, for not only were the rebels firing at him from the walls but I saw a party stealing round on our right to try and cut him off. When he did return I was so angry I would not speak to him however much I admired his enthusiasm and devotion to duty.'[7]

Thanks to the thoroughness of Gordon's reconnaissance, Tsingpu fell easily on 13 May. Besieging another walled city Staveley sent Gordon with a naval captain 'and a few bluejackets and marines' to report on the approaches. Attacked under the walls by Taipings who sallied out 'they owed their escape from destruction,' said Staveley, 'entirely by (sic) their coolness and by improvising such defensive cover as happened to be at hand.'[8]

Staveley was deeply impressed by Gordon's tactical skills and his leadership beyond the field duties of an Engineer. Then the rebels again threatened Shanghai and Gordon constructed defences against a possible assault, while Shanghai endured the 'dismal swamp' feeling of summer. As one officer described it: 'the stillness and murkiness of the atmosphere, the croaking of frogs, the stinging of mosquitoes, the noise of bats whirling through the rooms, big beetles flying about, and the stench of dead Chinamen poisoning the air'[9] – because the Chinese buried their dead in coffins above ground. Many of Gordon's sappers fell sick, often through buying bad liquor; several died, yet as Gordon wrote to Harvey early in August, 'If you are moderately careful you can get through the summers in comfort.'[10] He reckoned he had a good R. E. company, and unlike Colonel Moody he was ready to send his sappers to improve amenities in the International Settlement; in gratitude some civilians lent him a good house rent free for his quarters and Mess.

He needed officers to replace those who had fallen sick or been posted home: 'I am left alone while that dear old C. R. E. at Hong Kong has 3 subalterns and three older men.'[11] Then a tall, quiet yet athletic Irishman of twenty-two, Thomas Lyster, arrived from Hong Kong to join Gordon's solitary Mess. Lyster wrote home: 'There is another Engineer officer here, Captain Gordon; he is a first-rate fellow, and a very good officer ... Gordon is such a good hearted fellow that every one in any difficulty comes to him.' Gordon was equally appreciative of Lyster, 'as a friend and officer, and I can also say what is of infinitely more import – that he lived a Christian life; which in China is not easy.'[12]

The Taiping rebels were again menacing the district, robbing, burning and slaying. The British in Shanghai were forbidden by Palmerston's government to intervene beyond the thirty-mile radius. The only foreigners aiding the Imperialist troops up-country were some French troops, and Ward and his mixed crew of adventurers who led the Ever Victorious Army. Late in August Ward came briefly into Shanghai: 'a quiet looking man, with very bright eyes but is a regular fire eater.'[13] Ward resumed operations but a few weeks later he was mortally wounded near Ningpo, the Treaty Port about a hundred miles south of Shanghai. He died on 22 September 1862, leaving a large sum of money to the Union cause in the American Civil War, although he had arrived in China poor.

When news of Ward's death reached Shanghai the British Consul, Medhurst, suggested that a British officer be seconded to the Chinese service to succeed him. Staveley concurred and wrote to the War Office, with a copy to Sir Frederick Bruce in the legation at Peking. Bruce, however, wished to avoid British intervention in the civil war between Imperialists and the Taipings, while the American minister, Burlinghame, favoured Ward's deputy who had already assumed command: a twenty-six-year-old French-American adventurer from North Carolina named Henry A. Burgevine, whose father had been an officer of Napoleon and a general in the Spanish army. Burgevine lacked Ward's qualities and was a wasteful administrator and poor disciplinarian; though brave in battle he was indecisive, and inclined to drink hard when worried, then became violent. Somewhat reluctantly the Chinese governor confirmed Burgevine's appointment.

One month after Ward's death Burgevine and 1500 Chinese troops joined General Staveley, who had marched out of Shanghai to recapture the strongly fortified walled city of Kanding. Gordon's skill and courage in forming a bridge of boats across the creek under hot fire from the walls, and then leading troops into the breach caused Staveley to place Gordon's name first in the list of commendations and to recommend him for promotion; but Burgevine allowed his men to loot the fallen city. In November he angered the Governor (*Futai*) of Kiangsu, Li Hung Chang, by failing to march towards Nanking in support of the Imperialist army at a critical moment, until the danger had passed.

Late that month General Staveley sent Gordon with a strong escort to start a detailed survey of the countryside within the thirty mile radius. Gordon now had two other officers besides Lyster to share out the exploration of countless rivers and canals, towns and villages of the alluvial plain.

The Taipings had lately evacuated the area. Engineers and escorting troops alike were appalled by the sufferings of innocent villagers; Gordon wrote home: 'Words could not depict the horrors these people suffer from the rebels or express the utter desert they have made of this rich province.' He wished that non-interventionists in England could 'see the sights of this neighbourhood ... I am not particularly sensitive nor are soldiers generally but certainly we were all impressed with the utter misery and wretchedness of the poor people and our feelings not amiable towards our government for withholding the force from suppressing this rebellion which could easily be done by us in a month.'[14]

While Gordon was surveying, Burgevine continued to displease Li Hung Chang by failing to keep accounts, and he allowed his men, said Li, to be 'disorderly and mutinous, disobedient to orders, and a pest to mandarins and people.'[15] Li put pressure upon him by encouraging the Shanghai bankers to withhold funds. Staveley had sent a Captain John Holland of the Royal Marine Light Infantry, and several instructors, to help Burgevine but wanted yet more strongly to see a British officer replace him as the general in command of the Ever Victorious Army; on 12 December he put to Sir Frederick Bruce in Peking the name of Charles Gordon.

Staveley then took personal command of the troops protecting Gordon's survey, and told Gordon of his intention. On Christmas Day 1862 Gordon wrote a formal application 'for permission from Her Majesty to accept service under the Chinese Government,' which Staveley forwarded with a strong recommendation to the War Office.[16]

Burgevine's men were now mutinous because their pay was overdue. He promised them on 3 January 1863 to bring back the money. Next day he went to Shanghai with armed men, to the house of Yang Fang, Banker and mandarin, who was known to westerners as Takee (*T'ai-chi*.) During a furious argument Burgevine struck Takee, drawing blood; he seized 40,000 silver *taels* and had his men carry back the boxes by force.

The Futai, Li Hung Chang dismissed Burgevine from his command.

Takee, the mandarin whom Burgevine had assaulted, wrote to Thomas Wade, Sir Frederick Bruce's assistant (and eventual successor, an eminent Sinologist) that the new commander of the Ever Victorious Army should be 'a man of good temper, of clean hands, and a steady economist'; Wade passed this comment to Gordon in a letter of congratulation: 'I need not say how delighted I am for one that you are ready and willing to fill such a post.'[17]

Gordon told his parents that he was 'extremely doubtful of the Government at home approving of the gift of such a good appointment to an officer of such rank as I hold.'[18] He believed he was still a captain, not knowing for another six weeks that his promotion to brevet-major had already been gazetted on 30 December: brevet rank, the Army's way round the rule that promotion followed strict seniority of service; with a brevet an officer could be promoted over more senior captains to become a major in the Army, for meritorious service or for valour, while still a captain in his own corps: Gordon remained a captain in the Royal Engineers when a major in the Army, and after promotion to brevet lieutenant-colonel, even when promoted full colonel in 1872, he would be a regimental captain for a further three and a half months.

A more serious bar to the appointment was Bruce's conviction, already stated in a despatch to the Foreign Office, that British neutrality would be compromised if a British Army officer took service under the Emperor. Unknown to anyone in China, however, the steamer carrying Bruce's despatch had been wrecked in a gale off Ceylon: the mails were salvaged and dried out but reached London several weeks after Staveley's despatch to the War Office recommending Gordon. In ignorance of opposition from their minister in Peking the British government issued an Order in Council allowing Army officers to take temporary service under the Emperor.

Gordon had continued his survey, declining to supplant the Ever Victorious Army's temporary commander, Captain Holland; Holland soon suffered a severe defeat outside the town of Taitsan which Gordon might have avoided.

Gordon passed his thirtieth birthday without knowing his future. 'You must not think that I am going to be rash in this matter.' he wrote to his parents. 'I have thought well over it and consider that I should not act wisely in refusing the same. I wish you to be satisfied that I will not D. V. remain out very long and I am sure, when you consider all things, you will think I have done right.' His father regretted that a son of his should leave the Queen's service, even for a short time, to become a mandarin; but Gordon wrote: 'I think that anyone who contributes to putting down this rebellion fulfils a humane task and I also think tends a great deal to open China to civilisation, D. V.' He promised, ingenuously, not to 'act rashly' although he knew that he would be riding into danger: the 'D. V.' (*Deo volente*) which now appeared more frequently in his letters was no empty symbol.[19]

On 25 March 1863 Staveley returned from Hong Kong, where the Order in Council had reached him, and formally appointed Gordon to the command, under terms agreed with the Chinese. '*I cannot help* adding,' he wrote eighteen years later when Sir Henry Gordon was compiling his *Events in The Life of Charles George Gordon* . . ., 'that I am naturally proud of having selected your brother for the Ever Victorious Army and should feel gratified if you could bring this into your narrative.'[20]

Up to that time Gordon had done nothing outside the confines of British Army service. He was not a maverick, nor an adventurer like Ward or Burgevine, but under orders of the War Office; although on loan to the

Chinese government he remained a British officer, conscious that he represented the Crown while loyally serving China. He had not commanded more than an Engineer company of some eighty men.

On 25 March 1863 he went to the Ever Victorious Army's base, Sungkiang (Sung-Chiang), west of Shanghai on the line of the thirty mile radius, and took command of between 3000 and 4000 Chinese led by Americans with a few British, Germans and other nationalities, who received him in a surly spirit, resenting the dismissal of Burgevine. Gordon brought four regular British officers, to command each arm, and his future brother-in-law, twenty-seven year old staff-surgeon Andrew Moffitt, who some years later would marry Helen. Lyster had 'hoped to come ('Major Gordon is just the man I would go anywhere with. I am not sure that I should join if they were under any other officer.'[21]) but he was needed in Shanghai as Gordon's replacement.

Gordon met General Li Heng-Sung who, under the agreement, was nominally his equal. Then came an urgent order from the Futai to march to the relief of Chanzu, closely besieged by the Taiping general Chung Wang. Chanzu lay up a canal from Fushan, a former nest of pirates close to the southern shore of the wide Yangtze estuary, which must first be recaptured from the rebels.

'G. takes command,' runs Gordon's laconic manuscript note, written two years later for Samuel Mossman, editor of the *North China Herald*. 'Chanzu was closely beleaguered by Chung Wang. Fushan was partially surrounded by the Imperialist Forces with a portion of the Ever V. Army under Tapp who had been repulsed on the 17 March. G. starts with 500 extra men arrives at Fushan on the 2nd April captures place on the 4th April with loss of 1 officer and 3 men killed and five wounded.'[22]

So a long desultory siege of a vigorous, well-armed enemy was ended in two days, revealing Gordon's extraordinary power to lead what the Victorians called 'native troops.' This made a formidable combination with his well-known gifts for reconnaissance and his daring: 'We are all most anxious about Major Gordon,' wrote Lyster in Shanghai before the news of the victory. 'I trust he will get through it all right; he is so regardless of danger it makes one uneasy.'

Up the canal, Chanzu was now 'nearly at its last extremity'[23]: only the ruthlessness of the Imperial Governor prevented surrender. Gordon repulsed a counter-attack and pressed on up the causeway beside the canal, passing a mass crucifixion: thirty-five putrefying naked corpses of

Imperialists, some of whom had evidently been tortured by fire before being bound alive to bamboo crosses.

The Ever Victorious Army arrived before Chanzu to find that the Taipings had lifted the siege rather than face Gordon again.

CHAPTER SEVEN

The Ever-Victorious

The Chinese gave Gordon the name *Ko-teng*. *Ko* means 'offensive weapons' and *teng* means 'to rise'. Sir Thomas Wade the Sinologist and diplomat explained to Henry Gordon that as the Chinese have no alphabet they choose the characters (each a syllable) which sound closest to what they think is the sound of a foreigner's name: *Gor-don* became *Ko-teng*, and although 'offensive weapons rise' proved apt 'I should doubt,' wrote Wade, 'that they were chosen as referring to any qualities of the person ... In choosing *Ko-teng* for Gordon they have been more successful than they usually are.'[1]

Ko-teng Gordon, having relieved Chanzu, withdrew the Ever Victorious Army to Sunkiang. His need to take the offensive stopped him improving his command's organization; as he wrote the next year: 'I have had the disadvantage of the errors of construction to contend with the whole time.' Nor could he easily replace the commanding officers recruited by Ward. 'In themselves,' he wrote, 'they were not so very objectionable, but being ignorant uneducated men unaccustomed to command, they were not suited to set an example or control the men they had under them as officers.'[2]

With the four British officers he had brought in he improved discipline and tactics. He rendered detailed accounts to Li, paid men and officers regularly, and forbade on pain of death the looting on which they had largely depended; he took a cut in pay and refused the traditional bonus which the Governor wished to pay him for the capture of Fushan. He also banned liquor from the camps: hard drinking had been a characteristic of the Ever Victorious Army.

Within a short time he had weeded out incompetent commanders until, as he wrote afterwards, he had 'leaders who were zealous and painstaking and could be trusted.' – or so he thought. Carrying a note book he worked by 'frequent personal and minute inspection without the slightest attempt at formality.' Orders were generally given by word of mouth and formal ceremonies 'were as much as possible avoided (an advantage, as there were many Americans in the force), and each commanding officer, supreme in his command, felt himself trusted.' Gordon said that 'the arrangements were just such as any officer invested with absolute power and a little common sense would carry out,'[3] but as he recalled years later to Florence Nightingale, 'I gained the hearts of my soldiers (who would do anything for me) not by my justice etc. but by looking after them when sick, or wounded, and by continually visiting the Hospital.'[4] He was grateful to Staff-Surgeon Moffitt for creating a humane and efficient medical service. Moffitt, fluent in Chinese, also did much for the surrounding peasantry.

By 18 April 1863, after nearly four weeks, and two victories, Gordon could write home: 'My troops are in great spirits and would do anything. I think during the short time I have been in command that they have got confidence. The rebels are the greatest scourge to the country people. I trust within a short time and with Divine help to put them down.'[5]

Burgevine, however, had gone to Peking ('surreptitiously,' said Futai Li) and persuaded the American minister and Bruce that he had been unjustly dismissed. Bruce asked Li to restore Burgevine to his command as a matter of justice. Li Hung-Chang refused: Gordon had 'proved himself valiant, able and honest ... The people and place are charmed with him;' he wished to 'drill our troops and save our money,' and his men 'delightedly obeyed him ... I cannot therefore remove him without cause'[6], nor would Li contemplate a return to Burgevine's erratic ways.

Charles Staveley had left for England to recover his health (he rose to be a full general and a K. C. B.) and had been relieved by Major-General W. G. Brown. Brown immediately endorsed Li's decision and in a letter to Bruce praised Gordon, 'whose great ability and physical energy render him so well fitted for the command'. Should Gordon be removed, said Brown, 'the Force would likely become of little or no use, but perhaps a source of trouble.'[7] Li had asked the Throne to give Gordon temporary rank as a *Tsung-ping* (equivalent to brigadier-general) in accordance with the original agreement with the British. When the Imperial decree arrived it ordained that he should also receive a 'button of the highest grade' for his mandarin's cap.[8]

Li was his strong support. The details of their co-operation have been confused by an extraordinary hoax, *The Memoirs of Li Hung Chang*, published in 1913. Purporting to be a selection translated from Li's 'journal' or 'diary' it deceived many western experts: inconsistencies or factual inaccuracies were brushed aside by its 'editor', William Francis Mannix, as arising from difficulties of translation or transcription.

The book sold well, despite some questioning of its authenticity and even a statement to the publishers from Li's son that 'my father never kept any diary whatever in his lifetime.' The fake was not exposed until 1923, after Mannix's death, when his friend Ralph D. Paine published a second edition with an introduction. *The Story of A Literary Forgery*. Paine revealed that Mannix, a failed journalist with a string of petty convictions for fraud, and a slight experience of China, had composed the 'Memoirs' while serving a year's sentence for forgery in a Honolulu jail. He had been allowed books, from which he cleverly extracted background and events, but the 'journal', with its references to Gordon in Chapter Three came out of Mannix's head; yet writers have continued to quote as if these spurious 'Memoirs' throw light on Gordon.*

On 27 April Gordon received orders from the Futai to march against the strategic town of Quinsan while Li's brother would march to Taitsan, nearer the Yangtse estuary, which the Rebel commander, Tsah Yen Ching, had offered to surrender. Gordon took 2800 men. Two days later the Force had reached a village fifteen miles from Quinsan when a frantic despatch came from Li: after 1500 of his brother's troops had entered Taitsan the treacherous Tsah had shut the gates and made them prisoners, beheading at least 300 in cold blood. He sallied out to seize the Imperialist camp and his brother had escaped with a spear wound in his buttocks. Gordon must march at once on Taitsan.

In another two days Gordon appeared before its South Gate and at once realized why Holland had met disaster there in February: it was too well defended. Gordon moved the force along the canal which formed the moat,

*The fake 'Memoirs' were still being quoted as if genuine by a biographer of Gordon in 1988, yet any deductions as to Gordon's character are worthless and misleading. Allen (1933) and Wortham (1933) may perhaps be excused since the second edition with its exposure of the hoax was not well known in England. Elton (1954), Chevenix-Trench (1978) and later writers have little excuse. The forgery is discussed in detail by Professor Albert G. Hess in *The "Memoirs" of Li Hung-Chang – the Story of A Non-translation. Renditions*, Spring 1981, pp 155–167 (Chinese University of Hong Kong.)

towards the West Gate. On 1 May he made a reconnaissance and noted that the gate had no powerful defence in itself but was covered by two bamboo stockades enclosing two stone forts, sited 1500 yards west, beyond a ruined suburb: the creek leading to the West Gate was not even staked: the water could become an access to the walls by using a bridge of boats.

Next day, 2 May, the stockades fell easily after bombardment. Gordon then landed his guns in the ruined suburb and opened up on the walls, moving guns and boats steadily nearer, while infantry fire on the battlements weakened the defenders' response. By mid-afternoon Gordon judged that the breach in the pounded wall was wide enough for an assault. 'The storming party advanced' he wrote. 'In a moment the breach was crowded with rebels, who stood boldly up, and threw bags of powder, with fuzes attached, into the boats. The troops pushed on across the bridge – one of the boats of which had been sunk by the explosion of a powder bag – but could not mount the breach, the rebels presenting a forest of spears against their advance.'

In this furious fight the legend of 'Chinese' Gordon was born.

He led from the front, unarmed, smoking a cheroot and carrying his cane. Knowing by instinct that irregular troops must see their general, he ignored the enemy's bullets as he urged on his men, while keeping a cool grip on the battle: he ordered up two howitzers who fired over the heads of the stormers. The shells, recorded Gordon, 'mowed down the defenders of the breach in scores, though they still attempted to fire down at the storming party which lay in the ditch. The sounding of the "advance" made them show again, but after a time they got more wary, and another attempt was made to mount the breach, again to be frustrated. The rebel chief's snake flags still floated out on the breach, and till he left, it was said the breach would be defended.'

Gordon ordered a violent fire 'which hurled masses of brickwork on the crouching rebels. Another and third attempt by a fresh regiment ... was stoutly met by the rebels, and the contending bodies swayed on the edge of the breach for a moment, and then the stormers surged over and the place was won, the flags of the chief disappearing at the last moment.'[9]

Gordon wrote long afterwards that 'I used to pray as my men went up the breaches in China for their success; thank Him, if they succeeded, if not, was content; never wanted to know Him any closer, swung as a pendulum in wide sweeps.'[10]

The E. V. A. poured into the city. The bodies of several foreign supporters and three sepoys were found in the breach or (the accounts are contradictory) were killed by the Force in the hand to hand fighting: its officers had tended to be violent against compatriots who served with the Rebels. In the city they found an English deserter from the 31st Regiment, Private Hargreaves, badly wounded. 'Mr. Gordon, Mr. Gordon,' he cried, 'Don't let them kill me!' 'Take him out and shoot him,' shouted Gordon, to stop any E. V. A. Westerner putting a bullet through him on the spot. Then, in a low voice to one of his staff: 'Put him in my boat and tend to his wounds.' The man reached Shanghai safely and survived. That night Gordon scribbled an unsigned note to his parents: 'I have just taken Taitsan with not much loss of life and am thanks to Providence untouched. I will send details later. Your aff. son.'[11] Later he spoke of his losses as 'very heavy indeed' compared with those of the Rebels, and that during the twenty minute struggle in the breach he had felt 'very great doubts of our success.' 'Gordon said that in his experience in the Crimea he never saw anything like it,' recorded Lyster; and in an official report to General Brown, he called it 'by far the most dangerous service for officers I have ever seen, and the latter have the satisfaction of always feeling *in action* that their men are utterly untrustworthy in the way of following them.'[12]

Gordon made up his casualties by enlisting Taiping prisoners. They willingly shaved their heads in token of submission to the Emperor, for many had been conscripted by the Heavenly King and felt no loyalty. Gordon included some in his bodyguard company and even in his personal bodyguard of six 'wangs' as he playfully called them.

He then led the E. V. A. back down the causeway towards Quinsan, his original objective.

As he marched, an execution took place without his knowledge. Seven Taiping prisoners, alleged to have been the architects of the treachery which had led to the beheading in cold blood of 300 Imperialists, were sentenced to a degrading and lingering slow death allowed by the Chinese criminal code. The mandarins chose to carry out the sentence at Wokong close to General Brown's small force of British troops, with its hangers-on from the Shanghai Western community who had come to watch the battle or bring supplies. Military and civilians alike were disgusted to come across seven Chinese, stripped, and bound to stakes, with a flayed piece of skin hanging from an arm and seven small arrows piercing their torsos; the seven men were exposed all day and then beheaded.

Exaggerated reports of atrocities by the captors of Taitsan on their Taiping prisoners then appeared in the Shanghai newspapers and went to Hong Kong, where they were taken up by the Bishop of Victoria, Dr. George Smith, who protested to the Foreign Secretary without checking the facts. Dr. Smith had not lost his sympathy for the Taipings, whom he still believed to be sincere if somewhat heretical Christians, and he was supported by a strong lobby of merchants in Hong Kong who were making money by supplying them with arms.

Gordon soon knew that he was being abused in newspapers in China and in England, but did not flinch from the conviction that he served humanity by suppressing a cruel and wanton rebellion which had lost any claim to serve the people of China or the cause of Christ.

The Taiping lobby in England accepted, in time, that Gordon had not been involved in the executions but they never forgave him for his part in suppressing the Heavenly Kingdom. In 1885 during the adulation following Gordon's death, one of the Gravesend clergy who had known him well and had himself served in China as a missionary, was asked by a friend whether Gordon had ever stated 'that his Chinese policy against the Taipings was a mistake, and he repented of it ... If not I can only look upon him as a murderer of native Christians and a wild mercenary soldier.'[13]

As yet unaware of the controversy Gordon arrived before Quinsan, held by rebels. The Imperialist commander, General Ching (an ex-rebel) had built stockades near the East gate. Quinsan was a large city with walls four miles round, and wide canals outside the walls to form a moat, and a hill of three hundred feet, topped by a pagoda, in its centre. The defenders had access by canal from Soochow, their main base only sixteen miles away. Quinsan's walls were poor but the turreted East gate with its heavy gun, believed to be served by an Englishman, was too strong to assault although General Ching now wished to attack it.

Gordon's men were becoming insubordinate. Despite his strict orders they were encumbered by Taitsan plunder or had wandered away to sell it. 'Vain effort,' his notes run, 'to keep them together to attack Quinsan; forced through their behaviour to go back to refit to Sungkiang.'[15] He left his new steam gunboat *Hyson*, the most powerful vessel on the waterways, to guard General Ching's flank.

Back at Sungkiang he put the men to rigorous training. 'My time from morning to night is much taken up with all sorts of work,' he wrote home on 10 May, 'as in addition to leading the Force I have to instruct officers and men and to organize it, but we get on well together.'[16] With his spare frame and heavy smoking he could go long periods without bothering to eat: sometimes he would throw rice and meat into a bowl of tea and gulp down the mess, developing the habit which was to distress his landlady at Gravesend; other days he would seem to his bodyguard and staff to eat nothing, but would walk into the commissariat after they had gone to bed, and suck ten or a dozen raw eggs.

He was becoming a loner: he had been a normal member of a Mess, but now, with his officers scattered at their units, he lived by himself. He had hoped to replace the more ignorant, drunken or insubordinate foreign adventurers by British officers, until the War Office ordained that they must go on half-pay; most of them could not afford the risk when Chinese pay was notoriously irregular. Instead he took British privates and non-commissioned officers.

On 26 May Gordon brought the E. V. A. back to Quinsan after suppressing a mutiny among his foreign officers: he had reorganized the Commissariat to stop them stealing rice. The force arrived at their old camping ground near the East gate of Quinsan, to find that the Rebels had built stockades and breastworks which almost surrounded the Imperialists. General Ching had resisted fierce attacks but failed to destroy the Rebel stockades or to assault the town. Next morning Gordon took the stockades from the flank, losing one of his best British officers. The Rebels escaped across the wide canal in their boats and disappeared inside the walls.

The East gate looked as strongly defended as before. Ching had told Peking that he only needed to cross the canal to take the town; to save his face he urged Gordon to attack it next morning and when Gordon replied that he would reconnoitre the other sides of the town first, Ching was annoyed.

On 30 May, with General Ching and Li Hung Chang himself, who had arrived in expectation of a victory, Gordon embarked on the paddle steamer *Hyson*, commanded by the valiant Yankee Captain Davidson, and entered the wide canal which formed a semi-circle some miles to the south of Quinsan: 'an imprudent proceeding,' since the Rebels on the hill – which gave a view of thirty miles around – might have guessed his plans. The *Hyson* steamed on until they saw stakes which protected the junction with the main canal connecting Quinsan and Soochow. This junction was held weakly: if Gordon could capture its stockades and fort he would sever Quinsan from the Taiping base and induce surrender without much loss of life.

General Ching was 'sore as a bear' when Gordon again declined to make a frontal assault. Next morning, before dawn, Gordon sent Imperial sailing gunboats ahead to remove the stakes (which they did not attempt until he arrived). At first light he followed with *Hyson* and 350 men and some field guns in a colourful flotilla. They captured the stockades and a village and entered the main canal. The route to Soochow was a narrow causeway between the canal and a wide lake stretching many miles to the north. Gordon disembarked men to hold each captured stockade and was steaming on in the *Hyson* towards Soochow when they met a large party of rebels marching east to the relief of Quinsan. At sight and sound of the steamer, which made full use of its whistle and occasionally fired its 32 lb gun, the rebels turned and fled, pursued by *Hyson*.

Though there were now few of his men on board, Gordon took on 350 prisoners, 'rather a risk' since they might overwhelm the crew. Gordon also rescued a naked infant who clung to him for much of the remaining action: Gordon later sent him to Shanghai, arranged for a foster parent and paid for his education, calling him 'Quincey'. Quincey rose to be chief of police of the Shanghai-Nanking railway and founder of a family which, a hundred and thirty years later, included a woman academic in America.

Darkness was falling and Soochow not far away when *Hyson* turned back in case their route had been blocked by counter attacks: they heard heavy firing behind them and arrived in time to prevent some Imperialists being overwhelmed. Gordon steamed on towards Quinsan, when 'at the distance of two hundred yards we saw a confused mass near a high bridge. It was too dark to distinguish very clearly; but on the steamer blowing the whistle, the mass wavered, yelled, and turned back: it was the garrison of Quinsan attempting to escape to Soochow – some seven to eight thousand men. Matters were in too critical a state to hesitate as the mass of the rebels, goaded into desperation, would have swept our small force away. We were therefore forced to fire into them, and pursue them towards Quinsan, firing however very rarely, and only when the rebels looked as if they would make a stand.'[17]

The *Hyson* could have caused a massacre but Gordon refused to use his power: indeed he wrote next day to the British Consul that nothing but the 'absolute necessity' of preventing the rebels carrying the weak stockades by force of numbers 'justified our firing into them, but it was imperative and the rebels were desperate.' After securing the safety of the stockades Gordon found 'a dense mass of 300 rebels who gave up their arms and surrendered.'[18] His own loss was two killed and five wounded.

At daylight the country people rose against the fleeing Taipings and killed hundreds or drove them into the lake to drown, until Gordon eventually estimated that over 4000 rebels had been killed or drowned ('humanity might have desired a smaller destruction') and 8000 were prisoners. General Ching, meanwhile, had entered unopposed through the east gate.

CHAPTER EIGHT

Betrayed at Soochow

Gordon refused leave to loot. Quinsan should henceforth be their base: the key to the countryside and to Soochow, his ultimate objective, and strategically placed for his armed steamer. The Force would also be removed from the temptations of Sungkiang, to the disgust of the artillerymen, who refused to fall in on parade. They sent Gordon an anonymous proclamation threatening to kill him and the Western officers with the big guns and the Chinese officers with the small guns.

Gordon knew instinctively that faced with another mutiny he must act as a mandarin, not as an officer of the British Army with its slow procedures of arrest, court martial and confirmation by higher authority before sentence could be carried out.

He summoned the artillery non-commissioned officers, guessing that they were behind the mutiny. Through his interpreter he asked the name of the writer of the proclamation and why the men had not paraded. They pretended ignorance. He then said that if the name were not given, one in every five N. C. O.s would be shot. They groaned, and there was a corporal who groaned loudest and longest. Gordon seized him with his own hands and ordered the bodyguard to shoot him. They put him up against a tombstone 'just outside the West gate. Mark of bullet still there,' wrote Gordon more than a year later.[1]

He placed the remainder under arrest, ringed by his bodyguard, and told them that unless they gave the culprit's name within an hour he would carry out his threat to shoot one in five. He retired to his tent. Before the hour was up the name of the executed corporal was handed in; whether he was indeed the author of the proclamation or a convenient dead scapegoat, Gordon did not enquire. He was certain that his summary taking of one life saved many which would have been lost if the mutiny had taken hold.

Instead, mutiny became desertion. As he wrote laconically in his third-person notes: 'Men then desert. 1700 only out of 3900 remain – very disorderly lot: Ward spoilt them. G. recruits rebel prisoners, who are much better men.'

The hot weather was upon them and Gordon was content to train the Force. 'Humanly speaking I see every chance of the Rebellion being speedily crushed'[2] he wrote on 3 June; he had succeeded in his strategy of cutting off the rebels from the sea, and now was determined that the Ever Victorious Army and the Imperialist divisions should invest Soochow, the great silk city and Taiping base, so that it would surrender: 'never thought it would be necessary to take Soochow by force,'[3] he noted afterwards. Meanwhile he could protect the rich cornlands and restore freedom of movement on the creeks, canals and lakes: 'the people around are so grateful for their release that it is quite a pleasure,'[4] he wrote on 23 June.

The Imperialist General Ching, still sore at being deprived of personal glory, was a nuisance from a combination of jealousy and ill-planned pluck against the enemy and anybody around: he even fired on Gordon's steamer and had to be forced to apologize. When the Futai, Li Hung Chang, forgot the men's wages and did not pay the bills for supplies, Gordon dipped into his own slender resources, so that where Ward had made a fortune, Gordon would leave China poorer than he had arrived; but by mid-July he had determined to resign, since his situation was 'derogatory to my position as a British Officer'[5] He continued to plan his campaign.

Then he received a letter from Halliday Macartney, a fighting young Army doctor (born the same year as Gordon) who spoke Mandarin fluently and had entered the Chinese service, first as Burgevine's secretary and then on the staff of Li Hung Chang. Macartney warned Gordon that Burgevine was recruiting foreigners in Shanghai, whether to join the Imperialists or the rebels was not known. On 25 July[6] Gordon took his Force westward by water and the causeway, towards the Grand Canal, to cut Soochow's access from the south. That same day Burgevine wrote to Gordon: 'My dear Gordon, You may hear a great many rumours concerning me, but do not believe any of them. I shall come up ...* and have a long talk with you. Until then adieu!'[7]

Gordon was conscious that he had displaced Burgevine who was refused either employment or compensation. Gordon had tried to be friendly and

*Three words illegible.

had gone bail for him but was contemptuous of Burgevine's military skills, especially now that he was broken in health through poorly healed wounds.

Burgevine's letter must have reached Gordon on a march which led him by a series of surprise attacks to the surrender, with little loss of life, of Kahpoo and Wokong, with fifteen sailing gunboats and 7000 men, a useful source of recruits to replace Ever Victorious men who had deserted to loot. Soochow was now cut off except from the north-west, and Gordon had restored Imperialist access to the Great Lake (*Tai Ho*) which lay to the west: the Soochow rebels must make a long detour by land if they wished to keep touch with territory they held farther south, or with Shanghai and, its arms suppliers.

Gordon garrisoned the captured towns, returned to Quinsan and left by the steamer *Hyson* for Shanghai to hand in his resignation to the Governor, who received him graciously in his *yamen* that evening; but with no interpreter present, no business was done. Gordon made an appointment for the morning and went to the home of the Acting British Consul, John Markham. Markham said that most of Gordon's officers were in league with Burgevine. That night an urgent letter arrived by courier from Macartney in Sungkiang: his small steamer *Kajow* had been pirated away by Burgevine and a gang of Western desperadoes; the Imperialists had been too lazy to intercept it; Burgevine was last seen steaming across the lake in the direction of Soochow.

Gordon called for a horse. 'Although,' wrote Markham to Bruce, 'I tried to prevail on him to remain until the next day, he started at midnight, quite alone, to ride a distance of fifty miles. I have not yet heard of his arrival but as he knows the country thoroughly, I trust he has succeeded in reaching Quinsan in safety.'[8]

Hearing that Burgevine had reached Soochow and had been joined by as many as 300 foreigners (in fact only 103) despite the Imperialist blockade, Gordon knew that all hope of Soochow's speedy surrender had gone. He hurried from Quinsan to his garrison at Wokong and arrived in time to throw back a violent counter-attack led by Burgevine and his foreigners in 'Garibaldi shirts' (the red shirt popularized by Garibaldi and his legion.) 'We have had a tremendous fight for three days.'[9] Gordon suspended his resignation 'until all difficulty and danger vanished,' to the satisfaction of General Brown who wrote of Gordon that 'in this officer is combined so many dashing qualities, let alone skill and judgement, to make him invaluable to command such a force.'[10]

Gordon dubbed Burgevine's foreigners 'rowdies', 'the scum of Shanghai', but they brought the rebels strength in guns and leadership which would make an attack on Soochow too costly; although 'Burgevine's military knowledge is nil,' a defeat of the Ever Victorious Army 'would be disastrous ... I shall therefore act a good deal on the defensive,'[11] not least because the weather was very hot in August and early September. This policy was warmly supported by General Brown, 'who has been very kind and considerate,' but not by the Futai, or by Peking. Gordon received a letter in Chinese from the Futai which was poorly translated by his interpreter: 'Now the rebellion has been giving out a sign of being defeated, you will pursue forward at once ... As [the Force] is of Chinese soldiers, you being one of the Chinese officials are to take my advice to move your troops accordingly.' Gordon pencilled two large exclamation marks in the margin.[12]

Weeks passed without action. By the end of September, Burgevine had become annoyed by the Taiping's failure to give him high command. He opened secret negotiations with Gordon. Burgevine was disillusioned by the prolonged civil war. He wrote to Gordon on 3 October 1863: 'I am perfectly aware from nearly four years service in this country that both sides are equally rotten. But you must confess that on the Taiping side there is at least innovation, and a disregard for many of the frivolous and idolatrous customs of the Manchus. While my eyes are fully open to the defects of the Taiping character, from a close observation of three months, I find many promising traits never yet displayed by the Imperialists. The Rebel Mandarins are without exception brave and gallant men, and could you see Chung Wang, who is now here, you would immediately say that such a man deserved to succeed.'[13]

During the next ten days westerners from both sides met on a bridge which had been informally accepted as a no-man's land. A Shanghai newspaper reported: 'The frank and straightforward manner of General Gordon eventually led the principal men to conceive the advisability of withdrawing from what they saw was a hopeless cause.'[14] Burgevine, in pain from his wound, was drinking heavily again and urged Gordon to desert the Imperialists when he, Burgevine, deserted the Taipings; then to march with their joint forces to Peking, depose the child Emperor and seize the throne. 'The indignation with which Major Gordon received this wild and insulting notion,' reported Interpreter Mayers to Consul Markham, 'probably acted as a last argument in convincing Burgevine of the uselessness of his struggle.'[15] William S. F. Mayers, who became one of Gordon's close friends, had arrived with the amnesty requested by Gordon for Burgevine and his men.

A little later the Taiping Wangs (Generals) ordered these adventurers to bring their little steamer *Kajow* on a foray against an Imperialist port: during the fight the *Kajow's* magazine blew up, the ship sank, and Burgevine, accused of being drunk, shot his second in command in the eye.

Gordon meanwhile had received a rebuke from the senior Chinese general which Gordon's own interpreter, an adventurer called Henry Ballou Morse, known as Mei, translated in a way which suggests that language difficulties were always present: 'I could not find,' ran the translation, 'any reason why the rebellion Pai Chi Wen (Burgevine) if surrender with sincerity, has much disguise. As he is deceitful to be rebel, Major Gordon who is a noted British Military officer and now leading troops for China with full trust, must not offer Pai any favour, so as to avoid any corruption possibly done by subordinate, as well as to keep Major Gordon's name. It is to be remembered that our principal duty is to fight with rebels, and we shall easily be deceived if always acknowledging surrenders.'[16]

Nevertheless Gordon was sure that Burgevine's removal from the rebels, with his gang of foreigners, was an essential preliminary to coaxing the Taipings into surrender. A plan was concocted. The rebel general became suspicious and forbade all exit from the city: Burgevine and another westerner were stopped but not beheaded. Next day Gordon fired a pre-arranged rocket and moved his men close to the camp outside the walls, where the foreign sick and wounded lay. The Taipings opened fire and in the mêlée only thirty-three officers and men managed to cross the moat and escape. They were in pitiable condition 'and all testified great joy and gratitude at finding themselves within General Gordon's lines.'[17] He took nineteen of them into his bodyguard.

Gordon now negotiated with the Taiping Wangs but his hope of weakening their resolve by a mass defection was spoiled by their cunning ploy: they handed over Burgevine and his people 'with respect,' in a ceremony which implied an honourable transfer, not a mass desertion: 'the foreign officer Burgevine is very ill,' Moh Wang had written to Gordon, 'and is on his way to Shanghai for medical treatment . . .'[18]

Burgevine was sent down to Shanghai and handed to the American consul. After trying to seize another small steamer he was arrested but allowed, under the amnesty, to leave China, promising not to return; a promise which he broke the next year but failed to reach the Taipings beleagured in Nanking. Again the following year, with the rebellion almost over, he tried to reach the last unconquered Taiping Wang but was recognized by a foreign instructor and arrested. He escaped execution because he still held American citizenship although he had taken Chinese nationality. A few months later he was drowned in a river when a boatload (or some say an overhead cage) of prisoners capsized, or the cable broke, by accident or design.

His epitaph might be a sad letter he had written to Gordon from Japan: 'I have never sought to advance my own interests ... I have committed many errors in judgement no doubt, but you at least, will give me credit for purity of intention.'[19]

A young infantry lieutenant of the 99th Regiment (Lanarkshire, later 2nd Wiltshires) named Forbes Lugard Storey joined the E. V. A. from Hong Kong.

In front of a rebel stockade, one mile outside Soochow, Storey met Gordon: 'a light-built, active, wiry, middle-sized man, of about thirty-two years of age, in the undress uniform of the Royal Engineers. The countenance bore a pleasant frank appearance, eyes light blue with a fearless look in them, hair crisp and inclined to curl, conversation short and decided.' Looking back some thirty years later Storey wrote: 'I do not ever remember knowing before or since a man of such an extraordinary force of character, indomitable will, and great energy – the latter he imbued his companions with – and honesty of heart in all his actions. Without parading it, one could not help seeing and feeling that all his actions were governed by a strong current of religion; and though no doubt his strong will and temper made him do and say things which he afterwards repented, yet the force of circumstances and the peculiar position he was in must be taken into consideration.'[20]

The investment of Soochow was almost complete. Its strong, high walls stretched as far as the eye could see, protected by a canal seventy yards wide; but Gordon's Force of about 3000 men, and the larger Imperialist army of General Ching, whom Gordon now admired for his strategic skills, had steadily reduced the stockades which guarded the gates. There had been fierce actions, including one defeat (the result of treachery) in which many men and officers were killed or wounded. Gordon, with his cigar and his cane, was always to the front. When an American officer had been caught in unauthorized communication with the enemy (probably hoping to trade for personal profit) Gordon had told him that his punishment should be to lead the next 'forlorn hope'; but when he fell with a bullet in the mouth, it was into Gordon's arms. And when a Chinese soldier was too shivering with fear to aim, Gordon placed his shoulder as the man's rifle rest. Finally, on 29 November, the last stockade of stone, mud and bamboo fell and Soochow was cut off. An assault of such a city, with its garrison of 30,000 men would bring huge casualties on both sides, followed by sacking and burning, rape and massacre, which Gordon was determined to avoid.

All the time that he was planning and fighting he was in secret correspondence with the enemy chiefs urging Lar Wang and Moh Wang to surrender Soochow. Gordon did not scruple in the earlier stages to trade guns and horses to help win their confidence. In one letter the Taiping Wangs replied to Gordon: 'If Your Excellency should be willing to come to our side, we shall be delighted to work together with you ... Pray bear in mind that we both worship God and Jesus, and being of one religion, we have no intention of being false or harmful.'[21] Gordon's comment afterwards was that 'The head chief may know something of the Christian religion but I will answer for it that nine-tenths of the rebels have no real ideas on the subject.'[22]

While persuading the Taipings to surrender he was persuading the Imperialists to grant generous terms. Li Hung Chang, the Futai, arrived from Shanghai at the end of November, ready for the fall of Soochow; Gordon received the clearest possible impression that the Futai promised the Wangs their lives and that they could bring their armies over to the Imperialist side. Gordon was certain that if Soochow should be occupied peaceably, with no beheadings, the remaining Taiping strongholds would surrender speedily and the rebellion end.

General Ching, himself once a Taiping rebel, was now negotiating openly with Lar Wang; Gordon met Lar, at Ching's request, but had no part in the terms of surrender. One rebel chief, however, Moh Wang, whom Gordon admired as a valiant fighter, and was willing to take into the Ever Victorious Army, had opposed the other Wangs; he wanted Soochow defended to the last man.

On 2 December 1863 Gordon had his batteries ready to pound the walls, and pontoons to cross the moat. That evening Gordon and Ching agreed to Lar Wang's request that they postpone their assault until 6 December to give him time to overcome Moh Wang's opposition. Gordon again received the Futai's assurance that if the Wangs surrendered the city and the 'Long Hairs' shaved their heads in token of submission, he would grant good terms. When Gordon and Lar Wang met, 'I said I wanted to make the Imperialists and rebels good friends.'[23] The Wangs must trust Gordon's word that all would be well.

On 4 December two Frenchmen with the rebels came out of the city to report that the Wangs had all met at Moh's palace for a banquet and discussion, dressed in state robes and wearing their princely crowns; and that when Moh maintained his opposition to surrender, the others had killed him and cut off his head.

That night most of the rebels shaved their long hair and at 8 a. m. the following morning, 5 December, the North and East Gates were surrendered to Ching. Gordon immediately withdrew his Force a short way from the walls: he had no faith in their discipline if they were allowed into a city ripe for plunder. Instead he proposed to lay siege to the next rebel town. He went to the Futai, who had set up camp beside his barge on the canal below the walls, and asked that the men be given two months' extra pay as compensation for capturing towns without looting. Li refused. When no argument prevailed Gordon said he would resign: he would lay down his command at 3 o'clock that afternoon unless the Futai had changed his mind.

Gordon then entered the city with a small staff and bodyguard. The streets were empty, the shops shut, but no house was burning or looted, no women and children lay dead in the streets, no heads bled in the gutters. He went to Lar Wang's palace. Ponies ready-saddled were in the courtyard. Gordon entered the *yamen* or judgement hall where Lar Wang with some twenty other Wangs, 'very distinguished soldierly-looking men,' as Storey noted were standing dressed in valuable furs against the winter cold. Lar Wang assured Gordon that all was well. Gordon knew they trusted his word.[24]

He next went to the house of Moh Wang. In a large hall with high vaulted roof a great table stood littered with the remains of a feast. A sickly smell of withered water lilies pervaded the air. In the centre, across the table, lay the headless body of Moh Wang in gorgeously embroidered, bloodstained robes. Young Storey was removing the outer robe; in an undergarment he found Gordon's letters to Moh, splashed with blood, and handed them to Gordon, whom Storey saw 'much moved' by Moh's death. As none of Ching's soldiers would touch the body, Gordon ordered Storey to arrange decent burial.

Gordon went out of the city to his camp. 3 o'clock had passed. He was ready to resign but found General Ching fresh from the Futai with an offer of one month's pay only. Gordon's officers angrily refused it and wanted to march their men against the Futai. Gordon persuaded them to accept and march back to Quinsan. 'Ching told me at this time,' he wrote two or three days later, 'that the Futai had written to Pekin and that he had extended mercy to the Wangs.'[25]

Gordon woke next day, Sunday 6 December 1863, expecting the peaceful surrender of a great city, its stalwart defenders and innocent inhabitants. Instead, the day ended in suspense and danger, followed within hours by shock, misery and fury.

His men as they marched away hurled insults as they passed Futai Li's camp. Gordon gave orders for his steamers to be brought round to the nearby lake, having discovered that he might easily recapture the small steamer stolen by Burgevine's men, and went into the city, where he learned that the formal ceremony of surrender would take place at noon at the camp of the Futai, who had prepared a feast for the Wangs. Gordon, tragically, declined an invitation to attend since he thought the Wangs might be embarrassed, and he wanted to recapture the steamer.

While waiting for his own steamer Gordon went again to the palace of Lar Wang, whom he found cheerful. Lar suggested, without apparent premonition, that Gordon wait in Soochow but did not press when told that the business of the steamer was urgent. As Gordon walked towards the East Gate the Wangs in their finery trotted past him, laughing and talking, on their way to the feast.

Not long afterwards, standing on the top of the East Gate he noticed in the distance round the Futai's stockade a huge crowd which he supposed was the ceremony of submission and was not alarmed. Then a large body of Imperialist soldiers rushed through the gate, cheering as if seizing a vacated stockade. Gordon shouted his disapproval. General Ching joined him and they rode their ponies along the walls; but when Ching was vague and contradictory about the submission ceremony, and kept firing into the air, Gordon 'thought the thing so strange that I asked Dr. Macartney, who was by me, to go to Lar Wang's house, and to see him, and tell him not to fear anything.'[26]

On reaching the South Gate Gordon had become so uneasy that he left Ching and rode into the city. The streets were 'full of rebels, standing to their arms, and Imperialist soldiers looting.' Accompanied only by his interpreter he reached Lar Wang's palace at dusk: he found it gutted by looters and no sign of Lar. Lar's uncle about to escort the women and children to his own house entreated Gordon to come as their protector. When they reached the house it was already protected by street barricades and a large body of Lar's own men.

An extraordinary night followed. The Taipings would not let Gordon go. As the hours passed and he saved them from several bands of Imperialist looters he wanted more and more to send his interpreter to find Futai Li Hung Chang, take him prisoner and release the Wangs. Had the rebels in the uncle's house known what had happened at Li's camp the previous noon they might have killed Gordon, now virtually their hostage.

Sometime in the small hours they let his interpreter go, with a small escort, one of whom came back to report that the interpreter had been seized and beheaded (in fact, only wounded). Gordon finally got away, to look for his bodyguard, and was arrested by Imperialists and detained an hour. Released, he reached the Gate where his men were and sent them to the uncle's house. They found it gutted. The city was being sacked, against Gordon's solemn undertaking to the Wangs. Soon after daylight on 7 December he met General Ching and rounded on him furiously. Ching 'was most anxious to excuse himself but I did not listen to him. At this time I did not know the Wangs had been beheaded.'

Ching left Gordon, went into the city, shot twenty men for looting and sat down and cried. He returned to his camp and sent a Major Bailey, commanding his artillery, to Gordon by boat. Bailey told him that Ching was not to blame: 'that the Futai had ordered him to do what he did, and that the Futai had ordered the city to be looted.'[27] Bailey believed that Wangs had been beheaded but some might still be prisoners. He produced Lar Wang's young son, who pointed across the seventy-yard creek to where his father had been killed. Gordon went across and found six headless bodies 'gashed in a frightful way.' Lar Wang's body was not visible (it had been partly buried) but his head lay nearby, horribly cut about 'showing the brutality of the executioners.' Lar's son begged him to take it. Gordon wrapped it in silk, in a bizarre foreshadowing of the day nearly twenty-three years later, when his own severed head would be wrapped in cloth and carried to the Mahdi.

Believing he might rescue any survivors he took a revolver from one of his staff (normally he carried no arms) and went into the stockades: 'I thought that I could frighten the Futai into giving them up.'[28] Li, however, had anticipated Gordon's anger and gone into the city. Gordon wrote him a furious letter in the heat of the moment and left it in the Futai's boat. 'Gordon's ire, grief, and chagrin,' recalled one of his staff, 'at the treachery and broken faith exhibited towards the Wangs – they having by him been promised their lives, and further, the lives and property of all in the city guaranteed – no one but himself could or ever will fathom. He was beside himself.'[29] Not only had he been double-crossed, so that his solemn promise had been worthless, but, as he wrote later, 'if faith had been kept, there would have been no more fighting as every town would have given in.' The rebellion would have ended with little more loss of life on either side 'and not much injury to the inhabitants.'[30]

Gordon poured out to his staff the most violent and impracticable plans to revenge the Wangs and disgrace the Futai. Then the steamers came up. He boarded one, withdrew to Quinsan, went into his house and wrote a terse note to his parents, without ascription or signature: 'I have just returned from Soochow and you will I know be glad to hear I have fought my last battle with the Imperialists. They have in the most dastardly manner broken faith with the Rebels and beheaded their chiefs. I have no time for more as I am now deeply engaged in arranging matters.

'Kind love to all, Your aff[t] son.'[31]

Li Hung Chang did not return to his camp that evening but to Macartney's, near Fifty Nine Arch bridge, presumably to avoid Gordon's wrath. Next morning Gordon's letter was brought from the boat. Li asked Macartney to translate, telling him 'of the rupture which had occurred between him and Major Gordon.'

Macartney glanced at the letter and told the Futai that it had been 'written without due consideration, and under circumstances of extreme irritation,' and that the breach would be more speedily healed if Li knew nothing of the letter: Macartney believed that he was doing Gordon a service in not translating his wild threats to recapture Soochow and hand it back to the rebels unless the Futai resigned at once. The Futai asked Macartney to keep the letter, which he sent six months later to the new British Consul Sir Harry Parkes with an account of the incident: Parker gave it to Bruce who did not place it among his official papers so it has disappeared.

The Futai sought to justify his breach of faith. Some of his claims were specious; but not perhaps his remark, as reported by Macartney to Parkes, that 'he had begun to dread the result of his promised clemency' on the people he governed, if mercy were shown to those who had caused so much bloodshed. Then he said: 'He could not understand how Major Gordon should take the matter so much to heart. What was he to the Wangs, or the Wangs to him?' Macartney explained how Gordon cared about 'a *promise* having been broken to which he had been a party,' but Macartney missed Gordon's other point, that clemency at Soochow would have brought the surrender of the remaining towns and the end of the rebellion.

Macartney told Parkes that he was about to read Li a lecture on foreign ideas of honour when I was brought to a standstill by his advancing the undeniable fact that China was China and the foreign country the foreign country.' The Futai asked Macartney to go at once to Gordon and effect a reconciliation.[32] He arrived long after dark when Gordon was in bed. They had no conversation until the breakfast table next morning, with others present. Macartney's efforts were snubbed by Gordon, who added to his official report: 'The Futai sent Mr. Macartney to persuade me that he could not have done otherwise, and I blush to think that he could have got an Englishman, late an officer in Her Majesty's Army, to undertake a mission of such a nature.'[33] (This was printed in the Foreign Office Blue Book, to Macartney's hurt. Later, when all was sweetness and light again, Gordon acknowledged that Macartney had acted from highest motives, and apologized openly in the Shanghai press.)

Hardly had Macartney left on 8 December when Frederick Mayers the official interpreter arrived. Gordon's near contemporary and good friend, he had been going on leave up-country when he met the messenger taking the news to Shanghai, and had rushed to Gordon's side. 'The noble fellow,' runs Mayers' diary entry, '... recapitulates the whole history ... never have I seen so high wrought and generous a feeling – almost an agony – for the wrongs of others ... its climax ... when he suddenly threw aside a sheet and exposed the ghastly head of the murdered Ma Wang (*sic*).'[*]

Next day a senior mandarin, named Pwan, one of the principal landowners of Soochow, came from Li Hung Chang in another attempt at reconciliation, imploring Mayers, who interpreted, 'to do all in my power to appease Major Gordon's mind.' Pwan deplored the treachery and

---

[*]All efforts to trace the Diary of F. W. Mayers (1831–78) have failed. This heavily abbreviated quote was included in a letter from his son S. F. Mayers, dated 29 November 1931, to Sir Hesketh Bell (Royal Commonwealth Society Archives, Bell Papers C. U. L.) The Diary may have been destroyed in an air raid.

volunteered that it would indeed prolong the rebellion, but he was specially worried that Gordon's resignation would cause the Force to 'fall into disorder, and to desert most probably to the rebels.' E. V. A. officers were disgusted at the Futai; Gordon had only dissuaded them from changing sides by pointing out that they would prolong the agony of the Chinese people.[33]

General Brown, who had been on the point of embarking for Hong Kong, came instead to Quinsan and persuaded Gordon to withdraw his resignation because only he could control the Force, which Brown took formally under his own command. He ordered Gordon, as he himself wished, not to co-operate with the Futai and Ching until he was publicly exonerated from any part in the massacre of the Wangs. Gordon had been back to Soochow to recover Lar Wang's body, and rescue his family, but he refused to see Li Hung Chang, to whom Brown (Mayers' interpreting) was explicit in condemnation. Li was plainly relieved that Gordon would not resign, and as they were leaving he seized Mayers' arm, imploringly: 'I look to you to arrange matters and prevent a breach in friendship!'[34]

Gordon stayed distraught. Major Storey, four or five days after the massacre, found him 'in a truly sorrowful state; he could not speak from emotion, his eyes were full of tears, he did nothing but walk about the room in a distracted manner.'[35] He retained command with utmost reluctance. Moreover he expected to be roundly abused when the news of the massacre reached England, for not resigning. 'I do not care,' he wrote on 15 December. 'I know that I have acted to the best of my ability in the right course and then what may be said is immaterial. I am sure that there would have been twenty times the loss of life if I had not remained in command and twice as much misery.'[36]

That did not reduce his own, for as he wrote on Christmas Eve to the Secretary of State for War, Earl de Grey and Ripon: 'There was little doubt of the end of the rebellion if he had kept faith. I need not say how extremely this work has upset me and at the time it happened if I had come across the Futai it would have gone hard with him.'[37]

CHAPTER NINE

'The Admiration of All'

The Chinese loaded Gordon with honours for the capture of Soochow. In flowery decrees, one addressed to the public and one to Gordon personally, the Inner Council of the boy Emperor praised his 'thorough strategy and skill and . . . most distinguished exertions,' and conferred on him a 'medal of distinction of the highest class' to be worn like the star of a western order of knighthood. Li was commanded to 'compute, count and present' 10,000 taels of silver. Li tactfully sent them by the mandarin Pwan, who had shared Gordon's disgust at the massacre.

On New Year's Day 1864 Gordon went down to the West Gate of Quinsan to meet the procession of Pwan's coolies carrying the open boxes of silver from the canal, each box topped with a pair of ceremonial shoes laid on red cloth. Four small banners were carried too. He made the procession turn about and carry the boxes out again. He then went back to his house to await Pwan and the private Imperial decree, having prepared a table, lit by candles, on which Pwan placed the scroll of yellow silk, accompanied by a translation.

Gordon read the translation and then wrote on the back of it: '*Answer*. Major Gordon receives the approbation of His Majesty the Emperor with every gratification, but regrets most sincerely that owing to the circumstances which occurred since the capture of Soochow, he is unable to receive any mark of His Majesty the Emperor's recognition, and therefore respectfully begs His Majesty to receive his thanks for his intended kindness, and to allow him to decline the same.'[1] He signed it, kept the scroll (which Mayers retranslated for him) and two of the flags, handing back the other two because they had been presented by the Futai.

To refuse a generous present of silver from the Emperor was to insult the Throne; yet the Regent, Prince Kung, and the Imperial government seem to have been more impressed than annoyed. Gordon later presented the scroll and the decrees to the British Museum.[2]

In the early weeks of 1864 Gordon remained at Quinsan and its neighbourhood, keeping the Ever Victorious Army in training but not in the field against the rebels.

He was still in a state of shock. If later rumours of secret drinking had any foundation, now might have been the time. Some thirty years later Mayers' son, then a young man who had been brought up on his late father's 'unbounded admiration' of Gordon, made enquiries in Shanghai; he was told by 'quite trustworthy men' who had known Gordon 'that there were grounds for the secret drinking stories. Their account was that he had the habit of mixing gin with his tea. They had no doubt that he suffered from indulgence in this habit, but did not go so far as to say that he "drank to excess."'[3]

Their evidence is debatable, even if they were not unconsciously transferring memories of Burgevine. Gordon was not a teetotaller, and almost all Western men in the Shanghai of the Eighteen Sixties were inclined to gin and to brandy. Gordon, however, had banned liquor from his camps because of the hard drinking of Burgevine's officers; the only possible case against him would be that he defied his own ruling by secretly 'mixing gin with his tea.' Gordon certainly was a heavy consumer of tea, especially as Dr. Moffitt, wise before his time, had warned him that in hot countries drinking water must be boiled, a fact not yet grasped widely by the medical profession; yet Gordon was renowned for his candour and his refusal to dissemble,[4] and such drinking in secret would be out of character. The charge is not proven in Shanghai; it surfaces more seriously later in Africa.

A more serious charge was whispered at London dinner tables some years after Gordon's death: that he had become an opium addict in China. The rumours may be traced to Henry Morton Stanley, who had no liking for Gordon. Stanley apparently claimed that 'Emin' Pasha, the German doctor Edvard Schnitzer who had been on Gordon's staff in the Sudan and later governed a province had revealed that he took opium. Schnitzer, a Silesian Jew brought up as a Protestant Christian, was a physician in the Ottoman service, who had adopted Turkish dress and the name Mehemet Emin and practised Islam. Whatever Stanley's gossip, Emin Pasha made no such revelation when they were together some ten days in Central Africa during Stanley's celebrated 'Emin Relief Expedition.' Stanley's diary records merely a bizarre guess: Emin said: 'I cannot conceive how any mortal man could restrain himself from sexual intercourse. But Gordon was free from any carnal desire.'[5] Emin as a surgeon, wondered whether Gordon might have become an opium eater in China, since opium can cause impotence. Stanley would have been wiser to retort that no man of Gordon's sustained energy could have been taking opium.

At half past three in the afternoon of Tuesday 19 January 1864 Robert Hart, the young Ulsterman who had been appointed Inspector-General of Chinese Customs at the age of twenty-eight the year before, set out from Shanghai in two boats to reconcile Gordon and Li Hung Chang and thus 'to get Gordon to work again.' As Hart had written in his 'dearly beloved journal' the previous evening, that he would examine the question 'with perfect coolness and self-possession; and on its settlement may hang very important results.' When he resumed his Diary on 11 February he wrote in red ink across this paragraph: 'Successful in every respect.'[6]

Hart was unaware that Gordon's inactivity had been authorized by General Brown, for he mused: 'Were Gordon to resign the brigade would go over to the rebels; holding the command he refuses to fight; refusing to fight he disobeys orders; disobeying orders he shows the Chinese that even an able and reliable man, such as he is, is unmanageable.' This would prejudice China against a western-style military system. 'Quixotry,' he added, 'does not do at the present moment in China: an expediency that aims at the right – not an adherence to right that allows wrong to continue uninterfered with – is what is now requisite.'[7]

Hart's winter journey by water was not without fears, for two of Gordon's officers had lately been murdered on their way down to Shanghai, but he reached Quinsan safely at noon on his third day, only to find that Gordon had gone surveying on the far side of Soochow. Hart reached Soochow ('many skeletons and much ruin everywhere')[8] and was received by Futai Li Hung Chang in his new quarters, previously those of the escaped chief Wang of Soochow; Hart found them well built and clean, but 'awfully cold.' Li 'went into the details of the execution of the Wangs, and what he did seems to him right and necessary, and not the result of pre-meditated treachery. He wishes me to endeavour to get Gordon to meet him.'

They discussed measures to satisfy Gordon, which the Futai immediately acted upon while Hart resumed his chase, sailing through rain and wind and a dreary marsh, ice-bound for a few hours on two mornings, but always missing Gordon. On Sunday, 31 January, a week and a day after leaving Soochow, Hart came back to Quinsan, walking the last six miles in winter sunshine: 'was stopped at the gate, until Gordon, fortunately caught at last, sent out orders to admit us.

'Met Gordon for the first time: about 30 years of age*; slightly made; with a restless and very blue – light blue – eye. Had a long talk with him; *found the Futai had paid* all claims; and said Gordon – "You nearly missed me again; for I was near going up to Soochow to-day to call on the Futai." He asked me to go with him, saying it would increase my influence with the Futai; but I told him the first thing I should say to the Futai would be that Gordon had himself, before I met him, determined to visit H. E. He said, "You surely would not attempt to induce me to visit him." To this I made no reply: no use striking fire when things were found to be in trim.'⁹

They left by night, taking Lar Wang's adopted son. Next day, Hart saw Li Hung Chang alone first; then Gordon presented his officers and Lar's son. 'It was agreed,' recorded Hart, 'that Gordon should take the Force into the field after the China New Year, and co-operate *even* with Ching, unless told not to do by Sir F. Bruce.' The Futai would issue a proclamation taking the responsibility of the executions on himself, and 'showing that Gordon knew nothing about it.'¹⁰

Back in Shanghai three days later Hart wrote up his journal, concluding: 'Thus my trip, uncomfortable as it was, had been completely successful. Gordon had seen both the Futai and Ching, and had determined on future operations! *Never say die!*'¹¹

In due course Gordon received a letter from the Futai. The translation which is filed with the orginal has a quaint touch: '. . . The other day Hart requested us to prepare a public proclamation for Quinsan to let the people clearly understand that Major Gordon, who had moved his troops back to Quinsan, did not know of the execution of the Soochow false ruler, who has his head chopped off on account of expecting to be a high officer of his original men staying at certain good situation, and not agreeing to shave his head, although surrendered.'¹² The proclamation would be sent to Gordon when passed by Hart, and the Futai promised in future to 'try to save surrendered rebels from death,' and warned Gordon to beware of pretended surrenders.

Some years later Hart wrote in his journal that Gordon and Li 'were at

*Three days after his thirty-first birthday, 28 January 1864.

loggerheads in 1864 owing to bad interpretation,'[13] perhaps implying that Li claimed never to have uttered in Mandarin the unbreakable promise of clemency which Gordon understood from his interpreter's English. (Gordon had mastered words of command – probably in Shanghai dialect – and polite phrases, but for conversation he was dependent on 'our miserable linguists' until eventually Hart sent him a young Englishman, Hobson, so that he would have 'an honest tongue in another man's mouth.')

Gordon himself believed that the power of the Wangs, even when surrendered, had worried Li, who also wanted to loot Soochow because his troops had not been paid; and that General Ching was afraid that he might be supplanted by Lar Wang: Macartney claimed that Ching confessed before he was mortally wounded on 9 March 1864 that he had persuaded Li to behead the Wangs.

Whatever the truth, Gordon had given his solemn word to the Wangs and was not responsible for their deaths. Li's Proclamation to that effect was formally endorsed by the Throne, yet in the next century the Communist historian of the Rebellion attacked Gordon for murdering the Wangs.

Before Hart had left Quinsan Gordon mentioned a worry: that Bruce would not approve his taking the field again, since the question of withdrawing all British officers had been referred to London. 'He thinks,' recorded Hart, 'Sir F. will consider him unstable: I'm to write explaining matters to the chief: Gordon says the force *must* be broken up.' Hart reassured Gordon, and later wrote that 'Gordon ... will answer all enquiries and stop all condemnation by crushing the rebellion.'[14] Gordon wrote to Bruce that 'I am aware that I am open to very grave censure for the course I am about to pursue but ... I have made up my mind to run the risk. If I followed my own desire I should leave now as I have escaped unscathed and been wonderfully successful.' He wanted to dissolve his 'dangerous rabble' as soon as possible, and did not think the rebellion would last six months if he took the field but might drag on for six years if he left 'and the Government does not support the Imperialists.'[15]

In reply Bruce wrote a private letter in mid-February which 'Gordon does *not* wish it talked about, as it is enough to stamp him as a madman.' He did not preserve this letter, but another letter from Bruce, dated 12 March, and written with a formality very different from the avuncular tone of his private letters to Gordon, gives grudging concurrence, 'founded in no small measure on my knowledge of the high motives which have guided you while in command of the Chinese Force, of the disinterested conduct you have observed in pecuniary questions and of the influence in favour of humanity you exercised in rescuing Burgevine and his misguided associates from Soochow ...' Bruce applauded Gordon's perseverance, and his 'true humanity' in restoring the suffering inhabitants to their homes, and accepted that to leave his work incomplete would be 'a serious calamity.' He ended by urging Gordon to 'take care that your efforts in favour of humanity are not in future defeated by the Chinese authorities.'[16]

By then Gordon had been in the field again for nearly a month, having marched out of Quinsan in snow and hail on 19 February. He fought many sharp actions, gradually reducing the remaining rebel areas in a province devastated by the war. 'You have little idea,' he scribbled to Augusta on 25 February, 'of the misery this rebellion has brought on the country people around here. Hundreds die of starvation daily. In one house there were two living skeletons and seven dead. The poor creatures had not strength to take the bodies out. The Rebels had carried off all the rice and burnt their houses. I pray that before long they will be dispersed. They are now very weak, but as cruel as ever.'[17] And to the Acting Consul, Markham, he wrote a week later from another place: 'The people here were feeding on human flesh, and the country is covered with corpses.'[18] When he was able to bring them rice the starving remnants fought for it like wolves.

This campaign of the winter and early spring of 1864 was not easy, and was only won, in Storey's view, by Gordon's 'increasing watchfulness and attention. For months he rarely took his boots or clothes off at night: he would go into his boat and turn into a couple of blankets sewn up in the form of a sack'. Unlike Montgomery eighty years later who slept undisturbed, Gordon would jump out of bed at any disturbance, or if he heard more musketry or gunfire – or less – than he had ordered. And though Gordon was easily angered by inefficiency or disobedience, Storey noted that 'to his servants, all rebel boys and orphans whom he had taken under his protection, he was most kind.'[19]

When the Ever Victorious Army went into action Gordon was always in the forefront, unarmed, smoking his cigar, his bodyguard beside him, and the banners, inscribed in Chinese characters with the names of his victories. He had lived a charmed life, his men ascribing his safety to his 'magic' cane: they believed it deflected the bullets.

But on 19 March, a 'gloomy, cold and wet day,' Gordon assaulted a walled town named Kintang. The rebels were quiet and expected to surrender but Gordon's Chinese had announced after burning coloured papers that the day was unlucky. When the guns made the breach and the assault began across a stagnant ditch, the attacking columns met a furious defence from the rebels: 'their fire was very good and the showers of bricks something astounding.'[20]

Three times the assault failed, even when Gordon sent his flags of victory forward. His aide-de-camp, the younger half-brother of General Brown, was wounded in the thigh. Then a bullet struck Gordon just below the knee. He was carried to his boat and the bullet extracted. His second-in-command took over but Gordon sent message after message 'which rather hampered the temporary commander.'[21] By 3 p. m. the attack had failed 'with great loss to us who fall back;'[22] and having already heard that the rebels were marching on his base at Quinsan, Gordon ordered a swift strategic retreat by water, his officers giving their wounded general's boat a strong escort.

'I got a bullet in the leg,' he reported to General Brown's deputy, Colonel Hough, 'which lays me up but which has done no harm beyond loss of blood.'[23] Before his letter arrived, a rumour ran round Shanghai that Gordon was dead. Hart was distraught. 'I can't tell you how downhearted I was for a while,' he wrote to Gordon when the report had been contradicted, 'and how savage with myself I was that I had had anything to do with your taking the field again. My dear Gordon, don't expose yourself so much: for your own sake, do be *prudent*. By jove! if anything happens to you, I'll never forgive myself . . . Take care of your wound: rest, or come down to Shanghai and *convalesce*.'[24]

In the same letter he could rejoice: 'Hurrah! A thousand congratulations: I have just heard you are a Lieut-Col. in the Army. Bravo! *In the first place, that* will suffice; and, after it, will come something you may be sure. Hartman says you ought now to quit, else "Providence will be down on you": I hope, however, you have your guardian angels . . .'

Gordon made a swift recovery, being still very fit; but while he was unable to walk, directing operations from his boat, the Ever Victorious Army suffered a 'most disgraceful' defeat on 30 March. It was caused partly by Gordon's humanity. The Force had hemmed in some 10,000 poorly armed rebels, mostly Cantonese. For two days his men 'drove them like sheep.' Then Gordon realized that the driven rebels would soon enter an undevastated area; so he changed the direction of the drive by trusting two of his western officers to handle the infantry while he took the artillery by water to turn the rebel flank. The infantry halted before a breastwork. Failure to guard flanks or hold back a reserve 'allowed a plucky mob of men armed with spears and knives to inflict a most serious disaster on us.'[25] The Ever Victorious men 'fought like demons' but then broke and ran; two officers had been killed, three more were captured (and, Gordon thought, probably tortured to death) and 150 men, who were mostly ex-rebels, were prisoners too. 'I was nearly caught myself, never dreaming that the infantry would have got into such a mess . . . The Rebels all know me, and most of the chiefs have my photograph. I believe they would toast me if they caught me, but at the same time think they trust me to some extent.' His difficulty was 'how to attack such a mass of men with such a small force.'[26]

This reverse was disagreeable but not important. The collapse of the rebellion was in sight, to the dismay of critics in England who still thought the Taipings a Christian movement. When Gordon asked Hart to forward a laudatory despatch from Bruce 'as it would comfort my people to know I am not so universally condemned,' Hart told Henry Gordon on 22 April 'that even Sir F. Bruce's expression of approbation, forcible as it is, falls far short of Col. Gordon's merits. With the greatest ability and energy, in the face of great difficulties, constantly exposed to personal risk, with the overflowing generosity that sinks self and only considers others, he has been rendering such a service to humanity as is seldom heard of. Col. Gordon is now before Chancu-fu, and, thanks to him, that scourge of China, the Taiping insurrection will, in all probability, be pent up in Nanking before the end of May.'[27]

Gordon attacked Chanchu (Changhow) the day after Hart had written to Henry Gordon, but did not capture it until three weeks later. In the final assault a heavy gun, captured years before from a British ship was aimed right at him but the rebels had not kept their powder dry and it misfired.

Nanking, the rebel capital, must soon fall: Gordon foresaw great slaughter unless British gunboats intervened. He told Bruce he would not take the E. V. A. 'as I should find myself in the presence of so large a force of Imperialists that any attempt that I made to save the Rebels would be defeated.'[28]

Both Li and Gordon thought his 'rabble' should be disbanded now that the rebellion was almost over, because 'the Force is most dangerous when not actively employed.' Gordon had become weary of his post and especially of his officers, 'the quarrelsome devils who worry my existence with their petty jealousies and squabbles.'[29]

General Brown and the new British Consul, Sir Harry Parkes, disapproved, while the Shanghai merchants were dismayed; but Gordon was already showing the characteristic which would be the despair of cabinet ministers twenty years on: 'on these subjects I act for myself and judge for myself. This I have found to be the best way of getting on,' he told his mother the day before the capture of Chanchu. 'I shall not leave things in a mess I hope, but I think if I am spared I shall be home by Xmas.'[30] He would be leaving China as poor as he entered it 'but through my weak instrumentality upwards of 8 to 10,000 lives have been spared.'

Even as he wrote, a despatch from England was nearing Shanghai. The Prime Minister, Lord Palmerston, had told Queen Victoria on 23 April: 'Lord De Grey is to withdraw Major Gordon from the Chinese service in consequence of the treacherous conduct of the Futai.'[31] This did not imply the break-up of the Ever Victorious Army but Gordon had acted already: he would not allow it to revert to a man of Burgevine's stamp, and 'I can say now,' he wrote after the disbandment was complete, 'that a more turbulent set of men who formed the officers have not been collected together or a more dangerous lot, if they had been headed by one of their own style. I shall be censured for breaking up the Force, but the responsibility is my own and I could not in justice allow it to exist a moment longer than was necessary for the public safety.'[32]

He extracted generous gratuities from Futai Li for all, whether Chinese troops or foreign officers, but when Li wished to give Gordon a large sum in silver coin for himself, Gordon refused. As he wrote home, he had 'declined money in any shape and I think the Chinese Govt trust me more than any foreigner ever has been trusted. I have never cringed or yielded in any way to them and they have respected me all the more and I feel the conviction that I have been most favoured in being able to attain the position in China that I have, by my own exertions. Helen will exclaim at my refusing the coin knowing how dearly the family love it, but I could not take the money from them in their miserable poverty, and I feel correspondingly comfortable.'[33]

In the same letter of 2 June 1864, one day after the Ever Victorious Army had been fully disbanded and every man paid off, he told his parents that 'the Chinese Govt have conferred on me the highest military rank and the "Yellow Jacket" a distinction conferred on not more than 20 other mandarins in the Empire and which constitutes the recipient as one of the

Emperor's Bodyguard.' The Yellow Jacket, an equivalent of the Order of the Garter, was actually limited to forty: it had been instituted by the Manchu Emperors in the early days of their conquest following an incident in battle when forty of the bodyguard were dressed in Imperial yellow so that the Emperor would not be identified by the enemy.

Fourteen years later, in a memorandum of 10 May 1880, now in the archives of the Royal Engineers, Gordon revealed that 'the Chinese tried hard to prevent me having it, but I said either the yellow jacket or nothing and they at last yielded.' And in a letter to Viscountess Cardwell (17 February 1880) he wrote: 'It was very against the grain, that the Chinese gave me this yellow jacket, they were very averse to doing so, but I said "Give me the yellow jacket or nothing."'[34]

Possibly Li Hung Chang had offered the Yellow Jacket on his own initiative, only to find that the Imperial Council had no wish for a foreigner to receive the most exalted honour in the Emperor's gift; and that Gordon, perhaps for political rather than personal reasons, insisted. The mystery deepens with a letter written by Hart in Peking, dated 17 June, more than a fortnight after Gordon had told his mother of the award: 'Allow me to congratulate you. The Emperor has by a special edict conferred on you the Hwang Ma-Kwa, or yellow jacket, and has also presented you with four sets of Tutu's* uniform, which, you remember, you said you would like to have. Don't, like a good fellow, refuse to accept these things; the *government* has the very highest appreciation of your services, and wishes to show it in every way you will allow them to do so.'[35]

Li Hung Chang told Gordon, after he had returned to England, that 'of those from Western lands who have assisted China in military matters, you alone by your loyal and valuable service have become the recipient of this mark of gracious favour.'[36]

Gordon knew that many in England had sympathized with the rebels. When he sent home his journal of 1863 he did not want it published 'as I think if my proceedings sink into oblivion it would be better for everyone.'[37] He himself could not go home yet. Bruce had wanted Gordon to reorganize the Chinese army on Western lines. The scheme filtered down to no more than a Camp of Instruction. 'Gordon – much to his own annoyance – has volunteered for the work rather than let the measure fall through,' wrote Parkes to his wife on 3 July. 'All perhaps that will be required is that he

*A tutu was a provincial Commander-in-Chief.

should start the thing, and then some fitting officer may be found to take it off his hands, as he is very anxious to get away ... He stays with me whenever in Shanghai and is a fine noble generous fellow, but at the same time very peculiar and sensitive – exceedingly impetuous – full of energy, which just wants judgement to make it a very splendid type ... We have seen a good deal of each other when he is here, for as he is very shy I try as much as possible to dine alone, and we then tattle on on Chinese affairs all to ourselves.'[38]

Parkes, only two years older than Gordon, but knighted already for diplomatic services and for his sufferings as a prisoner in Peking, was a man of deep faith who had quickly won Gordon's friendship.

Gordon used these conversations to make Parkes 'feel that he should be more forebearing towards the Chinese than he used to be,'[39] for as Henry Gordon was to write twenty years later, 'No one ever took a deeper or more affectionate interest in the Chinese peoples and their true welfare and happiness than my brother both in his public life and in his private asservations.'[40]

Gordon set up the Camp after advising the Imperialists at the siege of Nanking after all: He was there when the Heavenly King committed suicide by eating gold leaf, and again after it had fallen easily. 'My troubles are now over,' Gordon wrote to Harvey in England, 'and I am living a delightful life in some hills near my old quarters at Sungkiang ... I am under the Commandant at Shanghai nominally, yet I never am bothered by him.'[41] He had Lieutenant Storey and two ex-officers of the British Army to assist him in teaching artillery and infantry drill, giving all his commands in Chinese.

Gordon soon grew bored with forming the Camp 'which,' wrote Parkes to his wife, 'is far too *slow* an occupation to be suited to his active and somewhat erratic tastes, and being unsuited he has not made a very good job of it.'[42] He relieved his boredom by completing the survey he had begun before taking command of the Ever Victorious, and saw only too clearly the misery and devastation of the once prosperous silk-growing district. He and Storey hurried back from surveying for the five hour ceremony at which the Emperor's representatives invested Gordon with the varied robes and insignia of a Tutu and of a Companion of the Yellow Jacket: 'silk dresses, robes, jackets, hats, caps, boots, shoes, fans, girdles, thumb rings of jade, and necklaces for all seasons and occasions.' All the time 'guns fired, crackers fizzed and burst, gongs were clashed, and huge brass horns brayed,' and mandarins kow-towed before him. 'Gordon's face,' wrote Storey, 'bore a sort of half-amused, half-satirical smile, and though he hated the whole ceremony and fuss, still, he entered into the whole affair with interest, asked about the various garments, and made comical allusions to his appearance in them.'

Just as the Yellow Jacket itself was put on, a 'fat old mandarin' preparing to kow-tow fell backwards into the water hole where the officers' beer and wine stayed cool. This was too much for young Storey. His guffaw made Gordon look 'rather angrily in our direction. When he saw what had happened he could not resist laughing. We pulled the old fellow out, had him rubbed down, gave him some champagne and brandy mixed, some cheroots, and ere long he quite forgot his mishap.'[43]

Soon afterwards Gordon was able to hand over to a Major Jebb. Trying to depart without fuss, after dinner one evening, he 'darted into his boat and closed the door,' but the Camp stockade was ablaze with Chinese lanterns, the Imperial troops lined the bank for a mile and a half, carrying banners, lanterns and blazing torches. 'Volleys of shell were fired, thousands of crackers let off, and horns and gongs brayed and clashed as the fast boat in which Gordon always travelled came along decorated with the flags he had so often and so successfully carried into action,' and towing his new suit: he had 'a great dislike to the sheen of new clothes,' although always spruce in uniform.[44]

He sent a brief note to his parents, probably sending it by the diplomatic bag and his brother Frederick in the War Office, but signed simply 'Son': 'The individual is coming home,' and did not wish it to be known, lest his ex-officers call on him for favours.[45] In Shanghai he received a laudatory address from the great merchant houses with seventy-two signatures.[46] Sir Harry Parkes sent off a copy to the Foreign Secretary 'with a covering letter pointing out that such acknowledgments were the only reward he cared to take in the country he has so greatly benefited.'

When Gordon called to say goodbye, over a cigar and a glass of port round the fire, Parkes could see that the stress and the incessant dangers, on an erratic diet, were catching up on Gordon. 'I hope he may have recovered his health before he reaches England, for he left us very poorly and much shaken.'[47] He sailed from Shanghai on 25 November 1864.

Historians would debate his importance in the defeat of the Taiping rebellion but the character and achievements of 'Chinese' Gordon, as he was now known in England, were already of the stuff of legend, which grew in the telling. Thus, eight years after Gordon had left China Queen Victoria's private secretary, Sir Henry Ponsonby, wrote to his wife: 'The ever victorious he was called ... his rule was I believe most severe for he treated princes and privates alike and this made him feared and respected by the upper and liked by the lower class of soldiers with whom he won a series of battles. Indeed he was never defeated ...'[48]

His battles in a small though strategic corner of China became in popular memory the conquest of vast provinces; and *The Times*, in a leading article of 1880, wrote that his brilliant victories had 'reanimated the empire when apparently on the point of dissolution.'[49]

The impression made upon the Western community and Chinese *literati* was well described in the journal of a twenty-one year old French royalist, the Marquis de Beauvois, who was equerry to Louis Philippe's youngest son, the Duc de Penthieve, on his journey round the world. They arrived in Shanghai little more than two years after Gordon had left.

They were told of a man 'who was both honest and courageous; he did not go to war for the sake of making a fortune, but saw his duty in this new career, and brought to bear upon it all the grandeur of his ideas, and all the purity of his character. Working sixteen hours a day, and influencing by his example the six thousand Chinamen as well as the new officers whom he collected round him, and changing in a few weeks the spirit of his troops, he came like a hero to end brilliantly, by seven and thirty successes, an unequal struggle.

'This man was Gordon; his name has gained the admiration of all, and it requires but few days journeying through the countries which were his battle-fields to find in all mouths words of reverence and honour for the brave English officer.'[50]

That passage, in de Beauvois' original French edition of 1868, was to be the link between Gordon in China and Gordon in the Sudan.

PART TWO

THE LIBERATOR
1865–1879

CHAPTER TEN

Where Next for Chinese Gordon?

Gordon had thought of coming home adventurously through the Russian Empire. He abandoned the idea from 'lack of coin,' for as Bruce had told the Foreign Secretary, when transmitting a highly eulogistic letter in which Prince Kung, regent of China, had begged Queen Victoria to honour Gordon: 'Not only,' wrote Bruce, 'has he refused any pecuniary reward but he has spent more than his pay in contributing to the comfort of the officers who served under him and in assuaging the distress of the starving population whom he relieved from the yoke of their oppressor.'[1]

Gordon came by sea, and thus again influenced history, this time by a tiny nudge: in Ceylon he had found a fellow R. E., Anthony Durnford, near death from heat apoplexy and sunstroke. Gordon nursed him 'and brought him back with me. He was in a sad state but now much recovered,'[2] as he wrote from Marseilles on 10 January 1865. Had Gordon not saved Durnford's life, the Zulu War of 1879 might conceivably have been avoided: Colonel Durnford's well-meaning policy in Natal was a cause of the conflict, in which he perished bravely at the disaster of Isandhlwala.

Gordon crossed France and reached Southampton to arrive unannounced at the elegant Regency crescent house, 5 Rockstone Place, where his parents, with Augusta and Helen, had lived since the general's retirement. Gordon did not stay long, for he must wait on the Secretary of State for War at the earliest opportunity. The military historian, Colonel Chesney, stated in *The Times* nine years later as 'a well known fact' that 'the Minister seemed hardly to have heard of his name, and to know nothing of his successes.'[3] Since Lord de Grey and Ripon had received at least one private letter from Gordon in China and had discussed him in Cabinet, the charge is unfair: moreover they evidently became personal friends, to judge from Gordon's later comments.

Gordon refused to be lionized: every society hostess would have snapped up Chinese Gordon but, as Harry Parkes had foreseen, 'a London whirl ... will possess little fascination for him. He is a reserved retiring man, and avoids glitter and bustle of all kinds.'[4] Moreover, he had not yet recovered his health: as he wrote to his friend Harvey: 'I am so very seedy from liver and ague' ... 'I am still suffering from liver'[5] (Victorians were inclined to ascribe all gastric complaints to their livers; Gordon's reference does not indicate over-indulgence in alcohol.)

One whirl was unavoidable. The Royal Engineers wished to give him a testimonial banquet in their magnificent Mess at Chatham. Gordon begged a senior officer 'to get the thing knocked on the head.';[6] he appealed to Colonel Harness, the commandant at Chatham, and asked Harvey 'to tell him how intensely I hate and abhor being complimented or having speeches made. I know it is the very worst taste I should shew and that I am everything that is to be blamed for not liking it, but that makes no difference in my nature. I tell you truly, there is nothing I would not go through sooner than go to Chatham. I am sorry for all this, but cannot help it. I will swear the sentiment was born in me and that I am not activated by pride.'[7]

His objections and his liver were overruled. At a great dinner on 18 March 1865 Colonel Harness proposed Gordon's health 'in stirring and vigorous language,'[8] supported by 'Old Fireworks,' Colonel William Gordon, soon to be knighted and promoted Major-General. Charlie Gordon wrote two days later: 'I could not but be highly gratified and honoured by the reception given me by my brother officers. My own part of the performance *will haunt* me to my grave ... Colonel Harness could not have been more civil or kind than he was, and he has paid me an honour I shall always value.'[9]

Gordon spent much of the spring and summer at Southampton and in London, writing up his China journal (the original having been lost at sea)[10] in great detail for Earl de Grey and Ripon, who could not read his handwriting and had it printed: Gordon went to heavy expense to recover the fount and destroy it; the journal was never filed in the War Office papers and is lost. He also travelled about, meeting old friends, with whom the playful side of his character, subdued in China, reasserted itself. 'I hear something of a cricket match, R. E. and R. A. against Army,' he wrote jokingly to Charles Harvey on 19 May. 'Now I am as you know a very good player and ought to be asked before Heneage. I am deeply mortified at this omission and expect you are at the bottom of it ...'[11]

He was entitled to fifteen months leave but requested only six, and was already discussing his next posting.

The Royal Engineers were in difficulty. If, as was generally expected, Gordon was to rise to the highest rank in the Army he must revert to the normal ladder of promotion: he was only thirty-two and a captain in the Engineers (although a Chinese general and a British Army lieutenant-colonel) and could not be placed over his seniors. Nor, at that age and rank, and having won distinction in foreign, not Crown Service, could he be given a higher honour than Companion of the Bath (C. B.). Gordon himself wanted to go abroad: he said he could not afford to stay in England more than a year,[12] and since he lived simply he must have been giving much of his income away, supporting little Quincey and other China waifs, and possibly aiding the dependents of some of the Ever Victorious officers who had been killed; and tipping nephews and nieces.

For some months he harboured a hope of returning to China to re-organize their army; then he thought of applying for a post (unspecified) 'in the centre of Africa'[13] or exchanging to India. Senior Engineers were eager to place him where he would like to go. He considered Dover, as second-in-command of a pleasant station, but it lacked good lodging or a place for the three dogs he had acquired and was too remote from Southampton for frequent visits to his ageing parents, whereas Aldershot was nearer. Then he accepted Dover after all, under his dear friend Harvey, to whom he joked: 'I am to go to Dover under a Captain C. E. Harvey, who I believe is a Tartar.'[14]

He never went to Dover. A suggestion of New Zealand ('The man to . . . stamp out for ever the Maori rebellion is Charlie Gordon . . . He is in some respects a born general')[15] came to nothing, but at the end of July he was staying with 'Old Fireworks' at Portsmouth where another guest was Colonel Chapman the deputy adjutant general in charge of Engineer appointments at the Horse Guards, who now 'asked me if I would like to go to Gravesend'; Gordon wrote to Harvey on 30 July, 'which I did, and I *believe* I am to go there. I look on it as a desertion of you and am sorry to be separated, but my funds are low and I think that I should be obliged to live much more expensively at Dover than at Gravesend, where I can be quiet . . . I hope you will not be put out by my not going to Dover.'[16]

Gravesend was a lieutenant-colonel's appointment and he would be his own master, completing the construction of new forts on both banks of the lower Thames and renovating old batteries to suit modern artillery: an ironic choice, since Gordon had written in China: 'The construction of a fort or barrack would be complete algebra and worse to me as it always was. It is not works that carry the day, it is the men who defend them and their leaders.'[17]

Thus, by almost casual change of plan, Gordon approached his happiest six years.

CHAPTER ELEVEN

The Gravesend Colonel

Gordon arrived at Gravesend on 1 September 1865, aged thirty-two years and seven months, and put up at the Clarendon Hotel on the river front as his official residence, Fort House, was under repair. 'I most heartily wish I was in the Celestial Empire again,' he wrote that evening to Harvey. 'I will *never* come back to this land again if I can get abroad . . . If I desert, do not be surprised.' He ended: 'Believe me, Yours truly in the dumps, *C. G. Gordon*.'[1]

Gravesend was still a fashionable watering place as well as a fishing and sea-going port, for the view downriver into the Lower Hope gives an illusion of being on the seaside. Gordon, however, hardly had time to explore before a telegram summoned him to Southampton: his father lay dying.

For nearly three weeks Gordon stayed in the pleasant Regency terrace house with its view over the Solent to the Isle of Wight, helping to amuse his father and relieve his suffering, yet feeling no particular grief 'for I have always had an innate idea that death was a gain, long, long ago'; but standing on the edge of eternity he found himself, after five years away from England and its full churches and family prayers, wondering 'whether Christ came for such a wretched, weak sort of religion as that usually followed by the Christian world – a religion of grumpiness, spite, unhappiness, pharisaism, etc. I thought surely, if He did come and suffer, He came for a more effective religion than that; otherwise it must be confessed that as far as our life in this world is concerned, His mission failed in enabling His followers to overcome the world.'[2]

As the old lieutenant-general grew weaker, his surviving family (William had died in New Zealand) were able to gather by his bedside before he sank into a coma and died at 3 p. m. on 19 September.

Gordon returned to Gravesend. His official duties occupied only the mornings and he was bored. He would walk out to a village in the neighbourhood and sit in the churchyard and think about his father and walk back. Then he was summoned again, to Gosport, where his brother-in-law Captain Neville Bayly, superintendent of ordnance factories in the south-west lay dying at the age of thirty-nine, having never fully recovered from a wound in the Indian Mutiny. He died on 21 October. Gordon stayed on for a month to support his sister Etta, who had a further bereavement when her infant youngest son died on 19 November.

This time of seclusion and sadness settled his mind to be done with superficial religion. 'God made me count the cost and conclude that His service should be *all* and that if *everything* was given up He would abundantly repay me in this world.'[3]

Gordon came back to Gravesend in the first week of December. After the thrills of China he was discontented with Thames forts. 'I do not much like the place, it is very quiet but that I like; there is little to be done however and that little I cannot say is very interesting. However I hope to get more reconciled after a time.'[4]

And soon he was not only reconciled but devoted to Gravesend, for he found a new vocation.

For a short time he took rooms at Mrs. Lord's in Harmer Street then moved into the attractive official residence which had been the rectory of Milton-next-Gravesend until the Army had bought it in 1797, renaming it Fort House. The oldest parts dated from the 15th century. Gordon found it too large for his needs until he discovered a good use for the space, and for the fine garden.

It stood close to New Tavern Fort, which dated back nearly ninety years to the war with France during the American Revolution. As Commander Royal Engineers of the lower Thames and senior officer of the Gravesend garrison Gordon had to oversee the civil contractors and the gunners who were modernizing New Tavern and the other forts on both banks, but he considered the forts a waste of money and the batteries badly sited: he annoyed the General commanding Chatham district when the Duke of Cambridge, as Commander-in-Chief, congratulated Gordon on a new battery and he replied: 'I had nothing to do with it, sir; it was built regardless of my opinion, and, in fact, I entirely disapprove of its arrangement and position.'[5]

By the spring of 1866 he had slipped into a routine. He rose early and took a cold bath and then spent an hour or more with his Bible and in prayer, 'visiting' his friends and all who he knew were in need. He refused to eat a large breakfast, although he never stinted his guests. When his excellent housekeeper Mrs. Mackley insisted that he needed eggs before his strenuous days he humoured her for a week or two but then suggested she give the eggs to the poor; she took the hint. Mrs. Mackley, a Scot, had been widowed twice and had sons by both marriages: her husbands may have been seamen who were lost at sea.

Gordon refused to do official business before 8 a.m.; if one of his subordinates broke this rule 'the Colonel's manner at such times was (to put it mildly) distinctly discouraging,' recalled young Arthur Stannard, who was articled to the civil engineer (and later married to a celebrated novelist.) Stannard remembered one early morning when two sergeants could not direct their workmen because a problem needed the Colonel's decision. Since neither would dare knock on his door at seven although they could see by his open window that he was up, they prevailed on Stannard's chief. The Colonel himself opened the door and on seeing Mr. Woodhouse half closed it again.

'"What do you want?" he said shortly, with an expression on his face which boded no good ...'

The even-tempered Woodhouse began to explain. '"By-and-by", broke in the Colonel, testily, and closed the door in his face.

'My chief retired, naturally somewhat nettled at this behaviour, but at eight o'clock the Colonel sallied forth, with a face as bright and a manner as cheerful and complacent as if he had never heard of the difficulty before, and at once settled the question offhand. And yet the sight of the men standing idly waiting for him must have touched his soft heart with a pang of regret that he had not come out when asked, for he took occasion to say, ere he walked away, that he was so sorry the men had been kept waiting; he did not know they were unable to get on with anything else until that particular job was done.

'"Ah" you wouldn't give me time to tell you that, Colonel,"my chief replied with a laugh; but all the same he vowed within himself that the Colonel should see many and many a sun rise and set before he found *him* at his door earlier than eight in the morning again.'[6]

After dealing with office work Gordon would set off for the River. He had quickly grown impatient with the slow pace of his predecessor's two-oared boat and preferred a four-oared gig. His favourite crew of Marsden (coxswain), Atkins, Elwick and Raspison, in the high hats, tail coats and buckle shoes of the Gravesend watermen, became the fastest oars on the river. They might wait for hours on the chance of being wanted, then would smarten themselves as Gordon hurried through the Ordnance Yard.

They would 'scurry along down the jetty and into the boat,' recalled Stannard, 'and almost before he was fairly seated have her cast off and their oars dipped. I believe they adored him in their hearts, but he certainly did take it out of their bodies. They fairly groaned within themselves when he chanced to take a down-stream journey with a tide running strongly up, for it meant a constant fire of impatient appeals – 'A little faster, boys, a little faster!' ... There was indeed nothing more remarkable about Gordon than his almost morbid appreciation of the value of time; he would not, of his own accord, waste a single moment; his own words, 'Inaction is terrible to me,' were in fact literally true.

'For a man of his small stature his activity was marvellous – he seemed able to walk everyone else off their legs, over rough ground or smooth. It was a most comical sight, for anyone with a sense of humour, to see him land at a fort and run up the glacis and round the works, followed by one or more of his own staff, my chief (a massive, slow-moving man), and two or three foremen, all "comfortable" in bulk. Whenever he paused, his followers would straggle up one by one in various stages of breathlessness; and invariably did he require to address his first remark to one of those who were furthest behind.

'To all of us, his subordinates, he was always scrupulously polite; but although there was no undue self-assertion or *hauteur* in his manner, it was never possible to forget, when he was on duty, that he was the Colonel-Commandant. He was extremely reticent and sparing of remarks when on the works, and always confined himself strictly to the business in hand.'[7]

After 2 p.m. Lieutenant-Colonel Gordon was inaccessible to the contractors: he devoted himself to works of mercy in the town, which like most mid-Victorian towns had extremes of poverty and wealth. Behind some good houses opposite the Fort and its garden were warrens of mean streets and alleys. The prosperous houses up the hill stood in contrast with tenements near the shore, where illness or loss of work could throw a family into destitution. Most of the children had no education; many old folk could not avoid the Workhouse.

Gravesend already had a strong social conscience. The nineteen churches ran many charities, sometimes in rivalry, but they could not meet every need, especially in a seaport.

Gordon, with his compassion strengthened by dedication at the deathbeds of his father and brother-in-law, began to visit the Workhouse and its Infirmary. He met a Miss Mary Broom who in a small house in Passenger Court, a short distance from Fort House, had a soup-kitchen for the needy and seemed to know whenever a poor person was sick or dying or in despair. She welcomed Gordon's help.

He had keys made to the wicket-gate of his large garden and handed them to elderly couples who could hobble about enjoying the lawn below the cannon on the ramparts, and watch the ships turning with the tide. He divided the vegetable garden into small plots which the poor could cultivate themselves.[8]

Inwardly, he was unhappy. His dedication had become a long dreary struggle[9] to bring his mind and body into subjection to God: 'Went to every sect, found no good. Slaved at prayer up in November at 4.30 a.m.'[10]

He wanted the fruits of the Spirit described by St. Paul, such as love, joy, peace and longsuffering; on Boxing Day 1865 he wrote to Augusta: 'I had been making a great mistake through the Devil's wiles, in continuing to pray for the Holy Ghost instead of praying for *more* of it (*sic*), the change and the result was marvellous. I had in fact been doubting God's promises.'[11]

He felt like a restless sea. 'The secret of our troubles is want of love to God,' he wrote in June 1866. 'If we have it to Him, we shall find it impossible not to have it to others. I can say, for my part, that backbiting and envy were my delight, and even now lead me often astray, but by dint of perseverance in prayer, God has given me the mastery to a great degree. I did not *wish to give it* up, so I besought Him to give me that wish; He did so, and possessed of that wish I had the promise of His fulfilment. I am sure it is our besetting sin . . .'[12]

He could 'see that the fruits of the Spirit could be only had by abiding in Christ or being joined to Him but how joined was still a mystery.'[13] Christ was 'a steadfast friend who never fails us,'[14] yet a Friend outside and not within.

The solution came unexpectedly on 6 September 1866, Gordon's Crimean comrade, Major Howard Elphinstone, V.C., R.E., who had become Governor to the sixteen year old Prince Arthur (afterwards Duke of Connaught) and lived with him at Ranger's House, Greenwich, reported to Queen Victoria: 'To-morrow a Lt. Col. Gordon of China repute, and an officer who has just returned from Bohemia and been present with the Crown Prince's army will dine here.' Henry Gordon, now commissary-general, also came over from Woolwich.[15]

Gordon disliked dinner parties and refused social invitations at Gravesend; but he was happy to oblige 'Elphin,' and later would sometimes ride on Woolwich Common with him and the Prince, who thought Gordon 'looks such a young man to have commanded such a number of troops.'[16]

Gordon took the short railway journey to Greenwich and walked up to the elegant red brick early Georgian villa where Chesterfield had written his celebrated letters to his son.

While dressing 'rather listlessly' for dinner Gordon's eye fell on his Bible, which had fallen open at the First Epistle of St. John. His eye caught the words of Chapter 4, verse 15: *Whosoever shall confess that Jesus is the Son of God, God dwelleth in him, and he in God.* 'Something broke in my heart, a palpable feeling and I knew God lived in me.'[17] As a Gravesend friend later reported, from Gordon's vivid description: 'Suddenly it flashed upon him that he had found a jewel of priceless value – he had found what alone could satisfy him, oneness with God: henceforth that was the key to his whole after life and he wondered he had never seen it before.'[18]

The indwelling of God became for Gordon 'the secret' which any man might know, the 'Koh-i-Noor diamond' which was his most precious possession and the source of all happiness and service. Back at Gravesend he discovered two books which strengthened his faith: *The Imitation of Christ* by Thomas à Kempis; and *Christ Mystical* by the seventeenth century Bishop Joseph Hall, whose commentary on the New Testament had led to the conversion of George Whitefield, the great evangelist. Gordon soaked up Hall's emphasis on the 'true, real, essential, substantial union whereby the person of the believer is indissolubly united to the glorious person of the Son of God.'[19]

Gordon was to develop thoughts which led him on unconventional paths. For the present, he held that the simplest belief, whether by an illiterate urchin or a colonel, by a washer-woman or a princess, that Jesus is the Son of God is enough for God to live in them, 'both in body and soul, transforming the whole man into the likeness of Jesus Christ, if they confess Jesus to be His Son.'[20] 'In the believer in Christ,' Gordon wrote to Harvey, 'God dwells, and His presence is felt by those in whom He lives. Some may not feel His presence as much as others, but He is in every believer whether manifested or not. The Veil over their hearts may not be quite rent, and so they see dimly ...'[21]

'You believe in your heart that Jesus is the Son of God?' begins the one-page tract which Gordon wrote at this time around his favourite verse, and distributed far and wide. 'Then God dwells in your body, and if you ask Him, "O Lord! I believe that Jesus is the Son of God; show me, for His sake, that Thou livest in me," He will make you feel His presence in your heart. Many believe sincerely that Jesus is the Son of God, but are not happy, because they do not believe *that* which God tells them: that He lives in them, both in body and soul, if they confess Jesus to be His Son. You believe this statement, yet do not feel God's presence? Ask Him to show Himself to you and He *will* surely do so.'[22]

CHAPTER TWELVE
Scuttlers and Wangs

Gordon now went among the sick and the poor with a light heart which helped in itself to relieve suffering. As he wrote to a friend, 'Man is apt to rest on the Redemption apart from the liberty which that Redemption gives. God did not redeem us to be feeble and weak, but He redeemed us for His service, to joy in Him, to know Him in His thick darkness.'[1]

His new happiness was plain. 'Gordon's face, all the time I knew him,' recalled the Reverend W. Guest, the Congregationalist Minister, and founder of a girls' school at Milton, 'wore an habitually serene aspect of peace, kindness, and of inward joy and strength.'[2] Not that he had become a saint overnight; Arthur Stannard, the young civil engineer, saw that 'in spite of the beautiful goodness of his heart and the great breadth of his charity, Gordon was far from possessing a placid temperament, or from being patient over small things. Indeed, his very energy and his single-mindedness tended to make him impatient and irritable whenever any person or thing interfered with his instructions or desires.'[3]

Yet Gordon's civilian clerk in the R. E. office, W. A. Lilley, not only became a devoted helper in all the charities, but a fervent admirer. 'The great charm of his countenance,' Lilley wrote, 'was the clear blue eye which seemed to possess a magic power over all who came within its influence. It read you through and through, it made it impossible for you to tell him anything but the truth, it invited your confidence, it kindled with compassion at every story of distress, and it sparkled with good humour at anything really funny or witty. From its glance you knew at once that, at any risk, he would keep his promise, that you might trust him with anything and everything, and that he would stand by you if all other friends deserted you.'

To the fashionable world of Gravesend Gordon seemed an ascetic. He had no retinue of servants, only the long suffering Mrs. Mackley and his

Army groom-orderly. He fed sparingly (but smoked heavily) and was known to push food into a drawer if someone in need should call; yet if one of his relations or Army friends stayed, they would be well fed with Mrs. Mackley's good cooking.

Gordon had no interest in money and was inclined to give without discrimination: no beggar was turned away. Although neat in dress, his watch chain was a woven strand of his mother's hair. He even gave up his favourite hobby of photography to save time and money for work among the poor; and if impatient with military subordinates he was endlessly patient and gentle with the bedridden and the old, not only in the town but in the surrounding villages, and would tell them long stories of his doings in the Crimea, Armenia and China 'which it was simply impossible for any well-to-do person to extract from him.'[4]

In 1867 his scope was extended when he met a young couple of independent means, the Freeses, for they introduced him to the Town Missionary, Thomas Jackson, retired from the London City Mission: Jackson had once collected a hall full of burglars to meet the great Lord Shaftesbury (then Lord Ashley) who helped many to emigrate and go straight. Now working in Gravesend, Jackson could tell Gordon of many more cases of need than he could find by himself.

The Freeses became Gordon's intimate friends. Frederick William Freese, of an Irish landed family, and his wife Octavia, who was Gordon's age, lived with their small children in the higher part of Milton about a mile south above Fort House. Freese was honorary manager of the Religious Tract Society's branch where Gordon had called to buy tracts and have his own tract printed. They invited him to Homemead, their house at the end of a row in Clarence Place, with a garden running down the hill.

'I had no idea, neither had my husband,' wrote Octavia, 'that he was in any way remarkable, yet I felt both amazed and puzzled greatly at our new visitor. Almost boyish in his appearance and in some of his utterances, yet with an eye and an expression that might have been a thousand years old . . .'[5] He talked fast and freely, yet was so reticent that the Freeses only discovered that he was 'Chinese' Gordon on his second visit; and Octavia always believed that it was she who had started his work among the poor by her introduction to Jackson.

She became his confidante and later his correspondent, while her husband and Gordon developed such a 'David and Jonathan friendship' that the Freeses would call Gordon 'David' to each other.

When their four year old elder son, Eddie, was accidentally burned on his hand, so severely that he nearly died, he never forgot Gordon's sympathy and kindness. 'Although only a small child at the time, I remember well,' he wrote in old age, 'the feeling of the air of love and indefinable mystery that seemed always to surround him. To my childish mind it was as if he were Our Lord and, even if I did not quite identify him with Jesus, the impression I have always had of His personality was founded on memories of Gordon.' Gordon gave Eddie a key to the garden when he was better. 'Every day I was taken to this garden, and the memories of its fruits and flowers have never left me. Here I used to play about among the guns and mortars, gather mulberry leaves for my silkworms, and gradually recovered my health.'

At first Gordon would come up to the Freeses several evenings a week and, wrote Eddie, 'spend hours disussing with my parents all things in heaven and earth with a depth of spiritual vision that made his hearers' hearts burn within them.'[6] Soon, however, he could only come occasionally. His evenings were absorbed by the philanthropy for which he is remembered best: his work among boys.

Mrs. Mackley the housekeeper had two sons whom she could not afford to place in a school. Gordon offered to teach reading, writing and arithmetic, and from this began his twice-weekly night-school for boys. When Mrs. Mackley's sons were ready he paid for their education at a local academy, but he now had about fifteen boys in three classes, each to a room, from beginners to good readers, taught by himself with the aid of Lilley, and a young man whom he paid, and sometimes the curate of Holy Trinity nearby, John Scarth. Gordon always mixed in some fun with the instruction, and would end the day with a prayer and a hymn; one of his favourites was James Montgomery's hymn about the prospect of heaven, *For Ever With the Lord*; and the boys would roar out:

> 'And nightly pitch our moving tent,
> A day's march nearer home.'

After a hunk of bread and a hot drink, the boys would be sent home each with a sixpence pocket money; and if the sixpence was swiftly waylaid at the sweet or cake shop he did not care.

Gordon was cheerfully indiscrimate in catching 'scuttlers,' as he called them, who were running around in the streets. Many were boys who worked on the shrimp boats. Some were (in the contemporary term) 'waifs and strays' who lived rough and dirty. They would be brought back to be scrubbed by Mrs. Mackley (who grumbled a little at this) or by Gordon, who would buy them a set of new clothes.

Sometimes, on his visits in the back streets, he would find a likely lad in an overcrowded tenement where a young mother, widowed or deserted, could not manage her numerous offspring: he would put him up in Fort House until he could place him in a lodging: or he would find a sick lad, carry him to Fort House, and nurse him. On at least one occasion he sat up all night with a delirious boy.

To Gordon, each boy was of infinite worth. A 'scuttler' was also a 'Wang' (i.e. King) as important as any Taiping rebel general. He used both nicknames and called smaller children 'doves.' 'They were always made heartily welcome,' wrote Lilley, 'and never patronised. Some of them had a very rough exterior, and came, as Gordon quaintly remarked, "with their gloves on"; but he knew the way to their hearts, and won their affections, so that they loved him exceedingly. Their roughness became changed into gentleness under his care, and they regarded him almost with adoration,' not least because he never gave up when they failed him.[7]

He took great pains to place boys in work. He became well known among the owners and masters of seagoing vessels, who would take on cabin boys or young deckhands on the Colonel's recommendation. Gordon would fit them out, to save expense to their parents. If a boy was particularly bright and had done well at sea Gordon would write to an influential friend to secure a nomination for a training ship.[8]

He knew that he was sometimes exploited: boys would squander their wages, or sell some of the gear he had bought them, when the ship put in at Southend before sailing up the Thames to Gravesend; after signing off they would soon be at the Colonel's doorstep. More often they made good, and Gordon would follow their progress as they sailed about the world. He placed a large map above a mantelpiece at Fort House, with pins stuck in the oceans wherever a Wang might be sailing.

When John Scarth left Holy Trinity (to return as incumbent two years later) Gordon wrote to him: '. . . as for the night school, it is a poor thing and the lads do not come for the greater part to learn at all but to play, in fact I do not think anything has flourished since your departure.

'Now I will tell you of the Boys. Brunt fell off the bowsprit of a schooner one dark night at 8 pm and is at rest. Wakefield is much as usual.' Several had gone on long voyages. 'Bullock still is here, one cannot rely on him, he is *notyet* sickened of the streets ...' And so the list went on.[9]

A lad of ten years old had found work at one of the forts, Coal House Point, waiting on the masons as they shaped the granite blocks for the guns. William Heal had run away from home leaving numerous brothers and sisters and a good mother because he was frightened that he might kill his alcoholic father when he next beat her up.

A few days after arrival, hearing a workman say that the Colonel was about, Heal asked who 'the Colonel' was. '"Who is he?" he answered. "He's the finest man in all God's earth – that's who he is." ...

'Presently I saw a gentleman walk along the staging; the engineers and clerk of the works were with him. For a time they looked at plans and discussed details; then they passed on, Gordon nodding or having a word with a man as he passed. He had a marvellous memory for faces, and as soon as he caught sight of mine he knew I was fresh on the job. He stopped and spoke to me. Where did I come from – where was I lodging? – was I comfortable? – touched me upon my head – said: "Be a good lad," and passed on. All the rest of the day I could see his blue eyes before me, and somehow I did not feel quite so lonely when I thought of his smile. Each week I looked forward to his coming. His day was a red-letter day to us all.'

Heal was already using the recreation huts which Gordon had organized at Coal House Point. Then Gordon invited him to spend the week-ends at Fort House, which he did for nearly two years, joining the 'rough young scamps' who lived there all the week. 'Saturday afternoon would be spent with him in the garden or study. He would chat about bees or flowers, or maybe take a hand with the ball. Sometimes he would read us a story or tell us one; we would sit at his feet or rest on his shoulders whilst he talked.' If, as often happened, gifts of fruit and flowers had come in from local squires and farmers, the boys would be sent round the backstreets and cottages to deliver them to the sick.

Back together in the study, one of them would be appointed to move the pins on the map above the fireplace under Gordon's direction. '"Charlie was here last week," he would say. "I expect to-day he would be about here." The pin representing Charlie was moved accordingly; so he would go on until every pin was mentioned. Then he would kneel and commend to the Great Father's care every boy represented upon the map. Then he would pray for the boys that were kneeling about his knee; he would tell God your name, and somehow God would seem to be another kind of God after you had listened to his prayers.'

In 1917, by then a substantial business man, Heal recalled to the well-known journalist, Harold Begbie, how Gordon would often talk 'about the power of God or the beauty of Christ. These conversations, and he was always encouraging us to ask questions, made a marked impression on our minds – they were so natural, so real, and so delightful. But the greatest impression made on my own mind came from solitary talks with him. I can never forget those talks. As long as I live they must be the greatest thing in my life. Nothing can ever exceed them.

'It was the power of those solitary talks which converted me. I know that owing to those words of Gordon, child as I was, I did, nevertheless, definitely give my heart to God, definitely renounce what we call "the world," definitely determine that I would fight my evil nature and live unselfishly. The words which impressed me were quite simple; it was the force of Gordon's personality behind them which gave them their extraordinary power. He made me feel, first of all, the meaning of that phrase, the Goodness of God. Goodness became to me, through Gordon, the most desirable of ideals. It became in God tremendously real ... Beauty and goodness were always associated in Gordon's mind. He gave us a distinct feeling that beauty and goodness went together.

'One thing, too, I remember: Gordon's teaching about the nature of forgiveness. All his emphasis was on love – the longing of God to forgive, and the creative power of forgiveness in the human heart.' Heal thought that perhaps Gordon did not quite capture the majesty and power and infinite mystery of God. God was just 'a great loving father agonising, as it were, to do all that He could for His children. And that was enough theology for us. We were under the spell of Gordon's personality. We lived in the magic of his mystery – enchanted. His power over us was something that can never be expressed in words.'

When, at the age of twelve, Heal heard that his father had been killed in an accident, Gordon advised him that his duty lay at home. Gordon's strong testimonial quickly secured a job. Heal earned enough to see his brothers and sisters through school while educating himself, then built up his own business, becoming a big employer while active in good causes.

As Begbie commented: 'If there had been no Gordon at Coal House Point, what had been the story of William Heal?[10]

Gordon was doing in miniature what already was done in Gravesend by the Ragged School.

Ragged Schools had started in England nearly thirty years earlier through the initiative of a crippled artisan in Portsmouth, and had spread over the land: Lord Shaftesbury was president of the Ragged School Union. They reached children missed by the National or Church schools: compulsory education was not enacted until 1870 and only slowly became a reality, as Board Schools were built to complete the system. At Gravesend on Sundays about 100 children were taught in the afternoon and 200 in the evening, by about 20 volunteer teachers. Two women taught a smaller number free on weekdays, all learning to read and write and being taught the rudiments of the Christian faith. William Freese was a strong supporter and a teacher.

In 1869 the Freeses moved from Gravesend to a house in its own grounds at Chislehurst, some twelve miles inland to the southwest, nearer London. William asked Gordon to take his place. Gordon was elected in January 1869 and joined the committee in 1869.

Except for W. G. Penman the town coroner and Mr. Paine, grocer and ex-mayor, the teachers were mostly shopkeepers in their twenties or thirties, all strong Christians. Thus Gordon joined Fenwick the tailor, Crowhurst the tallow merchant, L. J. Essenhigh of the hardware shop and others.[11]

They belonged to different churches, for the Ragged School movement was non-sectarian, but each was a faithful adherent of his denomination whereas Gordon, nominally a member of the Church of England, did not identify himself with any one church. He worshipped every Sunday but varied his choice. First, the Wesleyan Methodists; next he regularly attended the parish church, St. George's, famous for the tomb of Pocahontas, the American Indian princess of Tudor times, and always sat among the poor and not in a fashionable pew.

When an English Presbyterian minister, H. Carruthers Wilson, came to Gravesend to start a congregation, Gordon became a close friend and often attended his church. Gordon was also, unusually in that age, a friend of the Roman Catholic chaplain, Father Joseph Wyatt. (It was Wyatt who warned him against a plausible old woman beggar, in vain; but when she walked off with his tunic, hanging by the door, he had to put the police on her trail but refused to lay a charge when she was arrested. She was sent to jail for another offence – and was back for help as soon as she came out.)

Denominational loyalties were laid aside in the Ragged School, where Gordon did his weekly stint in the crowded rooms, on two floors, with an open stairway; and if he must be absent he would arrange a substitute, unlike more casual volunteers. As the minister of Zion Baptist church, W. Emery, said at the Ragged School annual meeting of 1869, 'It is not pleasant work; it is not a nice thing always to sit in the midst of a lot of dirty boys and girls; it is not always pleasant to hear some one singing "Pop goes the weasel" when you are trying to teach something better; it is not pleasant to go into the homes where there is filth and squalid ignorance and drunkenness.'[12] Gordon loved it.

'He had a class of some fourteen lads in one corner of the schoolroom,' recalled Penman at the time of Gordon's death. 'Their ages ranged from twelve to seventeen. They were the very roughest and the poorest we then had in attendance, but it was remarkable how entire was the control he had over them. Some of those lads he himself brought to the school; their parents were mostly of no occupation, or in some way served the boats on the river. Several of the boys were employed on shrimp boats.

Penman recounted how Gordon gave a home to some of 'the poorest and most miserable of the lads, feeding and clothing them, they employing their time in the garden, in chopping wood, and running errands. Three or four of them had scarlet fever while in his house; and yesterday I heard from the lips of one of these, now a man of twenty-nine, how the Colonel used to care for them in their sickness, and would sit with them far into the night talking to them, and soothing them, until they fell asleep.'

Penman mentioned Gordon's concern to place boys in work, afloat or ashore, taking them back when unemployed. 'He entered into all their concerns,' eulogized Penman, 'caring nothing for himself, he cared only to make them happy and industrious; while his chief aim was to lead them to the Saviour.'[13]

This might not be achieved at once. In 1951, a retired scrap merchant and town councillor in Southend, aged ninety-five, told an enquirer how Gordon had rescued him, clothed and tamed him. After Gordon had left Gravesend this William Scott had gone to sea, then stowed away to Australia. After many adventures he had returned, taken a shop in Gravesend, ruined himself by gambling and finally came to Southend in his later thirties. 'The influence of General Gordon never left me and Almighty God was good to me all through my troubles. The best thing that ever happened to me was when I was converted through the simple preaching of a farm labourer . . .'[14]

* * *

Gordon was equally at home with sons of his better-off neighbours. Thus John Robson came into his circle while still a schoolboy, and later became his pupil as the first step in an engineering career. On winter nights not devoted to the night school, Gordon would often invite Robson across to sit with him 'before his dining room fire when long and interesting conversations took place between us whilst he smoked his pipe.'[15]

In the eighteen-sixties, middle class mothers would not allow their sons to mix with poor boys – unless as voluntary teachers under supervision – and Robson, when recalling Gravesend, would point out that Gordon had two circles of boys, the poor 'who were the objects of his charity, and those who were his friends and companions. His greatest happiness was to see them playing in his large garden or playing at cricket on the Government land, indeed he often expressed these sentiments to my mother and invited us to come as frequently as possible' – and here they may have mixed with the poorer boys who certainly were allowed to play in the grounds of Fort House. Robson knew that several of these 'friends and companions' rose to fortune 'and a high position in life.' Another boy, whom Robson would not have known, was Horace Hutchinson, a general's son, of Northam in North Devon, whom Gordon met when staying with Hutchinson's uncle in nearby Westward Ho!

Fifty years later, by then a celebrated golfer and essayist, Horace Hutchinson recalled being given at the age of eleven Gordon's carefully chosen present of a taxidermist's set, and the fostering of a love of natural history. 'There was about him,' wrote Hutchinson, 'a boyish, almost a childish, simplicity and directness which gave him the power of appealing very intimately to a boy's mind and heart. To me, hardly more than a child, he would talk even then of God and of Jesus Christ as if they were personal friends whom we knew in common. He never had the least sense of embarrassment in speaking of his religion ...'[16] Later, when Gordon was visiting Augusta and their mother at Southampton he would stop off at Winchester to take Horace out from College.

To Horace, Chinese Gordon had 'all the glory and glamour attached to the hero,' but to the boys of Gravesend he was 'the Kernel,' (occasionally the words 'God Bless the Kernel' were seen scrawled on the fence of Fort House). Boys of both social classes instinctively recognized his sincerity; but in London clubs some who did not know Gordon personally suspected his motives and sniggered. They should have known that his practical affection for boys was open and admired: the canny Mrs. Mackley would never have allowed her sons to be friends of a man whose motives were mixed. Moreover his work for boys formed only one part of his wide ranging philanthropy for all ages and both sexes: he was surprised after he had helped a young middle class woman in trouble that her mother should call to know when he intended to marry her: he remarked that he had pushed a washerwoman's barrow for a quarter of a mile 'and she did not ask my intentions!'

As for subconscious leanings which a later generation would term 'homosexual', the German doctor Emin Pasha, in making his bizarre suggestion about Gordon and opium remarked that Gordon was 'free from any carnal desire ... without even appetite for sex.'[17]

From Gravesend Gordon once wrote to Augusta: 'There is a Miss Dykes here, the nicest girl I ever met. But don't be afraid, the dead do not marry.'[18] Mary Frances Dykes married Gordon's great Sapper friend Major John Donnelly.

CHAPTER THIRTEEN

A Scheme of Mercy

Although absorbed in good works Gordon was very much the efficient soldier. He kept in touch with Chatham – which he found 'in a state of change and muddle . . . I think it was in its halcyon days under Sandham and Archy and myself!!!'[1]

Sometimes he hoped to be summoned back to China. His interest was unabated. When Andrew Wilson, a journalist familiar with India and China wanted to write an account of the Ever Victorious Army Gordon showed him private papers and encouraged him, while tearing out of the draft any eulogies on himself. The book, however, was delayed by Wilson's return to the East and his ill-health and did not appear until long after Gordon had left England.[2]

Gordon also took much trouble to ensure that all his China officers or their next-of-kin received the medals issued by the Chinese government. He was disappointed that the Crown refused permission to wear them on British uniform, even though he had asked Burlinghame, the American minister in Peking, to intercede with the Foreign Office.[3] As for his own great gold medal presented by the Emperor, Gordon had been so appalled by the poverty in Manchester, still suffering from the shortage of cotton caused by the American Civil War, that when a fresh appeal was launched he scratched out the inscription on his medal and sent it to be sold anonymously for the fund: the parting was a wrench: 'Give away your medal' became his favourite phrase for sacrifice.

Some Chinese, then rare visitors in England, came to Gravesend. Gordon entertained them and was much amused and embarrassed when they kow-towed to him in the street on his casually mentioning that he had been given the Yellow Jacket. And when Hudson Taylor founded the China Inland Mission in 1865, Gordon showed sympathetic interest though he took no part in their preparations except to offer Taylor a large 'Magnetic Electric machine ... used by medical men for nervous diseases: it also serves as an amusement to those who have not been able to attend lectures on scientific subjects.'[4] He left it at Charing Cross station to be collected: it may have been his father's.

Gordon was doubtful about Hudson Taylor's determination to put his missionaries into Chinese dress, although this proved to be one secret of their eventual success, but he followed their early tribulations with sympathy. He wrote to Augusta in 1867: 'Mr. Taylor's mission in China has had chequered progress. They must lean more on the Lord, though it seems hard to say so when they are striving apparently so hard.'[5]

No summons to China came for Gordon. Late in 1867, the British government decided to send an expedition to Abyssinia, as Ethiopia was then known in Europe, to rescue British diplomats and others from the Emperor Theodore. Gordon longed to join, and had every hope since Napier, in command, had known him in China, and Staveley had a division. When the expedition was mounted entirely from Bombay Command, Gordon's disappointment drove him into 'the doles,' as he called depression: he even gave himself a short leave to Southampton where he recovered his spirits, bravely telling himself that the souls of Gravesend scuttlers were more important than Abyssinian glory. Then an appointment nearly took him from Gravesend.

His namesake and patron, Sir William Gordon ('Old Fireworks'), a bachelor nineteen years older than himself, treated him almost as a son, leaning all the more as the after-effects of Crimean wounds began to affect the general's mental stability. Charlie had stayed with Sir William on his rain-soaked estate in Lanarkshire and Sir William had invited himself for long visits to Fort House.

When Sir William was appointed Inspector-General of Fortifications, and thus head of the Royal Engineers, he implored Charlie to help him as Aide-de-Camp. After much soul-searching Charlie accepted; but as the grim, dull task loomed nearer he felt he could not bear to leave his scuttlers. He withdrew, Sir William only extracting a promise to be with him when his time came to die.

A few weeks later they went together to North Devon to stay with Sir William's sister, Mrs. Hutchinson, at Westward Ho! Soon Charlie became alarmed by the general's instability and took away his razors but returned them on the telegraphed insistence of the General's brother. A few days later

Sir William cut his throat, so inefficiently that he lingered ten days, devotedly attended by Gordon.

Gordon turned death beds into ante-rooms of heaven. 'Our old friend's sun set in perfect peace after a severe storm,' he wrote to Harvey. 'He suffered not more than many others would from their ailments and I cannot say that the past is anything but comforting to me. We were brought more together than ever we were before, and I cannot express what happy converse we had before his spirit fled. Thank God, to die would be joy to me, and I could therefore cheer him who was about to cross the river. The coming glory must far transcend this fading world's joys.'[6]

Gordon had come to believe (turning a blind eye to Scriptural passages to the contrary) that all would be saved through Christ's redemption whether they accepted or denied Him. 'I could not express how deeply I believe, by God's grace, in His universal salvation of the souls of all men,' he wrote at this time to Sir William's sister-in-law, who had an incurable illness. 'It gives the confidence which can speak peace in the midst of the most untoward circumstances, and never have I felt a doubt of the ultimate glory of my hearers, whatever they may have said to me. You will try and realise this view, and it will much cheer you. Day by day death will be familiar to you as the kindest of friends to you and to all others. The thousands who fall in battle are thousands liberated from prison to see the effulgent God of Love, whom you love and adore with more than your heart can express, and whom you desire to be more worthy of.'[7]

At Gravesend Gordon would go joyfully into the room where an old hag or a small child lay dying, in a one-room tenement or a smart home, and the pain and the sorrow would fade while the young Colonel was at the bedside. 'There have been many taken away of late here, and several more are dying. I like to be with them. It brings the future nearer to me, as if you were seeing friends off by a train to a place to which you will eventually go yourself; and I think you may send messages to those who have already gone, and to the Chief among ten thousand . . . What a comfort it is to feel that they are going to peaceful homes, that you can, as it were, give them before their departure a message to deliver to our Lord – though it is not necessary, as He is with us and in us.'[8]

As the years passed in his Gravesend backwater, and the Thames forts neared completion Gordon laid plans to extend his work among the poor. He dreamed of buying a house to be a refuge for the aged, presided over by Mrs. Mackley who would thereby have a home when he left. This private dream never became reality.

Then he suggested publicly the founding of a Mendicity Society to help the numerous mendicants or beggars who wandered the streets and hovered around his door.

At an enthusiastic meeting on 2 March 1869 at the Town Hall Colonel Gordon took the chair. A parson from Blackheath, where a similar society flourished, explained the scheme whereby householders subscribed, and were given slips of paper to hand to beggars instead of money; the paper to be redeemed at a central office which would weed out the false and help the deserving to find work or to return to their own towns. The Mayor of Gravesend, F. Leith, spoke in support, the principal clergy applauded, a committee was formed and the Gravesend and Milton Mendicity Society was established on 16 March and began operations on 1 May 1869.[9]

In September a much-travelled visitor to the town complained that he 'never was so annoyed and pestered by beggars ... No matter what part of the town you visit you are besieged by these lounging mendicants.' In November a public meeting of the society attracted a sparse attendance, to hear Gordon, as Secretary, report that 2027 deserving beggars had been helped and soon 'the professional beggar would find it useless to attempt to ply his trade in the neighbourhood' – provided that more householders supported the scheme.

Gordon's engineering pupil, John Robson, recorded that 'many gentlemen of the town promised assistance (they could not refuse when such a man appealed to them) but within a year or so they forgot their promises and left him alone to carry it on at his own expense. This was a great disappointment to him as it seriously curtailed the scope of the scheme and left the expense of its maintenance to a comparatively poor man; such was his frequent complaint to me.'[10]

On Saturday 22 October 1870, little more than eighteen months after Gordon's scheme was launched, the local paper lamented 'the downfall of the Gravesend Mendicity Society, which has collapsed solely on account of the deficiency in financial support. The promoters of the affair will, at least, have the satisfaction of knowing that the society has only suffered disintegration by the non-co-operation of their fellow townsmen, and not by any want of energy on their part.'[11]

That winter of 1870–71 was one of the hardest. The freezing conditions stopped work on the forts: Gordon enjoyed himself by transferring to paper his survey of the Lower Thames fortifications, singing as he plied his brush. Poverty increased in the town. With his friends the clergy, and the Ragged School teachers and all men and women of goodwill, he redoubled his efforts to relieve distress.

Soon after his thirty-eighth birthday he was told of his next appointment, to begin in October 1871: not to lead irregular troops in some far away campaign, but to be the British Commissioner on the Danube Commission which he had helped to set up in 1856. During the summer Gordon made arrangements for his numerous pensioners to receive his money regularly. He gradually dispersed his furniture, some of which would turn up at auctions long after, their value increased by the Gordon legend.

He would never be forgotten in Gravesend. Fort House was destroyed by a flying bomb in 1944 but the Gordon statue in Gordon's Memorial Garden is one among many reminders of the patron saint of Gravesend.

CHAPTER FOURTEEN

Danube Backwater

Gordon left for Galatz on 10 October 1871. The Freeses saw him off at Dover, Frederick Freese crossing the Channel with him. Gordon had hoped Freese would come out as private secretary, since both his health and his business were in trouble, but on his return home he had a seizure, and although Gordon kept the place open Freese declined the invitation, which his son, looking back many years later, thought a pity. So Gordon had no close friend; nor had he a dog, having failed to find either a setter or a pointer. He reflected that 'it is easy to send for a dog afterwards.'[1]

He travelled by Paris, Vienna and Bucharest. The onward journey was difficult because a flood had destroyed the railway bridges 'and I had to take carriages from one river to another as the gaps occurred.'[2] Galatz on the Danube, his old headquarters of the survey of 1856, was now the principal port of the autonomous (but not yet sovereign) principality of Romania under Prince Charles of Hohenzollern (later King Carol I). It had not changed much: 'a large, very ill paved, straggling town,'[3] with streets ankle deep in mud; a place of Greeks and Jews, and Romanians who were inclined to fall into debt to the Jews. Gordon found it unattractive but 'I have a good house,' he wrote to Mrs. Hutchinson at Westward Ho! 'and shall be able to endure I hope. It is not a house or place which can help us but our living Friend who minds no climate or place and whose presence in life is peace.'[4]

The Commission for the Improvement of the Navigation of the Danube had been set up by the Treaty of Paris in 1856, to make the Danube fully navigable and to ensure free and safe passage for the vessels of all nations. It had organized the necessary civil engineering in the Delta and now, as Gordon put it, was a cross between the Thames Conservancy and Trinity House, responsible both for maintainance and navigation. Gordon, however, had not been in Galatz six weeks before he realized that the

Commission 'is not what it ought to be.' The Turkish commissioner was also a provincial governor: the Austrian, Prussian and Russian were consul-generals in Bucharest; the French lived in Paris and came twice a year, 'so the management is left in the hands of the English and Italian commissioners who live in Galatz.'[5] The Italian was also a busy consul and often away, so that Gordon became the entire Commission in the eyes of the populace, 'a very invidious position,' he told the British Ambassador in Constantinople, Sir Henry Elliot, to whom he reported regularly.[6]

Gordon's predecessor, Colonel (later General) Sir John Stokes of the Royal Engineers, had been commissioner for sixteen years; they were old friends but Gordon found that Stokes had 'got into a groove,' running the Commission almost as a despot, ignoring absent colleagues. Gordon wished to bring them in partly because 'I do not want so much work. I am naturally lazy, and am of a disposition either to take up a thing entirely or else to take it *very* easy.'[7]

Twice a year all the Commissioners met at Galatz, a wearisome time, Gordon told the ambassador, because in such a body 'a compromise is all that can be expected on any question.' 'Your Excellency will have known,' Gordon commented on another occasion, 'how troublesome it is to have to deal with an obstinate Turkish colleague in the Commission when the local government and the views of the other Commissioners are often in opposition.' Gordon, however, found Ismail Bey, the Turk, 'most useful and reasonable.'[8]

Much more enjoyable than tiresome meetings were the travels which were part of the duty. Gordon was in his element. A winter journey which he described to the Military Attaché in Vienna, Colonel William Goodenough, involved 'the most dreadful roads,' and floods, and swollen streams, sometimes covered with ice, when Gordon would leave the carriage and walk. 'It is no joke walking over crackling ice with the view of fish swimming beneath you, the great sobs the ice gives, and the wild wail of wolves make it cheerful work. Here you may die without any fuss, for there are but few people about . . .'[9] When he slept in a hut the fleas were 'as big as canary seeds and same shape,'[10] and he kept finding himself addressing the peasants in Chinese instead of his few Turkish phrases. One consolation was the wild-life. 'I do not think I ever saw such countless masses of ducks and geese as there are on the lakes out here but they are yet very wild,'[11] he told Colonel Jenkins, who secured two spaniels for Gordon to take out on his next leave, ready for the shooting season.

Galatz was a cosmopolitan city. Stokes had been prominent in society and had entertained grandly. Gordon found 'so much title-tattle and such mischief making that it disposes one never to go anywhere.'[12] He preferred to spend his evenings alone in the well-furnished house (all expenses covered by the Foreign Office) to study the Bible and write. He sent home a stream of meditations to Augusta and maintained a vast correspondence with all his friends, especially those at Gravesend. When the Ragged School chairman forwarded a glowing resolution of thanks, Gordon replied at once in a long letter for reading aloud to the boys, written on 'the day of your school treat.' '... I can assure you I do daily twice pray for the welfare of the school and teachers, and I often think of you all, and would like to come among you.' He gave many details about the geography and history of Galatz and the inhabitants of the Delta, mostly refugees from Russia: '... though the surroundings are very dull, and the swamps they live in are dreary enough, the people look happy and seem to have no greater burthens than those who live in better lands; you see the same careful, loving mothers, the same careless Russian Willie Websters running about as in Gravesend. The Lord's ways are all equal, and to Him, they are as much valued as the greatest in the world, and the thus seeing them makes me think of your flock, and yearn for the time when He will bring us all together as one people with one God "a great multitude whom no man can number, clad in white robes, with palms in their hands" ...'[13]

He kept in touch, as far as he could, with his seafaring 'Wangs' and grieved when he heard of deaths by accident or disease. He corresponded with Miss Broom at Passenger Court about those of all ages who he was helping financially through her, such as a boy with a wooden leg, who could not decide whether to be a grocer or a tailor: 'the father must settle everything and let me know how much is wanted ... give a look at Mrs. Roberts now and then. Poor woman, she is worthy of help ...'[14]

He did not forget his middle class friends, sending Romanian stamps to ten year old O'Hara Steward, who had lost his father in '67, with a chatty if rather improving letter which concludes 'with many kind wishes, and a recommendation to think when you have any trouble that there is Someone who always listens and who can help you even to learn your lessons.'[15]

And always there was prayer. Again and again his letters far and wide will mention that he prayed for the recipient daily. Thus, he ended a long letter to Charles Harvey about local politics and the problems of the Commission: 'I should so like to hear you hold forth on the subject in your grand way.

How very much they neglected your education at Marlborough College. Kind regards to Mrs. Harvey and you are in my thoughts twice per diem at the morning and evening sacrifice.'[16]

In the last week of August 1872 Gordon was sent back to the Crimea with an old friend, Colonel Adye (afterwards Lieutenant-General Sir John), to report on the state of the military cemeteries. They found Sevastapol still in ruins and the forts and ramparts, which they had assaulted seventeen years before, 'mere crumbling earthworks.' The Russians 'though very courteous were evidently disgusted with our visit.'[17] The French had gathered the bones of 28,000 of their dead into one cemetery, but Adye and Gordon successfully recommended keeping the small cemeteries where the men fell. 'The whole scene is sacred and historical' and could be improved and maintained at little cost.

The two colonels, one nearly fifty-three, the other rising forty, had much time to chat while they sailed on *H. M. S. Antelope*. Adye found, as he commented in his memoirs published ten years after Gordon's death, that Gordon was 'actuated by one principle which is rare – namely a contempt for the accumulation of money. In fact, he gave it away almost as fast as he received it ... all his sympathies were with the poor and friendless.'

As to the Danube Commission, Gordon's views were 'rather peculiar. He explained to me that, as the river had been adequately dredged and buoyed, and as the lighthouse at its mouth was completed, there was really nothing more to do; and that the Commission was practically useless. As I understood, he had written to the Foreign Office to that effect, adding also that his salary was too large.'[18] His report would have been critical of Stokes and may lie behind a letter from Stokes to Sir Henry Gordon some months after Charlie's death: 'My relations with your brother were always of the most friendly character, and I can never forget the handsome way in which he endeavoured to repair what he thought was an injury he had done me. The injury done was to the interests of the Danube navigation that has never been repaired to this day, and never can be. The implied injury to me was amply atoned by his handsome avowal.'[19]

Adye and Gordon on their way back from the Crimea were kept in quarantine outside Constantinople. They then stayed a few days with Sir Henry Elliot at Thesapia on the Bosphorus, in his pleasant wooden summer palace which long afterwards was destroyed by fire; and here one September evening came a dinner party which was to change Gordon's life. Among the ambassador's guests was Nubar Pasha, the Armenian Christian, born in Smyrna and educated in Europe, who was in the service of Ismail, the Khedive (Viceroy) of Egypt under the Ottoman Sultan; Nubar had been Ismail's minister for foreign affairs and would twice be prime minister. They were looking for a successor to Sir Samuel Baker, the eminent British explorer who was governor-general of Equatoria, the southern Sudan, which he had annexed for Egypt. The Khedive was dissatisfied with Baker and had decided not to renew his contract when it expired in 1873.

Nubar found himself in a long conversation (in French) with a fellow guest, the British Commissioner on the Danube. Understanding that this man was an officer of the Royal Engineers, Nubar asked if the Commissioner knew any British officer in the Indian Engineers who might succeed Baker. The Commissioner, as he himself wrote later from Galatz, 'having already taken a dislike to this idle spot, I pricked up my ears,'[20] and expressed interest in the post for himself. After the conversation ended the German chargé d'affaires, von Radowitz, asked Nubar if he knew who the Commissioner was. Nubar said 'No.' 'It is Gordon!' Nubar looked blank. 'Chinese Gordon.' added the German. The epithet meant nothing to Nubar but to disguise his ignorance he murmured a knowing 'Ah.'

Back in Cairo Nubar looked up books about recent Chinese history. From the glowing tribute of the Marquis de Beauvois he realized that Gordon, who had not mentioned China during an hour's conversation ('rare modesty and such as I have rarely met') might be the man the Khedive sought to suppress the Slave Trade, and pacify the tribes of Central Africa, and open safe communication up the Nile to the great Lakes.[21] Gordon heard no more when he returned to Galatz. Towards the end of the year he went back go England on leave. His mother had suffered a stroke and he spent much time at Southampton in close attendance. And his younger brother Freddie had died at the age of thirty-six, leaving a widow, now living a few doors from her mother-in-law and Augusta. Her six small children used to joke, when they grew up, that their father had been very selfish to die so young leaving his widow to bring them up on a pittance; but they had a generous uncle Charlie who added them to his ever-growing list of beneficiaries.

Gordon was able to slip across the Solent to Osborne at the invitation of two close Sapper friends in the Royal Household: Sir Howard Elphinstone, Comptroller and Treasurer to Prince Arthur, who was now twenty-two and a highly efficient and popular captain on leave from the Rifle Brigade, and Sir John Cowell, Master of the Queen's Household.

'Yesterday Cowell had an Engineer friend here, Gordon by name,' wrote the Queen's Private Secretary, General Sir Henry Ponsonby, to his wife on 28 December 1872. 'I had heard of him, the ever victorious he was called . . .' At the Household luncheon he had talked of the Crimea and Romania and Turkey. 'This and much more was what he talked about. Elphinstone and Cowell immensely proud of him, and justly so.' Gordon then 'had a mysterious confabulation with Prince Arthur. So there may be something looming. But perhaps it is only to go with him to Rome where he is going for a month.'[22]

Gordon did not go to Rome but to Woolwich to see Henry, and on to Chislehurst for a day and a night with the Freeses, who had moved from Gravesend. 'So once more,' recalled Octavia Freese, 'we three met again and renewed our old intimacy and talked of everything, he all joke and geniality.' When Gordon said that he 'considered himself shelved at Galatz and wondered why,' Octavia suggested that he was like Moses in the desert, 'being prepared in solitude and loneliness for some great work that he was yet to do.'

That very day the exiled Napoleon III died at Chislehurst. Gordon had always been fascinated by the Emperor ('Kind-hearted, unprincipled') and when he lay in state Gordon came again with Henry. As old Crimean officers they wished to pay their respects. The Freeses and the Gordons 'all walked up the hill together. We were very full of spirits, being so glad to meet again, and went laughing and joking up the hill; but it was very characteristic of Gordon that as we neared the gate he suddenly became quite grave, and said to me, "You must not be so hilarious," and our tone moderated at once.'[23] Ten year old Freddie Freese never forgot seeing Napoleon in an open coffin 'like a figure of wax in full uniform covered with orders . . . Gordon was much moved and spoke on the way home of the vanity of all earthly ambitions.'[24]

He returned to Chislehurst briefly for the Emperor's funeral, then a few days later had breakfast with the Freeses on his way to Dover, 'and,' wrote Octavia, 'after burying some half-crowns in the garden for my little boys, with strict injunctions that they were not to be dug up till the next day, he went away, just sending me a postcard with nothing on it but this: "PS.CXXI"'[25]*

---

*'I will lift up mine eyes unto the hills, from whence cometh my help. My help cometh even from the Lord . . .'

Gordon was back at Galatz by his fortieth birthday, 28 January 1873. No word came from Nubar. Gordon had decided to resign. 'I shall not stop here over April 1874,' he wrote to Harvey, now commanding Engineer in Halifax, Nova Scotia. 'It does not and never did suit me to be here . . . I cannot stand being mixed up with a lot of men with whom one must discuss every detail on even the most trivial question.'[26] And the language barrier prevented him working among the poor of Galatz except through donations.

That summer the British government announced the forming of a military expedition for West Africa to stop the outrages of 'King Coffee' of the Ashanti, with his zeal for human sacrifices, who was harrying tribes friendly to Britain in the hinterland of the Gold Coast. Gordon was widely tipped as its possible commander; indeed, 'all the papers clamoured for his appointment,' as Sir Henry Ponsonby commented to his wife.[27] In a letter to *The Times*, 'A Student of History' (Colonel Chesney) called Gordon 'the finest soldier for irregular warfare which this age of warfare has produced . . . It is true that to send such a peerless soldier to the coast of Africa might be considered as throwing him away in one sense. But then in another sense we have already thrown him away. For Colonel Gordon has the misfortune to be an Engineer, and therefore, still remains merely Colonel Gordon,' in exile on the Danube. In a later letter to *The Times* Chesney admitted that Gordon's 'peculiarly retiring character' had contributed to 'the extra-ordinary neglect of a great soldier.'[28]

The War Office selected Sir Garnet Wolseley; though three months younger he was senior in rank and had seen more recent service in the field. Gordon did not grieve. As he wrote to Aunt Amy later that year, perfect peace must be based on the doctrine that God ordains all things: 'I accept that not a sparrow falls to the ground without His will, if so little a thing as that happens with His direction, everything that happens to us is with His will, and therefore I accept anything that happens as directed by Him and as far as I am concerned unavoidable.'[29]

Baker lingered in Egypt after his contract expired and did not leave until August. On 30 August 1873 the British consul-general at Alexandria, Hussey Vivian, telegraphed to Sir Henry Elliot at Constantinople: 'Viceroy begs me to telegraph to you that he wishes to offer command of the troops and government of the territory annexed by Baker to Colonel Gordon formerly in the Chinese service who will be armed with fullest powers.'[30] The Khedive assured the British government of his determination to organize the country thoroughly and to suppress the Slave Trade, and hoped that 'they will give their consent and assistance in securing Gordon's services.'

The ambassador forwarded the wire to Gordon, who wrote to him on 5 September that it was 'a difficult question to answer as of course it will depend very much on what our government may feel with respect to the appointment. I replied, "for my part" I would accept.' He would not 'throw up my commission for a service of the sort' or go against the government's wishes, nor leave before settling a successor.[31]

When the Khedive's telegram was forwarded by the Foreign Office to Balmoral, the Queen hesitated 'to give leave as Gordon seemed a man who would be required by her. Possibly on the Gold Coast.' 'We have had a discussion on "Ever Victorious Gordon"' Ponsonby told his wife, '. . . If he is such a valuable man I don't think we ought to allow him to be taken off to the Egyptian wars. I suggested this to the Queen.' If Wolseley fell ill 'or requires an active second-in-command would Colonel Gordon be thought of?' But Wolseley had taken out a brilliant ring of subordinates, most of whom rose to be field-marshals or generals, and the War Office and the Foreign Office told Balmoral that Gordon was not wanted. Lord Granville, the Foreign Secretary, who was at Balmoral, told the Queen that as Gordon wished to go 'it would be a gracious act if Your Majesty consented.'

Ponsonby commented: 'I suppose they know best what they want but I am sorry to lose just now the services of a man whose peculiar aptitude is in drilling foreigners and making them fight.' And Gordon's friend Sir John Cowell minuted: 'The Khedive is sharp in trying to get Gordon and as he G has never had any field for his talents since leaving China, it would be a relief to him to have a chance of doing good anywhere on a larger scale than the Danube work.'[32]

A few days later Gordon returned to England and saw his mother for the last time: her mind had nearly gone and he knew that he could do no good by lingering at her death bed. He wrote a note to Harry: 'In the event of my dear mother's death please give over to Augusta *everything* that may fall to my share, for her to do what she wishes with.'[33] The formal deed was not signed until three years later, but Gordon had no thought of keeping his share as a trust fund for ever-growing charity, perhaps keeping him out of debt: Augusta should have it all.

He returned sadly to Galatz. By his mother's death he would have lost 'any great desire to return to England,' he told Elliot, 'and if I do not go to Egypt I will I think go to India.'[34] Foreign Office consent came through.

Gordon saw his successor installed on the Danube, crossed the Mediterranean to meet his new master, the Khedive, then returned to England to prepare.

Since he would be leading a pioneering expedition rather than a settled government many young men applied, including John Russell, son of the famous war correspondent W. H. Russell, who wrote in his diary after meeting Gordon: 'A darling fellow all over. He said he would do his best for John.'[35]

Gordon avoided obligation to the Geographical or Anti-Slavery societies. James Grant, who had discovered the source of the Nile with Speke, called at Gordon's lodgings. Grant left his wife in the carriage and stayed so long that she caught a cold. Gordon also met the Reverend Horace Waller, a leading anti-slaver, who knew Central Africa and was now editing Livingstone's journals.

On the day that the news of Livingstone's death reached England, 28 January 1874, Gordon's forty-first birthday, he left for the southern Sudan, scattering post-cards to relatives; 'Goodbye. Isaiah[35]. C. G. G.'

CHAPTER FIFTEEN

Sudan Prelude

Khedive Ismail, three years older than Gordon, had large, thick ears and a ragged red tangle of eyebrows. His eye-lids drooped, one more than the other, and when listening he would appear to keep one eye closed while the other flashed intelligence.[1] Yet he had an extraordinary charm, and he charmed Gordon, both on the preliminary visit and when Gordon arrived in Cairo early in February 1874 to take up his post; but Gordon could not then decide whether Ismail's desire to end the Slave Trade was sincere, or humbug to please the Great Powers of Europe.

The Khedive appeared to be charmed with Gordon: 'What an extraordinary Englishman! He doesn't want money.'[2] Gordon had rejected Sir Samuel Baker's high salary because 'all the coin one takes is wrung out of poor people,'[3] generally by the *courbash* (a hippo, rhino or buffalo hide whip). Gordon contracted for such a modest sum that Ismail searched for an ulterior motive: Gordon might have a secret commission to spy out the southern Sudan for British annexation. The Khedive therefore (so Gordon came to believe) placed a spy on Gordon's staff, a boastful French-American Colonel, a Confederate veteran named Charles Chaillé-Long.

Gordon accepted Chaillé-Long but had already chosen a man he could trust: Romolo Gessi, the Italian-Armenian interpreter whom he had known in the Crimea. Gessi had fought under Garibaldi in the war of 1859 and had been in a timber business on the Danube when Gordon had met him again. Gessi, a swashbuckler who, Gordon thought, should have lived in the days of Queen Elizabeth, had agreed to leave a somewhat floundering business for the opportunity of adventure. He had already brought his wife and young family to Cairo: 'Gessi met me at the station, delighted to see me . . . wife not over-content.'[4] The staff was international, including young Willy Anson, a British admiral's son who was a Gordon family connection (not a nephew);

and an interpreter, Auguste Linant de Bellefonds, whose mother was an Abyssinian Christian and his father an eminent French engineer and explorer in the Egyptian service; two feeble Egyptian aides-de-camp who would rather have stayed behind but were foisted on Gordon; and an ex-slave trader, Abou Saoud, whom Baker had dismissed but Gordon was prepared to trust; he did valuable work before falling into disgrace again.

Gordon was now His Excellency Gordon Pasha, Governor-General of the Equator, 'so no one can or ought to cross it without permission of His Excellency,' he joked; but he refused to let his German servant address him as 'Your Excellency'.[5] Leaving Gessi to bring most of the expedition's staff and the heavy baggage up the Nile, he went on ahead with Long by the Red Sea to Suakin, across the desert by camel and pony to Berber and up the Nile to Khartoum, the populous city three miles up the Blue Nile from its junction with the White. Dominating the view from the steamer was the large white palace of the Governor-General of the Sudan.

Ismail Pasha Aiyub, a Kurd or a Circassian with fluent French, impressed Gordon favourably at first: Gordon was not his subordinate but answerable directly to the Egyptian government. Ismail Aiyub showed him the hospital and tried to entertain him with nearly nude dancing girls, only to find that the Governor-General of the Equator had slipped quietly away.[6]

Ismail Aiyub had greatly eased Gordon's onward route by organizing the penetration of the *Sudd*, the area of floating vegetation which had blocked the White Nile at a curve, far to the south of Khartoum, where Baker had been held up for months; Gordon and Long steamed through the *Sudd* without delay but the voyage to Central Africa against the current in a rickety paddle steamer seemed frustratingly slow. Gordon described it to Augusta in long journal-letters to be passed round the family: the crocodiles lying in the sand at evening, the monkeys coming down to drink, the hippos and the laughing storks, 'highly amused at anybody thinking of going up to Gondokoro with the hope of doing anything;'[7] and, as the ship reached the equatorial region, the stark-naked blacks, proud Shilluks and Dinkas, who regarded even a loin cloth as a sign of slavery.

By now Gordon found Chaillé-Long 'a regular failure,'[8] boastful, inefficient, and a spy. As soon as they reached Gondokoro, the neat capital of Equatoria, 680 miles from Khartoum, on 16 April 1875, Gordon ordered Long to make his way farther southward up the Nile to the court of King M'tesa of the Baganda, whom the Khedive hoped to make his vassal.

Gordon could do little without his full team and supplies, whether to explore, pacify or break the slave trade; and therefore returned at once to Khartoum, where the Governor-General was surprised to see him again so soon. The Khedive had ordered Ismail Aiyub to supply Gordon with all he needed; but Aiyub secretly wanted to continue the profitable slave trade and therefore to keep Gordon weak and dependent. As Gordon wrote later: 'The great object of my foe Ismail Pasha Aiyub was to keep me in this state and my great object was to break out of it.'[9] They kept up a running war of words, each sending frequent complaints to Cairo.

Gordon went on down to Berber to meet Gessi, the staff and the stores; but instead of taking all to Gondokoro he sent Gessi and young Willy Anson up the Bahr-el-Ghazal river to re-establish firm government and stop the slavers, while he made his own base at the town of Saubat where the Ghazal river flows into the Nile. He chose this as the best place to break the slave trade.

He had found the trade 'as brisk as ever,'[10] for slavery was the economic base of Egypt and the Sudan; Arab and Dongolese raiders would penetrate into the savannahs and forests beyond the borders, invade villages and seize men, women and children, making them march within forked wooden yokes, their hands tied to the bar which linked one captive to the next. Baker had stopped the slavers using the Nile but this had made more misery: 'the poor slaves instead of dropping down the Nile more or less comfortably, now have to walk over thousands of miles of blazing sand with the thermometer at 110°.'[11] Gordon had already lessened the demand for slaves by making ivory a government monopoly; traders would not want slaves to carry it if they could not reap the profit: Gordon loathed 'this indiscriminate slaughter' of elephants for their tusks and foresaw the near extinction of the herds.[12]

He caught slavers and released slaves, many of whom settled round the town. Eighty years later an English officer of the Sudan Defence Force heard an elderly man tell how his father had worked under Gordon: '"Gordoon" Pasha was a God, he destroyed the slave traders. My father said that "Gordoon" Pasha's eyes were like spears – no man dared tell him a lie. He was here many years, then he left us and the slavers came again but worse than before.'[13] Gordon stopped the trade in Equatoria, but his province did not extend far from the rivers: until he could control the whole Sudan the trade would not be killed.

After a frustrating wait for the steamers which he needed before he could explore farther south, he returned to Gondokoro in August, a place 'miserable to a degree' where it rained seven months in a year, and 'the poor natives . . . are more or less starved and have been so mistreated by the slave dealers, that they have no heart left. I hope to be able to give them peace at any rate, and make them more happy but it will be an uphill game, at present.'[14]

He sent his brother Enderby a photograph he had taken of a Dinka chief, six foot four inches tall, one of 'a lot of naked black creatures,' naked and unashamed, who would not wear clothes if given them but were 'quite aware of right and wrong.' The chief 'will reason that "*If I do wrong, I do wrong, but am not under the Pasha, it is my land*"' (touching the earth) "*and not anyone else's.*" I have been gentle with them, and I think they like me as well as they like a handful of beads.'[15]

Gordon's staff were falling ill, mainly with malaria. The place became a hospital and Gordon the nurse: 'I never saw such a gang, they get ill and quarter themselves on me.'[16] Several died, including Auguste Linant the interpreter. Gordon saved Russell's life and sent him back, to his indignation. Away in Bahr-el-Ghazal Gessi had nearly died, and Willy Anson had died in Gessi's arms, to Gordon's great grief when he heard. Gessi arrived at Gondokoro to make his report. Gordon wished to keep him but only Gessi could be trusted to build a dockyard at Khartoum and put together a steamer from parts rusting unused.

Gordon stayed reasonably fit. T. H. Huxley the scientist once asked Gordon 'Why he didn't have the African fever. "Well," he said, "You see, fellows think they shall have it and they do. I didn't think so, and didn't get it."'[17] When testy and shivering, he would pretend he was bilious. Later he was sent bottles of Warburg's Tincture (*Tinctura Antiperiodica*) a remedy mixed by a physician of Charing Cross which included aloes and alcohol, opium, quinine, rhubarb, cinnamon, ginger, etc. etc.[18] It caused such sweating that Gordon thought he was 'flowing away' but 'it certainly has given me new life and has a wonderful effect.'[19]

By October 1874 the expedition seemed almost at a collapse, except for the return of Long, whom Gordon soon sent away again to bring stores from Khartoum.

Then, on 14 November, arrived two officers of the Royal Engineers, Charles Moore Watson, an Irishman aged thirty, and the twenty-four year old William Harold Chippindall. Gordon, and most books, misspelt him Chippendall but usually called him Chipp. He had sent for both from England but forgotten about them; their coming therefore, after mapping the Nile on their way up, was a delight: 'first rate, well instructed fellows and a great help to me. I am so glad of their arrival,' he wrote to Harvey, 'for it leaves me free from all science and saves me going to the Lakes, lets me attend to the Province and revenue. My dear Charles be content, you would be a shadow here. I find my temper fretful, and it is weary work,' which he longed to leave.[20]

Watson and Chipp give a vivid picture of Gordon in Equatoria before they too were invalided out, Watson in February and Chipp in July 1875. In Khartoum everyone had spoken of Gordon as 'the one man who can get the White Nile district into order. It is really wonderful how he seems to inspire everyone with confidence, and from what I hear he seems to work tremendously hard,' wrote Watson to his mother. And a week after they had arrived he wrote: 'the more I see of Gordon the more I like him.'[21]

'He is very well,' wrote Watson that same day to James Grant, the Scottish explorer, 'and hard at work, and you know this country well enough to understand the kind of difficulties he has with the Arabs and Egyptian officials. I cannot but wonder sometimes at his patience. He appears to have won the confidence of most of the tribes in the vicinity, and now they bring in ivory for sale with the greatest confidence. Before he came, the Egyptians said you could not go half a mile from Gondokoro without an armed escort.'[22]

The two Sappers were sent South, intending to explore Lake Albert Nyanza. Gordon went with them up-river as far as Rejaf, and they saw, as Chipp recalled, his 'feverish impatience that everything should go right, which manifested itself by constant interference in all details,' a trait which Chipp mentioned in a letter after Watson had been invalided: 'He seems always to think that nobody but his blessed self can even screw a box-lid on. He is a fearful egotist in that way. But he is devilish kind to one, and really I fear he will almost spoil me for future service.'[23] But when Chipps' own health broke in July 1875 he wrote: 'I cannot tell you my sorrow at leaving Gordon, for with all his faults one can't help but love him.'[24]

Chippindall recovered. As he served in India they may not have met again, but both he and Watson, who became a great friend of Gordon, revered and defended his memory.

Watson and Chippindall had brought eight months' mail. Gordon disappeared into his hut to answer it within a week. Each day, when not on expeditions he would put time aside for a vast correspondence and, according to Chaillé-Long (but to no one else), would place a hatchet and a flag outside his door as a sign that he must not be disturbed.

Part of the seclusion he spent in Bible study. The Bible he had in Equatoria, the gift of Aunt Amy, became so worn outside and heavily marked within that he left it with Augusta on his return to England, and Augusta presented it in 1885 to Queen Victoria at Windsor, who placed it open in a glass case, with his bust beside it.

In his Bible studies he continued to develop theories which he realized were unorthodox* but they were built on the great cornerstone of his faith: the indwelling of Christ. Once, writing to Augusta, Gordon bemoaned his carelessness with money (he was strict with public accounts but not about his private giving) and he suggested that God could keep the books for him. 'It is a query if it is right to put this on Him but I think if you have a Friend of His might and wisdom, you cannot too much trust Him, and with His power, it is no trouble to Him and therefore the closer your intimacy, the better. I know these views are outrageous but I would take His own invitation to cast all my cares on Him, for He careth for thee . . .'[25]

Sometimes he used the Bible with confusing results, as Chipp recalled: 'he told me that when he was perplexed over any problem he used to pray about it and then open his Bible anywhere, and that the first text his eye lighted on he took to be an answer to his prayer. This habit was the cause of much confusion as he would often counter-order his first orders.'[26]

Chaillé-Long claimed in a book of 1884 that Gordon would disappear to meditate for 'days at a time,' a claim unmentioned in Long's first book of 1876 and conflicting with the facts recorded in Gordon's journal-letters and other sources, including the diary of Ernest Marno the Austrian botanist and explorer. In a book of 1912 Long inserted a brandy bottle beside the Bible (possibly transferring a memory of Marno's fellow-traveller the Austrian consul, whom Gordon found drunk at that time). The brandy bottle gave Lytton Strachey his cue; yet earlier (in 1908) Long had described Gordon as 'a unique figure, brave, high spirited, and chivalrous, the soul of honor. His purity of character was so marked that it has been mistaken by those who would have him saint before soldier.' Long added: 'I declare that Gordon never showed the religious side to me.'[27]

*see chapter 27.

The question, Did Gordon Drink, which was hovering long before Strachey, has been exhaustively examined in two books, of 1931 and 1954.* The subject surfaces at times in the rest of this story but may be summarized: brandy (Gordon usually called it cognac) was the normal social and medical drink in hot countries in his day; like Churchill he had a strong head but unlike Churchill he would go for long periods without alcohol. He never touched liquor in Equatoria and was annoyed with Watson and Chippindall for bringing him a present of a dozen of sherry;[28] and he never took brandy on his desert journeys. Those who worked closely with him claimed that he was always temperate: Chippindall, as the last survivor of the expedition up the White Nile, wrote in 1932 that 'I am emphatically of the opinion that the imputation on Gordon of drinking to excess is a base calumny.'[29] And secret drinking was impossible where Gordon served. Augusta put the matter in perspective: when a friend mentioned the rumours she replied: 'It doesn't really matter. Everyone who knew Charlie knows the truth.'[30]

To link his province from north to south, Gordon decided to place fortified posts beside the Nile from Lardo, where he had transferred his capital a short distance to more healthy ground than Gondokoro, to Lake Albert, if indeed the western branch of the Nile flowed out of the lake: no explorer had been that way.

The few Europeans who had travelled south of Gondokoro claimed that frequent rapids, often in narrow gorges, made the upper Nile unnavigable. Gordon did not wish to march through country in which the tribes might be hostile; he would go by river, hauling his small steamer and numerous nuggars (native barges) up each rapid. For the next three months after Chippindall's departure Gordon became an explorer (cockroaches in the sugar, mosquitoes one day and sand flies the next) who was also governor-general. He took his soldiers and their inevitable camp followers up the uncharted river, surveying as he went, hiring tribal labour (paid in cows taken as tax) to haul.

'A day of agony to me,' he wrote one August evening, 'We have got three nuggars through the Googi Rapids, as they are called; and such anxiety – it was really quite painful – ropes breaking, and nuggars going down a six-knot

*C. H. Allen *Gordon in the Sudan* (1931) and Lord Elton, *General Gordon* (1954).

current. I am really quite exhausted – more mentally than physically.'[31]

He told Augusta that he 'prays the nuggars up as he used to do the troops when they wavered in the breaches in China; but often and often the ropes break, and it has all to be done over again.'[32] Chipp, when he read that in print, dryly remarked that 'I do not doubt that he prayed; but he also used more mundane means, as I have seen him rushing at the black teams and beating them handsomely if they were slacking on the haul, it is true he only had a walking stick but he used it effectively.'[33] He led from the front. 'His (poor) Excellency,' he wrote, 'has to slave more than any individual: to pull ropes, to mend this, make a cover to that (just finished a capital cover to the duck gun).'[34] And always he had the work of the province. 'Up at dawn and to bed at eight or nine p.m.; no books but *one*, and that not often read for long, for I cannot sit down for a study of those mysteries. All day long worrying about writing orders ... obliged to think of the veriest trifle, even to knocking off the white ants from the stores, etc., that is one's life.'[35]

He was moving through tribes disposed to be hostile because Baker had fought rather than persuaded, and had failed. Gordon determined to persuade. 'If you would rule over native peoples,' he once wrote to the young son of a friend in Ireland, 'you must love them.'[36] Gordon poured out gifts, and courtesies, while worrying whether 'it is evil for us to invade an independent country or, they, the natives, to defend it.'[37] When he had to seize supplies which had not been offered by a chief to pay his tax he pondered: 'This is painful work for me, but what can I do, I must either throw up the whole matter and come down or else do this. All these questions are difficult ones of right and wrong ...'[38]

Only once did he have a serious fight, in a place of tall elephant grass and doora (a cereal like maize) beside the river. Hostile Bari attacked with spears. They refused a parley and later nearly ambushed Gordon as he walked. Ernest Linant (Auguste's brother) had just returned from the court of King M'tesa where he had found H. M. Stanley. Linant asked permission to burn the tribal huts in the nearby hills, which Gordon granted in order to distract the Bari from the steamer.

Gordon supplied his own bodyguard but Linant did not spot an ambush in the long grass. He was speared, and most of his men. On his body Gordon found Stanley's letter which the *Daily Telegraph* published, appealing for Christian missionaries at M'tesa's request. Despite such a setback, Gordon's policy won. An Italian who took up an official position in Khartoum two years after Gordon left Equatoria summed it up in his journal: 'Rarely indeed can it be said of Gordon Pasha that he resorted to force but there are numberless instances in which with gentleness and good manners and with gifts he succeeded in a month or two not only in making the navigation of the White Nile unrestricted and safe as far upstream as Gondokoro, but he knew how to retain the friendship of those peoples who, up till then, had been hostile.'[39]

Gordon had hoped to take his steamer and native boats ('nuggars') as far as Lake Albert but on 17 October 1875, after establishing his southernmost post he was on foot on the caravan road after passing above a gorge where the Nile narrowed, when he heard 'a noise of thunder.' A native guide led him by a difficult path; the noise became louder. Soon he looked down on the Fola Falls, a ten mile length of roaring cascades, so narrow that the whole river seemed to pour down two clefts in the rock. 'It is all over,' he said; not a nuggar could navigate the Fola Falls.

Gessi was on his way up. Gordon gave him the task of organizing the overland carry to a launching place for the steamer, with the honour of discovering whether the Nile did indeed flow out of Albert Nyanza, and then to be the first white man to sail round the lake.

Gordon stayed in the south to organize revenue and government. The British Foreign Office had quashed his plan for a chain of posts from the Indian Ocean to Uganda; Gordon therefore advised the Khedive not to attempt to annex M'tesa's Kingdom of the Buganda and instead sent the German doctor Edvard Schnitzer, known as Emin, to make a treaty of friendship with the King. Gordon did some final exploring; in September 1876 he turned for home.[40]

Gordon's old chief on the Danube and at Chatham, Edward Stanton, had been Consul-General at Cairo throughout Gordon's time in Equatoria, and a great help and correspondent. Through a mutual friend he told Henry Gordon that the Khedive was delighted with Charlie, who was 'in high favour with everyone in that country. I believe he will leave a name in Central Africa for ages.'[41] Gordon Pasha was not delighted with the Khedive who had neglected to send instructions for a year; and the governor-general at Khartoum continued to frustrate.

As Gordon steamed slowly down the Nile for Cairo and home, he could not make up his mind. In September he wrote: 'As far as I can see I shall come back here again and give up H. M.'s service. I have a field for the last years of my life.' Then he recalled how much he disliked it. 'How I hate this country and all the work' he had written; and: 'Oh my goodness! I do heartily wish it was over;' and, of the Egyptians, 'Oh dear, What a people to slave for . . .[42] Talk of two natures in one,' he wrote in November from Khartoum, 'I have a hundred, and they are none alike and all will rule; and whether it is the climate or not, I never know my own mind for two days consecutively . . . I wish I was more decided, but alas! I cannot be so, and I envy Gessi who knows his mind . . . I expect, having had for these past years, my blood at a high temperature, day and night, from year's end to year's end, must have some effect on one's temperament.'[43]

He was not sure whether he would enjoy home. He day-dreamed of lying in bed at Southampton until 11 a. m., taking 'little toddles to the Docks or the cemetery,' and keeping off 'those terrible railway journeys,' and dinner parties. He had been eating little and wanted '*oysters* when I come home, they are good for the brain, with brown bread and lots of them, not a dozen, but 4 dozen.'[44] As for church, 'It seems a very long three years, without a Sunday, every day is just the same. I do not know how I shall get on with the clergy or what denomination I shall join.'[45]

He would keep away from Baker and Grant and the geographers; he would seek out the anti-slavery men; and after a long leave would perhaps take another appointment abroad. By the time he reached Cairo his mind was made up: he would not renew his contract.

'When I went up the stairs of the Khedive's palace, you could have found no one more decided *not* to return, but when I went downstairs, *I had consented to do so.*'[46] The Khedive had exercised all his charm and had promised solemnly, if Gordon would return, to stop the irregularities of officials which had frustrated all attempts to end the slave trade. Gordon had placed himself in the hands of God, to 'let myself drift where He wills,' and took this promise as an indication of His will. Doubts followed quickly. He could not decide whether his promise to return was conditional or absolute. Nubar suggested Gordon should 'throw over' the Khedive and open up a country between the ocean and the lakes (in the manner of Rajah Brooke, the British Indian Army officer who became independent Sovereign of Sarawak in Borneo, but Gordon said he would not make the first move.

He arrived in London at 7 p.m. on Christmas Eve, at his old lodgings off the Strand, and in a characteristic gesture went at once to Bayswater beyond the Park ('the world's end') to comfort the sister and brother-in-law of the late Louis Lucas, a young explorer who had been a nuisance and then had gone mad.[47]

Gordon spent his five weeks' leave partly with Augusta, whose house was filling with African curios which he had sent or brought, but mostly in London. One evening a brother officer invited him to dine at their club with Colonel (later General Sir) William Butler, who left a vivid description of Gordon after his three years in the southern Sudan.*

Butler, particularly noted 'the indefinable expression' of Górdon's eyes, and found his conversation 'the best and cheeriest talk I ever listened to. Gordon's voice was as clear and vibrant as the note of an old Burmese bell, which has a great deal of gold in its metal. We adjourned to the smoking-room, and there the stream of thought and anecdote flowed on even better than before ... He spoke in low but very distinct tones, and his voice, varying with its subject, carried to the ear a sense of pleasure in the sound similar to that which the sight of his features, lit with the light of a very ardent soul, gave to the listener's eye. I never heard human voice nor looked into any man's eye and found similar tone and glance there, not did I ever meet a man who had equal facility for putting into words the thoughts that were in his brain ...'[48] Butler later wrote a biography of Gordon, which Augusta thought the best.

All this time Gordon was debating his future, whether to return or resign. Horace Waller sought to involve him in the scheme of William Mackinnon, founder of the British India Line, to create an East Africa Company, based on Zanzibar, like the old East India Company. The country would be opened for commerce and the Slave Trade be destroyed. Waller enthused to Mackinnon about Gordon: 'If you look closely you will see the spirit of a Clive in this man – let us try, by God's help, to make a Clive or greater if we can – less he is not and you will say so when you know him well.'[49]

Gordon was tempted, provided he set up the stations but not command the whole concession: 'I know nothing of concessions and would be sure to make a mess of it.'[50] He discussed terms of service yet could not decide whether he was irrevocably committed to the Khedive. On 11 January 1877 he sought the advice of the Foreign Secretary, the fifteenth Earl of Derby.

---

*Butler married Elizabeth Thompson, the painter (as Lady Butler) of military epics.

That evening Derby wrote in his diary about 'a visitor who really interested me, Col. Gordon, the successful commander of a Chinese army, and conqueror of the lake regions of Africa for the Khedive. He came to consult me as to returning to his command: where he thinks he is doing more harm than good, for the Khedive's officers ill use the people in every way as soon as his back is turned. He said he did not think the Khedive sincere in wishing to improve the country: or if so, he was capricious and not to be trusted: he, Gordon, had been left over a year without either supplies or instructions, which he ascribed to the Khedive being taken up with other objects and not caring whether the expedition succeeded or perished.

'He spoke of the unhealthiness of the interior where even Arabs fall ill; and evidently had had enough of the work. I told him I could not advise, it was a personal matter, but if he wished to retire I could not see who could complain, or what possible claim the Khedive could set up: he had not bound himself to serve for life. He seemed to agree, but I don't know what he will do.

'He is a small, thin person, with an unusually mild expression of countenance, a look as of great habitual patience (I noted the same expression, years ago, in the late Rajah Brooke); nothing about him very noticeable except bright wide-open eyes. His manner quiet and pleasant.'[51]

The Derby interview inclined Gordon to resign. Although 'sorely troubled in mind, for my brothers and some of my Army friends look on my action in thinking of Zanzibar as "gross treachery" to HH.,'[52] he telegraphed Vivian, who had succeeded Stanton at Cairo, to tell the Khedive that he would not be back.

Next day an affectionate but firm reply came from the Khedive, holding him to his 'solemn promise.' Gordon wavered. 'I am most variable,' he confessed to Waller. 'Maybe it is the effect of the African climate.'[53]

He decided to go back to Cairo but, on the advice of Gerald Graham and Charles Watson, to insist that he be given the whole of the Sudan. Lord Derby, when he heard, commented: 'I can hardly imagine the Khedive consenting; but if he refuses, Gordon has a fair excuse for retiring.'[54]

On 20 January Gordon changed his mind again and wrote out a telegram refusing to return. He asked the War Office to send it in cipher but the Military Secretary showed it to the Duke of Cambridge who 'emphatically' (probably with one of his famous oaths) 'said I must go back, and would not allow me to break my promise.'[55]

Since Gordon did not wish to resign his Army commission he had no alternative. The Duke, when Gordon went to see him, 'was very civil,'[56] but was not allowed the last word. That day, after Gordon had been to Woolwich and Gravesend, he put the matter in the hands of God, with prayer. As he wrote on a post card to Augusta: 'After preparation, (on return from Woolwich) tossed!! Head to go, Tail to stay. It fell Head!!! C. G. G. 21.1.77'[57]

CHAPTER SIXTEEN
The Governor-General

Gordon arrived in Cairo on the evening of 8 February 1877. Next morning when the Master of Ceremonies called to convey the Khedive's invitation to dinner Gordon broke protocol by sending his excuses, 'for I felt either I must resist these court approaches or I was beat.'[1]

The Khedive was charmed by the refusal. When an appointment was fixed, he sat on his divan and handed Gordon a *firman* which made him Governor-General of a Sudan much larger than before, to include his old Equatoria and other provinces, one being in a state of revolt. Gordon would control finance and be answerable to the Khedive alone, not to the Egyptian government: in effect he would be almost absolute monarch of a country the size of Western Europe, with powers greater than a viceroy of India.

An approach to Lord Derby by Gerald Graham had produced 'this most splendid concession' through intervention by the new British Agent and Consul-General Hussey Vivian, whom Gordon remembered kicking around at 'The Shop.' Thanking Vivian formally for 'the astounding authority His Highness has invested in me,' Gordon wrote that 'no one could possibly have imagined that such powers ... would be so full, and complete.' He looked forward with confidence 'to the total suppression of the Slave Trade in, and the opening out of these vast countries.'[2]

The Khedive asked Gordon to go first, as Governor-General, to the Red Sea coast, and up-country to a territory in dispute between Egypt and Abyssinia (Ethiopia). King Johannes (or John), who had succeeded Theodore as King of Kings or Emperor, had soundly defeated an Egyptian army the year before while Gordon was in Equatoria. Friendly relations had been restored but a brigand chieftain named Walad-el-Michael, who had deserted John and sided with the Egyptians, was causing trouble. Gordon must deal with him and also induce King John to sign a treaty.

In Cairo Gordon had met a twenty-four year old subaltern of The Blues, John Brocklehurst, whom he invited to join him in the Egyptian frigate put at his disposal. They became great friends during the voyage to Massawa, in the part of Eritrea which at that time belonged to the Sudan. Brocklehurst spent a few days shooting and then sailed back. The frigate caught fire in the Red Sea and several sailors were killed. Brocklehurst escaped with the loss of his luggage and Gordon's dress coat.

Gordon meanwhile had gone into the interior by camel, and by mule in the mountains, with escort and pomp expected of a governor-general, which he found trying, taking an amused comfort from the tendency of his sentries to fall asleep when guarding him at night. He was now a *mushir*, marshal of Egypt ('I and the Duke are equals!') with a splendid uniform of gold lace for formal occasions; he felt 'only very, very slightly elated by the honours and power given me,' mainly because of the confidence placed in him.[3]

They came to Keren in its almost impregnable position, which would become famous some sixty years later in the Second World War for the siege and capture of the Italian garrison. In 1877 the Egyptian garrison was small, while the rebel Walad-el-Michael commanded thousands. He was peremptorily summoned. Gordon described the scene in detail to Augusta in his usual journal letter, noting especially the priests of the ancient isolated Ethiopian-Coptic church, so suspicious of a different Christian that when Gordon spoke they lifted a cross to their eyes to ward off evil. Walad-el-Michael made his submission but Gordon had to tread carefully. As he wrote to Gerald Graham: 'We the Egyptians are like a flea among the warlike mountaineers who are all warriors. I have no troops to speak of, and my diet is humble pie, a diet thank God, Englishmen have not had to eat often.'[4]

King John could not be reached; he had gone to fight a rival. Gordon therefore set off on the long mule journey through the mountains and by camel through the lowlands, where he surprised his retinue by setting a powerful pace: forty-five miles a day, travelling in the early mornings and in the evenings until after sundown. At every stop the local people would crowd in with petitions or complaints, and every night the flying beetles would bite; he once counted eighty on his nightshirt when he lit his candle. They crossed the Atbara river, following the great trade route where the railway would run many years later, and finally went by boat down the Blue Nile to Khartoum.

Gordon was installed with ceremony on 5 May 1877 in the great square, filled by an enthusiastic crowd – a ceremony which would be repeated seven years later in very different times. His inauguration speech was brief: 'With God's help I will hold the balance level.'

Khartoum was a cosmopolitan town of Sudanese and Egyptians, Greek and Levantine merchants, and an underclass of black slaves from the south: every household kept slaves in domestic service. Most of the population followed Islam but Greek Orthodox and Coptic Christians, and pagans from the south made the religion of the people as mixed as their colour, for blacks, browns, and some whites mingled in the streets.

The governor-general's fine palace, set in a spacious garden on the waterfront, was Khartoum's biggest building, large enough for a potentate's harem and fancy boys, and hordes of servants. Gordon found most of the 140 windows broken when he arrived, by the fury of his predecessor's sister at her brother's recall some months previously. Next door, in another garden, stood the Austrian Roman Catholic mission, and nunnery, including an orphanage and a church where the organ was played by the Austrian consul, the large ginger-whiskered Martin Hansal who had brought Marno to Equatoria and been found drunk.

Gordon learned that a governor-general is 'guarded like an ingot of gold.' 'I have here a pomp which little suits me,' he wrote to Olivia Freese on 18 May, 'but which I must perforce keep up. I think the people like me and it is an immense comfort that while in the old regime, 10 or 15 people were flogged daily, now none get flogged. The people seem better and happier, a huge crowd stand around the palatial gates, but only a few are privileged with an interview.' He had a box placed for petitions. Bribes still paid to his clerk, a black Sudanese called Tuhami, were now put in the treasury (or so Gordon thought.)[5]

Gordon ended his letter to the Freeses: 'If I live and God blesses me as He has done I may make these people happy, to some little extent.' The greatest happiness would be the abolition of the Slave Trade. To effect it he must disband and replace the 6,000 Turkish *bashi-bazouks*, irregular troops who guarded the frontiers yet allowed the slave-raiders' caravans through. Gordon could not abolish slavery at once because the economy depended on slaves; but during his journey from Abyssinia he had thought up a scheme which would end it over the years. He sent this to Hussey Vivian in Cairo and it became the basis of the Anglo-Egyptian Convention 'for the suppression of the Slave Trade,' signed in August 1877: All masters must register their slaves, including runaways, before 1 January 1878, when registration would stop: no man or woman enslaved after that date would be the legal property of the master and could therefore run with impunity. Sales between masters would continue to be legal but the market for new slaves would decline since no sale would have the force of law. By the Convention, slavery would be abolished in 1889.

Gordon believed that 'with terrific exertions' he might in two or three years have a good army and a fair revenue, with peace and increased trade and an end to slave raiding;' and then I will come home and go to bed, not to get up again until noon every day, and I shall never walk more than a mile.'[6]

Meanwhile he must suppress the revolt in the distant western province of Darfur, without firing a shot if he could help it. He left Khartoum on 21 May, having already replaced his deputy by a man more amenable to his wishes, and now had ninety-seven days of camel riding ahead.

'As a camel traveller he is looked on as a prodigy,' Wolseley heard in the Sudan seven years later. 'He can even tire out the Bedouin and can get more out of a camel than other men.'[7] Gordon himself would joke that 'the Gordons and the camels are of the same race – take an idea into their heads and nothing will take it out.'[8]

He would race ahead of most of his army and descend in his gold-laced uniform and red tarboosh (fez) upon a lazy outpost. He pressed ahead through the sandy bush-covered desert. He was travelling in the hottest and driest month when he wrote from Oom Changa (Um Shanga) in Darfur to his friend Goodenough on 22 June: 'Of all the countries of the world, where there is misery, recommend me these sandy deserts. Philosopher as I am, and believer as I am, I often, even in my position, wish I were dead. None of you have an idea of the arid dullness of these lands.'[9]

One by one he relieved garrisons in the oases and restored peace. He avoided what he called 'collisions' whenever he could. Once a loyal tribe had gone to stop a rebel band which threatened the caravan road. Gordon and his troops were delayed, and he came up to find that his loyals had killed all 160 rebels, for three men wounded. He commented to Augusta: 'I wish people could see what the suffering of human creatures is – I mean those who wish for war. I am a fool, I dare say, but I cannot see the sufferings of any of these people without tears in my eyes.'[10]

He knew that corrupt administrators had caused the revolt, and he dismissed the bad and installed better. At one place he found that a mosque had been turned into a powder magazine. 'I had it cleared out and handed back with great ceremonies which have delighted the people: it is now endowed and in full swing.'[11] Strong Christian though he was, he held that 'the Mussulman worships God as well as I do, and is as acceptable, if sincere, as any Christian.'[12]

As he went from one oasis to the next he would pray for the chief he was about to win over, believing that prayer made a bond between men. 'God has prospered me in all my work,' he wrote to Sir Henry's wife, Rose, on 1 June, 'and I like to think He is the Governor General and I His adjutant for the moment. This takes all the weight off me. If things go as I do not think right, He knows best, for not only does He direct affairs but He has the power of carrying out. What a comfort! It is unspeakable.'[13]

He had to endure alarming moments when receiving the allegiance of Bedouin chieftains: 'They ride up at full gallop to you brandishing their swords and swearing fidelity, etc. One little chap rode up quite fierce with a huge sword, and muttered his fealty. I like to stand out among them alone to show I do not fear them. Sometimes they will nearly ride you down.'[14]

His conviction that nothing could happen outside the Will of God was never better displayed than in one of the most famous incidents in Gordon's career, on 2 September 1877 at Darar in Southern Darfur.

Many years before the Sudanese Arab named Zubair* had left Khartoum to trade in south Sudan, then a medley of black petty sultanates at peace with each other. According to Zubair they were cannibals, who would sell adulterers and robbers in the market for food or for slaves, 'so I bought all these men who were fit to carry arms.'[15] He raised 500 men, trained them, and then set about razing whole villages and sending the men, women and children for sale in Khartoum and Egypt and beyond. He built a large private army by enlisting the soldiers of every sultan he conquered, and became master of the Bahr el Ghazal region.

In the year when Gordon had gone to Equatoria, Zubair had allied himself with the Egyptian forces and invaded the then independent Darfur. He defeated and killed its native sultan and went to Cairo expecting to be made sultan himself; but Khedive Ismail, fearing his power, had detained him and sent him to serve as a pasha with the Turkish armies fighting Russia.

---

*His Arabic name also transliterated as Sebeyr or Zebeyr and in other ways: Gordon used one version in 1877–9 and another in 1884–5. For convenience I have standardized it to Zubair as per Hill's *Biographical Dictionary of the Sudan*.

His youthful son, Suleiman, had taken command of his father's armies and continued to make slave raids (*razzias*) to the south from his stronghold at Shaka, scorning orders to stop. On 31 August 1877, when the rains had come, Gordon heard that Suleiman had advanced on Dara with a large force of armed slaves, intending to overwhelm the weak Egyptian garrison.

Gordon started at once on his racing camel with an escort of 300 men whom he outpaced. As he sped south he saw the ravages of the slave traders and of his own Bashi Bazouks who stole boys and girls 'with as little compunction as a fowl.' Near Dara he rode into a swarm of flies and came on his garrison 'like a thunderbolt . . . a single, dirty red-faced man on a camel ornamented with flies,'[16] as he put it. When his people recovered from the shock they fired a salute.

Suleiman, son of Zubair, and his powerful army were encamped three miles away. Only bluff could bring them to heel. Gordon was a master of bluff: he had once gained a bloodless victory, on the Nile hundreds of miles south of Khartoum, or so Queen Victoria was told by one of his friends, by threatening to order up the British Fleet.[17]

At dawn Gordon put on his magnificent marshal's gold braided uniform ('my gold armour'), mounted a horse and 'with an escort of my robbers of Bashi Bazouks, rode out to the camp of the other robbers 3 miles off. I was met by the son of Zubair, a nice looking lad of 22 years and rode through the robber bands, there were about 3000 of them, boys and men. I rode to the tent in the camp, the whole of these chiefs were dumbfounded at my coming among them; after a glass of water, I went back, telling the son of Zubair to come with his family to my Divan.'[18] This moment was the inspiration of the sculptor Onslow Ford for his celebrated statue of Gordon, though for dramatic effect Ford conflated the two arrivals, placing Gordon in full dress on his camel, and forgetting the flies.

Gordon rode back to Dara and waited – for an assault or a parley. Then Suleiman and his advisers came, and entered fully armed, a rudeness by Arab etiquette. Suleiman, small and boyish, in a blue velvet riding jacket, accepted Gordon's coffee, 'and sitting there in a circle I gave them, in choice Arabic, my ideas: that they meditated revolt, that I knew it, and that they should now hear my ultimatum, viz, that I would disarm them and break them up. They listened in silence, and then went off to consider of it.' Gordon had not used an interpreter, but relied on his bad Arabic 'and a pantomine of signs.' Not surprisingly they had looked 'stupified.'[19]

Suleiman duly sent a letter of submission but until he retreated to his base at Shaka, Gordon could not be sure of peace or war, for three days: 'it is like a game of chess, and a long one it is, for the moves are made so slowly.' Gordon felt tired by 'the length of negotiations etc. etc. but it is better to be tired and wait than that one poor black skin should have a bullet in it.' He heard later that Suleiman's advisers wanted him to kidnap the Governor-General; and Gordon's advisers suggested taking Suleiman by treachery but he refused.

Gordon's state of mind fluctuated like a barometer, for he had no confidence in his troops. 'What a comfort to have God to help me, though my flesh would like good soldiers and a strong fort.'[20] At last, after one of the robber generals had deserted with his troops to Gordon, Suleiman left Dara in a rage. Gordon had already sent troops ahead and now followed Suleiman to Shaka and accepted his submission and the dispersal of his army. Since Suleiman declined to go to Cairo and pledge loyalty to the Khedive, Gordon ordered him to serve in a minor post in another province: Suleiman asked for a governorship but Gordon refused and Suleiman went away sulkily, plotting revenge.

Meanwhile (at Dara) a camel courier from Khartoum had brought 'a host of unpleasant letters.' The mail from England included tiresome misunderstandings by the Anti-Slavery Society who seemed to expect Gordon to abolish both the Slave Trade and Slavery at once: 'I cannot expect in three or four days to end a state of affairs which has lasted for 10 or 12 years. These Bassingaia or slave dealers and slaves never spare men, women, or child.'[21]

A letter from Khartoum accused his personal clerk, Tuhami, whom Gordon had made a Bey (Lieutenant-Colonel). He had been secretary to Gordon's three predecessors and was invaluable. Fluent in French and German he had become a great friend but power had corrupted him into the old ways. 'Fancy that my black Secretary took 3000L backsheesh!' Gordon told Augusta. 'Is it not horrible. I declare I never felt so miserable about a matter as I do about this, for he is a nice fellow and suits me perfectly in every way, and he is as black as a coal, with a little snub nose.'[22] Gordon replaced him by Berzati Bey who became 'for three years my brave and faithful friend, known by European scoffers as "the black Imp." '[23]*

Gordon thought of forgiving Tuhami until he fled from justice. A female slave who knew where the money was hidden died mysteriously in a well.

*Berzati was killed in the Hicks disaster in 1883.

Tuhami was caught, and when he could not repay the theft the court sentenced him to go in chains to a remote Equatorial station, where he lost his sight. Yet on Gordon's return in 1884 Tuhami Bey, retired in Cairo, showed complete devotion.

At 9 a.m. on 28 January 1878 an Italian of the Egyptian Postal Administration, Licurgo Santoni, who had come to reorganize the postal service of the Sudan, watched the arrival at Khartoum of the Governor-General who had already 'received me with infinite courtesy' at Berber. Gordon had been on another strenuous tour, first back to Keren where Walad-el-Michael had been tiresome, and then by camel to many places in eastern Sudan.

'The steamer carrying Gordon Pasha', wrote Santoni, 'came alongside at the foot of the residency where the government officials, consular agents and the native people awaited him in large numbers. He had scarcely disembarked when a battery of artillery, a military band and the troops, lined up along the roads leading to the residence of the governor-general ... celebrated H.E.'s arrival with an indescribable uproar. Most of the inhabitants of the city were lining the Nile banks and the boats, all of them beflagged, made an impression beyond imagining, with a mass of male and female Blacks – a truly African celebration.

'There was a splendid reception. All the military officers and civil officials were there to pay their respects, the religious notables, the commercial communities, the consular agents and so many others that it would be too laborious to recount. Even six stately elephants in the charge of their Indian attendants were in their review order and, as Gordon Pasha passed, the elephants saluted him by raising and lowering their great trunks three times in succession. The ceremony over, H.E. retired to the palace for a little rest.'

The elephants had been ordered from Cairo by Gordon for work in Equatoria. They were on their way to Gondokoro but did not prove a success.

Some weeks later Santoni summed up in his journal what he had learned of Gordon's first year as Governor-General of the Sudan: 'In organizing these huge provinces Gordon Pasha achieved the impossible, but as his exertions were not supported by his subordinates his efforts remained fruitless. This man's activity with the scientific knowledge which he possesses is doubtless able to achieve much but unfortunately no one backs him up and his orders are badly carried out or altered in such a way as to render them without effect. All the Europeans, with some rare exceptions, whom he has honoured with his confidence, have cheated him.'[24] Only Charles-Frederic Rosset, the German who had been Gordon's agent in Khartoum during the Equatoria years, proved faithful. He was the British and the German consul and Gordon had made him his Private Secretary. Gordon had promoted many Sudanese to be judges, local governors (*mudirs*) and magistrates but nearly all proved corrupt, wrote Santoni, and Gordon had to rely on Turks and Circassians.

Gordon could not stay long at Khartoum that winter, for Khedive Ismail needed his help in Cairo. Ismail's combination of grandiose schemes and personal extravagance had put Egypt deeply in debt to bondholders in France and England, including their governments. Half Egypt's annual revenue was absorbed by the high interest on the debt; civil and military salaries were badly in arrear. The bondholders had set up a Commission of the Debt and its members now demanded an enquiry into the Khedive's finances.

Gordon handed over to his deputy, a Circassian born in the Caucasus, and left in his government steamer on 7 February. 'H.H. was very complimentary,' he wrote to Harvey from near Wadi Halfa, 'and said he knows "no one who could advise him with respect to certain encroachments the debt commissioners have made on his authority, but me!"' Gordon comments that 'as you may imagine I do not know much about these things.' The thought of dining out depressed him. 'I don't care much about going to Cairo,' he added, 'For I drink cognac (which, up here, I never touch from month to month) and then I talk too much.'[25]

The Nile journey, however, refreshed him. He loved the 'stillness, clearness and silence of the winter atmosphere,' and as he sailed past palaces abandoned centuries earlier, he reflected, 'Why should man distress and worry himself with the trouble of a life so fleeting as ours is.'[25] At one point he obligingly gave a tow to the young Earl and Countess of Aberdeen on their honeymoon, but they slowed him up and after five days he cut them adrift: 'No invite to the Highlands, deer-stalking etc. etc. with the Earl!'[26] he joked.

While on the Nile Gordon wired to Cairo to cut his salary yet further; he had already been paying his own expenses when on tour and had bought seventy-two camels for himself and his entourage from his own pocket although entitled to charge the Sudan Treasury.[27] He was not therefore pleased when he heard that the Debt Commissioners were bringing in

Englishmen at high salaries. He wrote a paper urging that interest on the bonds should be suspended for a year, and the money go towards civil and military wages.

Gordon and his staff transferred to a train at the railhead. They arrived in Cairo several hours late. Gordon was at once driven to the Abdin Palace, dirty and unchanged, where the Khedive had delayed dinner by an hour. Before they went in, the Khedive drew Gordon aside and asked him to be president of the enquiry into the Egyptian finances and added that the Debt Commissioners had been so hostile to him that he wished to object to their being on the enquiry. Lesseps would support him. After dinner, Gordon and his people were put up in the magnificent palace where the Prince of Wales had stayed.

Next day the British Commissioner called – Captain Evelyn Baring, Royal Artillery and lately Private Secretary to his cousin Lord Northbrook when Viceroy of India. No two men could be more unalike than Baring and Gordon: 'When oil mixes with water, we will mix together!'[28] thought Gordon. Eight years his junior, born at Cromer Hall, not a terrace house in Woolwich, Baring had the 19th century gunner's contempt for a sapper. He stayed five minutes, telling Gordon that to exclude the Debt Commissioners would be unfair to the creditors, and begging him to realize they were not blind to the needs of the Egyptian peasantry.

Gordon noted: 'He has a pretentious grand patronizing way about him,'[29] and Baring showed it in the letter he wrote that evening to George Goschen, the future Chancellor of the Exchequer who represented the bondholders' interests but had returned to England: '. . . Altogether,' wrote Baring, 'he impresses me so far as an excellent, simple-hearted, and impracticable man about as much fit for the work he has in hand as I am to be Pope.'[30] Baring ignored Gordon's administrative and financial reforms in the Sudan; and when, as Earl of Cromer, he published his memoirs thirty years later he let the uninformed reader suppose that Gordon knew nothing of the Sudan before 1884.

The Debt Commissioners and the Consul-generals brought pressure on Khedive Ismail; instead of supporting Gordon he disappeared for three days into his harem. Lesseps put France before Egypt; Goschen, when Gordon wired his proposals, wired back rudely that Gordon had no standing in the matter. 'Such a time of it here with one thing and another,' wrote Gordon to Mrs. Freese on 10 March, 'but my Friend is with me and I am quieted with the knowledge of his rule.'[31]

By the end of March Gordon could do nothing more to prevent the Enquiry being loaded for the benefit of the international creditors. He left Cairo, unthanked or reimbursed by Ismail, labelled mad by the Consuls and Debt Commissioners for his proposal of a year's suspension of interest. 'A vacillating Viceroy, a corrupt entourage rendered any efforts I recommended useless,' he wrote to Gerald Graham from Suez. 'I will say my proposals seem to me even now, as having been good and reasonable and efficacious but they were not followed;'[32] and over the next four years resentment against the bondholders built up among the Egyptian civil and military until it erupted in the Arabi Rebellion.

'The more one sees of life ... the more one feels, in order to keep from shipwreck, the necessity of steering by the Polar Star, i.e. in a word leave to God alone, and never pay attention to the favours or the smiles of man; if He smiles on you, neither the smile or frown of men can affect you.'[33] Gordon took passage down the Red Sea to Aden and across to Berbera and made his way far inland to the holy city of Harar, deep in Abyssinia but, by the people's petition, temporarily under his rule. Gordon was only the second Englishman to reach it.

CHAPTER SEVENTEEN
Building a Nation

Gordon returned to Khartoum in June 1878 to a great welcome from 'my people.' He decided that he must stay in Khartoum to place finances and administration on a sound basis.

He had managed to reduce the deficit in 1878 but it was rising again. He rebuffed attempts by Charles Rivers Wilson, the Englishman (dominated by his wife) who was now Minister of Finance in Cairo, to extract large sums from the Sudan: 'I and the Cairo Council are daggers drawn, and I even go out of my way to snub them! Gordon could not stop country officials collecting taxes by the traditional method of the *courbash* or whip, which he had abolished in Khartoum, yet they seldom secured the full amount and much of that disappeared on its way to the treasury. 'I feel sure you would break your heart with the corrupt state of these employees,' he told Colonel Jenkins. 'The most severe examples seem to have no effect whatever, and they go on with their robberies, and slave dealing, just as if their successors (*sic ? predecessors?*) were not in prison.' He found a mistake of over a hundred thousand Egyptian pounds in the accounts. 'When detected, they said their mistakes often happened, it was no great matter!!! it was only the quarter of our Revenue. *I do not like these people*: they are not to be compared to the Chinese.'[1]

To economize, Gordon won the Khedive's consent to a withdrawal from the southernmost part of Equatoria, with the additional advantage of putting a gap between the would-be slave traders of the southern Sudan and the larger areas peopled by blacks. In the north he made another economy by cancelling the contract for a railway alongside the Nile, south of the existing line in Egypt. River traffic would be cheaper, and a combination of rail and river be best, but Gordon could not find money to build the railway; and thus he signed his own death warrant, since a length of railway in 1884 might have saved Khartoum.

Years later Sir Reginald Wingate, whose governor-generalship rebuilt the Sudan after the Mahdist years, read Gordon's report on the railway project and recognized (as Wingate's son wrote) 'Gordon's appreciation of financial problems . . . it is important to see him, in the Sudan, in his true light as a practical administrator in the service of the Khedive, and not, as he has been drawn in the English imagination, a combination of free-lance missionary and crusader.'[2]

Gordon tried hard to divorce justice from bribery and favouritism; and also reorganized the governorships of the provinces. He had wanted them ruled by natives rather than by 'Turks' or by Europeans, but could not find reliable Sudanese; and thus Rudolf Slatin, the young Austrian, and Frank Lupton, the young Englishman, joined his staff, later rising to governorships, which they would hold until made prisoners of the Mahdi. Gordon tried to recruit Sir Richard Burton, the great explorer and Arabist but Burton thought the salary too small and that he and Gordon would never work together. Others Gordon rejected because they soon 'got swelled heads or drank,' or could not stand the climate. He had to construct the lower levels of administration with what he could find. 'I always looked upon Gordon Pasha as a master carpenter, and anyone who served under him will heartily endorse what I now say,' wrote Augustus Wylde, a British trader who had travelled widely in the Sudan, three years after Gordon's death. 'No one ever turned out better work with the rough tools at his disposal. He had but little choice of servants; the majority of his subordinates would not have been suited to civilized services. He, however, made use of them, and gave the credit to those who did the work.'[3]

These months were long and lonely. His devoted staff of servants and his two cavasses (bodyguards) did not mind his bursts of temper; sometimes he boxed their ears or yelled at them, yet they loved him, knowing that he cared for them; he even nursed them, for that year was one of Khartoum's worst for sickness, owing to an exceptionally high Nile flood which caused hordes of mosquitoes. When all his servants were down with malaria and confined to their homes in the grounds, he fell sick himself. 'I was so seedy two or three days ago, in my vast lonely house, quite alone,' he wrote to Augusta on 23 September 1878, 'I used to wander up and down it, and think for hours. It is a very great comfort to me, never to have the least fear of death, when I am ill, and in that you'll be able to agree with me. What a blessing to have no need to be thinking of a wife and family, at such times (you had better not send this letter on.)'4*

To amuse himself he laid out a rose garden, and enjoyed the young elephant and the baby hippos, 'lovable animals,' who were in the grounds en route for Cairo; and the ostriches until they severely hurt a slave working in the garden: Gordon sold them and with the money bought the man's freedom and gave him the balance.5 Next door, at the Austrian mission, many of the Verona fathers and nuns were ill. Several died and the others were invalided to Egypt leaving only the bushy-bearded Daniele Comboni, Vicar-general of Central Africa and titular bishop of Claudiopolis. Gordon helped Comboni, arranging at his own expense for priests to travel up the Nile on the way to a new mission on Lake Victoria, and he refused to let Protestants set up a mission where Catholics had begun.6

Comboni was grateful that pacification had brought safe travel and swift communications, and when an Italian magazine used false information from men who wished to discredit Gordon, and asserted that he was encouraging the Slave Trade, Comboni wrote it a long and devastating rebuttal: 'Gordon Pasha is a tremendous enemy of slavery and I can testify to that . . . I believe that Gordon is a great man and quite capable of this great, laborious and difficult mission that he has undertaken. Let us hope that he does not get tired and may stay many more years in this office; humanity will be grateful to him.'7

Comboni deeply admired Gordon's personal life. 'This man who meditates on the Bible three hours a day, lives without a woman, like a perfect monk, and prays a lot.'8 Rivers Wilson once asked Comboni 'the cause of Gordon's extraordinary influence over the natives of Africa. To my surprise he replied simply: "His chastity." The possession of this quality, which was absolutely incomprehensible to the Arab, seemed to raise him to the position of a mystical and almost divine character.'9 After Gordon's death Comboni told his superiors in Rome that he believed him to be in a state of sanctity and that he kept his cigar case as a relic.10

Gordon also helped the three Anglicans of the Church Missionary Society who were using the Nile route, now safe, to reach the station already set up at the court of Mtesa in Uganda: 'They will want for nothing that I can do for them.' He sent practical hints on crossing the desert by camel to the Nile, including a caution to open bowels every morning, and advice that if any

---

*Once, when Gordon had called himself 'a donkey' for letting generosity outrun income, he had remarked: 'The only advantage in marriage is to be prevented from these extravagances.'!5

Sudanese was obstructive they should make a show of noting his name, saying that if he did not oblige they would tell Gordon Pasha. He added: 'I want you to like my people, not to look on them as utterly evil ... you are sure to succeed if you will entirely trust Him. Shut your eyes to Stanley, to Egyptian government, to all things, and nothing will go wrong, and you must succeed though it may not be as you would think the best way. You have counted the cost, and embarked in this work for His sake, and though inferior far, for our nation's sake you must go through with it.

'Are you missionaries? So am I! The letter must be one which he who runs can read: the *life*.'[11]

Although he wished they would settle among his naked Dinkas rather than at the court of 'this stuck up savage,'[12] Mtesa, he welcomed them warmly at Khartoum, which they found prosperous and bustling with trade. He urged them to start a mission among the pagans of the south, promising his special protection. 'How he loved the people!' wrote Charles Pearson. 'How to elevate, how to civilize, how to Christianize them, was his constant idea.' They were amused to see Gordon's cavass roll fat cigarettes, and insert one whenever the Pasha, chatting away, held up two fingers.[13]

As the three steamed south, Charles Pearson wrote: 'We often talk of you, and of the exceedingly pleasant time which we had at Khartoum. Your kindness to us will never be forgotten ... You perhaps do not know what a help on the way you gave us ... by the spur which communion gave to our missionary zeal. Our prayer is that, God may long spare you to govern the Sudan.'[14]

Shortly after the Anglicans had left Khartoum, Gordon heard that Suleiman, Zubair's son, whom he had made vice-governor of the southern province, Bahr-el-Ghazal, had rebelled and slaughtered three hundred soldiers. The private armies of slavers angry with Gordon had joined the revolt. The whole province might be lost and Khartoum itself be threatened.

Gordon could not take the field while administrative problems remained severe, but Gessi had come up, intending to make a private exploration. Relations had lately been cool because Gessi had passed false information to a magazine but he now accepted command of a small force, collecting more men as he travelled up river with orders to defeat and capture Suleiman.

Slave raiding and trading had continued. Even the Governor of Equatoria, young Ibrahim Fawzi, whom Gordon had trusted implicitly, was found to have used his troops to raid for slaves. He was recalled, tried, and sentenced to be shot. Wondering whether he might reprieve him, Gordon prayed and then tossed a coin: it came down for death. Gordon was relieved when his deputy, Geigler Pasha the German, intervened on Fawzi's behalf and he was sent south in chains. The story of a man's life hingeing on the toss of a coin reached Cairo, much embroidered. Fawzi lived to cross Gordon's path again more happily.

The Slave Trade was never far from Gordon's thoughts, especially as survivors of caravans, intercepted by his officers, would be brought to Khartoum, some almost as living skeletons, 'a terrible sight ... We have taken 26 caravans in the last three months, but it is useless. I telegraph to HH to let me shoot the dealers, he never answers, I did quietly hang one for mutilating a boy, but I cannot do that often without permission ... A bitter vicious feeling against HH and against these people fills me. I would hang all the slave dealers tomorrow but in doing so, I only cut at the branches, and I want to get at the root, i.e. I want to destroy the trade.'[15]

At last, at the end of February 1879, Gordon was free to leave Khartoum, going to Kordofan and Darfur, where another smaller revolt had started, then planning to work south to support Gessi, embroiled in a war of attrition with Suleiman's much stronger forces. Gordon, on his camel, with unreliable cavalry, manoeuvred to seize the watering places, thirty or forty miles apart, 'for if you take the watering places, they (the enemy) must surrender; only you must hold two, or three, at same time, for the enemy are like Gazelles, and double back on you.'[16]

He moved south and fought pitched battles, with heavy casualties on both sides. 'I no longer delight in war,'[17] he wrote to Augusta; but only by confronting the slave raiding tribes would he secure peace. He descended on Shaka, the stronghold of the raiders where he had accepted Suleiman's submission the year before, and this time he made every raider clear out, and dismantled the fort and the town. He wrote to Gerald Graham: 'You have little idea of what a difficult affair this slave suppression has been: I get sometimes mad with rage and terrible scenes pass between me and the slave dealers ... for I have a brutal cruel instinct in me which sometimes comes out'.[18]

Wherever he went, he broke up slave caravans. In one was a little black boy, Capsune, who described the scene later to Dr. Robert Firkin, one of the Anglican missionaries whom Gordon had entertained, who was now working in the southern Sudan.

Capsune had been seized by Dongolese Arabs who killed his parents and razed their village. After many cruel adventures he was in a caravan of captives, including other children, being marched through a country short of water. The exhausted slaves lay in huts while the Dongolese looked for water. Suddenly they heard 'that "Kurnek" (Gordon Pasha) was coming, and all was in confusion; the Dongolomees were in a state of abject fear; those who could escaped, while others tried to hide, but the soldiers surrounded the huts and thickets and several were discovered. The slaves were taken into the shade of a large tree, food and water by Kurnek's orders being given to them. "Children so thirsty; children very glad."

'The captured Dongolomees meanwhile had their hands tied behind them, their clothes taken away, and after receiving a whipping were allowed to depart and ran away "Quickly, oh, so quickly; stop for nothing but shut eyes and run." Kurnek then came from under the tree where he had been sitting and inspected the slaves and Capsune gazed with astonishment at the first European he had ever seen. The "White man's eyes" made the greatest impression on him and he says, "I shake very much, when I see eyes, eyes very blue, very bright. I think eyes can see through me and when I see eyes I frightened, and think I finished to-day". However, he was not finished, for after giving orders about the slaves, Kurnek called for his camel and rode on.'[19]

Gordon remembered Capsune as all head and extended stomach, nothing but two globes, one on top of the other. Dr. Firkin took Capsune to England, where he was presented to the Prince of Wales and brought up by Miss Rosalie Firkin. Gordon met him and they exchanged affectionate notes. He was taken back to Egypt and had just finished his education at a mission school when he died in November 1896.[20]

In May 1879 Gessi at last captured Suleiman's stronghold, Dem Zubair. Suleiman escaped but 'immense droves of slaves were released,' Gordon told the Anti-Slavery Society with some hyperbole, 'and the whole vast system of the Slave Trade utterly destroyed ... The slave dealers were killed by hundreds by the exasperated natives who retaliated for the cruel hunting to which they had been subjected.'[21] Gessi did not catch Suleiman until July; he attempted to escape and Gessi had him shot, some felt unjustly.

Gordon had made Gessi (now a Pasha) governor of Bahr-el-Ghazal, knowing that only prolonged good government would prevent a revival of slave raiding: Gessi saw a future for the people if they cultivated the cotton which grew wild, and dissuaded Gordon from giving up the province as an economy.

After their meeting, Gordon started back towards Khartoum. His health was breaking. The blood would rush to his head and he would think himself dying from angina pectoris; modern medical opinion doubts this, and ascribes the symptoms to nervous and physical strain.[22] His stamina remained astonishing. Rudolf Slatin found him exhausted under a tree at the end of a long ride, with sores on his legs, and revived him with brandy. Gordon remounted his camel and outpaced them all.[23]

He was weary of his 'long crucifixion', and in March 1879 had sent in his resignation, which Ismail refused to accept. Gordon was often angry with Ismail and called him 'the Incurable,' but Ismail 'supported me through thick and thin,'[24] against Egyptians who resented their loss of income from slave trading, and Europeans who resented his refusal to send money for their dividend. He knew too that the net was closing in on the Khedive.

On 26 June 1879 the Ottoman Sultan, under pressure from the Great Powers, ordered his viceroy to abdicate in favour of Tewfik, his son. When Gordon received the news, still on the road, he determined to resign. When he reached Khartoum on 21 July he heard that both Suleiman and his rebel ally in Darfur were dead. 'I am a wreck, like the portion of the *Victory* towed into Gibraltar after Trafalgar, but God has enabled me, or rather used me, to do what I wished to do – that is, break down the Slave Trade.'[25]

He left after ten days for the month-long journey down the Nile and arrived at Cairo on 23 August 'very cross at the dismissal of Ismail' and strongly prejudiced against Tewfik. At the private audience Gordon presented his homage 'and he told me to sit down, well a miracle had happened, here was a man with the talent, energy and (?) measure of the "Incurable", with a quality the latter did not possess, i.e. *honesty*. It was really quite astounding.'[26] Gordon left the palace having agreed to go, still Governor-General, to Abyssinia where King John was willing to sign a treaty of peace; indeed the American acting consul-general told the State Department that Gordon had been summoned to Cairo for this very purpose.[27]

CHAPTER EIGHTEEN
Cast Aside

Gordon saw King John at last on 27 October after thirty-eight weary days, riding a mule through 'interminable mountains, and sheep tracks which they call roads' from Massawa to the King's new mountain capital of Debra Tabor near Magdala, which Napier had captured eleven years before.[1]

The King dismissed the Governor-General of the Sudan and Khedive's envoy after three minutes. Next day he received him longer. 'What do you want?' asked the King. Gordon replied: 'Haven't you read the letters of His Highness and the French and English governments?' 'No.' The King ordered his head clerk to bring them and had him beaten with forty blows in Gordon's presence.

The King read the letters and said: 'You want peace. For that you must cede —' and he listed five districts, demanded a large indemnity and the despatch of an *abuna* (Coptic archbishop) from Alexandria to crown him.

Gordon asked him to put his demands in writing and allow six months for an answer from Cairo. When he added that Egypt was unlikely to agree to the terms the King said he would fight, and accused Gordon: 'You, a Christian English, wish to spill Christian blood.'

The King then said he was going to the hot baths, two days journey, and that Gordon must come with him. Gordon realized that 'the King's object was to drag me in triumph through the country.'[2] He declined. The King was angry.

A dialogue followed (so Gordon told the story): *The King*: "Do you know, Gordon Pasha, that I could kill you on the spot if I liked?"

'*Gordon*: "I am perfectly well aware of it, Your Majesty. Do so at once if it is your royal pleasure. I am ready." The King was disconcerted. *King*: "What, ready to be killed!" *Gordon*: "Certainly. I am always ready to die, and so far from fearing you putting me to death, you would confer a favour on me by so doing, for you would be doing for me that which I am precluded by my religious scruples from doing for myself – you would relieve me from all the troubles and misfortunes which the future may have in store for me."

'This completely staggered King John, who gasped out in despair: "Then my power has no terrors for you?" "None whatever!"' His Majesty went to the baths alone.[3]

The King disgusted Gordon by his cruelty, cutting off noses and ears and hands, putting out eyes; he 'is a man of most disagreeable expression, never smiles or looks you in face, suspicious of everyone, without friends, hating and hated of all.' His Christianity was equally horrid. He 'talks like the Old Testament, he [illegible – page torn at corner] the strictest sect of the Pharisees, drunk overnight, at dawn he is up, reading the Psalms. He never would miss a Prayer meeting, and would have a Bible like a portmanteau, if he was in England.'[4]

The King returned; he refused to release eight Egyptian prisoners, tried to bribe Gordon to desert the Khedive, then said: 'I will write a letter about this. Go to your master.'

'I saluted my dear Christian friend and bolted with precipitancy.' The letter proved to be insulting both to Gordon and his master, and the royal escort led Gordon and his party by the wildest and slowest route towards the frontier east of Khartoum.

When Abyssinian soldiers left him, he was able to send off a message to his people in the Sudan before one of King John's governors descended on him as he stood on the hill where he could see his own territory below, and forced him to return into the interior because the King would let him leave only by the route to the Red Sea. The governor hated the King, and said he was fast going mad; and hoped Gordon would conquer the country for Egypt.

It was now late November. 'We march for Massawa, bullied and hindered in all ways, passing snow and frost, give up tents and plod on: get free at Teeazzi River, under forced marches to Juntur, get arrested and plundered at Frontier: get released and arrive at Massawa on 8 December; out of 89 days, 79 on mule's back,' and a large expenditure on presents to the King and bribes to wayside chiefs.[5]

Gordon was now sick and desperately tired, with an erratic heart beat made worse by the thin air of the mountains, giving sudden shocks to the system so that he often believed he was dying. 'A teaspoonful of brandy (when you have it) stops it at once', he wrote,[6] but he had none. On his last night in the country, under arrest, he was made to sleep with an Abyssinian at his foot and one on each side. He was mightily relieved, on reaching Massawa, to find *H. M. S. Swallow* sent to rescue him.[7]

Worse was to follow. In his confidential report to the Khedive, which he wired ahead, he pointed out that though the Egyptians should keep Massawa, they could not afford to retain the detached province of Berber and Harar. He suggested the Italians should take it, especially as Italy might speedily deal with King John 'and benefit the whole world.' When he reached Cairo at the end of December, he found that this part of his secret report had been leaked to the press and caused an international furore. He was in disgrace.[8]

The Egyptian governors whom he had dismissed and the British officials who treated him as mad because he put the people of Egypt and the Sudan before England and France, had united to destroy him. The Khedive, in the manner of the East, where a man may be in high honour one day and in a sack in the Bosphorus the next, accepted his resignation with formal thanks and no hospitality: he had to stay at Shepheards* and since he hated the sight of food and would sit, after a few hurried mouthfuls, with 'tobacco and something to drink,' the gossips supposed him a toper. Even the doctor he consulted, who diagnosed nervous exhaustion and ordered complete rest, gossiped that there was no doubt at all that he was a secret drinker.**[9]

Gordon heard that a pasha whom he had twice dismissed from governorships would be the next Governor-General. The old miseries would quickly descend on the people of the Sudan, whereas, in Charles Watson's words, had Gordon 'been left untrammelled for some years, the Sudan would have had a good chance of entering into a condition of prosperity.'[10]

Gordon was in no state to continue, even if Cairo would let him. The new Consul-General Edward Malet, a rather humourless younger diplomat, wrote to Lord Salisbury, the Foreign Secretary: 'I have had a hard time of it lately with Colonel Gordon, who, I think, was rather off his head and I felt truly glad when I heard he had left Egypt. From Alexandria he endeavoured to send telegrams to all the ministers consisting of quotations from the Bible but his friends got hold of them and stopt them – one however to Riaz

---

*The hotel originally famous as the stopping place for travellers on the overland route to India before the opening of the Suez Canal.
**This story comes at third hand and may libel Dr. MacKay; if accurate, he may have jumped to conclusions from the state of the liver, while Gordon's condition may have temporarily accentuated his lisp into slurred speech.

Pacha is supposed to have got through containing simply the words "mene mene tekel upharsin".* I trust that thorough rest in England will put him right but I am sure he has need of it.'[11]

On 8 January 1880 Gordon wrote a brief note to Augusta from Alexandria before boarding his ship. He ended: 'My God has been so faithful! and kind! All thro' my troubles, that I can recommend Him to you.'[12]

---

*The writing on the wall at Belshazzar's feast, *Daniel* 5. *Tekel* means: 'Thou art weighed in the balances, and art found wanting.'

PART THREE

THE PILLAR OF CLOUD
1880–1883

CHAPTER NINETEEN

Congo or Zanzibar?

The steamer for Naples had already weighed anchor in Alexandria harbour when those on deck saw a caique being rowed fast towards her. 'It is Gordon Pasha!' cried several passengers. A few moments later Gordon climbed the ladder and jumped on to the deck.

Joseph Reinach, a young Frenchman of twenty-three, returning from three months of wandering in Syria, transferred his gaze from the Alexandria waterfront to 'the famous conqueror of the Tai-Pings.' 'He was a man of forty years,' he noted, though Gordon was nearly forty-seven, 'of medium height, very thin, a restless step, eyes very soft and vague as if lost in distant thought, and with that brick-coloured complexion which Englishmen acquire when long in the tropics; he looked sometimes dejected and sometimes angry.' Several passengers who had been long in Cairo showed him marked deference which he received coldly, and paced up and down like a caged lion, from poop to prow, smoking cigarettes. Towards evening he seemed calmer and when young Reinach was talking to the captain Gordon joined them. Soon Gordon and Reinach were smoking together.

Joseph Reinach was a promising writer and geographer with political connections: his patron was Gambetta, who made him secretary to the council of ministers on becoming French premier the following year. Reinach later entered the Chamber of Deputies. Gordon found him a sympathetic listener. For much of the three-day voyage 'the ex-uncrowned king of the Sudan' poured out in a mixture of French and English a vivid account of the Sudan and the intrigues of Cairo and the misguided policies of the British and French governments towards Egypt which had forced him to resign: 'To have quitted the Sudan before the time and to have abandoned his work half-finished to a successor without his belief or his indomitable energy, the thought was torture to him.' Reinach, a Protestant from Alsace, realized also that Gordon did not see his work in political terms: 'it was for the Gospel, for Christ, that he had been fighting.'

Gordon outlined astonishing suggestions for carving up the villainous Ottoman Empire, 'giving Constantinople to the Russians, Syria with Jerusalem to "la belle France," and Egypt to "perfidious Albion."'[1] This division, except for Russia's share, came to pass in broad outline in the next half century: but these ideas, when put into despatch to Lord Salisbury in 1880, convinced the Foreign Secretary that Gordon was mad. Lord Lyon, the British ambassador in Paris, who had to forward the despatch, was equally annoyed, especially as Gordon concluded it with the observation: 'Anyhow, it matters little; a few years hence a piece of ground six feet by two will contain all that remains of ambassadors, ministers and your obedient humble servant, C.G. Gordon.'[2]

Gordon profoundly mistrusted the Conservative ministers: 'the mountebanks; he never called Lord Beaconsfield and his friends by any other name,' noted Reinach. Their support of Turkey angered Gordon, who was unaware that this policy had secretly been reversed a few months earlier. He wanted to see the Turks' power broken; while on the ship to Naples he wrote half-jokingly to his Cairo friend Olagnier: 'I will go to Rome and see the Pope and obtain a brief to mount a crusade and preach against these people.'[3]

When the ship reached Naples Gordon visited the ex-Khedive Ismail in his pleasant place of exile below Vesuvius. Next day he brought Reinach to lunch there and afterwards they walked and went sight-seeing together. Gordon was still depressed: 'Neither the charming gaieties of the Chiaia, nor the quiet majesty of the ruins of Pompei, nor the marvellous view of Vesuvius smoking under the snow could distract him from his dominant thought: "I will not stay quiet unless something is done for my flocks in the Sudan."'

That evening Reinach took Gordon to the opera at the San Carlos; as Gordon had abandoned theatre-going his acceptance was further proof of his depressed state of mind, but when a troop of '*petites femmes á demi-nues*' danced a ballet, Gordon left in disgust, exclaiming, 'And you call that civilization!'

Reinach returned to the hotel at one in the morning and found Gordon – or so he claimed in a letter to Lord Cromer nearly thirty years later – in a state of undress, reading the Bible beside a half-empty bottle of whisky. Reinach's letter, written when he was a middle-aged literary and parliamentary figure, tells Cromer that Gordon *'buvait terriblement de brandy'*; Gordon had shocked him by calling for *'du cognac'* one morning at an hour when a Frenchman would have asked for *'un aperitif.'* Reinach's stories have been cited in isolation, as conclusive evidence that Gordon was a hard drinker; but the evidence loses some credibility in that Reinach published a eulogistic essay in Gordon's lifetime yet calls him in his 1909 letter to Cromer what Gordon had called Disraeli: 'a mountebank'. Gordon had many faults but no other contemporary critic ever suggested that he was a mountebank.[4]

Gordon's version of the Naples incident is missing, except for an edited extract from a letter dated Rome, 21 January 1880, printed by Augusta in her book: 'Fancy, I had an attack of "doles" for three hours! What a dire disease it is! However, I am all right now. At outside calculation, only some seventeen years' toil before my lease is out, and that will soon pass, whilst there is always a chance of getting off sooner. I cannot make up my mind to go to the Museum. I did go and see St. Peter's, and thought it poor!!! I went to Theatre San Carlo, opera *The Jewess*, but left after one hour and a half – could not stand it. I am not going to be hunted. I go direct to you and remain hid.'[5]*

Augusta's five-year-old nephew Freddie Moffitt, who was living with her and not with his parents nearby (probably because of Dr. Andrew Moffitt's ill health), was already well-disposed towards his famous Uncle Charlie because of the battle-axes, shields and chain-armour which had arrived from Darfur and now decorated the hall at Rockstone Place.

Early in February 1880 the famous uncle was about to land at Southampton by the packet boat from France, and 'I and the dog had been smartened up for the occasion,' recalled Freddie long after,[6] 'and the dog, having been tubbed, retired under the dining-room table to mark his disapproval of the proceedings, whither I followed him. The great man then arrived, and several old friends assembled to greet him. Having emerged from under the table, I made several abortive attempts to join in the conversation before being removed.'

Next morning at family prayers Gordon joined in the Lord's Prayer, 'and

*This letter is missing from the British Library's Gordon Papers. It was not in the relevant sequence in the Moffitt collection bequeathed in 1963 nor among the twelve letters to Augusta of varying dates between 8 January 1880 and 29 July 1882, purchased at Sothebys in 1969.

as it was my aunt's custom,' continued Freddie, 'to conduct the service to a silent audience I considered it rather a breach of etiquette. After breakfast I went into the garden to search for a hedgehog with whom I was on friendly terms. Suddenly Gordon appeared. Having bestowed a half-crown, by way of establishing confidence, with an admonition not to tell my aunt, he asked me if God dwelt in me. I promptly said, "No; he lives up there," indicating the sky. The answer was adjudged incorrect, but perhaps he was as satisfied with it as any other, for he was able to tell me God dwelt in me and looked out of my eyes and was in everything around me. I gazed at my hedgehog with renewed interest. This was the only time Gordon ever mentioned religion to me.

'The things which chiefly impressed my childish imagination were that he bought £1 worth of stamps at a time* and seemed to sit up all night writing letters. He smoked cigarettes at intervals in the basement by day and in his bedroom at night, blowing the smoke up the chimney, as he knew my aunt disliked the smell of tobacco, though perfectly willing to allow him to smoke wherever he liked.' Colonel Moffitt (as Freddie became) considered that the published letters and the information given to biographers by Henry and Augusta, both much older than Gordon, concealed the bright side of his character. 'My mother, on the other hand, was a few years younger, and they were together as children. With her he would laugh and joke about his escapades in the Arsenal as a boy. He would make an amusing tale out of scant materials . . .'

The arrival of Gordon brought a deluge of tips and gifts to nephews and nieces. He was disappointed that Henry, now Sir Henry Gordon K. C. B., living in Chelsea with his large family on a small pension, would not allow him to pay eighteen-year-old Albert's fees at an army crammer but he promised that for the two younger boys, Bill and Bob, 'a good telescope and field glass awaits each of them when preliminary examination is passed, and saddle, and gun, when the final examination is over.'[7]

Gordon went up to London to stay with Henry for the *levée* on 17 February at St James's Palace. All officers on promotion or return from abroad were required to attend in full dress, filing before the Prince of Wales to make their bow and converse briefly if the Prince desired. Gordon was tempted to injured pride when wrongly announced as *Captain* Gordon but as he bowed to the Prince and his three brothers, splendid with orders and

*i. e. enough to post 240 inland letters: Foreign letters cost more.

decorations and moved among the magnificent uniforms, he reflected happily: 'a mass of glitter, to be worms in 30 years time.'[8]

More important than a *levée* was his future. 'I was going to retire,' he had written to Colonel Jenkins on arrival at Southampton 'but as I am near being General I have taken 6 months leave.'[9] In the normal progression he would be promoted major-general in two years. He wished to serve abroad but after his trenchant opposition to their Egyptian policy he did not expect, or want, an assignment from the Beaconsfield administration which still had a year before it must go to the country. No one realized that the Cabinet was about to commit electoral suicide.

Gordon might not be welcome at the Foreign Office but he was by no means 'the hero on the shelf.' His services were much sought. Sir Bartle Frere, Governor at the Cape, had sounded him about taking command of the Colonial troops (as distinct from the Queen's, whose commander-in-chief was appointed by the Horse Guards.)[10]

Leopold II had already moved to secure Gordon.[11] As soon as his forthcoming resignation as Governor-General had been confirmed, Leopold had asked Mackinnon to approach him to set up a line of stations and hospitals from the east to the west coast of Africa through the 'high Congo', following up Stanley's great exploration. Mackinnon himself wanted Gordon for the East Africa Company he was planning if he could obtain a concession from the Sultan of Zanzibar, and was delighted to receive from Gordon, within days of his landing at Southampton, a brief letter: '3 years ago I gave you a memo of my ideas of what ought to be done to establish a sort of Hudson's Bay Company in Africa. Are you prepared to carry this out. If so I will be inclined to help as far as I can. I do not like Belgians. I could not dispute with Kings. I must be King of the territory as far as appointments go.' He wondered, however, if John Kirk, the British consul-general at Zanzibar, would be able to secure the concession from the Sultan.[12]

Mackinnon wrote back with such enthusiasm that Gordon replied with a note of caution, after meeting Horace Waller in London, who had shown him confidential notes of the Sultan's attitude. Gordon pointed out that he would have to retire from the Army, that such a Company would need to operate under a national flag, and that there was some danger of war, which 'would be the death blow to any company. I think I would not push this matter now. You see, my dear Mr. Mackinnon, you value me far, far too highly. My only merits are that I try and do my best, and I do not shirk from anything I set my hand to, but I am not wise, or discreet, and thank God, I know it.'[13]

He needed rest, away from a cold English winter, and was going to Switzerland to recover; on return, he told Waller, he proposed to go to Zanzibar at his own expense for two months 'to see how things look', and if all was well could go back permanently. The sea voyage would set him up and be a cheap way of passing his leave.[14]

Though King Leopold was Mackinnon's rival for the spoils of East Africa he did not scruple to urge him to convince Gordon that service in the Congo would enable him to continue and extend his influence on 'the countries which owe him everything.'[15] Gordon agreed to stop at Brussels on his way to Switzerland.

He arrived at his Brussels hotel on the evening of 1 March to find a huge card from the King inviting him to dinner ten minutes later (he wrote a hurried note to explain his absence) and no sign of his baggage. The King sent back an appointment for 11 a. m. next morning. Gordon was scribbling a running commentary to Augusta. '. . . Horrors, it is now 10.20 a.m., and no baggage! . . . Remember, too, I have to dress, shave, etc., etc. 10.30 a.m. – no baggage!!! It is getting painful; H. M. will be furious. 10.48 a.m. – no baggage! . . . 10.30 p.m. Got enclosed note from palace, and went to see the King.'[16]

The King was 'exceedingly kind' and Gordon stayed an hour and a half, and went twice again in the next two days, but their conversations convinced him, wrongly, that the King's plans were impracticable: the Sultan would not cede territory; England would object if the King tried to create his own Christian state in a supposed no-man's land between Zanzibar and the Egyptian Sudan ('*Query does any such territory exist?*'); and no European power, including Belgium, would let Leopold operate under its flag. Gordon declined as yet to enter Leopold's service but confirmed that he would go to Zanzibar at his own expense and attempt to persuade the Sultan to cede a port, either to Leopold's Association or Mackinnon's company, but 'I am not sanguine of success.'[17]

Gordon saw himself drifting into a dilemma: if he upset the King's ideas he would be virtually entering the Sultan's service, yet if, being now privy to the King's plans, he took employment under the Sultan he would be acting falsely.

With these questions unresolved, Gordon left Brussels for Berne to stay at the Legation with Hussey Vivian, the former Consul-General in Cairo who now was British minister to Switzerland. Gordon had joked that he would lie in bed until 11 a. m.; and he hoped he had 'helped to put healing balm on wounds of Vivian who, poor fellow, feels the trouble of perfect quiet after what he has gone through.'[18]

Gordon looked up the sons of Army friends who were being educated in Swiss schools including two of his brother Enderby's boys. (Enderby had retired as a full General). One of them, his godson Charlie, a 'bright, cheery boy' of fourteen had been unwell at school at Lausanne. Gordon went there and took him to a hotel where they could recuperate together by the shores of the Lake of Geneva: 'I like the quiet ... it is a new phase for me.'[19] The month's rest had already made the caged lion on the Naples steamer a little more of a lamb.

At Lausanne Gordon made a new friend: John Bonar, from Greenock in Scotland, who may have been introduced through Hussey Vivian, for he does not seem to have been staying in the same hotel. They went for walks, talking together as they strode up and down the celebrated hills of Lausanne and along the lake, with the magnificent backdrop of the snowclad Alps, 'the beauty of which he used to admire greatly,' wrote Bonar to Sir Henry a few weeks after Gordon's death. 'There was a peculiar and irresistible charm about him that at once won my heart,' continued Bonar. 'I well remember the kindliness of his manner and the brightness of his eye as he welcomed me when I used to enter his room.

'What at once, and always, struck me was the way in which his oneness with God ruled all his actions, and his mode of seeing things. I never knew one who seemed so much to "endure as seeing Him who is invisible."' Bonar compared him with Samuel Rutherford, the Scottish Covenanter in the 17th century, 'who walked with God as friend with friend' (Bonar was thinking of Rutherford in his letters rather than his controversies.) Gordon seemed to Bonar 'to live with God, and for God. His communion and fellowship were with Him, and wherever he went he made men feel the power of "the Endless life", which he lived under and enjoyed.'[19]

To balance this Presbyterian's observation of Gordon at the age of forty-seven, came another new friend and acute observer. A high-spirited Devonshire family had taken up residence in the modest Hotel du Faucon at Lausanne. The Reverend R. H. Barnes, vicar of Heavitree near Exeter, had been ordered a year's rest from parish work to recover his health, and had taken his wife, four daughters and two sons – ranging from nearly thirteen years old to two – to Switzerland, with the spinster daughter of a distinguished Oxford historian to help look after them; they also had an ugly Swiss nursemaid.

As the Barnes family sat by a sunny window in the dining room, the eldest girl, Violet, and seven year old Irene, who grew up to be distinguished actresses under the stage names of Violet and Irene Vanbrugh, became fascinated by an English gentleman and a lad sitting at a table by the door, who seemed to know no one and were 'wholly wrapped up in each other.'

'The gentleman,' wrote Barnes, 'was of middle height, very strongly built; his face was furrowed with deep lines; and his fine broad brow and most determined mouth and chin indicated a remarkable power of grave and practical thought. He appeared to be as gentle as he was strong, for there was a certain tenderness in the tones of his rich, unworn voice and in the glance of his delicately expressive blue eyes. By-and-by he spoke to me, and, because I was not in good health, offered to take such a walk as might suit my strength. We talked of the most serious subjects, and I was greatly impressed by the directness, simplicity, and earnestness with which he discussed them.'

Even when he learned the stranger's name, Barnes had no idea who he was, for Gordon is a common surname and few faces were well known to the public in the eighteen eighties. One day after luncheon, 'while he was smoking a cigarette' Gordon invited Barnes to his room. Having learned that he had visited Palestine and knew Arabic, Gordon showed him some documents; but Barnes, whose Arabic was too scant to read them, asked what they were. 'Death warrants!' said Gordon mischievously. 'Death warrants?' exclaimed Barnes, 'Why, who are you?' 'Don't you know me?' Gordon explained that he was still nominally Governor-General of the Sudan; but once he had signed these warrants his Governor-Generalship would be dead. Barnes then realized that his new friend was the celebrated 'Chinese' Gordon.

Their friendship grew fast. 'I have never known any one who had the same faculty of winning the confidence, love, and reverence of those who happened to be brought into relation with him,' wrote Barnes a year after Gordon's death, describing their intimate talks about the indwelling of God, with Gordon's emphasis on 'the intimacy of the relation which ought to subsist between God and man. Gordon 'had had a kind of spiritual power, which exercised a singular, fascination when one talked with him about the subjects on which he most frequently and most deeply meditated.'[20]

The children soon were devoted to him, both at Lausanne and in his visits to Heavitree in the next four years. Nearly seven decades later Dame Irene Vanbrugh recalled how Gordon 'seemed part of the pattern of our lives. My recollection of him is wholly unprejudiced, even after reading the uninspired version of his life written by Lytton Strachey, who obviously wrote of what he had read and heard, having never seen General Gordon nor felt the glamour of his personality. The clear blue of his eye, the quiet of his nature, the natural simplicity of his whole outlook impressed me. His guiding motto was: "Be not greatly moved".'[21]

The Barnes family found him a 'bright and agreeable companion,' and admired his devotion to his godson Charlie, a sharp lad but affectionate. The two Gordons shared each other's jokes. 'Uncle Charlie teases me a good deal,' young Charlie told his mother in the space left below his uncle's signature in their joint letter, and then described how they had called at the school and while the maid went to look for her mistress 'Uncle Charlie found one of those nuts we always have for dinner and just as he was cracking it Mme. Campart came in and so he put it in his pocket and eat (*sic*) it after. I am sure it had been in one of the children's mouths and that then it rolled out and was lost.'[22] Chinese Gordon came to no harm.

Barnes noticed then and later, that Gordon was at his best with children 'and they instinctively felt that in him they had a friend who understood them and whom they could trust and love.'

With women, he was much less at ease. Barnes's observation is revealing: 'When conversing with women he seemed to exercise even more than his usual self-control in the expression of his thought and feeling. His sympathy, geniality, and attractiveness became, as it were, veiled; and he was "himself again" only when the restraint was removed.'[23] Since Gordon could be wholly at ease when talking with Mrs. Freese and her husband, or with his sisters and sisters-in-law, Barnes' comment points towards a conscious preventive against female attractions. Rather than being sexually orientated towards men, as some writers have inferred from a selective use of sources, many clues suggest a man of normal male instincts who was determined to stay celibate. Gordon had frequently urged his bachelor friends, like Charles Harvey, to marry, and rejoiced when they did.

Charles Watson had announced his engagement a few days before Gordon had left for Switzerland. His letter of congratulation summarizes his attitude to marriage*: '. . . A man who is not married cannot know his faults; a man's wife is his faithful looking-glass; she will tell him his faults. Some men who have sisters may know themselves, but it is rare. Therefore I say to you (as I have said before), "*Marry!*" Till a man is married he is a selfish fellow, however he may wish not to be so. Remember that by marrying you are no longer free for quixotic expeditions; you are bound to consider your better half; nothing is more selfish than a married man seeking adventures which his wife *cannot partake in.* To me, aged, and having gone through much trouble, it seems that to marry in this way is the best thing a man should do, and it is one which I recommend all my friends to do. You say, "Why do not you follow your own advice?" I reply, "Because I know myself sufficiently to know I could make no woman happy."' To a married woman who asked why he had not married he replied, after a long pause: 'I never yet have met the woman who, for my sake, and perhaps at a moment's notice, would be prepared to sacrifice the comforts of home, and the sweet society of loved ones, and accompany me whithersoever the demand of duty might lead – accompany me to the ends of the earth perhaps; would stand by me in times of danger and difficulty, and sustain me in times of hardship and perplexity. Such a woman I have not met, and such a one alone could be my wife!'[24] . . .

When Gordon left Lausanne at the end of March he was no nearer a decision on his future. He had received a telegram from the War Office: 'Our government offers command of colonial forces' (in South Africa) but had wired back a refusal. Among his reasons were dislike of the inevitable rows with the Cape Parliament and the general commanding the Queen's troops; he would hate residence at Cape Town 'and necessary festivities which I loathe'; and he grudged 'the great delight of the present Government in England at my exile.'[25]

The Conservative government had now gone to the country for the slow process of a general election; voting took place over three weeks. Gordon decided to stay abroad until the result was known; if Beaconsfield won he would not return until his leave ended or a suitable opening came overseas. 'I have enough to live on,' he told Henry, 'but I cannot stay in England. It is a great relief to me, to be free, while I am well, and not over old.' When Henry and Enderby lobbied him for the Tories, Gordon retorted: 'I maintain that

*This letter (printed p. 101 of Stanley Lane-Poole's *Watson Pasha* (1919)) is missing from the MS. letters from Gordon to Watson in the British Library.

999 out of 1,000 *do not know* what they are talking about, when they defend Lord B.'s policy; if you say *you* do, let me *heckle* (ie Scotch for question) you.'[26]

Gordon and Charlie went to Berne at the invitation of Hussey Vivian but Charlie tired easily on expeditions, and would not eat at the long legation dinners. Gordon therefore took him by easy stages to Paris and sent him home, organizing his cross-Channel journey with great care.

'I was very glad to receive your note telling me Charlie had arrived safely,' he wrote to his sister-in-law Maggie from Paris. 'I feel very dull without him.' Though Charlie's untidiness had tried him sometimes, he liked 'his great affection for you all, his truthfulness and his speaking out' (qualities which others found strong in his uncle) and urged the Enderbys to make Charlie write to the Vivians and others. 'He will fight against it I know, but all these people were kind and it will not be much exertion. I never pretended to Charlie I was a paragon. It would be no good, for he is too quick; and I also wanted him to see it is nothing to acknowledge one's human failings. So you need not fret yourself to keep up appearance, for you will be sure to fail under such microscopes. I want C. to understand that in even a worldly point of view it is worth while being civil to outsiders (to one's own relations it does not matter so much). I have been far more helped by little people than by great. I take much more pains to *answer letters from*, and to help (if this is in my power) the *small* than I would the great. From this I consider I owe any success in the world. I would refuse a dinner with a king to give pleasure in taking tea with my old house-keeper . . .'[27]

He told the Enderbys to show the letter to Charlie, and wrote him a happy letter promising him a gun at seventeen and £100 'when you get your start in life, and telling him that he had left a towel behind. 'I asked you "what you could give to me?" You said nothing. Yes! you can, you can ask Him who lives in *your heart*, to give me a "humble, kind forbearing mind," to make me less proud, you will pay me back a millionfold for the straw I have given you. I do not want a hurried prayer on your knees, I want just a few words from your heart, even as you go down stairs. Now, my dear Charlie, be kind to your father and mother.' They would have been well off had they not had a large family. '*You* cannot pay them back, except *in love*.' Only in his postscript he did urge Charlie to write those letters, adding, 'make your mother pay postage'.

Charlie made his career in the Indian Police, and died unmarried in 1941.

Gordon in Paris horrified the British Ambassador by threatening to urge the French to find a governor-general for the Sudan to replace the Egyptian who was undoing his work and creating the conditions for revolt. Lord Salisbury, learning this, was the more sure that Gordon was a madman.

But by mid-April the Beaconsfield ministry had been defeated. Gladstone came in; Salisbury gave way to Lord Granville.

Gordon had hurried home, with a brief stop at Brussels, undecided between Mackinnon and Leopold, Zanzibar or the Congo. He still doubted Leopold's scheme. England might oppose it. He had drawn up a long memorandum at Lausanne to test Foreign Office reactions to a series of questions posed by Leopold, but had held it back unposted when the General Election was announced. He now sent it in as a personal and confidential paper. The memorandum passed slowly upwards, each desk expressing doubt or disapproval of Leopold's scheme as outlined openly by Gordon. The new Foreign Secretary, Lord Granville, saw no need to correspond with him ('One can never be sure that Col. Gordon is not under some misapprehensions arising from his enthusiasm') and determined to work officially through the Belgian minister in London.

King Leopold was annoyed: he had hoped to keep the details secret from his own ministers and to use diplomacy as a smokescreen. 'It is impossible to employ Gordon in negotiations,' he complained. 'It seems equally impossible to confide a secret in him.'[28]

However, when Leopold wrote this, Gordon was far away. His dilemma between the Congo and Zanzibar had apparently been resolved.

He had not taken the advice he had offered in an afterthought to Enderby, torn between Switzerland or Cheltenham College for his second son's education: 'If in doubt about Neville, toss up with reverence, "The lot is cast into the lap. The whole disposing thereof is of the Lord."'[29] He had relied as always on the conviction which he expressed on 29 April to Henry's step-daughter 'Coco,' who had run away from her husband and after his death had married another officer. In sending her a gift of money (as he sent to each of his nephews and nieces on coming home) he wrote: 'Remember that God rules every event, that man is only an instrument, and therefore you and your husband's future are in His hands. He has never changed ...'[30]

CHAPTER TWENTY

Passage to India

On 1 May 1880 Henry and Charlie went to visit an old family servant, Lizzie. On their return to Henry's house in Elm Park Gardens Charlie did not come in but started to walk towards the nearby lodgings which Henry had found for him in the Georgian terrace houses of Beaufort street, selected at Charlie's request for its cheap curtains which would not retain his clouds of tobacco smoke.[1]

As he walked away a hansom cab drew up. Sir Bruce Seton, a baronet who was principal clerk in the War Office stepped down and spoke to Sir Henry; Henry shouted to Charlie to come back and Sir Bruce Seton conveyed to Charlie Gordon a surprising invitation: to go out to India with the newly appointed Viceroy, the Marquess of Ripon, as his Private Secretary, sailing in two weeks. 'After some cogitation,' Gordon told Augusta that same evening, 'I have accepted,'[2] while offering Ripon an opportunity to withdraw the invitation because Gordon was the anonymous author of a letter to the press which had attacked the government of India's policy (at that period such letters were often unsigned). Ripon did not withdraw, and the dilemma between Zanzibar and the Congo seemed resolved.

Ripon and Gordon knew each other, although the acquaintanceship is not documented except for their official relations over the China journal in 1865 when Ripon was Secretary of State for War. They had a shared interest in the welfare of the poor, for when Gordon was at Gravesend Ripon was a 'Christian Socialist,' – a follower of Kingsley and F. D. Maurice: the term was unrelated to the later socialists. Ripon may have met Gordon in the company of his older first cousin, Thomas Gordon Hake, a long-forgotten poet who had been the family doctor and friend of Ripon's late mother*: her

---

*And said by the *Dictionary of National Biography* to have been related to her through his mother (Gordon's Aunt Hake') which would have made Gordon and Ripon relations. This is doubtful unless very distant.

home, Grantham House on Putney Heath, was one of at least four residences and estates which he owned, and Hake was still the local doctor.

Freddy, Gordon's younger brother, had worked under Ripon at the War Office. Fifteen years later Gordon had perhaps forgotten his comment when Freddy refused to be Ripon's private secretary: 'I am quite rejoiced at it. They are posts which require great subserviency in the holders of them, and offer great temptation, quite destructive in many cases of their peace, as they are so apt to make discontent.'[3] A Viceroy's private secretary, however, was far more powerful than a Cabinet minister's: Gordon's immediate predecessor, George Pomeroy Colley, who had left India for South Africa and his defeat and death at Majuba Hill the following year, had been partly responsible for Lord Lytton's controversial policy in Afghanistan.

Nevertheless, Gordon as an ex-Governor General soon found 'transition from a comet to a satellite is not over pleasurable to yours sincerely,' as he ended a letter to one of his friends.[4] To a clerical friend, however, he said that with perhaps only another ten years more of life, 'where I pass that period makes very little difference to me';[5] and to Augusta he wrote that he looked on the appointment as a man might who had only twenty-four hours to live and that 'I am a good deal independent of place whilst I have His presence.'[6] He was not about to adopt the 'great subserviency' of his long ago comment on private secretaries.

Ripon had been named by Gladstone as viceroy and Governor-General when Lord Lytton, contrary to custom, had resigned immediately on the fall of the ministry which had appointed him. Ripon was a radical, chosen that he might make the government of India more liberal, giving Indians more self-government and a higher role in the administration of justice.

Gladstone's choice was particularly bold because Ripon had recently become a Roman Catholic after withdrawing from public life to wrestle with his soul. When appointed Viceroy he had wanted as private secretary Colonel William Butler (who had been so impressed by Gordon at the dinner with Owen Jones in their club in January '77; husband of the celebrated artist) but Butler had been born an Irish Roman Catholic; Gladstone vetoed Butler,[7] since sending out two Roman Catholics would smack of a Popish Plot. Ripon then turned to Gordon, possibly on the advice of a former viceroy, Lord Northbrook.

Gordon was known for his passionate conviction that a Governor-General's first duty was to the people he ruled, not to the imperial power, though his style differed from the traditional ways of British governors and the Foreign Office warned that Gordon was too excitable for the post. The newspapers welcomed the appointment. The *Daily News* commented: 'There is something whimsical in turning Gordon Pasha – Chinese Gordon – into a Private secretary and sending him to Simla in the wake of a Roman Catholic Viceroy ... one who knew him well pronounced him to be a great man but decidedly mad. There is a deal of method in his madness, however, and whoever is opposed to him had better think more of his method than of his madness.'[8]

In Calcutta *The Friend of India* (which had been founded by Marshman, son of a missionary and brother-in-law of Havelock of Lucknow the Puritan general in the Mutiny) quoted a correspondent who believed that with the arrival of Gordon 'we shall have an end of favouritism, and all cliqueism will disappear from the face of official society.' Editorially *The Friend* was not so hopeful: 'If Col. Gordon were Viceroy he could not entirely eradicate these deep-seated diseases ... There is not in the world a man of gentler, kindlier nature than Col. Gordon; we know of no man more terrible to sham and charlatans. His mere presence in Indian official society will be a kind of shock which will send a shiver through all its vanities and artificialities, and may, indeed, in time create something like a revolution.'[9]

Lord Houghton, the liberal politician and literary figure, when introduced to Gordon while lunching with Ripon at Carlton Gardens warmly congratulated the new Viceroy 'on his great good luck in having such a Secretary: he was very glad Lord Ripon was going as Governor-General but almost more glad that Gordon was going as his Secretary.'[10]

In the Queen's Household, on the other hand, Sir John Cowell remarked to Ponsonby that he did not expect Gordon to go beyond the Red Sea, 'the whole appointment being in my mind so unsuited to him.'[11] And Gordon, though working so hard with Ripon that he was 'dead beat,'[12] had already regretted his decision. As he stated publicly a month later: 'Men, at times, owing to the mysteries of Providence form judgments, which they afterwards repent of, this is my case in accepting the appointment Lord Ripon honoured me in offering me. I repented of my act as soon as I had accepted the appointment and I deeply regret that I had not the moral courage to say so at that time.'[13] He was hedging already to his friends. 'I am only going on probation,' he told Waller on 6 May. 'The post is very unlikely to suit me'; and to Rose, Henry's wife, he wrote that he did not want people to think he would stay in India: 'I go out as *Private Secretary* or *Private Companion*, and am in no way bound to him or he to me.'[14] Lord Ripon, however, expected Gordon to stay at his side in India. Conscious that Gordon had recently wielded powers greater even than those of a Viceroy of India, Ripon tolerated his eccentric behaviour. When the Prince of Wales gave a farewell dinner to Ripon, Gordon declined the invitation. An equerry hurried round to Beaufort Street to say that a royal command could not be refused. Gordon retorted: 'I refused King John when he invited me to go with him to his hot spring in the mountains – and he might have cut off my head for refusing. I am sure His Royal Highness will not do that!' The equerry suggested pleading illness. 'But I am not ill.' The equerry begged for some excuse to take back. 'Very well then; tell him I always go to bed at half past nine.'

The Prince was amused, and invited Gordon to a mid-morning glass of wine: Gordon much enjoyed the interview, and reading the Prince's paper on military organization.*[15]

The Gordon family had a story that Ripon invited his personal staff to a dinner down at Grantham House. Gordon was put up in the lodge. He 'forgot all about dinner and had to be sent for and was found immersed in Red Books about India.' The Ripon family capped this story with another, that when they finally sat down, Gordon insisted on eating every course on the same plate, saying 'We shall have to rough it out in India, you know, so I may as well begin now.' Since all present knew that Gordon had been a Governor-General himself they presumably saw the joke.

On the cross-Channel steamer to France the Viceregal party travelled with the British ambassador who had been annoyed by the reference to coffins. Gordon sent a postcard to Augusta from Paris: 'Arrived safely, came over with Lord Lyons, 6ft by 2' 6", scowled at one.' But this was followed by another card, in pencil and undated but with the same postmark: 'Scowled not correct. Did not know one apparently.'[16] The recipient of the famous despatch about Governors-General and ambassadors soon to be buried had not recalled its writer's face from their brief meeting earlier in the year. The party continued by train through Italy and Lord Ripon wrote to his wife, who could not come until later because they would arrive in the hot weather: 'We are a very harmonious party and I like all the staff so far.'[17]

*The Gordon family tradition that the Prince had Gordon to luncheon tête-a-tête is disproved by the absence of his name from the Prince's social diary which he wrote up in his own hand, noting where he had lunched and dined and all who were present. (Royal Archives).

They boarded the P. and O. steamer, *Teheran* for the crossing of the Mediterranean, 'a beautiful passage with a perfectly smooth sea;' with the coast of Greece in sight Ripon wrote: 'Gordon has done some work which I have given him, very well; so far he and I get on capitally,'[18] and so did Gordon with Father John Kerr, Ripon's Roman Catholic chaplain, and young Lieutenant Eugene Brett, whom he used as assistant secretary: their friendship would lead Gordon into even closer friendships with Brett's older brother Reginald, the future second Viscount Esher. Also on board was Gordon's old friend and fellow-Sapper, Sir Andrew Clarke, a member of the Viceroy's Council, who wrote to his wife: 'Charlie Gordon is always near me. He is a very fine fellow, but is thrown away as a Private Secretary. I don't think he will remain very long in India unless he gets much interested in it and in the work ... Barrington Foote, who is the most amusing comical fellow I ever met, is keeping Lord Ripon and the others in roars of laughter on deck. Gordon is looking very angry, though at times he cannot help laughing.'[19] The aide-de-camp's stories must have been *risqué*: Ripon thought Foote 'a good fellow, but he is always telling and half acting comic anecdotes, which pall upon me very soon.'[20]

At Alexandria Gordon wrote to Augusta that 'Lord R. is all right but I do not think I shall stay more than 6 months, it is too small and restrained a position.'[21] They went overland to Suez, and Evelyn Baring and Edward Malet joined the train. 'How well I recollect,' wrote Sir Andrew Clarke a few years later, when Gordon's warnings had proved all too sound, his telling Baring 'that the action of the Cairo government would lead to grief in the Sudan.'[22] 'They were very civil,' was Gordon's comment on the conversation, 'and I expect were glad to hear I was off to India,'[23] especially as he had written a stiff letter to the young Khedive Tewfik on reading in the newspapers of the revival of the Slave Trade. 'I gave him a good wigging,' Gordon wrote to C. H. Allen of the Anti-Slavery Society, 'but I am bound to say Malet the Consul General and Baring declare he is truly sincere in wishing to put down the slave hunting, so I wrote him another letter to tell him, he will have credit till I hear how he behaves.'[24]

Gordon was now thoroughly restless. 'Going through Egypt finished him,'[25] wrote Clarke to their mutual friend Hugh Childers, the new Secretary of State for War (to whom Gordon had given a copy of *Scripture Promises* before leaving: it always stayed open on Childers' desk.) Egypt would inevitably have deepened the contrast between his present subordinate role and his former power, and he was miserable at the unhappy trend of events in the Sudan. Clarke had 'one constant struggle' to persuade him not to resign but wait until he could be offered more congenial work in India. They had many talks as the S. S. *Ancona* steamed down the Red Sea. Gordon wore his London frock coat to the astonishment of the others who sweltered in light clothes;[26] but the notorious heat of the Red Sea was nothing to a Sudan desert in summer.

One of Ripon's first tasks would be to confirm the new Amir of Afghanistan, placed on the throne when the second Afghan War had ended (as Lord Lytton had assumed) or to restore the deposed Amir, Yakub Khan, who was now interned in India on the suspicion that he had secretly instigated the mutineers who had attacked the British Residency and murdered Sir Louis Cavagnari and his staff; yet Yakub Khan had fled to General Roberts as he marched on Kabul to avenge the murders. A commision of enquiry had studied the evidence and had compiled a lengthy report. Ripon asked Gordon to make a précis and give an opinion.

He sat up much of the night and covered the report with comments in red ink. He concluded that no evidence convicted Yakub: 'He very likely was glad Cavagnari was murdered, but I could see nothing to show that he was implicated in the crime.' And three of the Viceroy's council had minuted the same conclusion.

If not guilty he should be restored; especially as Gordon thought wrongly that Yakub was the only man with a sufficient following to hold the country. 'Take him back yourself, my Lord,' said Gordon, as he recounted to his friend Major Donnelly five months later. 'You can easily do it with 3000 cavalry. If you succeed you will be looked upon as the greatest Governor general India has ever had; and if you fail and are killed you'll have a splendid marble monument put up to you! But,' Gordon told Donnelly, 'Lord Ripon did not see the merriment.'

He might not appreciate a joke but he concurred in Gordon's opinion, 'and told me to telegraph from Aden to his, Yakub's, keeper to meet him at Bombay.

'I said: "My Lord, I think that will hardly do, as you have not yet been sworn in and Lord Lytton is still Governor-General and may make a great fuss." Lord Ripon agreed, thought I was right and said the telegram was not to be sent.'[27]

At Aden Gordon wrote to Augusta: 'We have got here very well; Lord Rippon very kind. But I cannot say I like the berth, and I shall get away as soon as I can do so in a respectable manner.'[28] Four days later, on 28 May, he wrote again: 'After a hot voyage we are nearing Bombay, and there will commence a certain degree of purgatory in the way of festivities, which, as far as possible, I shall avoid. I am now quite composed, and have made up my mind to leave either in September or the beginning of October. I think it will not be a surprise to Lord Ripon, who sees I am too truculent for the post.'[29] Lord Ripon may indeed have begun to wonder whether Simla could contain two Governors-General, even if one were an 'ex-Ex,' but he continued to rely on Gordon. Gordon however had added to Augusta: 'Having the views I hold, I could never curb myself sufficiently ever to remain in H.M.'s service. Not one in ten million can agree with one's motives, and it is no use expecting to change their views.'[30]

The *Ancona* docked at Bombay on Monday, 31 May. The Viceroy-designate was received with a thirty-six gun salute, troops parading, bands playing and all the frills of a viceregal welcome which his Private Secretary loathed. They drove with a mounted escort of Indian cavalry through excited crowds to Government House at its splendid site on Malabar Point, overlooking the sea.

The Private Secretary looked with distaste at the magnificence which surrounded a British governor in India – the hordes of servants, the hurrying equerries, the scores of officials of every rank. That night the Governor of Bombay, Sir James Fergusson, gave a state banquet in honour of his new master-elect but Gordon had not packed his full dress in his cabin trunk and the luggage from the hold was not yet unloaded. The Governor's household, appalled at the thought of a Private Secretary, however distinguished, improperly dressed, fitted him up with other men's clothes as Maharajahs and British judges drove up. After the dinner Gordon fled, and was discovered in his room with his legs up as he studied papers, the inevitable cigarette in his mouth 'and his borrowed plumage on the floor.' As Clarke wrote next day: 'Gordon is not an ordinary man, and his mind and actions are not regulated in the same way as are other men's minds. He frets and chafes not only at what he thinks the finesse and lies of ordinary public life, but at its ceremony and its etiquette; a state dinner, or even to wait through an ordinary social gathering is irritating and annoying to him.'[31]

Several of Lord Lytton's staff had come down from Simla to greet the new Viceroy. Gordon soon had evidence that they would absorb Lord Ripon into their time-honoured system, for on the Tuesday night Ripon revived the question of Yakub Khan, and ordered Gordon to telegraph Yakub's keeper to meet the viceregal train at a convenient station on the way to Simla. As Gordon did not know which station would be best he went to the Military Secretary, Major George White of the 92nd Highlanders, who had won the Victoria Cross in the Afghan War and would go on to be the hero of the siege of Ladysmith and a field-marshal. When White heard that Ripon wished to meet Yakub's keeper he was 'awfully taken aback. Did I know what the consequences would be? Everyone in India would be staggered and so on – begged me to persuade Lord Ripon not to take such a step.'

Gordon did not think it would matter either way but agreed to let Ripon know of White's strong objection. Next morning Gordon sent in a note before breakfast. In a few minutes Ripon came out 'very indignant that anyone should have ventured to overrule his orders. He had no intention of being controlled and so on.

'All breakfast time he looked quite hurt and injured and indignant. After breakfast I left White talking with him in a beseeching way,' and presently Ripon came to Gordon, checked that the telegram had not yet gone and said, 'perhaps after all it may as well not be sent'.*

Gordon felt that Ripon had been snubbed and that it would get worse. 'Lord Ripon was being surrounded and guided by the very people from whom Lord Northbrook had begged me to keep him clear.' And although Gordon himself was ready to be snubbed 'if there was any use to it,' he was sure Ripon at Simla would be 'completely in the hands of the Lytton party. I felt I was *de trop* and could do no good and it was as well to give up as soon as possible.'[32]

Nor was that all. Ripon had been sent a book of poems by a Parsee of Bombay. As White told the story to Queen Victoria's Household at dinner in September 1884 when Gordon was besieged in Khartoum, 'Gordon was asked to acknowledge the gift and say Lord R. would read it with much pleasure. He left the room repeating to himself "Will read it

*After reading a garbled account of this incident in Boulger's *Life of Gordon*, Ripon wrote privately to Boulger in 1901 rejecting the story 'I had not made up my mind at all and it would have been very rash of me to have done so before I reached Simla.' (letter of 4 May 1901, Add Mss 43638 f 144.) This was written after twenty-one years; Gordon gave his version to Donnelly after five months, and he had not supposed that Ripon had made up his mind, merely that White prevented him discussing it with Yakub's keeper, or possibly with Yakub himself: Gordon's meaning is not clear.

with much pleasure – I know he will never look at it. I *cannot* write such a reply."[33]

Since telling white lies was as much a part of a Private Secretary's life as attending innumerable dinners, Gordon was more than ever certain that he should resign.

That afternoon Sir Andrew Clarke was still under the impression that Gordon would come to Simla, but while Clarke went for a drive with Ripon, Gordon brooded. He believed he could never do good in India. Making snap judgement on the British in India, based on the briefest experience, he considered 'the mode of life of Indian officials is effeminately luxurious, and must tend to deteriorate their efficiency for their position in India. I consider the salaries are twice as much as they need be.'[34] He felt, unfairly, that they 'only want to get through and retire.'[35] The Indian Civil Service would frustrate any reform intended by Lord Ripon so that Gordon would be useless to Lord Ripon in an impossible task and that no reform 'would ever be achieved in India without a Revolution.'[36] And he was conscious that the longer he stayed before resignation the more confidential papers he would read, gaining secret information, which he ought not to know if he were leaving Ripon's service; nor would he wait a few weeks and then concoct an excuse.

He wrote out his resignation and found Lord William Beresford, one of Lytton's equerries. As Ripon wrote to his wife next day: 'Yesterday evening just before dinner Beresford came to me with a letter in his hand and said that he had bad news for me. I immediately thought of you and Olly and my heart sank within me, but on opening the letter I found that it was one from Gordon resigning the Private Secretaryship. The announcement, therefore, which under other circumstances might have been disturbing, came to me as an absolute relief.'[37]

Clarke was astonished 'when just as we were sitting down to dinner Gordon told me, with a beaming face and in high glee, that he had done the deed, and sent in his irrevocable resignation to Lord Ripon!' After dinner Ripon and Clarke discussed how to announce the resignation without causing damage. Ripon was distressed, for he had 'in no way given offence, and he liked Gordon very much, and had all along been ready to yield much to Gordon's ideas and position.' They worked out a draft statement and Clarke saw Gordon. 'At first,' Clarke told his wife, 'he was very hard and uncompromising, though on some points he felt deeply and was terribly distressed. So after a long talk I left him late at night, or rather in the small hours.' Gordon may have insisted that his letter of resignation should be published; it does not survive but probably contained damaging comments on the Indian administration.

Early next morning Clarke 'found him altogether in a better mood.' Gordon saw Ripon for a few minutes, returned to Clarke's room and 'dashed off' a letter which 'went much further,' wrote Clarke, 'than was wanted in taking blame to himself, and in his testimony to Lord Ripon. But he entreated me to let him write as he himself thought best, and when he had written he would listen to no change or alteration in it.'[38] The letter, published in the *Times of India* on 4 June and, by cable, in the London evening papers that day, ended with a resounding tribute, unusual in an age of high barriers between Protestants and Roman Catholics: 'Depend on it, that this vast country will find in spite of all obstacles, great as they may be, that the rule of Lord Ripon will be blessed, for he will rule in the strength of the Lord, not of men.'[39]

'Yes, I ratted,' wrote Gordon to Henry, 'but I ratted so as to hurt Lord Ripon very little and we left the very best of friends,'[40] as Ripon himself confirmed in a letter to Childers: 'We parted the best of friends ... My respect for him has in many ways increased rather than diminished.'[41]

Gordon insisted on paying back his passage money (£68) although Ripon was rich; and, as his last advice, urged him to summon Baring from Egypt to reorganize Indian finances. Ripon did so, to the great advantage of India and of Baring's career; Gordon may, however, have hoped that Egypt would see Baring no more.

Ripon left Bombay for Simla that night. He did not meet Yakub or his keeper on the way, nor restore him to the Afghan throne: whether Yakub would have prevented the new outbreak of war the following month, leading to a heavy British defeat at Maiwand, the siege of Kandahar and Roberts' brilliant march to relieve it, can never be known. Yakub was not the cause of Gordon's resignation. 'A man might as well take an orang outang as Private Secretary as the undersigned,' wrote Gordon to a friend, 'but Ripon and I parted the best of friends, and we had a good laugh over the whole affair.'[42]

Gordon decided to go at once back to Aden by mail steamer to find a passage for Zanzibar. But that same night, at 3.30 a. m., he was woken by a messenger with a priority cable, forwarded via London, from Peking. China was facing war with Russia. The cable brought an urgent request: Gordon should 'come out at once,' conditions to be settled. Gordon wired that he would come 'and that I was indifferent as to conditions.'

'I telegraphed the War Office,' he wrote to Ripon, 'and I leave at once. I like, as your Lordship does, to trust in God in these matters. We are fools in the eyes of the world, but we are wise to do so, for even in this world, we gain by doing so.'[43]

CHAPTER TWENTY-ONE

Return to China

'I was a comet, I became a satellite, and now am, after an eclipse, a comet again,'[1] wrote Gordon in a letter dated 21 June 1880 on his way to China, where he hoped to prevent a war.

China and Russia were locked in dispute over a remote corner of Chinese Turkestan (Sinkiang) in the far northwest of the empire. Nine years earlier when a Moslem revolt against Peking had inflamed the border, the Russians had occupied the territory of Ili or Kulja, promising to return it when order was restored. They had not returned it, and when a high Manchu mandarin went to negotiate at the Tsar's court he was outwitted, and signed an abject treaty in September 1879 which ceded the territory. China was outraged, the treaty repudiated and the mandarin sentenced to death. One party in the Inner Council of the empire prepared for war, led by Prince Chun the father of the emperor, who once again was a minor. A more cautious party urged peace, led by Prince Kung and supported by Gordon's old comrade in arms, Li Hung Chang. Li was now viceroy of the metropolitan provinces and thus the most important mandarin of Chinese race; yet not being a Manchu he must tread warily: he could be summarily dismissed and even beheaded by the Manchu rulers.

As early as January 1880 the British minister, Sir Thomas Wade (Bruce's assistant in the Taiping years) had asked London whether British officers might be allowed 'to serve in defensive war against any Power except England? The Chinese Government still holds Gordon Pasha in high honour.'[2] The War Office, knowing that Gordon had left the Sudan minuted that it would be 'very desirable that that officer should, if he is willing, be so employed,'[3] but the Foreign Office pointed out the difference between a Chinese civil war and a war between China and Russia; to allow British subjects to help China would be a 'grave breach of neutrality.'

In Peking, as the crisis deepened, the Tsungli Yamen (Chinese Foreign Office) asked Li Hung Chang about Gordon. Li doubted at first whether the British Government would permit him to serve, but in May he authorized Robert Hart, the commissioner of Imperial Customs who had helped their reconciliation after the Soochow massacre and had become a good friend of both, to summon Gordon. Not knowing that Gordon was on his way to India, Hart sent a cable to London in May, care of his agent, C. A. Campbell. When Campbell read of Gordon's resignation he took the cable out of his drawer and forwarded it to Bombay, so that in the small hours of 4 June, in Government House, Bombay, after seeing Ripon off to Simla, Gordon received the telegram from Campbell asking where to send an important message from China, to be sent in cipher.

Later that morning Gordon read the deciphered wire from Hart in Peking: 'I am directed to invite you here. Please come and see for yourself, this opportunity for doing really useful work ought not to be missed. Work position, conditions and all will be arranged with yourself, here, to your satisfaction. Do take 6 months leave and come.'[4] Gordon immediately wired Campbell that he would sail at first opportunity: 'As for conditions Gordon indifferent'; and to Colonel Grant at the Horse Guards he wired: 'Obtain me leave till end of year. Never mind pay. Am invited to China. Will not involve government.'

He bought a passage on a cargo steamer to Ceylon to catch the China mail but a flurry of telegrams followed before he could sail: Grant: 'Must state more specifically purpose and position you go to in China.' Gordon: 'Am ignorant. Will write from China before expiration of leave.' Grant: 'Reasons insufficient your going China not approved.' Gordon thereupon wired his resignation from the Army, saying that he could not 'desert China in her present crisis' but if asked would counsel peace not war; and to Henry he wrote before he boarded the steamer: 'I will not take service unless HMG give me leave *but I will leave the Army*.'[5]

He told the Bombay press that 'my fixed desire is to persuade the Chinese not to go to war with Russia,'[6] and sailed for Ceylon. Colonel Grant had now consulted Hart's Agent in London on behalf of the Duke of Cambridge, and when Gordon's ship anchored off Colombo he was handed yet another wire: 'Leave granted on your engaging to take no military service in China.' Gordon wired back: 'I will take no military service in China. I would never embarrass HM Government.'

'So we've lost him,' noted Hart in his journal when he read the news of

Gordon's promise, 'unless, indeed I induce him to stay as *Sec*, or in some civil capacity, and draw military advice from him *sub rosa*.' Accepting that Gordon 'acts like a good subject' Hart was disappointed, having gloated the previous day: 'Gordon's coming said to have created some consternation in St. Petersburg.'[7]

Gordon had missed the China mail and enjoyed a restful voyage in the cargo ship, with his Private Secretaryship quite forgotten, to Penang and Hong Kong, where an A. D. C. came on board to invite him to stay at Government House. He declined, but promised to come up the following day to see the Governor, Sir John Pope-Hennessy, a noted supporter of the Anti-Slavery Society: the Governor would come down from his summer residence on the Peak.

That day, 4 July, was a Sunday. Gordon paid a morning call on a naval acquaintance, Captain East, R. N., whose ship *H. M. S. Comus* was in harbour. Gordon went on board, to find the ship's company fallen in for Sunday Divisions 'I came in for the sermon and part of the Communion, getting in behind all the men,' and was amused when the parson, preaching the 'usual empty sermon' at the Sunday service attacked Colonel Gordon for quoting Scripture in his letter to the press about Lord Ripon, not knowing 'when he prepared his sermon that I would be one of his congregation!'[8]

He could not stay for lunch if he were not to keep the Governor waiting. Reaching Government House on a very hot day 'I nearly died,' he wrote, as he discussed affairs on an empty stomach. Later he sent for one of his Ever Victorious Army interpreters; a youth he had named Quincey, whom he found had grown into a 'first rate young fellow with a very pretty little wife and three nice little children.'[9] This could not have been the foundling baby, rescued during the battle for Quinsan whom Gordon had adopted and named Quincey: he would have been only nineteen.

The Emperor's Viceroy at Canton had sent an invitation for a visit. Gordon transferred to a small steamer and arrived in Canton late on 5 July. He had now become convinced that China could never win a war with a first-class power while the capital remained at Peking: 'it is too near the sea.' If they turned their army into a large guerrilla force they might hold a well-armed enemy at bay, but he doubted that China would allow him to reorganize their armed forces.[10]

At Canton he was put up by one of Hart's subordinates, the local Commissioner of Chinese Customs, an Ulsterman named McKean. Gordon had never met the McKeans, but once again he showed his extraordinary gift for making deep friendships quickly with those who shared his faith. After returning to Hong Kong he wrote to the McKeans as if he had known them for years, from Government House: 'Look at the address and *marvel*. I got here after a good passage, nice Captain, and was met by letter from H. E. 'Come up to "Peak." As I was *dead*, I declined and said I would come up on the morrow. I then was invited to above address to sleep. I said "Yes" and tomorrow H. E. comes down and we spend day together. Pitman came down ("I do not like thee, Dr. Fell, the reason why I cannot tell") and then Palmer, R. E. a nice honest fellow . . .'[11] Pitman had been in the *Slaney* gunboat in 1861 and must have crossed Gordon in some way.

He moved his baggage to the Shanghai mail (and had a story about that) and then after dark set off to dine at Palmer's and got lost: 'Wandered for $1\frac{1}{4}$ hours in town, *swore*, a thing I have not done for months, not able to find House. By expenditure 4 dollars, I got to House.' He described their conversation on military matters at dinner and then, switching as he so easily did from secular to sacred, he went on: 'No person like Mrs. McKean to pour out my griefs to. My dear McKean, you have no conception how I yearn for the future life, how I groan over the tugging of a corrupt body after me. The world has gone from me' and he switched back to an amusing account of the Captain of the Macao packet.[12]

He reverted to this yearning, which echoed St. Paul and many saints down the ages, in a later letter to McKean: 'To look on death as a blessing is to live a resurrection life, and as it were, to leave the grave far behind you.'[13]

Gordon sailed from Hong Kong on 8 July, accompanied by a bamboo *chaise longue* thoughtfully provided by the Governor so that he could sleep on deck in the sultry nights, and reached Shanghai, where Hart's brother met him and put him up. The town and his old comrades were both much changed; he visited the cemeteries of Ever Victorious casualties and arranged for the E. V. A. Memorial to be repaired and felt sad.[14]

While Gordon wandered around Shanghai, Hart in Peking was writing him a letter after re-thinking the position, as he recorded in his Diary: 'Gordon pledged not to serve – Russia irritated at the thought of employing him – England requiring him not to serve – his conditional leave, etc. etc.: all show that I had better keep out of such a thing as meeting him at Tientsin; so I tell Gordon to hold his tongue, and that it will be best for him to come to Wade *first*, and postpone visiting *Li* till afterwards.' Hart sent off the letter, to be handed to Gordon on arrival, but four days later had doubts: 'After all, anxiety may have driven me too far, and I may be doing wrong in trying to stop Gordon . . . so I have written to tell him to consider himself quite free to decide for himself as regards movements, doings and language.'[15]

When Gordon's ship called at Chefoo on the Shantung peninsula, before sailing on to Tientsin, he was handed Hart's first letter. 'Your telegram of the 16th of June from Galle,' he read, 'ties your hands so completely that *it will be a good thing for you not to talk any kind of business to anyone until you have seen the British minister.*' Gordon might pay a visit of ceremony to Li, 'but considering the view Russia takes and the action our Government has taken, the *British Legation at Peking* is the only spot in China where your presence will not cause an immense amount of, for China, most embarrassing criticism. In fact, it would be well and *best* for you to come to *Peking first* and visit *Li* afterwards. Sir Thomas Wade is sending an invitation. Please accept it. The advice I give you is most important at this critical juncture.'[16]

After reading the letter Gordon disembarked at Chefoo for a day, at first deciding to turn back at once; 'but then I did not see the reason why I should not go on, so I did so, and was met at Tientsin by a letter from Wade and two ditto from Hart.'[17] As he explained later to Wade, 'he was irritated by what he regarded as an assumption on the part of Hart of a right to dictate to him,' though Wade thought that Hart had no intention of dictating.[18]

Gordon was even more irritated by the letter from Wade which he opened at Tientsin on 21 July, for Wade warned him in friendly terms that if war broke out he must 'quit Chinese service or change nationality.'[19] On reading this, as Gordon wrote to McKean, 'I went to see Li, and there whether for weal or woe, told him I would stay with him, and threw up my commission in H. M. Army. All things are destined for the best, and the events of this life are of ephemeral importance.'[20] He telegraphed to Colonel Grant at the Horse Guards: 'I am staying with Li Hung Chang, trying to keep peace between China and Russia to the utmost, because war would be disastrous to China, but will not desert China in trouble; therefore, with the object of being free to act, resign commission.'[21]

Hart commented: 'From his talk and doings, I think he's a bit crazy. We must wait and see';[22] Li, however, was deeply moved, writing to his superiors in Peking: 'With a view to utilizing foreign talents, I ought to keep him here and discuss with him all relevant matters, so as to be benefited by his experience and knowledge ... Gordon is loyal and sincere at heart, unmoved by venal considerations. In times past he made illustrious records in Kiangsu and Egypt. In spite of his distinguished reputation, he is still

frugal and diligent as before, and I find him most congenial. He will do his
utmost to help us in case of an emergency. When the Russians hear about it,
our position will doubtless be strengthened. This will not hurt the general
situation. Hart is afraid of Russian anger, but I am sure that you realize that
this is only his usual attitude of timidity and caution.'[23]

Li and Gordon had a long talk, in which Gordon even touched on religion.
Whatever their past differences, they found close and affectionate
understanding, as Li spoke of his enemies at court. Li knew 'it was useless to
go to war with Russia. But, said he, "I have said as much as I dare. If I say
any more I shall probably lose my head."' Gordon assured Li that he would
advise peace yet if war came he was 'willing to go up in the grand blow up of
the magazine.'[24] Gordon commented: 'Nothing can exceed Li's kindness.
He and the Ex-Khedive are men one would willingly die for.'[25]

The *literati* of Tientsin were delighted at Gordon's arrival: 'Our deliverer is
come.'[26] They gossiped in the tea houses that the British government had
sent him, even as Wade was cabling the Foreign Office suggesting Gordon's
prosecution under the Foreign Enlistment Act unless he changed his
nationality, but the Foreign Office snubbed Wade for his presumption.[27]
Meanwhile Hart heard from his subordinate commissioner of Customs at
Tientsin, the young German Detring, a story that Li had gone in disguise to
call on Gordon at midnight, and that Gordon was telling the consuls that his
presence was 'a guarantee of peace'; Hart doubted that Gordon could
persuade the Chinese to climb down in face of Russian threats, the only way
to peace. Rumours circulated that Detring himself was urging Li to stage a
cop d'etat at Peking to dislodge those in favour of war. ('I suppose he has a
coup under consideration,' noted Hart.) Gordon had coldly returned Hart's
letters since he would not be taking his advice.[28]

On the morning of Wednesday 28 July Gordon arrived in Peking with an
interpreter supplied by Li with strict orders 'to translate every word,
pleasant or unpleasant, according to the rules of propriety or otherwise,'
when Gordon should meet the Emperor's Inner Council.[29] ('So we are
destined to see queer moves in August,' noted Hart. He added: 'Detring says
Gordon's feelings to me are not very kindly. G. thinks too highly of himself,
notwithstanding all his self-sacrifice.')[30]

Gordon stayed at a hotel in the city, not at the British Legation in order to
be independent and not to embarrass Wade, but accepted Wade's immediate

invitation to luncheon.[31] Staying at the Legation were the Honourable Thomas Grosvenor, First Secretary of the Legation (son of Lord Ebury) and his young American wife, Sophie, who was 'particularly delighted when I heard he was coming as I had never met "Chinese" Gordon before.'

'He arrived,' Sophie recalled some years later to Lady Wade (who was in England at the time) 'with his Interpreter about 12 o'clock hardly spoke at all till lunch was announced and was so anxious to get done and be off that he could hardly eat anything and long before the rest of us were finished he half rose from table and said to Sir Thomas – "Shall we go away and begin work?" Sir Thomas laughed and said something about "his friend being as impetuous as ever – but he thought they might have some coffee with Mrs. Grosvenor first", and they all Sir Thomas, Gordon, my husband and the Interpreter came into your old sitting room beyond the yellow drawing room for coffee. I can remember it all as distinctly as if it were yesterday and my disappointment at being able to get so little conversation out of the great Gordon! He was with Sir Thomas until late that afternoon, nearly dinner time in fact.'[32]

Gordon and Wade had known each other for years and Wade was one of Sir Henry Gordon's oldest friends; but the interview turned stormy. Lady Wade wrote after Sir Thomas's death, 'my husband thought it necessary to perform, as he told me, the most painful duty of his life – namely, to tell Gordon that if he led the armies of China against Russia he would fall within the penalties of the Foreign Enlistment Act, and to warn him most seriously that he might have on his conscience a war between Russia and England, which might only too probably follow. Gordon's anger at this language was great ...'[33]

'He was extremely indignant,'[34] Wade recalled to Sir Henry; and since Gordon's efforts were strongly for peace and he did not intend to enter the Chinese service,[35] he had reason to be annoyed with Wade's assumptions. Moreover Gordon thought Wade was 'in such a state of mind while I was in Peking – begged me not to let it be known, not to leave my card anywhere, I said to him, "My dear Sir Thomas Wade, what does it matter, neither you nor I will in all probability live more than 10 or 12 years longer, and what does it signify if we shorten that."'[36] (Gordon had less than five years to live and Wade fifteen).

Gordon had evidently given notice that he would undiplomatically bully the Emperor's councillors into conceding Russian demands rather than fight a war they could not win, for at dinner that night, after Gordon had left,

Wade praised him as a man and for all that he had done for China but regretted 'that in their interview that day he had been so excitable and totally impracticable.' A young Third Secretary then mentioned that when he had corrected an obvious error of grammar in a memorandum which Gordon had drafted in French, Gordon 'was very much annoyed,' which showed 'he was evidently over-tired and excited.'[37]

Gordon's state may have impaired his memory of the interview, for two months later he told Donnelly that 'Wade had strongly urged him to take up Li and turn out the wretched lot who administered affairs at Peking.'[38] Wade later publicly denied 'any idea of the kind,' and when the charge was repeated after Wade's death, Lady Wade wrote a second rebuttal to *The Times*. Yet Sir Henry Gordon told Wade in 1885 that he had a note in his brother's handwriting recording his surprise that a minister accredited by one sovereign to another should 'venture to think of such a thing. Wade said, I do not want to upset the Emperor only to get rid of the Emperor's advisers.' Any remark could have been only a throw-away in the heat of argument, for Wade seems to have been puzzled by Gordon's memory, and told Sir Henry after a night's reflection that perhaps he had said words to the effect that Li would lose his head if he tried to stage a coup.[39]

Gordon also claimed that the French minister had echoed Wade's sentiments while the German minister had even urged Gordon 'to march on Peking and depose the Emperor,' and that Gordon had replied 'that I was equal to a good deal of filibustering: but that was beyond me – and what was more, I did not think there was the slightest chance of such a project succeeding.'[40] Whatever Von Brandt's exact words, Hart noted (two days after Gordon's interview with Wade) a report from his German commissioner of customs that '*Von B* advises *Li* to "vote for peace" and to *enforce it if necessary*.'[41]

The morning after Gordon's stormy interview he went to the Tsungli Yamen, only to find that all high officials had gone to the funeral of Prince Kung's wife. He was received next day, although neither Prince Kung nor Prince Chun was present. Relying on the deep respect in which he was held, Gordon laid aside oriental courtesies and told the councillors brutally that 'they could not win a war against Russia unless they burned Peking and removed emperor and capital to some remote province,' which would be fatal to the dynasty.

'We had a long discussion. I told them it was no use, they could not make war.' The interpreter 'got into such a fright at the words I used that he upset his tea. At last he declared he could not repeat such expressions as I employed, so I took the dictionary and looked out "Idiocy" and pointed that out to them.'[42] (Wade heard that 'G went very, very savage with the Peking officials, and more than ever devoted to Li.')[43] 'They asked me what would I recommend. I said, "Make peace," and wrote out the terms. They were in 5 articles and the only one they boggled at was the fifth about indemnity. They said this was too hard and unjust. I said, That might be, but what was the use of talking like that. 'If a man demands your money or your life you have only three courses open to you, you must either fight, call for help, or give up your money.' He showed again that they could not fight and that no great power would help them against Russia.[44]

At the end of the discussion he believed that they would reject his advice, and this was their first reaction. They informed Wade that 'Gordon's visit had not been altogether satisfactory. However great might be his military ability, his knowledge of the world seemed limited. His conduct had been strange.' They were determined 'to have no more to say to him as a political adviser.' Wade commented to the Foreign Secretary in London that Gordon's mind was no longer perfectly sound. 'A long life of isolation, under circumstances well calculated to disturb coolness of head, has, I fear, told upon his reasoning powers. His nerve is perfectly unshaken, but his judgment is no longer in balance, and, if I am rightly informed, his very devoutness is dangerous; for he has taught himself to believe, more or less, that, in pursuing this course or that, he is but obeying inspiration.'[45]

To Henry Gordon, years later, Wade suggested that 'Gordon's very virtues ... were in a way responsible for his defects.' His extraordinary energy and single-mindedness had led him to great achievements in China and the Sudan, so that for 'a great portion of his middle life he was either commander-in-chief of a large irregular force, or governor of a large irregular country; wielding power almost autocratically, and necessarily acquiring day-by-day great confidence in himself; the last tendency quickened no doubt by the sincere belief that seeking counsel as he did of his God and his Bible, his judgement in all things was certain to be directed aright.'[46]

At the time, in 1880, Wade concluded that Gordon could not work with the Peking mandarins after nearly quarrelling with them. Gordon himself returned to Tientsin convinced that they would not listen to his advice and that he had better leave China. In the event, the Treaty of St. Petersburg, signed during the next February with a Chinese delegation advised by

Gordon's old comrade Sir Halliday Macartney, followed Gordon's suggestions; the Russians in return gave back most of the territory and accepted a lesser indemnity.

Not knowing that his advice would be heeded in the end, Gordon left Peking two and a half days after his arrival, having paid a brief farewell call on Wade but avoiding Hart (who had not been in the city when he had arrived). Hart was hurt: '*You* and *I* OUGHT to have met and talked.'[47]

Gordon had thought Hart to be the cause of the trouble by propping up corrupt councillors while fearing to give offence by advising concessions to Russia. On the road to Tientsin he wrote him what Hart called an 'angry letter.'

Back in Tientsin Gordon intended at first to stay for a while as Li's adviser. 'Things are in a fearful muddle,' he wrote to Charles Allen of the Anti-Slavery Society on 4 August. 'Chinese will not make up their minds to make peace. I know in the long run that war could be fatal to the dynasty, and they know it. However, I have given them a good frightening and I hope they will decide. If they make peace one may hope to get away in a few months and then for the slave trade.'[48]

A few days later he began to feel that he could do little good and that his presence, as a provocation to the Russians, might do harm. Li urged him to stay. Li ignored Hart's hint that Gordon 'though a great soldier, need not necessarily be much of a statesman'; and Li would have been unimpressed by Wade's remark which Hart recorded: 'G, he says, touching his head, is gone there'; nor would he have been bothered by Hart's second-hand comment on 10 August: 'Gordon is still at Tientsin. Very eccentric, spending hours in prayer, then acting on inspiration.'[49]

With Gordon still at Tientsin Wade remained on edge, confused by contradictory impressions. He was convinced that Gordon had hoped to lead the Chinese to war with Russia yet he reported to the Foreign Office a comment by Gordon that if no other method could frustrate the pro-war party he would 'persuade Li, if I can, to march on Peking, and assume charge as Guardian of the Emperor: of course, I do not know if he will do it.' Gordon was sure, however, that Li had neither the desire nor the means to stage a coup.[50]

Gordon declined to stay in China. He promised to return if war broke out despite their efforts, and he furnished Li with sheaves of ideas about China's future. During an affectionate farewell he refused to accept more than a third of the sum which Li offered for his expenses and trouble.

'You will like Li Hung Chang,' he wrote to Sir Samuel Baker, urging him to come out to China. 'He is a splendid Barbarian and likes to hear the truth' – 'Barbarian' being written no doubt with tongue in cheek, since Li would have used the term for Gordon and all 'foreign devils.'[51]

Before sailing from Tientsin Gordon posted a friendly letter to Wade, and another to Hart, withdrawing his 'angry' letter. Hart wrote to his London agent on 11 August: 'Gordon, poor fellow, after throwing up his commission to throw in his lot with Li, has now said good bye to Li, and is on his way home again, and after waiting to denounce me at the Legations and refusing to come near me when in Peking, has now written to withdraw his letters, as he found he was mistaken. Much as I like and respect him, I must say he is "*not all there*." Whether it is religion or vanity, or softening of the brain – I don't know, but he seems to be alternately arrogant and slavish, vain and humble, in his senses and out of them. It's a great pity.'[52]

At Shanghai Gordon received a telegram from the Horse Guards: 'Leave cancelled. Resignation not accepted. Return England forthwith.'[53] He cabled back that they might have trusted him; he was already on his way. At Aden in September he received another cable withdrawing the order to return and granting him six months' leave.

He had left Tientsin believing that he had failed to save peace, that he had lost his commission (not that he valued it) and had quarrelled with two old friends. Six months later he would know that China and Russia had signed a treaty along the lines he had suggested to an unwilling Yamen; he had received a most friendly letter from Hart, ending 'I am delighted to know your commission is safe. Of course we'll meet again!' and they were 'as fast friends as ever.'[54] When Wade returned to England on retirement Gordon was one of the first to call, and shake him warmly by the hand. They found that the Peking episode had in no way affected their friendship.[55] And when Gordon's younger friend, Reginald Brett, had opportunity to examine the Foreign Office papers he gave his opinion that Gordon's intervention in August 1880 had been the main factor for peace.[56]

CHAPTER TWENTY-TWO

Island of Distress

On 30 November 1880 Sir Charles Dilke, Under-Secretary of State at the Foreign Office, sent a memorandum across Downing Street to Number Ten with a note at the top in his own hand: 'Colonel Gordon was here to-day and left this, Mr. Gladstone.' The Prime Minister's private secretary, Edward Hamilton, studied it and attached another note: 'Memorandum of Colonel ("Chinese") Gordon on *Irish Question* sent by Sir C. Dilke,' He then summarized it under three headings on a small piece of paper and sent it in.[1]

Gordon had not expected to visit Ireland when he had left China. He had returned to Hong Kong and stayed some days with the Governor and Lady Pope-Hennessy at Mountain Lodge. Sir John later recalled how 'we wandered together in the Chinese villages at the Kowloon side of the harbour. He visited the Tung Wah Hospital to meet the committee (the leading Chinese merchants) and he earnestly supported the policy of having some of them on the Legislative Council.

'He spoke strongly against Downing Street for having so long allowed the branding, flogging and general oppression of the Chinese. He did not like the British, German and American merchants who had been permitted by an order of the Governor in Executive Council, many years before, to keep the Chinese out of the best business region of the town of Hong Kong, and who had induced the Colonial Office to sanction severe laws against the Chinese.'[2] 'This quiet unobtrusive man,' runs another Hong Kong resident's memory, 'with the light and sparkling eyes. His high ideal of life rendered him perfectly indifferent to death.'[3]

Gordon now wished to go back to the oppressed of Africa. He sent a telegram from Hong Kong to Khedive Tewfik, in Cairo, asking for a reply to meet him at Aden: 'Has slave trade in Sudan ceased, on answer depends my visit to Sultan Zanzibar.'[4] As Gordon sailed west his future was being discussed in both Zanzibar and Brussels. The Sultan wanted him, on condition that the British government would introduce and support him; King Leopold wanted him, yet reckoned that he was 'in absolute dependence on the English government,' and perhaps must take Belgian nationality before opening up the Congo. The King therefore made no offer; yet Gordon held that his earlier promise to Leopold precluded service under the Sultan. The British Consul at Zanzibar, John Kirk, believed that Gordon's rule in the interior would bring great benefits of peace and order, but the Foreign Office might not approve; when Gordon wired from Aden, Kirk sent an equivocal reply.[5]

Gordon decided to sail for England. He might then go to the Congo, or Australia or even to Borneo, he told Augusta from the ship (Rajah Brooke's second-in-command was on board), 'but God knows best. It is odd to have lived one's life out ere it is finished'. He wanted to 'leave England for good. I never could stand that country, and would never care to serve in her military service ...' The next eleven lines of the letter are scratched out beyond reclaim, probably by Augusta.[6]

He landed at Southampton on 21 October 1880, to learn that his widowed sister Etta Bayly, long subject to fits, had died three weeks before. He would stay for the present with Augusta, now left alone,[7] but went up to London for the day to report to the Horse Guards, meet Sapper friends and learn who was getting what; and then again, to call on Lady Ripon at her own behest. He called and she was 'not at home'. 'She appears to have gone out of her way to snub me but it was like water off a duck's back.'[8]

He had about fifteen months to wait before his promotion to major-general; a new Royal Warrant on pay and allowances was due in February, shortly before his leave would expire, and he decided to 'rusticate' in Ireland until the Warrant's provisions should indicate whether he might go on half pay or continue to serve during his last year as a colonel: 'I can do nothing more in England or in the East, at any rate at present,'[9] he told Waller.

He left Southampton in the first week of November, knowing from the newspapers that Ireland was gripped by agricultural distress and civil strife, with evictions by the mainly Protestant landlords and murders by the Catholic peasantry. Parnell's new Land League, aiming to give all land to the tenants and to break the rule of England, was sweeping the country, while the word 'boycott'* was just entering the language.

---

*When Captain Boycott, agent of a hated landlord was ostracized by his community.

Gordon stayed a night near Chepstow with Colonel and Mrs. Jenkins, and another near Pembroke Dock, where few were left to remember him after twenty-six years except the ferryman, who recalled his splashing across the creek, and Mrs. Kelly, widow of the parson. He landed at Cork on 13 November and took the train towards Bantry Bay, where he had an introduction to a Captain White, an old friend of Henry Gordon.

The railway went no further than Drimaleague, where the passengers transferred to horse-drawn coaches for the last eleven miles and he found himself next to an elderly gentleman who introduced himself as Mr. Payne, Lord Bantry's Agent. As they drove through the hilly countryside, sodden after two of the wettest autumns, and Gordon saw the poor farms and the cabins of the peasants and occasionally the grand house of a landlord, glimpsed through bare trees, Payne told him of bad harvests, and of the agitators who encouraged farmers and cottagers not to pay their rents. Payne as a magistrate thought Habeas Corpus should be suspended.

Gordon refused Payne's invitation to stay, nor did he call at the great Georgian mansion, with its celebrated art collection, where the seventy-nine year old Earl of Bantry lived, though Gordon had known him long ago as White-Hedges before he had succeeded his brother: their father had been raised to the peerage for defeating the French invasion of Bantry Bay in 1797.

Gordon continued his journey through the magnificent scenery of the Bay to reach Glengarriff, where Captain White lived at Coomhola Lodge. Gordon stayed at Roche's Hotel, according to his custom, but soon made friends with the Whites. Captain White, a relation of Lord Bantry, had married beneath him: his wife was not received in society but they lived happily with their boy and girl and Mrs. White's sister, Miss Dudley. Gordon made a particular friend of little Edward.

Glengarriff is one of the loveliest places in all Ireland but Gordon was appalled by the misery on the 'huge estates' like Lord Bantry's 69,000 acres. As he called at cottages or talked with passers-by he heard of raised rents which farmers could not pay in a wet year, of cruel evictions and imprisonments; and he sensed 'a gulf of hatred between landlords and tenants, far beyond the question of rents.'[10] 'I felt much for the people,' he told Colonel Jenkins, 'and did not care to accept the civilities of anyone,'[11] and never took his gun out of its case to shoot snipe. He had intended to stay in Ireland, and on 15 November had sent a postcard[12] to Augusta asking her to post him a tin of tobacco when a large order was delivered, but two days later he wrote that 'none of the Whites or Bantry people want me except Captain W. of Coomhola so I shall devote myself to looking into the state of the people.'[13]

He very quickly decided that he had heard and seen enough and that his duty was to throw his prestige into waking up public opinion and officialdom in England, and to suggest a remedy for Ireland's troubles.

He sat down in Roche's Hotel and wrote fast. He wrote his conclusions to his old friend Erskine Childers, Secretary of State for War, and to his old acquaintance Lord Northbrook, First Lord of the Admiralty, who sent him a friendly and serious reply;[14] he wrote at length to Colonel Donnelly, knowing that he would pass the letter to *The Times*; and he wrote the memorandum for the Prime Minister. His idea adapted Parnell's Land League proposal and gave it a strong moral twist. Gordon had seen little of Ireland but knew from the press, and what White had told him, that his view of conditions in Bantry was valid for all the west.

By 30 November he was back in England and calling at the Foreign Office for Dilke to forward the memorandum to Gladstone. Gordon had wasted no words, nor paused to eliminate possible exaggerations.

'The peasantry of the Northwest and Southwest of Ireland,' contended Gordon, 'are much worse off than any of the inhabitants of Bulgaria, Asia Minor, China, India or the Sudan.

'That they are a heartbroken, listless, miserable lot, without a kick in them, that they live or it may be called exist on the verge of starvation, that they are patient, and enduring of their miseries to a degree that is astonishing.

'that their present position is one that is a scandal to our country and indeed to the world's civilization.

'that an unfathomable gulf of non-sympathy separates them from their landlords to whom they are little better than serfs.

'that no hope of alleviation can be hoped for, as long as the landlords have any finger in the pie.

'that the fact of the people's misery is a fact and it is quite useless tracing it further than that the existing relation of landlord and people has produced this state of things, which is detrimental to the Unity of the Kingdom.

'So I would say:

'Be just to the landlords, and let H M G buy up their rights and make them stand aside for good and all.'[15]

Gordon proposed that the Government should set aside £80 million to buy up the landlords in the eleven worst affected counties, calculating the sum as twenty years' purchase. A Wasteland Commission should administer these counties through stipendiary magistrates brought in from outside, and the landlords should have no part in the Poor Law or in public works. The Government should set up an Emigration Commission, if necessary, and should endow a Catholic university. For the rest of Ireland, the Government should ensure what were already known as 'the three F.'s: Fixity of tenure, Fair Rents, and Free sale.'

He then made his original and strongly moral point: 'In 1833 H M G paid 20 million to enfranchise the West Indian slaves, the money was paid down, it left the kingdom, nothing was got for it except the blesssing of God, on the extinction of an iniquity. 20 million in 1833 is worth 30 million now: if the W and N W and S W of Ireland is enfranchised from misery, the lost 50 million is well spent. In this question, you must go to the root; no half measures will do, they will only embitter feelings, and will be the more serious, for the Irish people will see that all hope of the Government aiding them, is gone.'[16]

He added a postscript: 'N. B. In the whole of the speeches, letters or pamphlets published by the landlords, you may look, in vain, for one particle of sympathy shown by the landlords to the tenants. The tone breathed by the landlords, is one of hard cold selfishness, both towards the tenantry and towards their country.'

He added that this plan would detach over two million people from the agitators: 'they would have nothing more to seek from agitation.'[17]

Gordon's letter to Donnelly appeared in *The Times* a few days later, making the same points in a more literary manner, and received wide notice. *The Times* leader described it as 'the heroic method of dealing with Ireland,' and the *Pall Mall Gazette* stressed its importance in awakening the people of England to their responsibilities, while a nationalist newspaper in Dublin rejoiced that 'one of the most remarkable men of our own or any time' had reached views similar to those of the Irish Land League. A London evening paper, however, sneered that 'Colonel Gordon, having for the moment abandoned his Chinese and Egyptian friends, has turned his attention to Ireland, and in a letter published this morning gives the experience of a superficial glance at the disquieted island.'[18]

Nor was Downing Street impressed. After enquiries, Gladstone's staff decided that Gordon 'is not clothed in the rightest of minds.' His suggestion, however, was taken up in a modified form in the Irish Land Purchase Bill which became, after his death, the Conservative's Ashbourne Act of 1885.

Gordon took no further part in Irish affairs but he did not forget the friends he had made, especially little Edward White. On Christmas Eve he thanked Edward for a nicely-written note and sent him a pair of field glasses to encourage him to stay in the countryside when older. 'You are daily in my thoughts with all your family,' wrote Gordon. 'I trust God will help you and them to bear the little worries you have to undergo. He will bring good out of evil, and my dear little friend, mind he is a kind loving Father, and would love you to speak to Him in little short prayers, when you need help, which you often will do. Jesus lives in you, and is thus near, very near your little heart.'

Two Christmasses later, in another letter to 'Master Edward White' Gordon wrote: 'You may not have thought it but I assure you, my dear young friend, that I have prayed *daily* for you all, ever since I met you in Ireland, and I am much pleased at your recollecting me which however as Jesus hears us, is not wonderful when we think that *He lives in each of us.*'

And two years later again, shortly before leaving on his last journey to Khartoum, Gordon enclosed an illuminated text: 'What time I am afraid I will trust in Thee.' *Psalm 56:3*. He wrote on it: 'To my dear little brother in Christ, Edward White.'[19]

CHAPTER TWENTY-THREE
'Take, Eat'

Having abandoned Ireland Gordon sent a wire to Horace Waller inviting himself to Twywell Rectory, where he had stayed briefly in January 1877. He wanted 'to think of the things unseen,' he told Augusta.[1] He took the Midland Railway for the ninety-mile journey from Euston to the market town of Thrapston in eastern Northamptonshire, changed to the Kettering branch line and arrived at the tall Georgian sandstone rectory on 7 December 1880.

He stayed with the Wallers and their young family only three weeks and five days yet he left such a strong impression on the country people of the Nene valley that thirty-five years later a writer in *Chambers Journal* understood that 'General Gordon spent his holidays at Twywell . . . lived for long periods at Twywell, known and loved by every man, woman and child – especially by the children – in that and the adjoining villages . . . A question about the parish churches, and Gordon appeared in the replies. What about those iron-furnaces in the distance? and Gordon was in the answer.'[2]

They called him 'the little blue-eyed Colonel.' He would discuss affairs with Thomas Found the stationmaster, William Hughes the shoemaker, Aaron Percival the parish clerk of this small parish of less than a thousand acres, and five hundred souls. He was friends with the tenant farmers and the schoolmaster, yet on the days when old Mrs. Baker took in her neighbours' wet washing, straight from their coppers, he would turn her mangle. He walked the lanes and the fields to chat with the diggers at the ironstone quarries during their dinner hour, or call in at the farm labourers' cottages. Wherever he met need he would give, and on one occasion when he had walked across the shallow valley and over the river, intending to return by train (changing at Thrapston) he found he had nothing left for his fare and walked back.[3]

In the evenings he had long discussions in Waller's study, a pleasant well-proportioned room to the right of the front door. The heavily-bearded rector and the slender colonel with his small military moustache and short whiskers talked far into the night about the slave trade and about theology. Gordon had concluded that 'the female W. is more spiritual than the male, who is wrapped up, to some degree, in Church and other dogmas, which are adamant,'[4] but as they talked, Waller led Gordon to a discovery which would profoundly affect him.

Waller had noticed that Gordon's devotional life, for all its intensity and delight, did not include the Sacrament of Holy Communion. He said 'he had communicated in times gone by, but attached no importance to it.' Waller thought it 'singular' that Gordon did not hold the two Sacraments of Baptism and the Supper of the Lord 'to be part of our Saviour's working plan for establishing and maintaining His Church.'

Gordon 'gladly courted strong persuasion; I enlarged on the significance of the Jewish Passover, and pointed out the utter necessity there was of adopting the means appointed by God before Israel's deliverance, if the stroke of the destroying angel's sword was to be escaped, and showed how our Lord took the adherence to the Passover memorial on the part of the Jews as a foundation on which to build up the Holy Sacrament of His last supper.'[5]

They discussed 'fully and studiously the perplexity raised in the disciples' mind by the extraordinary announcement of Our Lord,' as recorded in the sixth chapter of St. John's gospel: 'Whoso eateth my flesh and drinketh my blood, hath eternal life; and I will raise him up at the last day ... He that eateth my flesh and drinketh my blood, dwelleth in me and I in him.'[6] As they talked, they suggested to each other that the fading out of the Passover and the 'vivid appearance of the Holy Communion' in Christ's actions and words at the Last Supper, seemed like the dissolving views at a lantern lecture, 'where one picture slowly and gradually takes the place of the other.'

That night, Gordon realized that he had missed part of Christ's plan. Early on the Sunday morning, 12 December 1880, he went to the early Celebration in the little sandstone church and communicated for the first time for many years.

He had been brought up on the tradition which took the Sacrament only four times a year, but now he wanted to communicate at every opportunity, and 'his energy and activity of brain,' said Waller, 'poured like a torrent into a new conduit,'[7] as he wrote off to Augusta and at once began work on a pamphlet, *Take, Eat*, in which he contrasted the serpent's words in the Garden of Eden which led to man's fall, with Christ's words at the Last Supper; but he emphasized that Communion in itself was not the way of salvation, but for encouragement and strength.

Christmas was now near. Gordon took the train the few miles to Thrapston and came back with a sack of toys which he carried round the cottages. He bought a Christmas tree for the school, rigged up lights and emptied more of the sack so that every child should have another present, and he joined in the decoration of the church by making devices, used for many years after, and by weaving ivy-leaf wreaths, helped by the schoolmaster's small daughter. At Communion on Christmas Day he would not sit in the rectory pew but among the ironstone labourer families.[8]

On Boxing Day, Gordon exchanged the Rectory for the Home Farm, three hundred yards away up a muddy lane, to lodge with Mr. and Mrs. Freeman. The Wallers had already invited friends or relatives; Gordon was glad to be going to Home Farm for the last ten days of his visit to avoid dinner parties and because 'W. I see takes the orthodox way, and my ideas are heretical,' besides 'I am *cold* here and rather bothered by interruptions to my work.'[9]

He transferred his boys' Bible class to the Freemans' parlour. Then came a snowfall, and a day later the carol singers, for carols were sung between Christmas and Epiphany, not in Advent before Christmas Eve. Gordon flung a half-sovereign out of the window but the children could not find it in the snow and decided to return in daylight; but a smart lad came back with a lantern and a kettle off the hob, to Gordon's amusement.

Gordon was not only working hard at his pamphlet but had entered on a fresh spiritual experience. 'Ever since the realization of the Sacrament,' he would write to Augusta five months later, 'I have been turned upside down. The process dates from the time I was at Thrapston and began the subject. I may say that I never could have thought so many holes and corners would have been searched out. Scarcely a quiet day elapses without something being brought out which I had thought did not exist.'[10]

Each time he was going to Holy Communion he 'searched out' a failure or weakness to offer as a sacrifice. He gave these the apt codename of Agag, from the king of the Amalekites in the First Book of Samuel who had been defeated, and should have been destroyed for his crimes, but was spared by Saul. When Samuel was about to carry out the sentence 'Agag came unto him delicately. And Agag said, Surely the bitterness of death is past.' Samuel hewed him in pieces before the Lord.[11]

On 4 January 1881 Gordon left Twywell, staying a few days at Thames Ditton, then taking lodgings in Victoria Grove, a little south of Kensington Gardens; later he moved to his old lodgings in Beaufort Street near Sir Henry. He began to read widely in theology; he went regularly to Holy Communion, and when Holy Week came he was 'revelling in Communions. I think more and more of the value of the Sacrament,' he told Waller. He also sat through the Three Hours service on Good Friday, finding the meditations at a high church 'very fine and very earnest and spiritual and not sensational.' He sought voluntary work in the East End slums, but when he visited a possible vicar, Harry Jones, finding Mrs. Jones 'a fine strapping woman who would eat Mrs. Waller on toast,' Gordon decided that they did not need him; he then tried the London City Mission and found 'some work at Lambeth I am glad to say.'[12]

Meanwhile he had printed *Take, Eat* at his own expense. Augusta, as always, followed where Charlie led but neither his brother Staveley nor Aunt Amy liked it and Mrs. Freese, with her Church of Ireland background, was alarmed that Gordon was teaching the Roman doctrine that the bread and wine becomes Christ's body and blood materially, not spiritually. Gordon denied this in a long involved letter: 'To a worthy receiver ... that little piece of bread, that sip of wine when taken into his body is to that body the flesh of Christ and the blood of Christ ... as far as all the effects and benefits and power which the latter have. The very fact of its being such a simple act – foolish to man, wisdom to God – shows some remarkable mystery ... The Lord's supper is His Levéee. It is there He embraces man and offers Himself to be embraced by man ... I have no time to write more. Only remember that I have never thought much of the Communion till lately and never saw its great import. It is the tree of Life ...'[13]

Olivia Freese stayed sceptical and relations between them cooled a little after they had discussed the matter at the Charing Cross station for half an hour. He felt more inclined to scoff than to be versed. 'I cannot help thinking,' he confessed to Augusta, 'I am peculiarly formed; i. e. that I am, and have been always inclined to value my opinions more than any one's else; also that I am very selfish, inasmuch as I like in a general way, and not individually ... what a frail creature I am.'[14]

Charles Watson, his young colleague in the Sudan, now a captain and in charge of stores at the India Office, before going on to win fame in Cairo a year later by his recapture of the citadel from rebels, was more discreet: he did not oppose Gordon's views on Holy Communion. Gordon admired him as 'a very quiet fellow ... a *very* clever *discreet* officer';[15] And Watson helped Gordon destroy another Agag: the temptation to rush into print on every national question. 'Yesterday afternoon, at 4.30 pm.,' Gordon told Augusta, 'Agag died very happily, he is a nice fellow but too insidious. He was *smothered*. I promised Watson not to write any more to any papers about *anything*, so that is over.' A day later, when Gordon was annoyed by some act or announcement by Gladstone's government, 'Agag came mincing but it's no use, Watson pushed him down, and he is smothered, poor fellow.'

Gordon wanted Augusta to send up another case of cigarettes. 'I am not going to put on mourning for Agag, but really I think he was not so bad, mark the past tense, for he is most assuredly dead.'[16]

Agag was not dead, although Gordon would not realize this for a month or two.

The first four months of 1881 formed the only prolonged period between 1871 and his death when Gordon was in or near London. He continued to avoid social lion hunters although, as he once remarked, 'It appears that in society if one poses as a personage one gets abused, if one avoids society, one gets the same. It makes little difference to me, for I am a strong believer in man not having any free will.'[17]

One hostess whose invitations he accepted was the philanthropist, Baroness Burdett-Coutts ('a nice old thing'). He attended a small dinner party at her home in Stratton Street soon after she had announced her surprising engagement to Ashmead Bartlett (she being aged 66 and he 27). Gordon's old friend from China, Sir Harry Parkes, now minister to Japan, was there with his daughter, and Admiral Sir Harry Keppel, who had also served in China: 'I spoke what words Christ my Saviour gave me to B. Coutts and Lady Keppel,' Gordon told Augusta.[18]

He also received an invitation to luncheon, on any day he chose, from the Poet Laureate, Alfred (not yet Lord) Tennyson in the London house he had taken for the winter. Gordon, who had enjoyed the poems in the Sudan, did not reply but arrived suddenly and asked for Tennyson's son. When assured that they were alone 'he glided spirit-like into the dining-room where we were already seated. Going straight up to my father, he said in a solemn voice: "Mr. Tennyson, I want you to do something for our young soldiers. You alone are the man who can do it. We want training-homes for them all over England."' Tennyson replied that they were already interested in a projected camp for gentlemen's sons to be prepared for the Army or the colonies. Gordon agreed to head it, if founded, provided that the sons of the poor should be admitted. After Gordon had left, Tennyson told his son that he was struck by Gordon's 'look of utter benevolence and bonhomie.'[19]

Plans for the camp were dropped when Gordon went abroad but after his death Hallam Tennyson sent Augusta an epitaph in verse which his father had written, and added: 'I am also glad to be the first to tell you that a Gordon Camp is to be founded for training poor boys for the Army ... We have felt it as a kind of legacy from him to try and establish it either at Aldershot or in some military centre;'[20] and he listed the names of the 'strong committee' which founded the Gordon Home as the national memorial.

The welfare of soldiers had already brought Gordon the friendship of Florence Nightingale. During Gordon's brief stay in England the previous spring he had called at her home in South Street, Mayfair, where she spent her days on a sofa; she was a 'permanent' invalid who planned and directed her reforms in nursing, the Army, and Indian affairs by reading and writing letters and reports, and conversing with all manner of callers.

Gordon had wished to discuss a long paper written by a cousin who was married to a Colonel Hawthorne of the Royal Engineers; it drew attention to the inefficiency and callousness of the ward male orderlies who were the only 'nurses' in most military hospitals. Miss Nighingale was unable to receive Gordon that morning but sent a kind message and when he forwarded the paper she underlined in red the words in his covering letter: '*the truest way to gain recruits to our army would be* by so remedying the defects and alleviating the sufferings of soldiers, that universally should it be acknowledged that *the soldier is cared for in every way* ... To my mind,' Gordon went on, 'it is astonishing how great people ... can remain year after year heedless of the sick and afflicted.'[21]

Miss Nightingale took up the cause. She was unable to move the War Office but the incident had led to friendship and in the early months of 1881 Gordon was several times at South Street. They discussed reforms and, no doubt, their theological opinions, for on 25 January he told her he was prepared to die, and even to forfeit 'my eternal existence' if that would 'give you and all others the sense that they are all risen in Christ even now ... Such is the love I have for my fellow creatures.'[22]

Their talk was not always on an exalted level. Once he touched on a favourite theme: 'Yesterday I saw Miss Nighingale,' he wrote to a friend, 'and said, "You and me, Miss Nightingale, are at a disadvantage in the world, we are not married, we have no looking glasses to tell us our faults."'

Miss N. looked astonished, and thought it was a proposal. What I meant was that unmarried men and women have no one who cares enough about them to say the truth.'[23]

The friend to whom Gordon wrote was Thomas Gibson Bowles, the thirty-nine year old founder-editor of *Vanity Fair*, the social and gently satirical weekly which had already become a feature of later Victorian England especially for its Men of the Day series. Each number included a full page coloured cartoon-portrait drawn by *Ape*, the Italian born artist Pellegrini, or by his more famous colleague and successor *Spy*, Sir Leslie Ward. With this gentle caricature came a page of biography and assessment in friendly criticism by *Jehu Junior*, who was Gibson Bowles himself. Each cartoon usually delighted its subject and his circle, and would be framed and hung and handed down to descendants.

Gordon appreciated *Vanity Fair* and Bowles's other magazines: 'They keep people in order, who could not be touched in any other way,' but when Bowles made an approach on Gordon's arrival home from India and China he was rebuffed: '*I do not like* to be put before the world in any way. Kindly do not put it down to pride, my refusal.' Bowles persisted; Gordon met him, was charmed by their fellow feelings on politics and imperial affairs, and agreed to be 'put before the world.'[24]

Gordon said he would neither look at the picture nor read the pen-portrait but he asked Henry to send Bowles brief notes on their family history, and offered his own of himself, guaranteeing that his friends would agree to it: 'Gifted with instinct of a woman without judgement; impulsive to the right path, or the wrong, as moved by emotions; practically, and with reason, preferring to gain the hearts of men than £'s sterling, estimating the one more worth than the other; to be trusted in some places, yet utterly untrustworthy in others, one of those inconsistent characters the world is so familiar with.'

'Now,' he ended his letter, 'that is my opinion and I ought to know best.'[25]

Bowles ignored it, and kept most of his criticism for the refusal of successive British governments to use Gordon in high command. The picture appeared on 19 February 1881 as Number 141 in the series, and the pen portrait began: '"Chinese Gordon" is the most notable of living Englishmen.' *Jehu Junior*'s long account of Gordon's life ended: '... He gave excellent counsel to the Chinese Government, returned again to England, and is now the grandest Englishman alive, and a Lieutenant-Colonel of Engineers in the English Army waiting for his promotion ...'

Bowles used 'grandest' in the Scottish sense of 'excellence,' and to make his point of neglect he ignored the fact that the lieutenant-colonel of Engineers had long been a full colonel in the Army list.

Bowles finished with a heart-felt flourish: 'Colonel Gordon is the most conscientious simple-minded and honest of men. He has a complete contempt for money, and after having again and again rejected opportunities of becoming rich beyond the dreams of avarice, he remains a poor man with nothing in the world but his sword and his honour. The official mind, being incapable of understanding this, regards it as a sign of madness. And as it is found that besides being utterly without greed he is also entirely without vanity or self-assertion, he is set down by the officials as being "cracky" and unsafe to employ in comparison with such great men as Lord Chelmsford, Sir Garnet Wolseley, and Sir George Colley' (who a week later was defeated and killed at Majuba through his own fault).

'He is very modest and very gentle, yet full of enthusiasm for what he holds to be right. This enthusiasm often leads him to interfere in matters which he does not understand, and to make in haste statements he has to correct at leisure. But he is a fine noble, knightly gentleman, such as is found but once in many generations.'[26]

The Army and Navy Gazette gave 'every praise to the pen-and-ink sketch of the man,' but was appalled by *Ape*'s picture; 'a more feeble, drivelling, semi-idiotic personage could not be imagined, or anyone more unlike "Charley Gordon."'[27] Gordon had taken the trouble to draw a sketch to show Pellegrini how his orders and decorations should appear, though he disliked wearing them. He had also asked Augusta to provide a photograph, but no photograph came near the truth, in the opinion of Demetrius Boulger, then a young journalist on *The Times*, who had written a *History of China* which earned him Gordon's acquaintance at this time; later he over-edited Gordon's letters and produced a ponderous official biography. Boulger contended that in photographs Gordon looked robust but in the flesh fragile, despite his powers of physical endurance, and that the impression of fragility was 'heightened by the exceedingly gentle and benevolent expression of his light blue eyes, which lit up his otherwise plain and ascetic features, and which seemed to change with every emotion of his active mind. He was brisk in all his movements, had a difficulty in remaining still, and like a thoroughly wound-up racehorse seemed anxious to be off at an instant's notice to carry out the great projects of every kind which constantly passed through his mind for the honour and greatness of

England, and the amelioration of the people in China, Egypt, and wherever his varied services had given him an interest in the soil.'[28]

Gordon gave two sittings to Pellegrini, and laughed that 'Ape' thought him 'all eyes'. Gordon talked much of the things of God as he saw them, which perhaps distracted the presumably Roman Catholic Italian. In the end he drew Gordon as he had seen him from the window walking along Mortimer Street to the studio, an enormous cigarette in his hand, in top hat and frock coat shown smarter than they were: George Curzon, the future Viceroy and Foreign Secretary, then an Oxford undergraduate, was introduced to Gordon as he walked along Pall Mall, and though profoundly impressed by their conversation he noted Gordon's 'seedy black frock coat, trousers that did not come down to the boots, and a very dilapidated black silk topper with a particularly narrow brim and silk mostly brushed the wrong way.'[29] In the cartoon his head was accurately shown bent forward, a tendency which Gordon believed to be caused by his *angina pectoris*: he looked deep in thought, and his eyes were the most prominent feature of his face.

One reader of *Vanity Fair* was Reginald Brett, elder son of the Master of the Rolls who would become Viscount Esher, and brother of Eugene, Gordon's young friend on the voyage to India. Brett thought the cartoon indeed captured Gordon, as he glimpsed him walking up Tilney Street in Mayfair to spend yet another hour in Brett's home, eagerly discussing the issues of the day: 'He would generally come in the morning, a queer figure, with a loose comforter round his throat, and a hat – by no means a good one – tilted back on his head; the eternal cigarette between his lips. He was of small stature – very small, like so many great men – and of spare figure. He would have passed unnoticed anywhere, except for his eyes, which were of that peculiar steel-like blue common to enthusiastic natures, more especially when the enthusiast is a soldier. He would lounge into the library, and stand – for he hardly ever cared to sit – for hours at a time, leaning against the mantelpiece, or walking up and down the room.'[30]

Regy Brett was then aged twenty-eight. Being Parliamentary Private Secretary to Lord Hartington, Secretary of State for India, he had met Gordon before Ripon's voyage, and a call followed naturally on Gordon's return.

As the second Viscount Esher, Brett would become a close friend of

Edward VII and an important if enigmatic figure behind the scenes of Edwardian politics, and chairman of the Esher Committee which reorganized the Army. In this winter of 1880–81 his private secretaryship left him plenty of leisure when the House was not sitting and he welcomed Gordon's visits. 'From no one I have ever known have I learnt more of what is best worth knowing, than from your brother,' he wrote to Sir Henry after Gordon's death.[31]

'His talk,' he recalled many years later, 'was as fresh as a spring morning, full of humour, and his language as simple as the book of Genesis. Complexity of thought, confusion of ideas, prolixity of speech, were impossible to him. He saw with wonderful clearness, perhaps sometimes not very far.

'He detested cant, and although he could be strangely indignant, and was deeply roused by faithlessness, his charity knew no bounds. Repentance made up, in his eyes, for every crime. Hence his judgement of men was variable and often appeared inconsistent. Although it occasionally amused him to be deceived, he was rarely taken in. His religion was never obtruded, but it was as much part of his daily life as smoking cigarettes. He literally walked with God, and if it were not disrespectful, one might almost say arm in arm with Him.'[32] (Gordon had remarked one day that he believed in the God of Abraham 'and as I came to your house He walked with me arm in arm up South Audley Street.')[33]

Brett and Gordon had much discussion on Indian affairs. Gordon particularly deplored the inflated salaries of senior British officials and soldiers, which had been reasonable in early days but were no longer necessary. 'I would not alter the pay of private soldier (*sic*) in India, of European Regts; all other ranks I would, I should make an onslaught on the Doctors etc. etc. etc. ... The cutting down must be done from home, in conjunction with Baring. Even Baring could not stand up against the Indian Howl if it was known he was working it.'[34]

Gordon, a 'rigid economist' as Brett found, strongly supported the efforts of Baring, whom Ripon had appointed to his Council on Gordon's recommendation. Gordon set out his views in a long letter to Brett and turned it into a pamphlet. The *Morning Advertiser*, remarking that the 'English people are always interested in everything said and done by Colonel Charles Gordon, R. E.,' commented: 'There is no doubt, whatever may be the faults and flaws in his privately printed pamphlet, Colonel Gordon is right in the main ... and all unnecessary expenditure of public money is extravagance.'[35]

Gordon put to Regy Brett on 1 March 1881 that he and other rising politicians, the future 'successors of Gladstone etc.', should 'form some sort of community, and acquainting yourselves with all the ins and outs of our relations with our colonies and Foreign powers prepare yourselves for the mantles of those now in office,' whom he considered a lacklustre 'hand to mouth set', dominated by their officials.

Instead of dinner parties and treats Brett and his friends should work at this. 'Six united men with honest intentions would carry enormous weight; there is no doubt, but that in the recess, you must not go to Scotland etc. to shoot, but must go to the Colonies etc. I would have a regular dept for each man, and a president, and no needy man should be engaged.'[36]

Five days later Brett replied: 'I have thought well over your scheme and I have mentioned it to one person, an old friend and a member of the H of Commons. I have arranged that we will try and find one more who could be trusted,and we will then give your plan a trial, and if it is found possible to work it quietly and usefully we would enlist another recruit and so on.' Brett ended: 'Although not very sanguine about its success I think this plan if followed conscientiously would keep a few of us from "drifting" and would add something to the store of knowledge which in the hands of honest men is their title to govern.'[37]

Regy Brett did not, however, visit the colonies: he preferred racing at Newmarket; but his friend Albert Grey, afterwards fourth Earl Grey, was impressed by Gordon's idea, which was one of the spurs which set Grey on his career as a colonial pioneer and, later, as Governor-General of Canada.

Brett admired all that he heard of Gordon's work among the poor, and rejected hints from some who did not know Gordon that his concern for the boys of Gravesend had not been pure. Brett was a good judge for he seems to have been bi-sexual, later falling in love with one of his own sons, although probably without physical action. And when Lytton Strachey in 1918 portrayed Gordon as addicted to drink, Regy was outraged: 'It is an absolute lie that Gordon drank!' he wrote to Sir Philip Sassoon.[38]

As winter turned to the spring of 1881 Gordon was still on leave, unclear about his future.

The past was not forgotten. He had been down to Gravesend and had come back with empty pockets so that he told Penman in March that he could not afford to return for the Ragged School celebration; but 'since I left I have daily been in spirit with you and others I knew there wherever I have been.'[39] He asked Augusta to give the School his captured Taiping flags.

He was always happy to meet brother Sappers. Contrary to suggestions in later biographies his relations with the Corps were excellent. Colonel Fitzroy Somerset, ten years older than Gordon, told Sir Henry in 1885 of the 'affection and esteem felt for your brother Charley by all his brother officers ... He and I have been friends for years, and I have always had the greatest admiration of his deeds of valour, of his integrity and modesty.'[40]

One of Gordon's Crimea pals, James Browne, was now Commandant of the Royal Military Academy at Woolwich. 'Charlie often visited me here,' General Browne told Sir Henry some months after Gordon's death, adding a touching story: 'Over my own little sitting room chimney piece were 3 engravings, beautiful ones too of undressed women, really works of art in every respect, two by Trigres, one by Lefèvre. He said you ought not to have these here – you would not allow a cadet to have them in his room (Well, I think I should allow a cadet to have them, but I said nothing.) The day I head of the poor chap's death I sent the 3 upstairs.'[41]

The Sudan was never far from Gordon's mind, and he was bitterly upset by a letter from Gessi showing that all their efforts to suppress the Slave Trade had been undone by the Egyptian rulers in Khartoum. He worked closely with Waller, Allen and the Anti-Slavery Society, but when Sir Henry wanted Judge Scott, who had forwarded Gordon's Sudan letters to Augusta and had used them for articles in *The Times*, to edit extracts for publication he was indifferent: 'I do not care a jot about whether the book comes out or not, you may do as you like,'[42] he told Henry. (Sir) John Scott, as a paid official in the Egyptian service, then decided that he should not edit letters which criticized the Egyptian government and handed on the task to his brother-in-law, Dr. George Birkbeck Hill, a retired schoolmaster who had written the Life of his uncle, Sir Rowland Hill, originator of the Penny Post, and would later edit a new edition of Boswell's Johnson.

Gordon stood aloof, except to provide maps and a six-page note of his aims in the Sudan,[43] and to insist that there should be no praise or blame of himself or anyone else. He sent replies to a few queries but refused to read the proofs; and thereby prepared a small rod for his own back since Chaillé-Long, when *Colonel Gordon in Central Africa* was published in the summer of 1881 after Gordon had left England again, easily recognized himself as the name behind the — of a highly critical remark. Long turned against

Gordon, whom he had previously fawned upon, and denigrated him to whoever would listen or read.

When Birkbeck Hill was writing his preface in April Gordon had still not decided where to spend his remaining year as a colonel. He did not wish to retire and become a slum worker. As he told the young Scottish aristocrat, Ion Keith-Falconer, then a Cambridge undergraduate, 'secular and religious work, running side by side ... is the proper work for man.'[44] Florence Nightingale urged him to go to India but he replied on 25 April that his public life was over because he could 'never aspire to or seek employment where one's voice must be stilled to one particular note,' and he would not accept the shibboleth of the Indian or Colonial official classes: 'To me, they are utterly wrong in the government of the subject races. They know nothing of the hearts of these people, and oil and water would as soon mix as the two races.'[44] However, the so-called Gun War had broken out in Basutoland. He cabled the Cape Colony government, whose invitation to a command he had refused in 1880, offering his services. The Cape sent no reply.

He had long wanted to spend a year in the Holy Land, then a somewhat barren and under-populated part of the Turkish province of Syria, where he could explore the sacred sites and meditate in quiet, and where 'small means may do much good.' He decided that the time had come. The news got about. 'Is it true that you are going to Syria,' wrote one friend on 28 April. 'Why can't you settle down and give us the benefit of your society and counsel?'[45]

Then a letter from his old friend 'Elphin' changed the course of his life.

CHAPTER TWENTY-FOUR
Gordon's Eden

Aldershot 1 May 'My dear Charlie I heard yesterday from Cooke to say I was next on the roster for Mauritius. It is the first I heard of it and it has quite taken me aback ... It is quite impossible for me to start abroad.'

Colonel Sir Howard Elphinstone, V. C., had continued as Comptroller to the Duke of Connaught; and Mauritius, an over-crowded mountainous island in the Indian Ocean, about the size of the Isle of Wight, with one mail steamer a month and no cable, was as remote as could be from Osborne and Windsor. But Cooke had thought: 'it is worth while your asking Charlie Gordon whether he would go as your substitute;' so Elphin continued: 'You and I are sufficiently old friends that you will not take it amiss my asking you about this.'[1]

Elphinstone sent the letter by hand to Southampton on Sunday 1 May. That night Gordon telegraphed acceptance, provided he might refuse the quite high sum which Elphinstone should pay, by law, to his exchange. Elphinstone hurried to the Horse Guards on Monday to complete the formalities and wrote from Buckingham Palace to Gordon that evening that the Duke of Cambridge 'seemed very glad to hear that you were going to rejoin and do regular R. E. work.'[2] Next day the Queen received a note which ended her sudden worry over Prince Arthur: 'Lt-General Sir Henry Ponsonby presents his humble duty to Your Majesty. Sir Howard Elphinstone has found an Engineer officer Colonel Gordon ("Chinese Gordon") to take his place at the Mauritius, so that he now remains at Aldershot.'[3]

Gordon was thrown into depression by the thought of exile to Mauritius, so readily accepted to help an old friend. In a few days he crossed to Le Havre to place an eighteen-year-old nephew, the late Frederick's boy, in a mercantile house. Herbert had already roughed it in a sailing vessel to China and had a good character, but possibly a quick temper since his uncle nicknamed him 'the porcupine';[4] later he became a schoolmaster in Marseilles. Gordon stayed on, awaiting the Messageries Maritime steamer which served Mauritius, and the depression lifted 'through His mercy and I feel quite content about it.'[5] Then he learned from a letter forwarded by Henry that Romolo Gessi had died in the French hospital at Suez on 30 April.

Gessi had suffered dreadfully when his Nile convoy, returning from his governorship in the Southern Sudan, had been marooned in the Sudd. The Egyptian authorities had been so slow to respond that some four hundred of his men had died of starvation or cannibalism. 'A mere skeleton and broken in spirit he had reached Khartoum and Suakin but the heat of the Red Sea had tried him a good deal,' wrote his friend Count Louis Perinazzery, and neither medical help nor devoted friendship could save him. He had received a letter and enclosures from Gordon in April and 'was very much pleased with them and hoped he could answer them himself. With poor Gessi disappears all the filantropical (*sic*) work you (?)tried in Sudan. He was the only obstacle to the slave trade and to the return of ancient abuses.' The Egyptian Governor-General and his cronies 'will have a fine time ruining the country.'[6]

'Gessi!' mourned Gordon, 'Gessi! Gessi! how I warned him to leave with me! when at Toashia how I said, "Whether you like it or not, or whether I like it or not, your life is bound up with mine!" He knew me to the depths. I almost feared this in one way. However, Gessi is at rest. It is God's will.'[7]

Meanwhile Gordon was continuing the spiritual saga begun at Twywell in December. 'I cannot help going on about the Eucharist,' he wrote to Augusta from Le Havre. He called it a 'deadly weapon against envy, malice and uncharitableness, it is a love phitre for one's enemies ... The more frequently one communicates the more one realizes fresh depths in it. *It is not a question* of *Salvation*: that thank God, is long past, but it is a question of *Sanctification* in the flesh. I look on salvation as a finished work, but sanctification is a progressive.'

Then he told her how he had examined his life: 'I used to wander, as it were, through my heart, finding nice walks and splendid palaces, in which I reposed. Then came the downfall of my Egyptian palace; it was mouldy, faded and despicable; motives were discovered to be wholly earthly, and I turned from the ruins with disgust. Then I wandered into the last-visit-to-China palace, and it was splendid. However, only two or three days and that appeared tattered and mildewed, so I have no pleasure in that ruin.'[8]

And now, on 18 May 1880, at Hotel d'Europe, Le Havre, he reported an even greater sacrifice: 'Then came the smoking and drinking which I former (sic) enjoyed. I have to-day smitten that immense serpent, a yellow brindled one, and for months no spirits at all, and only 15 cigarettes a day. Terrible trouble with that snake, however there is the pledge for 6 months with trust for strength to keep it, in my diary.'[9]

Early on 24 June 1881 the French mail steamer *Godavery* dropped anchor in the fine harbour of Port Louis, capital of Mauritius, with its picturesque backdrop of hills. An hour or two later Lieutenant E. J. S. Boyce, the young acting Commander Royal Engineers, was sitting in his office at the Barracks when there entered 'a smallish man in mufti looking as if he had just stepped off Piccadilly.' He introduced himself as Colonel Gordon come to take over the command, which had been vacated some months before by Colonel Barry. Boyce had received no warning, and neither the new arrival himself nor a hunt in the Army List gave a clue as to which of several Colonel Gordons this might be, 'and I am sure,' recalled another officer, 'that it was several days before anyone on the Island knew that we were entertaining unawares the famous "Chinese" Gordon.'[10]

Mrs. Murray, wife of the elderly General, wrote to Gordon at once but he declined their 'great kindness in asking me to stay. I fear I am incorrigible in that respect, I have lived the life of a recluse for years and after nearly 50 one's habits are difficult to change.' He had obtained a furnished house 'and hope to get into it on Monday.'[11]

As soon as he had settled in the house, he unrolled the map of the world on which he still kept the little flags which showed the movements, inevitably much out of date, of his Gravesend 'Wangs' who had gone to sea, now men in their twenties.[12]

· He messed with the officers of the three companies of the 58th Regiment (2nd Battalion Northamptonshires) and the few Sapper and Gunner officers. The 58th had been thinned out by the Zulu war of '79 and the disastrous First Boer War of February '81: with the exception of Major Buchanan. 'We were all boys,' recalled C. M. O'Donel nearly fifty years later. 'Gordon took to us as if he belonged to the regiment.' The young officers found that Gordon was most energetic in his duties but off duty he was 'simplicity itself and with a sense of fun that was boyish,' continued

O'Donel. 'Living quarters were in a house outside the barracks, and he liked to have one or more of us there after dinner where we would spend hours talking and listening. But Gordon listened more than he talked. On these occasions he smoked cigarettes of a calibre such as I have never seen before or since and sipped at intervals at a long "peg". His talk was never about his own achievements. I remember once remarking, in the hope of leading him on, that the Soudan must be a tough country to campaign in. He said, "It's a question of water. You fight to get possession of a well, and then you fight again to hold it." That is as near as he ever came in my hearing to saying anything about his life which had been so full of adventure.'

When one of the subalterns wanted more knowledge of military topography Gordon undertook to instruct him in the use of the plane table. 'I can see them both now,' recalled O'Donel, 'out on the barrack square with its well-kept walks and big shade trees, Gordon in a black morning coat and tall hat, demonstrating rapidly, then picking up the table and moving at a trot to the next station, our man sweltering behind him. Then Gordon, having imparted the lesson for the day, would dash into his office as if the safety of the Island depended on his speed.'[13]

The subalterns did not like to ask why he wore London clothes in the tropics. Mauritius seemed 'pleasant' to Gordon after Sudanese deserts but when the hot weather was coming he noticed that the men of the 58th had been sent without tropical kit. War Office permission and payment would have taken months, so he ordered cotton uniform for them all and paid the bill himself.

An elderly naval sloop, H. M. S. *Fawn*, lay in Port Louis harbour for some weeks: a screw-driven steamship with auxiliary sails and yellow and black wooden hull. Captain Pelham Aldrich and his crew soon met Gordon, 'and we had the good luck to get on most friendly terms with him,' recalled Herbert Purey-Cust, son of the Dean of York. Cust, a future admiral, was then a lieutenant of twenty-four. 'Gordon always shunned the gaieties of society,' continued Cust, 'but what he delighted in was to get together a party of young fellows and make long expeditions on foot or by rail or road to places of historical interest, of which there were many in the island. He always ran the show himself and drew up elaborate route orders of times and places, and even details of health precautions to be taken, such as where overcoats and changes of socks should be left in the morning and be picked up on the way back in the evening, though he personally always contented himself with an old black morning-coat and a pot hat!'[14]

Gordon had a reason for the expeditions: the War Office had commissioned him to report on the defences of the Island and its dependencies. Before he had arrived he had urged Brett and others not to neglect Mauritius, which had seemed to lose its strategic importance as a coaling station with the opening of the Suez Canal: he pointed out that the Canal could be blocked up by an enemy, as indeed happened seventy-five years later. He soon saw that 'this place is utterly without defence,' as he wrote to Elphinstone in a long letter written soon after his arrival.

'My dear Elphin,' he wrote, 'It is only fair to let you know what you escaped. They say that HRH, in one of his furies with someone, said to the Adjutant General: "Send him to Hell". That the Adjutant General said, "we have no station there, your Royal Highness"; on which HRH said "send him to Mauritius". There is an old Major-General here, 70 in October. The Procureur-General died the other day of abscess on the liver; White, the Paymaster died yesterday, both were taken ill just as I came here; at the funeral of White, no arrangements, all higgledy-piggledy – General with cocked hat on backwards, etc., etc. (I thought the RE were the only people who did these things). A Colonel RE here is a farce, there is three quarters of a battery, three Coys of the 58th Regt. and five Sappers! There is a Colonel RA also.

'My arrival was a sort of thunderbolt among them and still more as I persisted in going to a hotel. The General's wife is a dragon.

'This place is utterly without defence ...' He had put up a preliminary report 'but I suppose it will be considered facetious.' (It was not: the Governor, Napier Broome, promptly set up a committee under Gordon's chairmanship.) 'If,' Gordon continued to Elphinstone, 'you want to find a place where things have been let go to sleep, I recommend you to try Mauritius.'[15] Gordon later told Henry, ex-head of Ordnance, that 'the only place or Dept. I have not found sunk in the deepest of slumber is the Ordnance Store Dept.,' under an official who was 'a rarity, he has shown such zeal, when no inducement existed to do so.' Gordon hoped the man would soon be sent to a more important station than this 'poor decaying place.'[16]

The larger proportion of whites in Mauritius were French-speaking Roman Catholics, but Indians now formed the majority race, having been brought in as indentured coolies on the sugar plantations on the ending of African slavery. The Bishop of Mauritius, Peter Royston, had been a C. M. S. Missionary in South India. The Bishop and Gordon became warm friends, despite Gordon's hasty criticism, later retracted, that the missionaries lived too comfortably; and the two would meet for Bible study in the vestry of St. James's Cathedral, a former powder-magazine, now topped with a spire and a tower.[17] Their discussions must have been lively as Gordon's religious views were soon reported to be 'cranky'. He worshipped in the Cathedral, although disapproving when the clergy administered the Sacrament in buff boots. On ceremonial occasions, when he must wear full dress, he would hold his hat in front of his dazzling array of medals. He usually sat at the back among native Mauritians but sometimes shared the fifth pew of the South transept with John Ackroyd, a magistrate a year younger than himself, who noticed 'When he knelt in prayer he rested his arm on the front of the pew, that it shook with his strong emotion.'[18]

Gordon found a small Chinese community. The leaders were delighted when he left his large red visiting card upon them, with his Chinese name in gold letters. Very soon he had started a Bible reading for Chinese which became so popular that it had to move to larger premises three times. He also visited the Indian camps with an Immigration official, Owen O'Connor, who shared his love of Thomas à Kempis.[19]

Gordon quickly won the hearts of Mauritians of all races, and the British officials and traders looked on him as an endearing mixture of efficiency, benevolence, faith and eccentricity: the story went that once when he took a hired carriage to visit a family the driver looked so astonished at his tip that they made enquiries and found that Gordon had given his entire quarterly salary, just received. As this would have been £295, paid through his bank, not in cash, the story is surely apocryphal, if in character.[20]

The Crown Colony of Mauritius in 1881 included the neglected Seychelles archipelago, 934 miles to the northwest on the mail steamers' route. Soon after Gordon had arrived at Port Louis a despatch came from home, ordering him and the senior naval officer to report on the Seychelles defences.

Gordon leaped at the opportunity. He had heard about a mysterious tree, known colloquially as the Coco de Mer, which grew wild in only one place on earth: a valley in the beautiful and fertile Island of Praslin, second largest of the Seychelles but only eight miles long. The fruit of the tree was shaped in such a way that he wondered if it could be the tree of the knowledge of good and evil which had stood in the Garden of Eden.

As an Engineer and a believer Gordon never held that Science need conflict with Religion. He had become friends with T. H. Huxley, who said of Gordon: 'Of all the people whom I have met in my life, he and Darwin are the two in whom I have found something bigger than ordinary humanity – an unequalled simplicty and directness of purpose – a sublime unselfishness.'[21] Gordon had not been dismayed when Darwin's theory of the origin of species seemed to destroy the early chapters of Genesis, and he was inclined to Charles Watson's view that man had existed, 'formed of the dust of the ground,' as in Genesis, Chapter Two, before God 'breathed into his nostrils the breath of life, and man became a living soul.' Gordon had hoped he might have found the site of the Garden of Eden in Africa, and now he might discover it in the Seychelles.[22]

He sailed in September, taking two boys, Frank and James Brodie, sons of his near neighbours on the Champs de Mars in Port Louis. At Port Victoria on Mahé, the principal island, they stayed with the acting Chief Civil Commissioner, Cockburn Stewart. Gordon walked and sailed about the mountainous island, with its forests of palm trees sweeping down to the sea. He decided swiftly that to strengthen the land defences would be absurd; the islands could only be protected by sea power. He was then ready to explore Praslin. With Stewart, the Brodie boys and some others he started early and sailed the twenty-six miles between the islands. As they neared the white beaches, edged with forests of palm trees and backed by rounded, sandy-coloured mountains, the beauty was entrancing. They entered the coral reef and landed, and began the walk to the valley of the Coco-de-Mer, first along the coast and then up the mountain. At one point they had to cross a stream. Gordon, recalled Frank Brodie, 'took off his boots and socks, tucked up his trousers and carried me over his back – he then showed me a faint scar of where a bullet had entered his knee during the Chinese campaign.'[23]

They passed through a tropical jungle which blotted out the sun: then the trees thinned and soon they were standing on the slopes of the beautiful Vallée de Mai, awed by the magnificence of the *Lodoicea Sechellarum* trees which were a hundred feet tall. High up on the trees hung the huge fruit, which take seven years to ripen: the double coconuts which had been washed upon distant shores and thus called Coco de Mer. When he examined the male and female trees and the heavy fruit he was sure he must be near Eden. With his love of the Old Testament in which shapes and objects, such as the design or furniture of the Temple, are given mystic meaning as 'types' of spiritual truth, the shape of this unique fruit looked to him extraordinarily apt. As he described it, accurately, to (Sir) William Thiselton-Dyer, then assistant director of the Royal Botanic Gardens at Kew: 'The fruit is shaped like the human heart, the bud or stem which attaches it to the branch like the male organ of generation. When the husk is taken off, the inner double nut is like the belly or thigh of a woman.' He gave more detail and concluded: 'In a word, its lines are those of the male and female organs of generation, and it is a fruit which cannot fail to attract attention by any one seeing it.' Gordon secured a good specimen of the fruit, which he gave to Kew; he drew accurate pictures and later made a model, also now at Kew.[24]

The fruit hung too high for a woman to reach ('she took of the fruit thereof, and did eat') but 'oddly enough,' as Gordon remarked to Dyer, Praslin island had its very own serpent, three feet long, and not found elsewhere. Gordon drew a picture of the serpent shinning up the tall palm tree to fetch the fruit. Furthermore the humble bread-fruit trees grew nearby and could be the tree of life.

By now the party were very hungry as Stewart had forgotten to bring any food (Frank Brodie unfairly blames Gordon but Stewart was host) and they returned to Mahé famished. Gordon was now most excited but had to postpone further research because they found that the mail steamer was in quarantine owing to cholera in Aden and on reaching Mauritius they had to stay three weeks on Flat Island.

Frank Brodie, Gordon and the director of railways shared a room with only two beds. Gordon insisted that Frank have the bed and he a mattress on the floor. 'He used to go out at about 4 o'clock in the morning by way of the window (our room opened on to the dining-room in which about half a dozen people slept during the night) to some quiet place to say his prayers, &c.' recalled Brodie. 'He was religious, but he never paraded the fact, quick-tempered but with a good hold over himself. Very kind-hearted to children, always had a lot of small change in his pockets for them. He had a very winning smile, and always seemed cheerful.'[25]

Back in Mauritius at last, Gordon had much discussion and correspondence with William Scott, director of the Royal Botanic Gardens at Pamplemousse. He also pored over maps, ocean charts and the Bible and concluded that the Garden of Eden, now submerged, lay close to Praslin. 'I found I think Eden in the Seychelles Isles,' he wrote to Colonel Jenkins as to many others, 'and the two trees of life and knowledge, both very wonderful, the latter is only found in Seychelles throughout the world, it is the most curious tree you ever saw, or thought of, and is full of types, so the other is, but this is a humble tree and would be passed by a non-observer. The Four Rivers flowed *into* Eden so I believe the text will allow, and the Indian ocean was once a continent before flood.'[26] He sketched a map to prove his point.

Fashionable scientists were not likely to accept Gordon's theory. They rejected the Garden and the Fall as unhistorical. Unable to foresee the next century, they believed that man was on an upward march to perfection. Nor was the theory accepted by Biblical scholars.

Apart from giving unending interest to Gordon, his discoveries had one important effect, for the Governor wrote to the Colonial Secretary, Lord Kimberley, suggesting that a learned society raise the sum 'for which the Coco-de-Mer Valley in possession of the old Scotch sailor Campbell might be bought. I may mention that a well-known and very gifted officer of Her Majesty's Service, who lately visited Seychelles, has elaborated a theory by which the island of Praslin is very pleasantly shown to have been the Garden of Eden ...' Broome described the palm to Kimberley and asked that steps be taken to preserve it from destruction 'for the mere sake of the straw now obtained from it'.[27]

Dyer and Sir Joseph Hooker, Director of Kew, had already been alerted by Gordon. A Mr. Button was made supervisor of government lands in Seychelles. And when, nearly a hundred years later, Seychelles became a tourist attraction for its beauty and climate, the islands promoted themselves as 'General Gordon's Garden of Eden.'*

'Gordon's memorandum on the defence of Mahé, Seychelles, is an extremely able document and shows his rapid grasp of a subject,'[28] noted Sir Hesketh Bell after studying it in the Book of Confidential Despatches. Bell was Governor of Mauritius from 1915–24 and had always been interested in Gordon. 'I came upon many traces of Gordon's work there, and, in the confidential files at Government House, found several remarkably interesting papers typical of his extraordinary vigour of mind and peculiarity of temperament.'[29] Gordon had recommended drastic changes, including the separation of the Seychelles into a separate colony. The Colonial Office took

---

*A fine specimen of Coco de Mer fruit is displayed at the entrance of the Paris Natural History Museum.

twenty-three years to agree. He also examined the whole question of Empire defence, from the Mediterranean to Borneo.

Meanwhile he had kept his pledge. 'Spirits are knocked on the head altogether,' he told Augusta, 'to my great gain. I think they are a deadly poison to the soul.'[30] On 18 November his six months' period of abstinence ended. After ten days he renewed it for another six months, 'but it did not do. I was always open to attack on that flank and was praying for strength against it.' At early Communion on Christmas Day he 'took up a sacrifice, one of the children of Anak ... so to-day I have given it up altogether, and mean DV to take no wine at all.'[31]

Whatever Gordon might feel, his friends and neighbours in Mauritius regarded him as 'a very temperate man – any report to the contrary is not true. All the time I knew him,' recalled Ackroyd, 'I never saw him in the least affected by indulgence in wine or spirits: in fact I never saw him take anything but a little claret or Sauterne and never any strong spirit.'[32] The 'peg' which Gordon sipped when chatting with the young officers in his own house was of brandy, O'Donel recalled, not whisky, which was then just coming into favour in the tropics; but possibly Gordon had his servant put in a drop of brandy to colour the soda water for politeness sake, for Gordon did not parade his abstinence.

When Harold Nicolson in a broadcast in 1931, enlarging on Strachey, pilloried Gordon as addicted to secret drinking, Sir Hesketh Bell made public and private enquiries of survivors from the Mauritius of 1881–2.

Their verdict, like Ackroyd's, was unequivocal. Archdeacon Buswell 'assured me that Gordon, far from being an intemperate man, was very abstemious. They had been close friends all the time that Gordon was in the island, and he would certainly have known if Gordon was a "secret drinker".'[33] And a retired officer, G. R. Grier, sent the *Sunday Times* his memory of Gordon in Mauritius 'as always smiling and cheerful, full of energy and vitality. I feel sure that to anyone knowing him at that time the statement that he was given to secret drinking would have appeared ridiculous. If he had been subject to this habit it would certainly have been known. Nothing of daily household life could be kept secret from the many Indian native servants to be found in almost every house out there.'[34]

Even stronger evidence came from the son of O'Connor, assistant chief of police, who had become a particular friend when Gordon discovered him to be a fellow-enthusiast for Thomas à Kempis. They would go for long walks together on Sundays. 'I remember distinctly,' wrote J. R. O'Connor, 'my father telling us many a time, General Gordon's dislike for anything which savoured of spirits or wine, how he used to upbraid Charles Bruce for drinking brandy at his meals and how he used to sermonize the Irish priests, whom he met at my father's table, for indulging too freely in whisky and wine whilst he only drank cold coffee or lime juice most of the time. Another favourite drink was the milk from the coco-nut.'[35]

On 24 January 1882 General Murray and his wife left the island and Gordon became acting Commander of the Forces and ex-officio Member of the Legislative Council, 'a most fortunate circumstance for our colony,' wrote *The Mercantile Record and Commercial Gazette*, 'that it should possess in the midst, and forming part of its administration, so high and remarkable a man as Colonel Gordon.'

Gordon at once used his influence to strengthen the national movement and help persuade the Colonial Office towards revising the Island's antiquated constitution. He would have refused the permanent command. Although writing to a friend in early February that 'this place is a very nice one and I am quite glad I came here,' he was longing to go to Palestine.[36]

On 10 March the *Mercantile Record* was 'extremely sorry to hear that the Hon. Colonel Gordon will be shortly replaced ... It is not often that persons so remarkable as he come to Mauritius. The Government should beg of the Colonial Minister that the Colonel may remain in Mauritius.'

Early on 1 April the monthly mail steamed into Port Louis harbour, carrying not only a large number of letters for Gordon and his usual stack of London newspapers but three official cables. One gave news of his promotion to major-general, effective 6 April.* This implied, in the usual way, that he would be on half-pay, available for recall if required. But another telegram, dated London, 28 February, cabled via Durban, re-routed via Aden to catch the steamer, stated that the new government of Cape Colony had asked for his services 'should he be willing to renew the offer made to their predecessors in April 1881 "to assist in terminating the war and in administering Basutoland"'; and that Her Majesty's government sanctioned this employment and authorized him to leave Mauritius immediately. The second official telegram, almost as long delayed, had been cabled direct from Cape Town on 3 March: 'Position of matters in

*In fact, gazetted 24 March.

Basutoland grave, and of utmost importance that Colony should secure services of someone of proved ability, firmness and energy ... It is very important you should at once visit Colony to learn facts ... leaving your future action unimpeded.'[37] Gordon must abandon his plans to sail to Natal, visit Zanzibar and then spend his year in Palestine.

The *Mercantile Record*, commenting that 'the whole Colony will regret his departure,' assumed that Napier Broome, the Governor, would have lent him a steam tug had the hurricane season not started. However, a small sailing schooner of 321 tons, the *Scotia*, Captain William Duncan, master, was about to leave for Cape Town with a cargo of sugar. That very afternoon, 1 April, as the Captain's wife wrote in her diary: 'At 4 pm a letter came to say that Colonel Gordon (Gordon Pasha) was going as passenger with us to Cape Town. It took us all by surprise. We felt rather put out at having a passenger at all, and more especially such an illustrious one. However, we have to make the best of it.'[38]

Gordon had time only for a quick discussion with Napier Broome, who had been Lieutenant-Governor of the Natal and was soon to embark on his memorable governorship of Western Australia; and to hurry round his charities with last gifts, and to tip his numerous honorary nephews and nieces wherever he called to say good-bye: he embarked with one rupee.[39]

He had sent a message that he would do so on the afternoon of 3 April, but by nightfall he had not come aboard. Just before midnight the Captain and his wife heard a footstep outside the cabin door. Gordon told them, with apology, that to escape a planned gala farewell he had walked twelve miles into the country and stayed out until dark, then walked back. Next morning, however, a whole procession of friends and children visited the *Scotia* before she sailed.[40]

Gordon had scribbled a quick note to Augusta, enclosing the telegrams. He asked Boyce, his second-in-command, to whom he gave his Royal Engineer's cocked hat, to assure her that he was 'perfectly well and in very good spirits at having another important duty to add to his list.' Boyce added: 'I cannot tell you how much he is regretted here or how much his absence is felt by all that know him or had the honour to serve under him. Personally I have lost the most thorough commanding officer that I have ever served under and a most kind friend, but I trust I may yet at some future date have the pleasure of serving under him again.'[41]

CHAPTER TWENTY-FIVE

Commandant-General

Within a day of leaving Mauritius the *Scotia* ran into a swell and Gordon retired seasick. The weather improved and 'the General's health and spirits improved proportionately,' Captain Duncan told a journalist some years later. 'He was a great smoker, and, seated in a big easy-chair, which had been placed on deck for him, enclouded in cigarette smoke, he would sit for hours during the heat of the day, and talk in the most entertaining manner. At nightfall he would, when in the humour for it, keep the watch company on deck, and while away the tedium by drawing liberally from his never-ending fund of stories, and very occasionally he would touch on his own past history and future prospects.'[1]

Then he fell ill again, after foolishly sitting on deck in the rain. 'Our guest has been very sick,' wrote Mrs. Duncan in her diary. 'He is still suffering, and all the while we have had comparatively fine weather. It is hard to say what will become of him when it is rough. He is not improving in health, far less in spirits. *He desires to be landed at the first port we reach*! It is surprising that he has lost heart so soon. How many kinds of courage there must be!' And she thought of his dangers and privations in China and Africa. The sea turned rough, and Gordon lay miserable, not least because sea water had seeped into the fresh water tanks and damaged his digestion. 'It was a very long weary passage,' he wrote to Augusta afterwards, 'and I was very seedy for some days. A sailing vessel is indeed a trial.' Like many a landlubber in a storm he said he had never been so ill in his life and offered his Captain £50 if he would make for land with all possible speed.

By 13 April Mrs. Duncan could record: 'The General is better, and is getting on splendidly!' 'His free and easy manner returned to him,' recalled the Captain. 'His merry laugh and cheery word could be heard both fore and aft, and his cigarette-case, which had remained untouched for a week or more, was again often appealed to. He had a great love for nautical expressions, and used to vie with the crew in his frequent use of them. The most ordinary story he made amusing by padding plentifully with these.' He spent part of each day reading rapidly through his month's supply of *The Times* and two other London papers. Fortunately this batch had crossed an instruction to Augusta in March to '*Stop all the newspapers* ... Newspapers feed a passion I have for giving my opinion'[2] – a sacrifice he could hardly maintain in South Africa. Meanwhile, he read them avidly: 'not a single item, however trivial,' recalled the Duncans, 'escaped his notice.' He would give a digest – and no doubt his opinions – each evening. When he had read the last newspaper he worked through the Captain's excellent library. One day he told the Duncans about his discovery of Eden in the Seychelles: the cautious Scots were not convinced; and he opened a heavy trunk marked 'Stationery,' and showed them coco-de-mer wood from old chest-of-drawers he had tracked down in Mauritius.

On Sundays he spent the morning with his Bible, making copious notes, and then would meditate, his eyes shut. Sometimes, on any day, he would break off a conversation to sit for an hour gazing out to sea with a far-away expression, perhaps pondering the Basuto problem after reading the despatches in *The Times*, or seeing it in the perspective of his faith. As he had scribbled in an undated, ungrammatical note in Mauritius: 'I am drawn to God (He draws me) with an affection that even if He was not Almighty I prefer Him. I would like any trouble with Him, than anything away from Him. Nothing, nothing could compensate His absence.'[3]

The General had already become a favourite with the crew, and the Captain noticed that any who fell sick or injured 'were his especial care. He spoke kindly and cheeringly to the poor fellows, and either read to them himself or saw that they were supplied with literature. They were the first he asked after in the morning and his last care at night.'

The Duncans had found that the General's 'habits were of a strictly temperate nature': he had not opened the case of champagne or the bottles of sherry which he had been given as leaving presents; but on 2 May, when they saw the lights of the Cape of Good Hope and later had rounded it and entered Table Bay, 'We ... had a glass of wine with the General to congratulate each other on the event.'

After twenty-four hours hove-to while the authorities decided whether crew and passenger need be put in quarantine, and Gordon had spent the day writing his thoughts on Basutoland, he landed, dead tired, on the evening of 3 May. Mrs. Duncan wrote in her diary, 'We will miss the General's company much,' and afterwards the Duncans said that had they known he would become 'the Hero of Khartoum' they could not have loved him more. Gordon 'made my way unnoticed to a hotel,' certain that God had 'ruled for the best in delaying my passage . . . Now the pillar of cloud and fire, how will it move?'[4]

'Gordon is as mad as a March hare,' said the Governor and High Commissioner to the Prime Minister after Gordon had called, and to an official: 'Gordon is certainly a military genius, but about religious matters he is quite mad; you will see.' Gordon had evidently been talking about the Garden of Eden.[5]

The Governor, Sir Hercules Robinson, one of the finest Colonial governors of the time, had been Governor of Hong Kong during the Taiping rebellion and Gordon's victories. Gordon's visits to the Robinsons at the Cape were not without incident. When they gave a dinner in his honour, as he told the Duncans on his last visit to the *Scotia*,[6] 'I was offered the arm of my hostess, and buckling on to the port side, I made good headway for some time. As we approached the door of the dining-hall, I could see that it was too narrow to allow berth room for two clippers under full sail. I therefore dropped behind, and allowed my hostess to sail ahead, but, failing to keep a proper look-out, I stupidly planted my foot on my escort's dress-tails, and rent the garment. For my heinous blunder I received a wild look of disapproval, and I shall not easily be forgiven.*

Robinson and his Prime Minister, Thomas Scanlen, were put somewhat in a quandary by Gordon's arrival without warning nearly three months after their first approach to the home government, for the situation in mountainous Basutoland had changed. Those Basutos (Sothos) who had agreed to hand in their guns (the 'Loyals') were no longer being attacked by those who refused to disarm; but Masupha, the half-brother of the weak Paramount Chief, Letsie, held the mountainous citadel from which their late father had ruled, and refused to acknowledge annexation by the Cape. The government had appointed an official whom the Basutos trusted, Joseph Orpen, as Acting Governor's Agent and hoped to rule through British magistrates as if the land were as peaceful and settled as the Cape. At the

---

*by Lady Robinson (née The Hon. Nea Arthur Ada Rose d'Armour Annesley.)

same time the Scanlen ministry had asked the Colonial Office in London to rule Basutoland direct, a request which was refused in a despatch which arrived a few days after Gordon.

Orpen saw no need for Gordon except as an unofficial adviser. Orpen called on him at the Royal Hotel with a pile of Blue Books and was charmed: 'I saw a good deal of him and the more I saw the more I liked him. I thought him very eccentric but transparent, honest, kind and lovable. I still think so of him. He had two natures, one of them was the result of malady for which he was hardly responsible,'[7] wrote Orpen at least twenty-two years later, in a long unpublished account in which he justified his own course; for a dispute soon arose, partly because Orpen regarded Gordon as a lovable eccentric of no consequence, while Gordon was being led to believe that the Cape government regarded him as the key to Basutoland's future, even if he could not be given the post of governor which he had assumed would be his. The Prime Minister offered him the post of Commandant General instead but, wrote Scanlen, 'being much occupied with public duties at that time I saw very little of the General personally.'[8] They did not make sure that each knew the other's mind.

Gordon had not wanted to command the colonial forces which included tribal levies with their white officers, but not British regiments stationed at the Cape. He foresaw endless trouble from their idleness and had no wish to be responsible for suppressing native peoples. Then he talked with members of the Government, especially with John Xavier Merriman, Minister of Public Works and Crown Lands, who had been born in Somerset, near Taunton, where Gordon had been at school: Merriman's father had come out to South Africa as Archdeacon and later Bishop of Grahamstown. Gordon found 'the Colonial Government very well inclined towards the natives, indeed their ideas are very considerate.'[9] He therefore accepted the post, still believing that his main mission would be to pacify the Basutos and that he would be 'leaving at once for Basutoland . . . I hope by God's active aid to obtain balm and heal their stripes,' he wrote to Waller. 'Then a knowledge that the prayers of you and Mrs. Waller and your chicks are with me. What a great imperishable comfort is God's presence, it floats over one over the waves of the troubled sea of life.' On the same day he wrote to Mackinnon that he had taken the post 'not for war purposes, for the Colony has had enough of war (the late one costing four million with little fruit) and go up to Basutoland next week.'[10]

Merriman hurried to Orpen 'very much pleased about Gordon's

appointment, and said: "You will see, Gordon will conceive something original and striking, to be off some night, for instance, and capture Masupha and bring him in prisoner, or something of that sort." It was, I think, the same day and soon after this, that I heard of Gordon's talking in this same way, and I became uneasy.'[11] Another portent of future conflict came when Orpen took Gordon to call on the Minister for Native Affairs, the thirty-two year old Wilhelmus Sauer: 'Mr. Sauer, as it appeared to me, received him very frigidly and unresponsively.'[12]

Gordon also asked to see the exiled King of the Zulus, Cetewayo, living at a farm near Cape Town since his capture at the end of the Zulu War, three years before. Orpen was shocked when Gordon told the Zulu ex-king 'that he was writing to the Minister for the Colonies at Home to recommend that Zululand should be given back to him to rule. That advice was a great mistake.'[13] Lord Kimberley accepted it: Cetewayo was back on his throne before the end of the year, after a visit to Queen Victoria.

On Ascension Day, 18 May, after 'a nice Communion,' Gordon slipped out on his own to visit Cetewayo again 'and felt for him. I tried to cheer him, for years ever since Isandwhala I have prayed for him.' He gave Cetewayo an ivory handled stick which he had been given by a sultan exiled in the Seychelles for whom he had done a kindness.[14] The next day, 19 May 1882, Gordon left Cape Town – and did not reach Basutoland until September.

The direct route to King Williams Town, the commandant-general's headquarters, was by sea. Gordon begged to be allowed to go by land. He set off, therefore, on 19 May by train, the first leg of a roundabout journey, with Joseph Orpen and Orpen's secretary and a military secretary of his own: Lieutenant-Colonel Philip Homon-Ffolliott, late of the 59th (Buckinghamshires). Gordon had taken a smaller salary to get him.

Much of the first day's journey Gordon spent talking religion 'very earnestly' to Homon-Ffolliott and ignoring Orpen, who listened politely. The train stopped at Touw's River station for supper. The four men had parted on the platform to go to their own compartments for the night. A few moments later the Colonel came back with a message: '" Mr. Orpen, General Gordon requests me to tell you that you have acted to-day as a Christian gentleman, and he has behaved very badly to you and is very sorry." I was startled and said: "Please tell General Gordon there is nothing whatever he has done that can possibly give me any pain." Colonel Homon-

Ffolliott said: "Oh, I am going to have an awful time of it!" So he afterwards had, but he loved Gordon all the same.'[15]

Both men found Gordon frequently irritable; but after they had reached the end of the line at Beaufort West, where they spent Sunday, and were travelling onward by Cape carts, four-in-hand, Gordon explained that he had been suffering from the after-effects of the sea voyage and the contaminated water, and only now felt able to discuss Basutoland.[16]

As the carts drove across country to strike the next railway, Gordon made Orpen describe the history of Basutoland (Lesotho) sometimes called the 'Switzerland' of South Africa; how the great chief Moshesh had formed the Basuto nation out of several tribes broken by the Zulus and Matabele, and had ruled from his mountain fastness of Theba Bosigo; how the Boers of the Orange Free State had encroached on his lowlands until he had put himself under the cloak of Queen Victoria; Basutoland had eventually become a dependency of Cape Province. Moshesh had been succeeded by his weak eldest son Letsie, already old, who was unable to control a rebellion and civil war which broke out in 1879 when the Cape Government unwisely sought to disarm the Basutos after disarming the Zulus: it was to end this 'Gun War' that the Sprigg ministry had sought Gordon in 1880.

A compromise had been patched up by the 'Governor's Award' of 1881 but Letsie's powerful half-brother Matsupha continued to defy him and to raid the defenceless 'Loyals' who had handed in their arms. The war had petered out, with Matsupha unbeaten, defying the Cape Government and the Paramount Chief from Thaba Bosigo. Orpen put great faith in his own white magistrates, supported by the Cape Mounted Rifles, to pacify the country.

Gordon absorbed Orpen's information and read the Blue Books and much of a report which Orpen had written. At Port Elizabeth they parted but Gordon unexpectedly followed Orpen a day later to his home at Grahamstown and produced a memorandum to send to the Prime Minister on the right course for Basutoland.

Orpen 'certainly did not approve of the propositions contained in it.' Gordon wanted to summon the Basuto to a national *Pitso* or assembly to air their grievances and chart a united course for the future under their Paramount Chief, to whom the rebellious Matsupha could be reconciled. Orpen considered that the Basutos had no grievances and that the choice was either a 'just administration' under his magistrates or 'tolerating tyranny of chiefs.' Gordon's proposal 'was wholly opposite to the understanding on which he was to join me in Basutoland, and the suggestions in his paper were wholly opposed to the policy of Government previously announced to Parliament and therein agreed upon.'[17]

From then on, during the winter months of June, July and August, the two were at polite loggerheads, until Gordon urged the Cape Government to remove Orpen (whom he had earlier described as 'a just, kind gentleman') while Orpen was exasperated by the memoranda which Gordon sent to Cape Town, culminating in his draft Convention which would virtually give Basutoland a status similar to a native state in the Indian Empire. Gordon had already sent a message to Masupha without telling Orpen. Meanwhile Gordon worked hard as Commandant-General to reorganize the colonial forces, having first recommended his predecessor for a decoration, 'one of those delights of the Military heart' which he scorned for himself.[18]

When Gordon had first reached King Williams Town on the Buffalo River, 700 miles from Cape Town, he had met Colonel Brabant (later General Sir Edward) an Englishman who had won distinction in the recent Native wars and had been a Member of the Cape Assembly before reverting to farming and part-time soldiering: he was later to win fame in the South African War for his defence of Jammersberg Drift. Brabant had been ordered to share his knowledge of natives and native warfare.

'I was naturally delighted to be placed in such intimate relations with so famous a man,' recalled Brabant. 'I must confess to a sensation of surprise and almost of disappointment on first meeting him, his appearance was not such as to give you the impression of his being the great soldier he really was. Of small stature and somewhat shabbily dressed, I looked at him with a feeling of astonishment that this could be the man who had quelled a mutiny among his irregular troops in China, by dragging the ringleader out of the ranks and shooting him with his own hands. (*sic*)

'But before I had known him long, I came to the same conclusion that his countrymen generally have done, viz, that he was a great military genius. He was, it is true, very eccentric, even to the point of making one doubt his absolute sanity, but on questions of military or civil administration with which he was at that time concerned, he was as sane and sound as any living person.'[19]

This sane but eccentric new Commandant insisted on reviewing troops in a top hat and old frock coat. He would take down the names of any he met during the day, to pray 'for each one separately and individually. Of course after a time the task became a heavy one, and then his temper became affected, and his military secretary would resent his irritation. He would then say "Oh I see what is wrong", and would wipe out the existing list and begin a new one.' Poor Homon-Ffolliott had already been weaned from one normal military courtesy; he must not address Gordon as 'Sir' without a forfeit of a shilling, for Gordon was wrestling with 'Agag' in the form of pride.

Brabant found that Gordon 'would consult the strangest people on the most important subjects. I have known him go into the hotel yard where he was staying and consult the hotel keeper upon a vital military question. He was absolutely free from any small or petty prejudices, and would listen to advice from anyone – no matter what his station in life – who, he thought, could throw some light on the matter in hand.'

In one matter he was far ahead of his time. Before leaving on tour he told Brabant to draw up estimates for a native army, effective and much cheaper than a mixed force of Europeans, Coloureds and native levies.

'He went into full details,' recalled Brabant, 'and to my horror proposed that a portion only of the regimental officers should be Europeans, the remainder being natives. I said, "I think , General Gordon, that it is my duty to tell you that such a scheme will never work in this country, where the prejudice as to colour is so strong; and that no white man would ever consent to being commanded by a native, however good the man might be." The General's reply was, "I did not ask you, Colonel Brabant, to give your advice as to the principle of the scheme, but to assist me in carrying it out."'

He was away three weeks, travelling by horse, Cape cart and foot throughout the Transkei. When he returned to King Williams Town Brabant brought his detailed estimates: 'As soon as I got into the room however, he said, "Brabant, I have discovered that you were perfectly right in what you told me with regard to the colour prejudice. I have given up the idea of raising the force we talked about."'

He had found much to correct in both civil and military affairs, and wanted the Transkei to be given its own government, so that decisions could be made quickly. When his reforms were blocked or ignored he put in his resignation but was persuaded to withdraw it by John Merriman. Gordon had travelled to Port Elizabeth to consult him. Merriman wrote back to Scanlen the Prime Minister on 30 July that Gordon 'is a queer fellow but I like him as much as ever I did ... He is a most curious mixture of action, clear-sighted business method, combined with the strange faculty of dashing off these impulsive memoranda. I think he is eminently a man of action and our habits of procrastination which are inseparable from government irritate him.'[20]

Gordon would have agreed. A month earlier he had written in a letter to his paymaster-general, young Arthur Garcia: 'I know myself, and I know what I am capable of, I cannot brook restraint for any time, and this I would unfairly have to do in any position under Colonial Government or Imperial Government.'[21]

Gordon succeeded in one reform, persuading the Cape government to put military finance, supply and transport under direct civil control and to create Garcia Inspector-General of the Colonial Forces. When Ffolliott returned to the Cape, Garcia became Gordon's private secretary also. The Garcias admired Gordon equally as an official and as a man. 'Often,' wrote Mrs. Garcia, 'to my embarrassment, he would insist on having my two small children brought from the nursery to sit next to him at luncheon, when he would attend to their wants and forget his own. He was the most abstemious of men in every way . . . Tea was his favourite beverage, and as he was a hard worker and never would give himself time to go to the hotel for tea, my husband usually brought him round to our house for it.' But when he was inadvertently taken into a ladies' tea party he gulped down the slop basin and fled.[22]

At last, in September 1882, after prodding the ministry in Cape Town, and refusing the most pressing invitation yet from King Leopold to take over in the Congo, Gordon was allowed to set out for Basutoland.

CHAPTER TWENTY-SIX

Mountain of Night

On 14 September 1880 Joseph Orpen, as Government Agent, met Wilhelmus Sauer, the Minister for Native Affairs, and General Gordon at Mafeteng on the western borders of Basutoland. Garcia and other officials came too. On their way up through the lower country with its Boer farms, Gordon had a happy time distributing Dutch translations of his Gravesend leaflet; a consignment had reached him from Augusta. Since most of the Boer farmers were solid Calvinists the leaflet may have seemed a curiosity.

As for Sauer, Gordon was in two minds about the tall young politician, writing to Mackinnon: 'I like Colony and Colonist and Colonial government very much, every one has been civil to me and I have got on first rate. I am now well up in Native affairs ... Government is weak in some ways. Sauer is a stumbling block to them,'[1] and might be soon replaced; yet in sending Sauer a memorandum of views on the Basuto problem, he could write: 'I believe that by your skilful management (I am not flattering) you will tide over this affair, but it will not solve the question.'[2] He recommended involving the British Government.

On 15 September the party drove into Basutoland to Morija. Orpen had alerted the people. As he and Sauer rode together in a horse waggonette, 'Chief after Chief with their followers came up to us along the road to escort us some distance; there were altogether some thousands and, through some mis-management which I greatly regretted, Gordon in his wagonnette got during part of the way into the rear and he was overpowered with dust, and became as I soon heard very irritable.'[3] Irritable he might be, but he was impressed by the Basuto: 'they are a fine people, the best blacks I have ever seen.'[4] Sauer, on the other hand, did not even thank them for their cavalry escort and was frequently rude to chiefs.[5]

Morija was a mission station of the Paris Evangelical Missionary Society, which long ago had won the confidence of the great Moshesh. Gordon and Garcia were guests of the resident missionary, the Reverend Adolphe Mabillé, who told Gordon that Masupha was incorrigible and must be put down. Next day Sauer held an *indaba* with the old Paramount Chief, Letsie, whose great place lay a few miles higher up, and his eldest son and heir, Lerothodi. The *Indaba* added to the confusion: Sauer seemed to be drifting, while Gordon, whom Orpen thought had no right 'to interfere or utter a word,' seemed first to repudiate force and then to urge it, saying to Lerothodi that his chance of being Paramount Chief was 'not worth a shilling' unless Masupha's power was cut down quickly. Sauer then held a second, private meeting without Orpen or Gordon, at which he urged the Chiefs to summon their followers and assault Masupha in his mountain fastness.

Whatever Gordon may have said at the *indaba*, he disliked this policy of using one chief against another. He had an instinct that the chiefs were more united than appeared; and more than ever he wanted to allow the Basutos to govern themselves. The thought of further warfare distressed him, as Mabillé discovered the next day, a Sunday, when he brought Gordon to hear the Sunday school singing. Gordon suddenly left the church. Mabillé hurriedly followed him and found him weeping: 'When I saw all those dear little children singing so sweetly and thought of our going to destroy them, I could not bear it.'[6] Mabillé assured him that there would probably be no bloodshed.

Gordon was also distressed by seeing natives with too little clothing for the cold of the mountains in early spring. He took blankets from the army store, telling Garcia: 'Don't be angry, my dear fellow . . .' As Garcia's senior officer he had the legal right to commandeer them and Garcia sympathized: 'even sheepskins are insufficient to protect them from the cold.' Garcia was also deeply impressed when one day he happened to see Gordon at prayer in the beautiful early morning, his cloak flapping in the breeze.[7]

They travelled on to Orpen's Presidency at Maserv on the Caledon River and stayed with him one night: Orpen woke Gordon early to show him a bright comet, visible for the first time that dawn. They rode off early, Gordon making a detour to visit an Anglican mission, where he wrote a confidential paper, *The Basuto Embroglio*, advocating self-government under a resident commissioner.

They were all to meet again at Thlotse Heights, a village with a magistrate's compound and a small fort, in the lovely scenery of the Leribe, with the snow-capped Maluti range behind (*Leribe* means 'undulating' and the village of Thlose Heights changed its name to Leribe). Sauer and Orpen had summoned two more Chiefs.

The district had suffered grievously in the Gun War. The parliamentary Commission on compensation was taking evidence at the very time of Gordon's arrival, and thus he met Cecil Rhodes, a millionaire at twenty-nine from the Kimberley diamond fields and Member of the Local Assembly for Barkly West.

Rhodes took to Gordon at once: 'It is curious,' he told a mutual friend of much his own age, at the time of Khartoum, 'but somehow he exercised a strange influence on me. He united spiritual ideas or sentiment with tremendous activity, and had such a belief in his own way of doing things as to amount to obstinacy. He was a ready listener but self-willed to a degree. We got on, however, capitally together, for we both believed in moral suasion (as he called it) rather than force in dealing with native chiefs . . . He had a wonderful power with natives!'[8]

They took many walks together. Gordon urged Rhodes to stay on with him in Basutoland, sorting it out together, but the mutual friend, Edward Arthur Maund, who as an army crammer had lived near Augusta in Southampton before joining Rhodes in Africa, thought they would have been 'too obstinate about their own convictions,'[9] whether in Basutoland or later in the Sudan where Gordon wanted Rhodes to join him; but both wanted justice for native races.

They discussed religion. Rhodes, an agnostic, did not grasp Gordon's views. He thought that his supreme confidence in the Future Life amounted to spiritualism; and as Maund commented, found it 'weirdly mysterious' that religion should enter into every act of Gordon's life. 'Extraordinary man,' Rhodes muttered, 'and yet so practical. I should think he alone understood himself. Neither the World nor the Authorities understood him. His ideals and methods were above them.'[10]

Thlotse was an Anglican mission station of the Society for the Propagation of the Gospel. As soon as Gordon was free from official duties – at breakfast next morning – he dropped in on the missionary, the Reverend John Widdicombe, for a long discussion about the troubles of Basutoland, and on the next day, wrote Widdicombe 'he came and stayed with me four hours – four of the most delightful hours I have ever spent in my life. The General smoked his cigarettes, and I my pipe of Transvaal, while we discussed

Mission work and its methods, gradually sliding off into Theology, and ending with the symbolism of the Old Testament ritual.

'I have never yet met a man who knew the Bible – more especially the Old Testament – as he did. He was simply *saturated* with Scriptural knowledge ... I felt humbled and ashamed in the presence of this man "mighty in the Scriptures": a layman, great in his own profession of arms, who had nevertheless found time, amid manifold duties and distractions, to study the Word of God so thoroughly that he put me, a commissioned ambassador of Christ, entirely to the blush.

'Now and then in these conversations his own well-known peculiar views came out; but they were at the worst quite harmless – at least, so it seemed to me – and on the essentials of the "faith once delivered to the saints" he was sound, orthodox, and Catholic to the core. He struck me as really humble minded, and penetrated with the mind and spirit of Christ.'[11]

The high church parson was pleased at Gordon's 'intense longing for Communion.' Widdicombe noted 'a dash of fatalism ... augmented by his natural tendency to mysticism,' but also Gordon's intense and fearless desire to be an instrument of the Divine will, coupled with a conviction of his own unworthiness: 'it was this humility of soul, and this realization of his own frailty, which impelled him to cast himself daily and hourly at the feet of Christ in self-abasement. He longed to be like Christ, and have the mind of Christ, that he might be able in the spirit of Christ, and of Christ alone, to do the Father's will. And it was this aim that kept him *straight* as well as courageous. Without it I can imagine him becoming a fanatic: with it he was a devout soldier of God; an enthusiast if you will, but no fanatic.'

Widdicombe, who was close to his people, found that Gordon understood their plight. Widdicombe begged him to remain, 'telling him that, at such a crisis the future of the country was in his hands, and that if Masupha could be induced to listen to anyone, I felt sure it would be to him.'

Next morning Gordon paid a last call on Widdicombe with a generous gift of money for his work. They went into the church and prayed 'for each other, for the work of the Mission, and for poor torn, distracted Basutoland, still bleeding from its wounds; after which I said some collects from the Prayer Book, ending with the Apostolic Benediction. Half-an-hour afterwards the General was on his way southwards to Masupha.'[12]

Gordon was encouraged, since Widdicombe knew Masupha's character, that his own instinct was right: he could solve the Basuto problem through meeting Masupha. That evening, after the party had ridden down the Caledon river to Morija, Sauer gave his consent. Afterwards Orpen contended that Sauer gave his consent reluctantly, while Gordon said that he went at Sauer's request. Misunderstandings at the time and selective memories later confuse the story. Sauer undoubtedly made Gordon write him a formal letter stating that he was going in a private capacity to find out whether Masupha would accept Government policy (which Gordon loathed) and to bring back the Chief's wishes for Sauer to consider. Gordon's letter concluded: 'I understand I have no power to make any promises whatever to him.'[13]

Meanwhile the Paramount Chief's son Lerothodi, acting on Sauer's orders at their private meeting, had brought together an armed force. Gordon understood that this force would be held in reserve and not move against Masupha unless the peace mission failed. Sauer may have intended this but even his best friend Merriman called him 'the Bumbler.' Orpen urged him to countermand his permission, alarmed at what Gordon might do. Sauer retorted that Gordon could do neither good nor harm: Masupha would be polite 'and laugh at him in his sleeve.'[14]

Gordon took only Garcia and a Captain Nettleton to walk into the mountains to Masupha's impregnable kraal at Thabu Bosiga, 'the Mountain of Night,' from where his father had ruled. They went unarmed. When, earlier, the Leader of the Opposition had claimed that Gordon plotted to seize Masupha by a dazzling feat of arms, Gordon had wired to Merriman a resounding denial: '. . . and ask Mr. Sprigg to believe that I should not like even for a moment, to act as a madman for the sake of making a claptrap reputation.'[15]

As they walked up the trail Sauer, in the valley, had discovered that Lerothodi could not expect to feed his warriors or keep them together for more than a day or two. Sauer therefore agreed that the chief might advance on Masupha the next day. Orpen was horrified and wrote a formal letter pointing out that 'General Gordon and party will run the risk of being detained and possibly murdered.'[16] He then rode away, as previously planned, to Morija.

Gordon reached the Paris society's mission station below Thaba Bosigo at 10 a. m. Masupha's friend Theophile Jousse was away. His young French assistant, Pasteur Keck, went to Masupha and returned in two hours with

Masupha's sons. Gordon handed Keck a long letter for Masupha, written while waiting.

After expressing admiration for Basutos and saying that he would not fight them ('If the Colony fights then I will go away') the letter faithfully repeated Sauer's demands and then turned them on their head by encouraging Masupha to ask for magistrates of his choice, adding: 'I think you can ask government to order the magistrates to consult with you on all large matters, to treat you with all proper respect as a great chief.' Instead of Masupha the rebel, Gordon was approaching him as a high contracting party, whose best course was to be friends with Queen Victoria.[17]

Next morning Masupha himself appeared with two hundred tribesmen. Gordon honoured him as an equal with a carefully prepared speech.* They found a mutual respect. Widdicombe believed that the negotiations would have succeeded, and an Englishman who knew Masupha wrote to *The Times* in 1885: 'The late General Gordon divined his character marvellously, and was the only man Masupha had the slightest regard for.'[18]

Masupha withdrew to his fastness to consider his answer. That afternoon one of Sauer's staff walked into Theba Bosigo mission with a letter: Sauer ordered Gordon to leave before the following morning because Lerothodi's force would attack at dawn. Gordon was astounded. He sent an immediate message to Masupha to hold his answer until 'these hostile movements cease.'

All night long Masupha's scouts reported Lerothodi's advance while Gordon, in anger, realized that the negotiation was dead. Masupha sent down a message of astonishment that Gordon should leave, and professed that he had decided to accept the Government's terms, yet Gordon could not stay in face of Sauer's order. He sent a last message, not to 'allow any rumours to interfere with your decision.' Then he wrote out a wire to be sent to the Prime Minister, with copy to Merriman: '(From) *Commandant General, Thaba Bosigo*: As I am in completely false position up here and can do more harm than good I am leaving for Colony whence I propose coming to Cape Town when I trust government will accept my resignation. *C. G. Gordon, Major General.*'[19]

By dawn, rain was pouring down. No attack came. Gordon, Garcia and Nettleton walked back towards the river valley. Lerothodi's force had

---

*The Cape Governor claimed that Gordon had fallen on Matsupha's neck and called him a dear brother in Christ, 'which was not according to protocol'!

melted away in the rain but Gordon, when he met the chief, upbraided him for trying to start a civil war.

Sauer sought to see Gordon. To avoid him, Gordon sent a curt note that having completed his military inspection in Basutoland he was returning to the Colony. Gordon refused to sit in the same train compartment, or stay in the same hotel: Colonel Brabant noted that 'General Gordon came back from Basutoland believing himself to have been very badly used.'[20]

Scanlen hurried ahead to give the Prime Minister his version, so that when Gordon offered to remain as Commandant General until Parliament met, Scanlen wired back that since Gordon would not fight the Basuto it would not be in the public interest.

Gordon returned to Cape Town, saw Scanlen, and wrote him a letter taking 'the entire responsibility': 'in my communication to Masupha I did not even attempt to follow the wishes of the Government, nor did I in the least weigh my words with a view to suit the Government. I acted entirely on my own responsibility, and was and am perfectly convinced that what I said was and is now the best thing that could be done.'[21]

Gordon's unexpurgated comments on Scanlen, Orpen and others cannot be known because Augusta scratched out more lines in his letters from South Africa than in any other part of the correspondence. He sailed for England an apparent failure and had lost the Congo too: 'I might have answered the King "Yes", considering the sequel of my career in Cape Colony.'[22] Yet within three months the Cape government had granted Basutoland autonomy, 'the Gordon policy without Gordon,' as the *Cape Times* wrote on 27 December. In 1884 the Imperial Government agreed to make Basutoland a British Protectorate. It thus escaped the apartheid of the next century and in due time became independent as Lesotho with Letsie's descendant as King.

CHAPTER TWENTY-SEVEN

Gordon's Calvary

After a few weeks in England Gordon sailed for Palestine on 26 December 1882 in the British India liner *Quetta*. Her ever-generous owner Mackinnon gave him free passage.

Gordon had lain low in England except for visiting his brothers and sisters: 'Three invalid sisters, one ditto brother with my small finances, prevent my going about much,'[1] made convenient excuses. He could not, however, put Egypt and the Sudan out of his mind, for while he was in South Africa Arabi Pasha had rebelled against the Khedive, to Gordon's glee, for he hoped Arabi would govern for the people of Egypt rather than the foreign bondholders; but Gordon's friend Wolseley had been sent out with an expeditionary force and had defeated Arabi at Tel-el-Kebir while Gordon was in Basutoland. British domination of Egypt became inevitable.

Gordon gave much thought to making the occupation a blessing rather than a curse. In London he called on Reginald Brett. 'I had a long talk with Chinese Gordon yesterday,' minuted Brett to his chief, Hartington, about to move from the India Office to be Secretary of State for War, 'and I send you the notes I made . . . He sent you all sorts of messages but was afraid to call'; Hartington pencilled a query against that.* Among many suggestions on politics, postings, and the Slave Trade, Gordon urged that a British Governor-General be appointed to the Sudan and he named Sir Charles Wilson – whose delay in advancing more rapidly to the relief of Khartoum two years and two months later would be blamed as one of the causes of Gordon's death.[2]

'Give as much autonomy as possible,' Gordon urged for the Sudan. '*ie*, don't employ Turks or Circassians, but natives as far as possible.' The

---

*Brett's note carries no name: it might have gone to Dilke, but Hartington is the more likely.

Sudan was already simmering with revolt against the corrupt and inefficient Egyptian pashas who had ruled Khartoum since his departure nearly three years before. A religious leader in his early thirties named Muhammed Ahmad, a descendant of the Prophet, had proclaimed himself the Mahdi or Expected One and had called on the people to throw out the Turks. The Mahdi had massacred an expedition sent to arrest him in the Nuba hills. Gordon had privately expressed sympathy with the unrest. Thus he had told Orpen when they first met in Cape Town (or so Orpen recorded many years later) 'that his own mission to the Sudan had been a mistake and he was often unhappy about it, but his great comfort was that he had sown the seeds of a rebellion which eventually would drive the Egyptians out of the Sudan. It is strange,' commented Orpen, 'that he should have, but a few years afterwards, been killed in the service of that same Khedive whom he detested, and fighting against the rebellion he had expected, and believed he had sown the seeds of, and to which he had looked forward with hope.'[3]

In London Gordon went to breakfast with Wilfrid Blunt, the celebrated writer, a Sussex landowner and notorious philanderer who supported nationalist movements everywhere, and his wife Lady Anne, Byron's granddaughter. The Blunts had an estate in Egypt and championed the defeated Arabi's right to a fair trial. Lady Anne wished she had known Gordon sooner. Having heard from Gladstone's secretary that he was 'not clothed in the soundest of minds' she wrote in her diary as 'a distinct impression' that Gordon 'does not appear to me to be otherwise than in perfect possession of perfect common sense ... But he is a man of ideas, utopian or "mad".' Wilfrid Blunt saw him as 'a little, quite unmilitary man, not specially distinguished except for his clear gray-blue eyes, and his singularly frank, unconventional manner. There was nothing in the smallest degree assertive about him, or which could give a stranger the idea of his being a leader of men, or a man accustomed to authority and importance in the world. His conversation was pleasant without any special grace of manner, and he impressed me principally with an appearance of extreme natural goodness and honesty of speech,' with 'much wit and pleasant humour in discussion.'

They discussed Egypt for two hours. When Gordon said he was going to Palestine Lady Anne was convinced that he was being sent by the government on a secret mission of enquiry 'into the state of the Mussulman world.'[4]

Gordon certainly had a mission of enquiry in mind when he reached Jerusalem in pouring rain on 17 January 1883 and put up at the Hotel Jaffa Gate. Jerusalem was a tumbledown city; for the Arab inhabitants Turkish rule meant, in the American Consul's words, an 'iron hand, oppression and suffering, ignorance and degradation.'[5] They had little employment except from the trickle of foreign tourists, and often lived on charity from the various Christian churches and groups. The smaller number of Jewish immigrants, mainly from Russia, were even poorer.

Gordon walked round the city, 'about two hours quiet walking,'[6] and saw the wailing wall and the Pool of Bethesda, but his chief aim was to settle the site of Golgotha or Calvary ('the Place of a Skull') where Christ had been crucified. Gordon was already doubtful of the traditional site beneath the Church of the Holy Sepulchre as a result of his reading, and poring over maps, and possibly discussion with officials of the Palestine Exploration Fund. Gordon must already have been familiar with the findings of Otto Thenius in 1842, for he went straight to the Skull Hill on the north side beyond the strong medieval wall, which Thenius had suggested.

On the very next day, 18 January, he wrote to Augusta: 'I feel, *for myself*, convinced that the Hill near the Damascus Gate is Golgotha. I trace its position from the ordnance map of Jer. The black lines are the contours. From it, you can see the Temple and Mount Olives (*sic*) and the bulk of Jerusalem. His stretched out arms would, as it were embrace it: "all day long have I stretched out my arms." Close to it is the slaughter House of Jerusalem, and quite pools of blood are lying there. It is covered with tombs of Muslim. There are lots of rock hewn caves, Jeremiah's Grotto is a large grotto, gardens are all round it, a lot of roads are near it.'[7]

He was already calling Skull Hill 'my Golgotha.' The more he studied the ground and the Bible the more certain he grew: he worked out that the ridge running south west from this hill to the Temple area, where the mosques now stood, had the form of a human skeleton and he saw a mystic meaning.

The house at the Damascus Gate had been taken by an American family, the Spaffords, who led a small group known as 'The American Colony,' devoted to good works and to awaiting the Second Coming of Christ. They welcomed him to sit on their flat roof, meditating and gazing towards this green hill. He had now rented a small house a few miles away in the village of Ain Karim, traditionally the birthplace of John the Baptist. He would ride in by the bridle path on a white donkey. Whenever he came, Mrs. Spafford would warn her five-year-old daughter Bertha not to disturb him, 'but I would creep up the roof stairs,' remembered Bertha, and crouch behind the chimney; there I would wait. My vigil was always rewarded, for at last he would call me and take me on his knee and tell me stories. He was not very tall and had fair, curly hair, and I remember how blue his eyes were, and the blue double-breasted suit he wore. I did not know General Gordon was famous, only that he was my friend and I loved him.'[8]

Bertha Spafford Vester, as she became, would also claim with a laugh that Gordon had taught her to swear, because he had told her parents about his servant, 'Joseph of Arimathea' who 'asked every morning: "General, sir, what shall we have for dinner?" "Well, Joseph, what have you got?" "I have chicken, Sir General." "Then have chicken, Joseph." This was repeated daily, until one morning the general saw Joseph approaching and anticipated him by saying, "Damn it, have chicken for dinner." The general gave one of his hearty laughs and said: "And now you see, Mrs. Spafford, why I do not want chicken." I was taking all this in, and soon after, when asked about my supper, which was invariably bread and milk, I said, "Damn it, have bread and milk." To my utter consternation I was punished. For many years I puzzled why, when General Gordon said "damn," Mother had smiled, but when I said it, I was spanked.' Gordon was unaware of her fate. He continued to gaze at 'Skull Hill.'

He wrote to many of his friends of his conviction that this hill was Calvary. He drew maps to prove it and discussed it by post with the Palestine Exploration Society. Some agreed, others disputed, while Charles Watson pointed out that in the Bible the Place of a Skull was not described as a hill.

Nevertheless, 'Gordon's Calvary' soon led the field as the most likely alternative site, and became a fixture on maps and in guide books.

Below 'Gordon's Calvary' lay gardens, and in one was a rock-cut tomb. Gordon did not mention it in his letters, except possibly in one of the untraced 'deluge' of papers and plans which he poured on a Swiss-German architect in Jerusalem, Dr. Baurath Conrad Schick:[9] when Schick surveyed the tomb some years later he described it as 'suggested by the late General Gordon to be the sepulchre of Christ'; and a group of English people raising funds which bought the land made strong use of his name. The Garden Tomb became a centre of pilgrimage and Christian teaching, for whether Gordon was right or wrong about the site of Calvary the tomb gives a moving sense of Christ's sepulchre after the first Easter morning.

Although Gordon did not refer to the Tomb he had an unshakeable conviction that Christ had risen from the dead, and 'full and happy sense of Assurance,' as Prebendary Barnes recognized, that 'Jesus is the Son of God.'[10] His death on the Cross and the Resurrection from the Tomb made possible 'the indwelling of God in us' which was the key to life for Gordon and 'opens out fields of delightful thought which never fade ... No earthly glory,' he told Sir Samuel Baker, 'can be so entrancingly interesting as the study of the great things of Scripture when enlightened by the knowledge that God dwells in our bodies.'[11]

He loved to think about Christ. In a letter from Jerusalem in February to the boy Edward White in Ireland he wrote that Palestine, being under the Turks, had not changed much 'since the time when our friend the Lord Jesus came to visit us. We did not treat him well, did we, we grudged Him everything, even the ointment for his burial, yet He came to deliver us, and He has forgiven all our unkindness, and would only desire us to remember that unkindness in order that we might feel more drawn to Him in love.'[12] Gordon then told Edward something of his researches in the Dome of the Rock and elsewhere as he fitted the symbolism of the Old Testament to the facts of the New.

He was not in the Holy Land for topographical research alone. From his little house in Ain Karem he wrote to Harvey in Chatham that when he had been 'shelved again' he had wanted the vacuum 'to be filled by our Lord. His society, so to speak, the increased sense of His union, must be better than being Governor-General of the Sudan, &c. Then I again set my face to give up all, all, and seek the increased union! So now you know why I avoided you and others – it was because I was in that phase.'[13]

All the way from England to Port Said on *S. S. Quetta* he had been seeking this deeper union, describing his meditations in an immense letter of twenty-two sides in purple pencil.[14] The meditations continued in Palestine as he offered up his faults, especially his quick temper, his pride (no one else thought him proud) and his tendency to criticize people behind their backs. On 6 February '*smoking knocked off*, never, DV, to be resumed, as yet it has not been my greatest trial. I can say that as for the flesh, I do not care for anything, but I have not yet reached the point, when I *would desire to be despised*.'[15] He told Harvey that giving up smoking 'was a sore thing, and I did not give it up as a penance, but because one has no right to misuse one's body, which is God's Temple'.[16] His resolution failed: he smoked again in less than a year.

He was now spending the daylight hours discovering for himself the sacred sites, or sometimes walking up a nearby hill from 'where I can see the sea and Jaffa and also the Moabite mountains and Jerusalem and Bethlehem,'[17] and many other Biblical places.

In the evenings he would sit in his little house and by the light of an oil lamp write pages to Augusta, to Sir John Cowell, and especially to Prebendary Barnes of Exeter, who collated them into subjects and later published them as *Reflections in Palestine*: Gordon in Khartoum saw the proofs but had no part in the editing.

The original letters have a spontaneity and immediacy which disappears from the printed page. The humour and sparkle which made Gordon's friends love his company are missing, so that readers in later generations could be misled into supposing him a gloomy man with none of the assurance and joy of the Resurrection.

The Prebendary, as a sound Anglican, must have blanched a little at some of Gordon's assertions. He believed in the pre-existence of every soul; not in transmigration, although occasionally in letters he had toyed with that, but in the sense of Wordsworth's *Ode on Intimations of Immortality in Childhood*: 'But trailing clouds of glory do we come/From God who is our home.'

Gordon saw the soul as placed in the 'sheath' of the body at birth, to be awakened through union with Christ: 'In Adam all souls and bodies stood, fell, and died; in Christ all are made alive, or raised or awakened from a dormant state . . . The dormant Divine existence is awakened never to sleep again, and I believe that the now raised and quickened soul will grope its way out of its shell; it will contend with the body, often being nearly extinguished but never quite, till the body gives up the struggle in natural death' – and the soul returns home to God, where Gordon longed to be.[18]

Gordon implies that man's physical body is in lifelong conflict with his soul: an idea promoted by certain mystics down the ages but rejected by the great theologians as heresy, untrue to Scripture. When St. Paul called on the Galatians to 'Walk in the spirit and ye shall not fulfil the lust of the flesh,' the Greek word translated *flesh* in the Authorized Version is traditionally held by scholars and linguists to refer to those attitudes and desires in the mind and the soul which are in conflict with the Spirit of Christ, and not to bodily temptations alone.

Gordon sought to be true to Scripture; but his ideas were honed in long hours of studying the Bible alone, in Africa, almost without books, by the light of his spiritual experiences. Later he read widely. Some of his views are original, such as the parallel between Adam's 'First Eating,' of the forbidden fruit, which brought evil into the world; and the 'Second Eating,' of the Body and Blood of Christ in the Sacrament, which strengthens the awakened soul. Most of his theology, however, seems an unintegrated mixture brewed from early Christian Fathers, Gnostics, medieval and 17th century mystics, Evangelicals and Tractarians.

A reviewer of Gordon's *Reflections* wrote in *Blackwoods Magazine*: 'What does it matter? Whatever he says is full of the divine love and consciousness, the very breath of holiness and truth. If we cannot follow him, what does it matter'.[19]

Gordon founded no school of thought. His more peculiar views may be left on the wilder shores of theology. As John Widdicombe in Basutoland had recognized, the heart of Gordon's gospel was sound: redemption through the Cross; the Resurrection; and 'union with Christ by the indwelling of the Holy Ghost.'[20] 'Christ is all in all,' he wrote to Cowell. 'He is the key to the Scriptures';[21] Gordon expected mystic light on Christ not only from almost every Bible verse but from every site.

He was thoroughly enjoying himself: 'I am living a very quiet life indeed,' he wrote to Henry, 'wandering over the hills and I see no one, my books are enough companionship. I expect that people are pretty mystified as to what I do.'[22] The French consul certainly was: he sent spies to trail him, and Gordon took an impish delight in outwalking them. Like Lady Anne Blunt, the Consul believed him to be on a secret mission for the British government, but Gordon's only strategic contribution was to support the recent curious advocacy of T. Henley for a canal through Jerusalem, the Jordan Valley and the Dead Sea, to link the Mediterranean and the Gulf of Akaba, thus outflanking the Suez Canal. That would allow the British to leave Egypt – and conform to a verse in the Prophet Zechariah: 'living waters shall go out from Jerusalem; half of them towards the former sea, and half of them towards the hinder sea.'[23]

When summer came he went farther afield. 'I have just come back from a long ride through the country to Haifa,' he wrote to an old China acquaintance, 'and then back by the Plain of what I suppose is called Sharon. The flies in the plain troubled the horses, however it was not too hot.' He loved 'that clear light that makes the East so attractive to me'; and the foliage and the colour of the rocks.[24]

In Haifa he met a celebrated English satirist whom he had known slightly in the Crimea and China as a young diplomatist. Laurence Oliphant had been a society swell and had written a brilliant novel, then suddenly disappeared to America to marry into a strange philosophical sect. The Oliphants migrated to Haifa. Gordon commented, 'They have odd ideas which I do not fathom.'[25]

'We were much taken with him,' Alice Oliphant wrote to her mother after Gordon and Laurence had reminisced 'like two old friends. They say it must be because they are each considered "one of the craziest fellows alive!"'[26] Laurence Oliphant told Augusta: 'What was so extraordinarily attractive in him, was his underlying meekness and contempt for himself except as an instrument for Divine ends. The absence of all cant combined with this intense desire for service however humble, made me feel him to be the most Christ-like man I ever knew.'[27]

In July Gordon moved down to Jaffa on the coast, as more central for exploring farther from Jerusalem. He looked out all the British and American residents and invited them to his hotel for a Bible reading. He found a Church Missionary Society post under the Reverend J. R. Longley Hall. Gordon took services for him twice, and attended a missionary conference at Gaza. One morning Hall needed to call on Gordon during his hours of study and prayer and saw the list of those for whom he prayed daily. Hall believed it ran to two or three hundred names of people of every sort, from Kings and Queens down to some of the humblest persons on earth.[28]

Gordon sometimes used the services of an American, Rolla Floyd, an ex-Mormon from Maine, who had made the first wheeled vehicle in Palestine in modern times and organized a carriage service between Jaffa and Jerusalem. One wet day an Englishman named William Greene overtook Floyd riding an Arab steed, escorting a carriage with two gentlemen. 'Do you know who I have got in the carriage? ... The celebrated Chinese Gordon.' He introduced Greene; Greene became well acquainted with 'this wonderful man, who the more I knew of him the more I admired him.'[29] Greene was helping a clergyman named Friedlander to settle destitute Jews from Russia. Gordon called on Friedlander, heard the need, went to his hotel and came back, said Greene, with 'a large bundle of clothes of every variety brought out for personal use,' together with a sum of money for the Jews.

Gordon's year in the Holy Land was nearly up. He did not wish to be idle but realized, as he told Harvey, that he was 'difficult to employ';[30] he could not brook the restrictions imposed on a general officer who was answerable to Parliament.

PART FOUR

TOO LATE

1884–1885

CHAPTER TWENTY-EIGHT

'Gordon for the Sudan'

On 19 October 1884 William Mackinnon sent a telegram to Gordon in Jaffa on behalf of King Leopold, and a letter to Sir Henry Gordon in London. As the letter explained, Henry Morton Stanley was coming home from the Congo after laying the foundations of the African Association's new state and did not wish to renew his contract as administrator; 'and as the work,' Mackinnon told Sir Henry, 'has become very important and requires a man possessed of great powers of organization and other qualities such as few men except your brother possess the King hopes he may be induced to accept the position. He will have entire control of the enterprise.'[1]

Gordon would have 'willingly and gladly'[2] accepted the King's offer in October 1882 had he not been engaged in South Africa; when the invitation was renewed after Gordon's return to England, he stalled, wishing to go to Palestine.[3] Now he could accept. He wired Henry to ask whether the War Office would give permission. After some delay a telegram arrived on 25 October from the Military Secretary, expressed rather oddly: 'Secretary of State decides to sanction your employment on the Congo.'[4]

Gordon could not leave at once because his nephew Willie Anderson was on his way out and wanted to be shown the sacred sites. Then, at Gaza on the night of 15 November, a letter from Henry told him that the Foreign Secretary, Lord Granville, did not want an officer on the active list to go to the Congo: As Granville explained to the Queen's Private Secretary later, 'the object of the association is excellent,' but it would soon collapse as King Leopold would not subsidize it much longer:[5] Granville, like Mackinnon, Gordon and, indeed, Stanley himself at this time believed that Leopold acted from admirable motives (the spread of civilization, the suppression of the slave trade) and not, as historians now believe, from a cynical wish to amass a vast fortune.

Henry learned that the War Office had already sent a telegram to Gordon: 'Secretary of State declines to sanction . . .'; and the Turkish telegraphist, probably with very little English, had misinterpreted the tapping of the morse code: *declines* had become *decides*.[6]

Gordon at once wrote to Mackinnon: '*I promised the King to go if he wished it*, and if His Majesty does, *go I will*.' He would resign his commission and enter Leopold's service 'for good and all. If I go to the Congo I go for ever, that is certain . . . Let H. M. know I am for sale for life for £500 a year'[7] – a far less sum than Stanley was paid.

Gordon finally sailed from Jaffa on 11 December but bad weather forced him into Haifa and he did not reach Genoa until 30 December. He saw in the new year of 1884 in a train, working through his prayer list, as he came overnight by Milan and the St. Gotthard tunnel to Brussels, arriving on New Year's Day. 'I am all right,' he scribbled to Augusta. 'Peace and tranquility I am glad to say.'[8] As he had written to Cowell some months earlier: 'To be A, governing huge countries, or B, occupying the smallest place, are the same in reality, for Christ rules events as much with respect to A's government as He does in B's little affairs. A and B, as far as the actual government, are as flies in a fly wheel, their motives of action are the only things which are of real import.'[9]

At Brussels he was received by King Leopold, tall and handsome with his long brown beard, on 2 January. 'He was very kind'; the King would compensate him for the loss of his pension and pay his debts, for Gordon did not scruple to run up debts (mostly to friends) in order to finance his long list of pensioners – old and young: he was helping numerous nephews and neices; and as he wrote once to Watson asking him to order some presents: '"Refuse being godfather." It is sheer ruin!!'[10]

Gordon agreed to leave for the Congo early in February, first returning to England to resign his commission. But while in Brussels he received a letter, dated 4 January, from his dear friend Wolseley, a peer since his victory at Tel-el-Kebir, and the effective head of the Army as Adjutant-General under the Duke of Cambridge. 'I hate the idea,' wrote Wolseley, 'of your going to the Congo. You have had enough of liver-grilling climates, and the world does not seem bounded with the clear horizon that would warrant – if I may venture to say to an old friend – our very best man burying himself amongst niggers on the Equator. Of course, if you will go there, all will go right for King Leopold, and I am very anxious his project should succeed, but I think he might attain his end without taking our best man from the English Army

– You see I write to you frankly, just as I feel.'[11] Wolseley promised to help Gordon retain his commission; and he said he would like to talk about the Sudan, 'as things can't go on.' Wolseley did not disclose in this flattering letter that Gordon's name had already been put forward as the one man who could solve the worsening crisis in the Sudan.

When Gordon had been on his way to the Holy Land a year earlier he had been tempted to divert to Cairo and offer his services to restore the Sudan to its native sultans; he believed that once independent the tribes would desert the Mahdi or not join him. By June, with the Mahdi's strength increasing, Gordon was sure that Britain 'underrated the nature of the movement in the Sudan.' He told Oliphant in Haifa that 'the whole affair should be settled by a civil commissioner, who should at once be sent by England to the Mahdi to arrange with him the terms upon which the Soudan should be rendered independent of Egypt.'[12] Oliphant believed that had Gordon been sent then, he might have effected a settlement.

The Egyptians did not wish to surrender the Sudan. They sent Hicks Pasha, a retired Indian Army colonel, to Khartoum to command their troops. When Cairo reinforced him with peasant conscripts, dragged in chains from their homes, he set out early in November to confront the Mahdi and was betrayed into an ambush. Hicks and his troops fought until their ammunition ran out, when they were overwhelmed and butchered. The victorious Mahdi was immediately joined by tribes which had kept quiet.

News of Hicks's disaster reached Britain on 22 November. That day a Sapper colonel who had served under Gordon in China and was later a general and M. P., wrote a suggestion to Sir Andrew Clarke, who ranked as the senior Sapper: 'Now, there is one man,' wrote Colonel Bevan Edwards, 'who is competent to deal with this question – Charlie Gordon. He would not work under the Khedive, but, if he was asked to assist the Khedive, working if possible, directly under the Government at home, I think he would go. His name alone would do wonders; but no time should be lost.'[13] He should be given supreme powers as governor-general and if necessary a division from India: the southern Sudan could be abandoned but Khartoum and the east coast kept safe.

Clarke sent the letter to Erskine Childers, now Chancellor of the Exchequer, with a strong endorsement: 'If the Mahdi is a prophet, Gordon in the Sudan is a greater. He will be in London in a day or two, as he is *en route* to the Congo. How well I recollect his telling Baring when we were passing with Lord Ripon through Egypt that the action of the Cairo Government would lead to grief in the Sudan. I was gratified to hear Wolseley speak the other day in even stronger terms of admiration and respect for Gordon than even I would do.'[14]

Childers passed this eagerly to the Foreign Secretary. Lord Granville cabled the suggestion to Sir Evelyn Baring, Gordon's old antagonist over Egyptian finances, who since September had been British Agent and Consul-General in Cairo and effectively the ruler of Egypt. Baring replied that the Khedive's prime minister was afraid of employing Gordon 'as being a Christian.'

Gordon's name was already being pressed on Baring independently by Major General Sir Evelyn Wood, V. C., the first British Sirdar (commander-in-chief) of the Egyptian Army, who had been appointed on Gordon's recommendation, through Brett, to re-create it after the Arabi rebellion.[15] On 11 December, the very day that Gordon left Jaffa, Wood wrote to Queen Victoria, who was fond of him and his wife, that he had never met Gordon (they realized later that they had met under fire in the Crimea) 'but after allowing for all his peculiar views about religion, Sir Evelyn believes his account of Egyptian-caused misery in the Soudan is accurate, and that he is the only man who could do anything up there at this moment without a good army. It is right to add the Pachas here allege the rising in the Sudan was all originated by Gordon!'[16] And certainly Gordon could write to a friend from Brussels on 3 January: 'I feel for the rebels and am proud of their prowess.'[17]

By then, the British Government had decided that Egypt should evacuate the Sudan.

Gordon left Brussels and arrived at Charing Cross at 5.30 p. m. on Monday 8 January, reaching Southampton and Rockstone Place at 11 p. m. He found a telegram from W. T. Stead, the celebrated editor of the *Pall Mall Gazette*, one of London's evening papers, asking for an interview to discuss the Sudan. Gordon wired next morning that his views were not important enough to warrant Stead's journey. Stead, who had pioneered the idea of the political interview and was acting entirely on his own initiative, would not be put off.

'Today came a Mr. Stead and invaded me,' Gordon wrote to Sir Samuel Baker. 'I told him what I had to say about Sudan ... This is all I mean to say.'[18] Gordon had summoned as witness his devoted friend Captain John Brocklehurst of the Blues, afterwards Major-General Lord Ranksborough. Since their first meeting in the Sudan in '77 Brocklehurst had married and had fought in the battle of Tel-el-Kebir and was now thirty-one. He had never met Stead. They sat in Augusta's sitting room, drinking her tea, the thirty-four year old Stead on a couch covered with a leopard skin. Gordon spread a map of the Congo on the floor and spoke of the coming destruction of the Slave Trade, but showed 'considerable disinclination,' recorded Stead 'to express his opinions' on the Sudan until it was 'represented to him very strongly that he of all men now in the country was best acquainted with the Sudan and therefore best able to speak with authority.'[19]

Gordon then spoke 'with the utmost clearness and emphasis' for two hours on the causes of the disaster and the difficulties to be faced. Gordon talked fast; Stead did not take notes, but Brocklehurst, who went back to London with him, was amazed by his accuracy when he checked the proofs next morning.

The rebellion in the Sudan, said Gordon, was 'entirely attributable to a single cause, and that is, the grossest mis-government.' He was convinced (wrongly) that the Mahdi was not 'in any sense a religious leader ... The movement is not religious but an outbreak of despair. Three times over I warned the late Khedive that it would be impossible to govern the Soudan on the old system, after my appointment to the Governor-Generalship. During the three years that I wielded full powers in the Sudan, I taught the natives that they had a right to exist. I waged war against the Turks and Circassians, who had harried the population. I had taught them something of the meaning of liberty and justice, and accustomed them to a higher ideal of government than that with which they had previously been acquainted.' As soon as he went the oppression returned, with inevitable consequences since 'their cries were unheeded in Cairo.'

But Gordon deplored the decision to evacuate Khartoum and the eastern Sudan, essential to Egypt. 'Even if we were bound to do so we should have said nothing about it. The moment it is known that we have given up the game, every man will go over to the Mahdi. All men worship the rising sun. The difficulties of evacuation will be enormously increased, if, indeed, the withdrawal of our garrison is not rendered impossible.'

The rebellion could be ended by negotiation, and 'the government entrusted to a man whose word was truth,' to rule for the benefit of the Sudanese. 'The Sudanese are a very nice people. They deserve the sincere compassion and sympathy of all civilized men. I got on very well with them,' he wrote, and he hated the thought of a Turkish reconquest. The long interview ended with Gordon's assurance that he did not wish to press his opinions and had been reluctant to say anything about this very difficult crisis; but 'when you appealed to me, I did feel moved at the thought of the poor Sudanese, whom I knew so well and loved so much.'[20]

The next afternoon 'all London' was reading the article headed, *Chinese Gordon on the Sudan*, accompanied by a powerful leader headed, *Chinese Gordon for the Sudan*. Until then, Gordon's name had been almost forgotten by the general public. When *Colonel Gordon in Central Africa* had been published in 1881, sales were small: Birkbeck Hill had 'looked for a gale; there was not more than a breeze . . . For a while the sale went slowly on, but at last it ceased altogether.'[21] Only in 1884–5 did the book become a best seller.

Stead's article made Gordon's name resound once more. *The Times* and other papers took up the cry, Gordon for the Sudan. The Foreign Secretary cabled Baring again, and again received a negative reply although Baring now wanted a British officer to arrange the evacuation. Evelyn Wood, looking back one month later, thought Baring's 'doubt of Gordon Pasha's appointment comes from the impossibility of inducing him to carry out any line of policy of which he does not approve. This arises from a very noble frame of mind, but it is obviously a drawback.'[22]

Gordon did not read Stead's article; he was not reading newspapers at that time, even in the train to Exeter on the day *The Times* repeated it. He was on his way to stay with Reginald Barnes and his family at Heavitree vicarage on the south-eastern edge of the city. 'We were all assembled in the hall to greet him when he arrived on a dark January day,' recalled Sir Kenneth Barnes, who was then aged five, 'and a characteristic little incident, not to my credit, then occurred. He hoisted me up in his arms, and this friendly gesture prompted me to ask him: "What have you brought me?" My father was horrified, but our famous guest saved the situation by buying me a box of Scottish soldiers, and playing on the floor with me.'[23]

Two members of the family were much influenced by Gordon's visit, for when Prebendary Barnes mentioned to Gordon, in their long talks together, his concern that each child should find the right career, Gordon said: 'Be very sure that, as far as is possible, you let them follow their own bent.'[24] Violet discovered years later that this remark had guided her father not to oppose her wish to go on the stage, a most unusual step for a clergyman's daughter: and thus 'Violet Vanbrugh' and her sister 'Irene Vanbrugh' became eminent actresses in their day. All the Barnes family remained devoted to Gordon's memory: 'A genuine mystic of unsullied personality.'[25]*

Gordon slept in a pleasant room looking across to the high ground of Woodbury Common. Next morning he attended Holy Communion and then went into the city to call on the Bishop of Exeter, Frederick Temple, the next archbishop, who was either amused or shocked when Gordon said that Christianity would advance rapidly in Africa if only the church permitted polygamy.[26]

They drove on, down Fore Street and across the Exe, to see the memorials to Gordon's grandparents in St. Thomas's church. A legend grew in Exeter that just as they reached the porch a telegraph boy, sent on from Heavitree, handed Gordon a wire from Wolseley; and that Gordon turned and never entered the church.[27] The wire, however, was not sent from London until the following day.

That afternoon Gordon and Barnes went by train to Newton Abbot to stay with Sir Samuel Baker at his country house, Sandford Orleigh. In the carriage as they drove from the station Baker urged Gordon to return to the Sudan 'as Governor-General, if Her Majesty's Government should require it. Gordon was silent,' recalled Barnes, 'but his eyes flashed, and an eager expression passed over his face as he looked at his host.' Barnes guessed that Gordon wanted to go but was committed to the Congo, where he could kill the Slave Trade at its source. Barnes's impression was confirmed late that night: 'When we had retired, he came to my room, and said in a soft voice, "You saw me today?" "You mean in the carriage?" "Yes; you saw *me* – that was *myself* – the self I want to get rid of."'[28]

He had already urged Baker to go to the Sudan as Commissioner-General. Gordon would have been amused and horrified had he known that about a year earlier Baker, when fishing for a baronetcy (without success) had told the Prince of Wales' Secretary that he would only take it if a similar honour went to Gordon for his attempt to eradicate slave hunting. 'Colonel Gordon

---

*When the vicarage became a retirement home it was renamed Gordon House.

(*sic*) who has worked for five years in a pestiferous climate with his life in constant danger, has been utterly disregarded.'[29]

Gordon returned to Southampton on the Saturday. Here he found Wolseley's telegram, forwarded from Heavitree, and wired back that he would come up on Tuesday. He found also that he was being 'hunted' by the press, and decided to escape to Brussels as soon as he had seen Wolseley, and lie low until he left for the Congo.

On the Sunday he probably worshipped at St. Mary's, the parish church, for he sent a note next day to Canon Basil Wilberforce (grandson of the Emancipator and later Chaplain to the Speaker) asking to be remembered at his prayer meeting: 'I would rather have the prayers of that little company gathered in your house to-day than I would have the wealth of the Sudan placed at my disposal. Pray for me that I may have humility and the guidance of God, and that all spirit of murmuring may be rebuked in me.'[30]

After final preparations for the Congo he went up to London on Tuesday 15 January and saw Wolseley, who told him that he would not be 'turned out of the army,': a way had been found to keep him on the active list, on leave, while in the Congo. They then discussed the Sudan.

'On the 15 January 1884,' runs Wolseley's memory of the interview in a letter to Sir Henry more than eighteen months later, 'I asked him if he would go to Suakin to enquire into the condition of affairs in the Sudan – I told him he ought to go if the government asked him. He said he would go although he denounced the notion of giving up the Sudan as the silliest of silly, weak policies.'[31]

In a more guarded report to Lord Hartington, written nearer the time, Wolseley recorded Gordon's conviction that it would be better to evacuate than to reconquer 'if such reconquest was to entail again handing it over to the government of Egyptian pashas;' and that he believed the Mahdi's power would melt away if English officers were appointed to govern the eastern Sudan.

Wolseley also implied in this report (4 February 1884) that the suggestion of the fact-finding mission to Suakin came from Gordon himself; if sent, he would advise whether to evacuate or to 'constitute some settled government ... in this latter case,' noted Wolseley to Hartington, 'he might recommend his own reappointment as Governor-General. From the first he expressed an earnest desire to help Mr. Gladstone's Government.'[32]

Gordon left Wolseley, called on Henry, Brett, Donnelly, and Baroness Burdett-Coutts, who gave him her letter-case as a keepsake. He would have called on the Prince of Wales had he not been at Sandringham.

He still thought he was going to the Congo: 'it was just on tapis that the Govt. would want me; but so very doubtful that it seemed unlikely.'[33] Next morning, with Brocklehurst, he left for Brussels and at Dover scribbled a pencilled note to Wolseley: 'If any hitch of any sort arises either at home or in Egypt, the latter is very likely. As my friend, hesitate not a moment to bury the whole matter of yesterday, for *I* only know it, outside W. O.

'I would not have the very slightest flutter of hurt on subject and would never mention it.'[34]

They reached the Hotel Bellevue in Brussels, only to be handed a telegram from Lord Wolseley, despatched at noon: 'Come here at once can you start this evening so as to be with me early tomorrow telegraph at once saying hour tomorrow I may expect you.'[35]

Gordon took time at Brussels to write to the widow of Colonel Jenkins, who had died recently: '... I feel much for you my dear Mrs. Jenkins in your solitude, and pray earnestly that the Comforter will raise you and be ever with you.'[36]

Gordon and Brocklehurst recrossed the Channel overnight, arriving at Knightsbridge Barracks at 6 a. m., Gordon 'very tired.' He washed and shaved and went to Wolseley who explained that Baring had agreed to his going to the Sudan. Baring had telegraphed: 'I would rather have him than anyone else, provided there is clear understanding with him as to what his position is to be and what line of policy he is to carry out. Otherwise, not.'[37]

Wolseley explained the policy, but the future would show that neither he, nor the members of the Cabinet who were about to meet Gordon, nor Baring in Cairo, were clear as to what it was. No Cabinet had met for months as Parliament had been in recess since the summer. Gladstone was at Hawarden Castle, his country home near Chester. Granville secured his sanction by telegraph[38] but Gladstone did not consider the start of Gordon's mission important enough to record in his staccato diary.*

The four Cabinet ministers known to be in London gathered to interview Gordon in Hartington's room at the War Office overlooking Horse Guards Parade. Hartington, able but indolent, who was to break with Gladstone

---

*The scene in the Charlton Heston film when he, as Gordon, is interviewed in Downing Street by Sir Ralph Richardson as Gladstone, who says 'Don't you do a Billy Hicks on me,' is fiction.

over Home Rule, was sending Gordon on a mission of peace, not war, to evacuate the garrisons; Granville, the weak Foreign Secretary, known as 'Pussy', was sending him to Suakin on the Red Sea to report on the whole situation – how to evaluate, secure good government, even counteract the Slave Trade – and to 'act under Baring's instructions to perform such other duties as may be entrusted to him by the Egyptian government.'[39]

Dilke, the radical (Local Government Board), whose political career would shortly be destroyed by his involvement in a divorce case, was so sure that they were sending Gordon to Suakin only to report (Dilke had objected to Baring's request for an executive officer) that he convinced himself later that Gordon had exceeded his orders even by going to Khartoum, and had deceived the Cabinet as to his intentions.

The fourth minister was Baring's cousin, Lord Northbrook, First Lord of the Admiralty who, as the Queen recorded in her Journal a few days later, knew Gordon well 'and says is an extraordinary man, with an enormous power over uncivilised people. His attempt is a very daring one.'[40]

Wolseley brought Gordon in to the Cabinet ministers. Gordon's account next day to Augusta was succinct: 'They said "had I seen Wolseley, and did I understand the ideas"? I said "Yes" and repeated what W. said to me as to their ideas which was "they would evacuate Sudan". They were pleased and said that was the idea, would I go. I said "Yes", they said "when,", I said "to-night" and it was over ...'[41]

Granville immediately sent a cipher telegram to the Queen detailing Gordon's instructions and wrote to her that Gordon 'is rather optimist than otherwise. He does not believe in the Mahdi, or the real fanaticism of the Arabs or in the probability of a massacre. He has great faith in time. Lord Granville trusts he may be in the right but it is an anxious moment.' To Hartington, next day, Granville remarked: 'We were proud of ourselves yesterday – are you sure we didn't commit a gigantic folly?'[42]

Gordon left the Cabinet ministers. Wolseley offered him a staff officer and he chose Colonel J. D. Hammill-Stewart of 11th Hussars, who had toured the Sudan garrisons early the previous year: he was discovered in his club and agreed to go though he had no time to fetch his uniform.

Gordon wired King Leopold and wrote a letter to apologize that the Congo must wait a few months. Had Gordon ruled the Congo its history would have been happier – unless he had swiftly resigned on some matter of principle.

He also wrote another note to Canon Wilberforce at Southampton: 'Offer thanks at your next prayer meeting. When I was upborne on the hearts of those Christians I received from God the spiritual blessing that I wanted, and I am now calmly resting in the current of His will.'[43]

The Duke of Cambridge, who as commander-in-chief should have been present at the Cabinet committee, had been on a shoot in Richmond Park with three friends 'and did very well killing 178 birds. Home by 5.15,' he recorded in his Diary. Here he learned of Gordon's mission: 'a very wise step but should have been taken long long ago.'[44]

At 7.45 p. m. the Duke of Cambridge went to Charing Cross station. In a scene made famous by prints the Commander-in-Chief, the Foreign Secretary, the Secretary of State for War and the Adjutant-General said farewell to Gordon and Colonel Stewart. Lord Granville bought his ticket. The Duke held open the carriage door. Gordon's nephew Bob dashed up the platform with Uncle Charlie's uniform in its case. Wolseley discovered, almost as the whistle blew, that Gordon (as usual) had no cash. Wolseley emptied his pockets and handed over his gold watch: they had already exchanged cigarette cases as keepsakes.*

Gordon was cheery, encouraging them all with his optimism. The doors clanged shut, the 8 p. m. mail train steamed out into the night ten minutes late.

The Duke, later that evening, called on his aged mother at St James's Palace. Her lady-in-waiting, Lady Geraldine Somerset, recorded his remarks in her diary in her usual uninhibited style: 'The Duke brought us a very great piece of news; that Chinese Gordon *has been sent* out to Egypt by the Govt! actually!! *at last* and when well nigh too late! very *probably* altogether too late. So like this Govt, after resisting all the advice these many months to send him out, to wait till he was not only engaged to the K of the Belgians to go to the Congo, but had actually started, positively was at Brussels, whither he had gone but yesterday – *then* to make up their minds to send him to the Sudan! he arrived here this morning and started tonight. The Duke went to the Station to see him off. If only Khartoum may not have been taken before he gets there!!! The Duke found him sanguine as to getting there in time, altogether as to his success. God grant him to be right.'[45]

---

*Gordon was smoking again.

CHAPTER TWENTY-NINE

Cairo

On the morning of Thursday 24 January 1884 the P. and O. steamer *Tanjore* entered Port Said harbour.

Across Europe and the Mediterranean Gordon and Stewart, who had only known each other by reputation, had found a mutual respect rather than affection. Both were ascetic in their tastes, and had a love for the people of the Sudan, but Stewart was a cool and reserved Scot who acted from calm judgement rather than intuition. He would be an excellent staff officer for the impulsive Gordon.

'Colonel Stewart is a capital fellow and knows the Sudan well,' Gordon had written to Northbrook during the journey, while Stewart wrote to his sister Haddie that Gordon 'is a charming chief and companion and I am sure we shall work hand in hand.'[1] Stewart felt confident 'that we shall come out of the affair with flying colours and with God's blessing pull England out of a serious difficulty. We do not mean to fight but to negotiate and use our personal influence. I am convinced Gordon will come well out of the affair and pull the chestnuts out of the fire.'[2]

As Gordon and Stewart came on deck they saw *H. M. S. Carysfort* anchored close by with steam up, ordered from Malta to take them down the Suez Canal and the Red Sea to Suakin. Then a steam launch came alongside the *Tanjore* and Gordon saw Charles Watson, now a lieutenant-colonel, and with him General Sir Evelyn Wood. Watson was glad to see Gordon looking fitter than when they had last met in '81, and as the Crimea veterans renewed acquaintance while he deciphered telegrams, he reflected that 'it is curious to think that Gordon had sent Sir Evelyn to Egypt, while Sir Evelyn had really been the means of getting Gordon sent to the Sudan.'[3]

Wood handed Gordon two letters. Baring wrote: 'I was exceedingly glad to receive Lord Granville's letter informing me that you and Stewart were coming to Egypt. I feel confident that you may both render very great services as regards Sudan affairs.'[4] He urged Gordon to change plans, coming to Cairo for consultations and to pay his respects to the Khedive. His request was backed by another letter from Gordon's great friend Gerald Graham: 'My dear Charlie – Do come to Cairo. Wood will tell you, much better than I, why. Throw over all personal feeling, if you have any, and act like yourself with straightforward directness. You have no personal aims in this matter, and therefore no personal feelings must be allowed to interfere . . .'[5]

Since Gordon had been ordered to act on Baring's instructions he had little choice, and soon was in the steam launch for the five hour canal journey to Ismailia where a special train awaited them. That night, at 9 p. m. Gerald Graham was at Cairo station with a few others, having hurriedly left an R. E. dinner at Shepheard's Hotel on hearing that the train was due half an hour early.

'It was a great sight,' wrote E. A. Floyer, head of the Telegraph Department, 'as tall Graham, some inches over six feet, grasped both Gordon's hands with "Charlie, dear boy, how are you?" and "Gerald, my dear fellow, how are you?" answered the little man joyfully.'[6] Graham drove with Gordon and Wood to the Sirdar's splendid residence, *Maison Duke of Sutherland* where Gordon was to stay.

Next morning Baring told Gordon that he was not to be merely an observer for the British government but Governor-General again, for the duration of the evacuation and to establish a settled administration to govern the Sudan after it ceased to be an Egyptian dominion; Gordon at that point believed that the Sudan should be a confederation of independent sultans[7]. He was given full discretionary powers and a substantial credit, for as he had pointed out to Northbrook, 'I fear great distress to the European employees who want to go to Egypt,' and he would need funds to allay it.[8]

He then called on the Khedive Tewfik, and apologized for calling him 'a snake' in the *Pall Mall* interview which had offended the Khedive when he had read it in *The Times*. The Khedive, forgiving and friendly, gave him his *firman* of appointment, sitting on the same divan on which his father had sat when handing Gordon his *firman* of appointment as Governor-General in 1877. Tewfik also gave Gordon a secret *firman* announcing the independence of the Sudan and the evacuation of the garrisons, to be made public when he thought best: its terms had been drafted by Gordon and Baring.

Next day Tewfik assured a French journalist, Baron de Malorte, that

Gordon was now the 'arbiter of the situation. Whatever he does will be well done; whatever propositions he will make are accepted in advance; whatever combinations he may decide upon will be binding for us; the Khedive has placed unlimited trust in the Pasha's judgement.'[9] But Gordon was not only the Khedive's representative and Governor-General; he was a British Commissioner, expected to follow the instructions and waverings of the Liberal government in London, who might not accept his propositions. As Wolseley remarked five months later to Gladstone's private secretary: 'instead of allowing Gordon to go out, as originally intended, to Suakin merely to *report* on the state and outlook of things in Sudan, he was waylaid by Baring at Port Said, brought up to Cairo, and despatched to Khartoum as Governor-General – a distinct departure from the terms on which he left England.' All subsequent troubles, said Wolseley, stemmed from that.[10]

Gordon was optimistic; but Stewart wrote that day to a friend, E. Hudson, 'I am leaving tomorrow for Khartoum on what I will not disguise from you is a dangerous expedition. I am going in the company of a very distinguished officer, Major General Gordon, who is at the same time an Englishman of the very noblest type, on a mission of very considerable importance ... if we come to grief it will be in a good cause.' ...[11]

Gordon meanwhile was making a round of courtesy visits. He called on Nubar, now Prime Minister again. He called on the commander of the British army of occupation, General Stephenson, who wrote to his sister next day and gave a clear statement of Gordon's view of his task: 'He told me ... that his mission consisted in employing the best means in his power by using his influence with the different tribes or otherwise, to effect the withdrawal of the different garrisons, civil population, with their women and children etc., from the Sudan with as little loss as possible.

'Most of the tribes are in rebellion,' continued Stephenson, 'and it will be an operation of difficulty and serious danger unless the wild tribes can be conciliated. Gordon is the most likely man to exercise this desirable result, and should he fail we must not be surprised to hear of loss of life among the fugitives during their retreat.' After describing Gordon's appearance Stephenson added: 'he is thoroughly disinterested, never thinking of himself, and imbued with a deep religious feeling. He will enter upon his mission with his life in his hand, trusting to his fearless nature and the recollection of the influence he exercised a few years ago in that country.'[12]

He called on Sharif Pasha, who had resigned as Prime Minister rather than agree to the evacuation; and in Sharif's ante-room Gordon came face to face with Zubair Pasha, the one-time conqueror of the Bahr al-Ghazal and later of Darfur.

Zubair had been kept an exile from the Sudan for the past nine years. Gordon had regarded him as 'the greatest slave-hunter who ever existed',[13] and had believed him to have instigated the rebellion of his son Suleiman, which had ended when Gessi had defeated and captured him and had him shot. Gordon had suspected that Zubair's father-in-law was secretly behind the Mahdi's rising, which he still did not see as a religious movement. He had therefore sent a telegram to Baring a day before reaching Egypt, asking that Zubair be exiled to Cyprus, and had prepared a long paper to support his request.

Meeting unexpectedly the tall Sudanese whom Graham described as 'that man of smooth words but cruel deeds, with a hideous face suggestive to me of a death's-head tenanted by a demon,'[14] Gordon had an immediate 'mystic feeling' that Zubair was the man to rule the Sudan. 'He would be accepted on all sides and . . . end the Mahdi in a couple of months.' But Zubair might be filled with malice towards him for the death of his son and the confiscation of his property.[15]

Gordon therefore proposed that he and Zubair should face each other in the presence of Baring and Nubar. They were joined by Wood, Watson, Stewart and Geigler Pasha, the tall German with a long ginger beard who had been Gordon's deputy and had lately returned from the Sudan. This council would decide whether Gordon might take Zubair.

They gathered after lunch at Baring's house. When Zubair entered, Gordon held out his hand. Zubair refused it, putting his own hand behind his back. Young Reginald Wingate, Wood's A. D. C., standing at the back of the room, thought Gordon looked furious, but it would only have been for a moment. The interpreter, Aranghi, sat between Gordon and Zubair while a young secretary, Samuel Davies, took shorthand notes in English.

Gordon asked Zubair to make any complaints. He replied: 'I want to know why my property in the Sudan was confiscated.' 'Because you wrote a letter to your son, Suleiman, inciting him to revolt,' replied Gordon. Zubair denied it, and after argument, Wingate was sent to find the letter, attached to the Court Martial proceedings in the Egyptian War Office archives. It was not produced at the meeting.

Soon they were arguing about Suleiman's execution for rebellion and for shooting 200 Egyptian soldiers. Zubair hedged, and then said he was not responsible for Suleiman when he was a bey under Gordon Pasha. 'I treated your son with every consideration,' said Gordon. 'I did my best for him.' 'But you killed my son whom I entrusted to you. He was as your son!' 'Well, well, I killed my own son. There is an end of it.'

At the close of their confrontation Zubair stood up and drawing his finger across his throat he said: 'If it can be proved that I incited my son to rebellion in the letter, I do not want to live. Put me to death with the sword!'[16]

When Zubair had left the room Gordon read out his reasons for wanting to take him to the Sudan. He then left, for the *ad hoc* Council to decide. Wood was astonished that Gordon could change his mind so quickly but Watson said that this was quite usual. Watson brought an urgent message from Gordon's ex-secretary, the blind Tuhami Bey, who had been on the special train at Gordon's request and was now helping the preparations. He begged that either Zubair or Gordon be sent but not both: Zubair would pursue his blood feud and have Gordon killed. Wood had heard the same from Tuhami. Stewart thought Zubair had shown animus against Gordon during their argument. The Council decided that Zubair must stay in Cairo.

Had they truly known Zubair's mind their decision would have been different. A few days later Zubair gave Baron de Kusel, a naturalized Englishman, his version of the meeting at the Agency: 'He told me that all the doubts that he had had concerning Gordon's connection with the death of his son were now removed. He was satisfied that Gordon had acted in absolutely good faith, and that the fault lay with Gessi, and some others. He also said that Gordon had inspired him with absolute trust, and that he hoped in future to be looked upon as one of his friends … I am convinced that Zubair meant what he said.'[17]

Instead, that afternoon at Baring's house, more seeds of disaster were sown. The two pashas, Sudanese and English, were summoned back. Zubair was told that he could not go to Khartoum; if Gordon came back safely he might be allowed to go later.

Gordon was deeply disappointed. His first proposition, far from being accepted in advance had been rejected. That morning, in a brief note to Augusta to tell her he was leaving for the Sudan that night, he had written: 'I feel quite happy, for I say, if God is with me who can or will be hurtful to me? May He be glorified, the world and the people of the Sudan be blessed, and may I be the dust under His feet –'[18] but not under Baring's feet, when so much was at stake.

Gordon was thrown into gloom. Even visiting Lady Baring's nursery to see their 'chicks', and later Wood's 'chicks', could not cheer him. At the farewell dinner which Lady Wood gave, he seemed remote and silent. As they all got ready to see him off at the station, he took off his evening dress coat and waistcoat and presented them to Wood's butler, saying he would never need them again.[19]

He had exactly one year to live.

CHAPTER THIRTY

Nile Journey

They travelled over night by train beside the Nile to the rail head at Assiout, where Thomas Cook had laid on a special steamer. Gerald Graham, with his A. D. C., Lieutenant W. Angel Scott of the Cameron Highlanders, was accompanying Gordon and Donald Stewart for the eight-day journey up the Nile to Korosko, where they would disembark to cross the desert. Also on the special train was the young rightful Sultan of Darfur, whom Gordon hoped would help form his federation of sultans.

The Sultan, however, was both disappointment and comic relief. Gordon having rejected his request for a few days' delay to collect his harem, the Sultan had held up the train at Cairo by arriving with a party of twenty-five wives, brothers and hangers on. Gordon did not like to leave them behind and sent for extra carriages.

At the railway station Gordon had still looked upset by Baring's refusal to allow him Zubair; the Sultan's antics may have helped him to recover, as also the knowledge that he had left behind a note to be given to Baring when he had gone, to say that he might decide on a personal visit to the Mahdi and not be heard of for two months, if taken hostage for Zubair.

When the train drew into Assiout in the morning, Gordon and the English officers were astonished to see the Sultan of Darfur step down in gorgeous array of gold-laced uniform, with the broad sash of a newly-awarded order across his chest. Ignoring the Governor-General he pranced towards the paddle steamer 'with long and rapid steps, followed by his motley court of ragged and dirty women and men,' and hitching up the ribbon 'which would perversely attempt to slide off his shoulder.' He 'took possession of the main deck cabin' recorded Stewart, 'but was very speedily and ignominiously expelled by Gordon Pasha' who ordered him to take off his uniform.

Returning after breakfast as 'an unsure, unintelligent and badly-dressed native' he stood humbly before Gordon who told him he would certainly be murdered on the way if he travelled in gold braid; he must not wear uniform until he had recovered his throne (he never did, and took to drinking gin.)[1]

They started on the river journey. They steamed all day and anchored for a few hours the first night. They slept on deck in the cold desert air and by some mischance Gordon missed the warm cloak which Watson had bought for him, and could not sleep.

Yet next morning Graham was writing to his wife and watched Gordon talking animatedly in his bad Arabic ('utterly regardless of grammar,' said Graham) to the black Ibrahim Fawzi, whose life had once hung on a toss of Gordon's coin. He was now thirty-two. Gordon had specially asked for him and delivered him from the exile imposed for having fought under Arabi. 'Gordon's face is smiling while he talks,' Graham wrote, 'his eyes twinkle with fun at some point, while by his gestures with his fingers he seems rallying the "Arabian knight" or laughingly pushing some question home. This was the morning after his cold, sleepless night, when many men would be apt to be cross and ill-humoured.'[2] It was also his fifty-first birthday.

He could be cross. Graham described an incident when Stewart agreed with Graham against sending a plan of operations to Cairo, 'saying "Speech is silver: silence is golden." This annoyed Gordon, whose nerves are irritable, and he said he would write it out himself ... At luncheon he reappeared in much better temper, saying he had written a letter to the Mahdi.'[3]

Graham saw these brief bursts of temper in their true proportion: 'His usual aspect was serene and quiet, and though at times a ruffling wave of constitutional impatience or indignation might pass over him, it did not disturb him long. The depth and largeness of Gordon's nature, which inspired so much confidence in others, seemed to afford him a sense of inner repose, so that outer disturbance was to him like the wind that ruffles the surface of the sea, but does not affect its depths.'[4]

On the third morning they disembarked for the short railway journey round the First Cataract, to Philae where they arrived amid 'a great rush and considerable confusion.' Before re-embarking on a second steamer they met the Roman Catholic priests and missionaries who had been withdrawn from Khartoum. Stewart thought Monsignor Francesco Sogaro, Comboni's successor as vicar-apostolic, 'very timid and frightened,'[5] expecting a tribal raid. Gordon promised to telegraph to Cairo although convinced that Philae stood in no danger.

As he said good-bye to Sogaro and asked him 'not to forget me in your prayers,' Gordon made a remark which would seem commonplace a hundred years later but was unusual then: 'Catholics and Protestants are but soldiers in different regiments of Christ's army, but it is the same army and we are all marching together.'[6]

As the river voyage continued, Gordon used up his energy in drafting a stream of memoranda and telegrams as he thought his way towards solutions, based on his profound knowledge of the Sudan and Stewart's more recent information, although Stewart was alarmed at some of Gordon's ideas.

The telegrams to Baring contradicted each other. As Charles Watson commented to Augusta after Gordon's death, he might seem vacillating to many who did not know him, 'but, as you know, the real fact was that he always used to write down his thoughts just as they came into his head . . . It was one great difference between him and the majority of people that he wrote exactly as he thought at the moment without considering whether it agreed with what he had said before, or what he might say afterwards. His real opinions changed very little, however much they might seem to vary.'[7]

Baring, so precise and ordered in his ways, who would never draft a paper until clear in his mind, grew exasperated by Gordon's contradictions, and began to think that he was drinking. Lieutenant Angel Scott knew better: 'I saw much of Gordon all the way up the Nile,' he recalled forty-seven years later, by then a retired lieutenant-colonel and a member of His Majesty's Bodyguard of Gentlemen at Arms, 'for boats were small and slow in those days. During this time, to the best of my belief, I never saw a drop of spirits pass his lips.'[8/9] Baring would have been wiser to heed the view of his cousin Northbrook, who commented to Granville that Gordon 'says all the foolish things that pass through his head but his judgement is excellent.'[10]

Baring would shake his fist at Evelyn Wood 'whenever my favourite "runs off the rails",' but Wood recognized Gordon's fundamental consistency, whatever his passing opinions. 'There is certainly no man like him in the world,' he wrote to the Queen while Gordon was still on his way to Khartoum. 'It must be admitted that with all the grandeur of Gordon Pacha's character he is very changeable. Nevertheless he has one fixed idea in his head where it has remained for years. "Free the Sudan from Turkish or Egyptian Pachas and their misrule." '[11] And his consistency in another vital point was testified by an old acquaintance whom Gordon met by chance at Luxor, where the steamer took on coal and Gordon strolled up to the hotel to keep away from the dust. Archibald Sayce, the Oxford philologist and orientalist, happened to be in. 'He told me,' recalled Sayce in his *Reminiscences*, 'that he had undertaken the mission very reluctantly, as he considered himself under an engagement to King Leopold to go to the Congo. Lord Granville, however, had appealed to him as an Englishman and a Christian, and that was an appeal which he could not reject. He had therefore travelled in post-haste with the object of bringing the Egyptian garrisons from the Sudan by means of his personal influence, "if that were possible"; otherwise he would be "supported by troops." This was evidently the belief under which he had accepted his mission; in fact, with all his enthusiasm he possessed a large amount of common sense, and none but a fool or a British politician ignorant of all things Eastern would have accepted his mission upon any other understanding.'[12]

On 2 February, the eighth day of their journey, they reached Korosko where Graham said a sad farewell, convinced he would never see Gordon again, as Stewart and he set off on camels across the wild and desolate Nubian Desert by the caravan route which cut across the great Dongola loop of the Nile and avoided the next three cataracts: an empty land of dark ravines and volcanic hills. Graham and Scott climbed one for a last view through field glasses: Gordon riding beside Ahmed, the handsome young son of the Sheikh of Berber, 'on a beautiful white camel. At the head of the caravan rode Ahmed's brother, both armed with the great cross-hilted swords and shields of rhinoceros hide. These swords, together with a couple of very old double-barrelled pistols with flintlocks, made up the Arab armament. Gordon carried no arms, but Stewart had a revolver. Before Gordon left he gave me a long, heavy, silver-mounted kourbash, or Sudan riding-whip, of rhinoceros hide, and told me to say that was a token that the reign of the kourbash in the Sudan was over. In exchange he took my white umbrella, having lost his own.'[13]

Back on the steamer Gerald Graham jotted down, that very day, his impressions of his old friend: 'It may seem a paradox to say so, but it seems to me that although Gordon never regulates his conduct by the opinion of others, he yet has an intense longing for human sympathy. His impatience is only a symptom of the intensity of this longing. His habit of rushing into print on subjects that move him, is another symptom, wrongly ascribed to vanity by those who don't understand him. But what he demands he gives freely, and this explains his great power over natives. It is the same with children. Gordon is a man all children would instinctively worship, for he loves them so. He told me that he has cried over the misery of the natives, sometimes before, and with them, and to their simple minds, a man with so much power and so much feeling for them must be indeed a new revelation. You can see his kindness shining in his face when the natives crowd round him kissing his hand. He never shows impatience with *them* ...'[14]

Two days later Graham wrote to Sir Henry Gordon: 'He is much more cheery and confident than he was when he left Cairo, and looks forward to constructing a government and army out of native materials as if it were the simplest thing in the world. He certainly has an extraordinary influence over the natives, the secret of which seems to me to be that he is really fond of them and enters into their feelings while at the same time he shows an energy that must appear to them superhuman.'[15]

This energy was now devoted to camel riding after a lapse of more than four years. For six days, sometimes riding for sixteen hours, Gordon and Stewart endured the extremes of heat and cold through a land of gravel and sand with only one well of blackish water: their men carried all supplies. Occasionally they met caravans coming the other way, including a dismissed Mudir (governor) returning to Cairo: 'this man looked both wretchedly ill and greatly frightened of Gordon Pasha,' noted Stewart.[16]

On the last march, shortly before reaching the Nile again at Abu Hamed, Gordon mounted a fresh camel, 'a bull-necked brute, and off he went full speed with me. I was in a state of mind, not for my bones, but had I fallen, it would have been a very bad omen and done much harm with these superstitious people, I am glad to say I kept my seat, and I shall indulge in no more of these displays.'

They found 'the people very civil, and glad to see me, they are in no panic at all.' He hoped that 'the country will be quiet in a month.'[17]

Gordon and Stewart left Abou Hamed encouraged. Gordon wrote to Barnes that he was 'glad to have come, for somehow I think God will bless my mission, aided as I am by so many prayers. His glory, the people's welfare, my humiliation (*i.e.* an increased sense of His indwelling in me, which is the sequence of a humble heart, to be *nothing* in this world, the dust of His feet, for who has caused Him greater pain, greater shame, than myself, who had so much light?)'[18]

After three days riding along the Nile they approached the second city of the Sudan. 'We had a great public entry into Berber,' wrote Stewart to his mother, 'the streets crowded with people and lined with soldiers. Many followed us on camels, donkeys, horses etc. etc., so that the dust was really awful.'[19] Flags were dipped, drums beaten, a guard of honour lined the entrance to the Governor's house.

An Italian adventurer, Guiseppe Cuzzi, who was now a clerk in a commercial house and had known Gordon in the Sudan earlier, hurried round and found the great hall crowded. 'Everybody, old and young, pressed around him to welcome him, and to express their joy on his coming. Everyone, even the poorest, was admitted,' wrote Cuzzi. 'Many held petitions in their hands. As was his custom, Gordon accepted these, and without even glancing at them, he gave to the bearers one or several gold coins. Others, who also had some demand, went down before him to kiss his hands and feet, and to put their requests to him. He had kind and consoling words for everybody, and whenever he was requested, he at once helped with money.'

Gordon greeted Cuzzi 'in the most friendly manner,' appointed him his personal representative and British Consul and invited him to join him and Stewart for dinner. 'Gordon was an excellent companion, and we sat together in very stimulating conversation far into the night.'

Cuzzi recalled in his memoirs Gordon's emphasis that his mission was 'to restore order in a peaceful way. When I said that in spite of his popularity this would not be possible, and that peaceful conditions could only be brought about through force and military, he replied: "For that eventuality I have one hundred thousand men at my disposal."

'I found this figure rather high and expressed my opinion that if these were good troops, it should be possible to defeat the Mahdists with even a tenth part of them. General Gordon made his statement with so much confidence that it gave me the impression that he was sure that he could at any moment count on extensive military help from England.'[20]

That night Gordon's telegrams poured out again. 'As he got farther from civilization,' recalled Floyer, 'he became immensely contemptuous of the elaborate mystery of cipher in which the Government wrapped up their communications. "Write in plain language," he would cry, "and give them to Floyer to send," and on his arrival at Berber the whole night was spent in receiving long and interesting messages on an immense number of subjects.'[21] The electric telegraph, tapped out in Morse code, carried a two–way traffic, including a sharp order from Baring forbidding any attempt to visit the Mahdi; Gordon sent back a meek promise to obey, perhaps losing an historic opportunity.

One telegram arrived in cipher, to be decoded by Stewart, who brought to Gordon the alarming news that Valentine Baker Pasha, Sir Samuel's brother, had been defeated by the rebel Osman Digna at El Tib near Suakin. Baker's Egyptian troops had proved worthless and Baker only escaped the carnage by charging through a line of enemy horsemen when the battle was lost beyond reclaim.

The road between Berber and the Red Sea, the shortest route for the evacuation of Khartoum, was thus closed, and moreover the sea route to India would be threatened if Suakin fell.

Gladstone's government dithered. At Windsor the Queen, upset already by an absurd rumour that Gordon had been captured, scrawled an agitated note to Ponsonby: '...It is *our prestige*, the British name, wh. is humiliated our *safety* in India and *every*where in the Colonies wh. is being *imperilled*. It is *really* too *dreadful*! Pray cipher strongly and write to *any* one of the Govt. who has *any spirit* or *feeling* for Great Britain's honour *left*!

'Most thankful Gordon is so far safe.

'The Queen feels her blood boil at the want of spirit & energy & haste.

'Oh! for a Palmerston or a Beaconsfield to be here now.'[22]

In Berber, Gordon spent a sleepless night planning and praying and meditating. At 5 a.m. he woke Stewart and told him that he had decided, against his own earlier convictions, to publish the secret *firman* at once, that the Sudan was to be independent of Egypt. He hoped to spur the leaders into forming local governments under himself as British Commissioner. He knew the risk, since some of the notables were in touch with the Mahdi; but no political decision in Cairo was secret: every Pasha had already told his wife.

When he assembled the notables in secret conclave that afternoon the *firman* 'caused the most profound astonishment,' noted Stewart, 'but, in so far as one can judge from what they said, nothing could exceed their delight.' More confidential enquiries suggested that the publication might have been a mistake,[23] as Gordon himself came to believe later.

He also despatched a letter to the Mahdi, offering to recognize him as governor of Kordofan and to give him a large sum if he would send back the Darfur garrison unharmed: Gordon had Rudolf Slatin Pasha's position much to heart (not knowing that he had been forced to surrender already) and had accused Stewart of 'cold blood' when he had suggested that if they could rescue Slatin the garrison would melt into the surrounding populace.[24]

At 5 p.m. that evening of 15 February, Gordon and Stewart went on board the little government steamer *Taufikieh* for Khartoum. Cuzzi watched the extraordinary scene: 'General Gordon, "our father", as the Sudanese called him, had embarked and stood on deck, surveying the crowd of thousands who had come to bid him farewell. After a cordial leave-taking, I was one of the last persons to leave the vessel which soon after started moving away. Weeping and crying loudly, and waving their hands vigorously, a crowd of men and women followed the boat along the bank, while Gordon stood on the bridge and waved good-bye with a kerchief. Soon he had disappeared from our sight – disappeared for ever. I am the last living European who talked to him down here.

'Slowly I returned to the town, full of melancholy contemplations, and accompanying with my thoughts the hero who was hurrying towards his doom, so undaunted and fearlessly.'[25]

CHAPTER THIRTY-ONE

Return to Khartoum

Four days later, at 9.30 a.m. on Monday 18 January 1884 Gordon and Stewart landed at Khartoum to a tumultuous welcome: 'received,' as Stewart wrote, 'by all the officials in gorgeous uniforms standing in front of a massive background of natives.'[1]

They walked through a guard of honour to the Divan or government headquarters where the *firman* of appointment was read aloud from a specially erected pulpit by a *ulema* (Moslem jurist or theologian) and Gordon addressed the crowd through an interpreter: 'I am glad to see you. It is four years since I was here and the Sudan is miserable and I am miserable! And I want your assistance to put it right! I might have brought numbers of troops but I have come here without troops and we must ask Almighty God to look after the Sudan if no one else can. Almighty God will give us help and guide us in the right path.'[2]

His proclamations had already been distributed; he confirmed that he would remit half their taxes 'and I will not interfere with your holding slaves.' (When the British press telegraphed for explanation he pointed out that it was a self-evident fact that he would not be in a position to liberate slaves in 1889, as laid down in the Treaty of 1877.) He introduced Stewart 'as my brother and my *Vikul* (Second-in-command).' After the ceremony he went inside. The people flocked in, pressing on him to kiss his hand. Later when he walked in the streets the women crowded round to kiss his feet, and more than once they threw him by mistake, to his great amusement.

He ordered a bonfire in the middle of the square. The debt books and the kourbash whips and clubs, and the stocks for inflicting the bastinado were brought out and flung on the flames. He ordered the gates to be opened, all to pass freely. Stewart went to the jail. 'Here I was literally mobbed by the two hundred and odd prisoners packed like sardines.' Gordon joined him and

288

gave him authority to enquire into all cases. Debtors, prisoners of war, boys and all who had served their sentences were set free, their chains struck off, while Gordon visited the widow of his second Sudanese secretary, the 'Black Imp,' killed with Hicks, and gave her a large present of money: 'as Basuti is not here I will take his place.'

That night Gordon paid formal visits and formed a Council of Twelve Notables for defence and administration. The city was bright with illuminations as the people rejoiced: 'Our saviour has come,' 'Our father has returned.' *The Times* correspondent and acting British Consul, Frank Power, heard the cries again and again in the streets. Power, who had been miserable, rejoiced too. Even twenty-four years later his then chief in Cairo, Moberly Bell, could recall 'the extraordinary effect which Gordon produced on the morale of Power and all with whom he came in contact when he first got there ... I remember how the entire change of tone impressed me at the time.'[3]

Frank Power, an Irishman aged twenty-five, an adventurous journalist of powerful physique, who would have been killed with Hicks had not illness kept him in Khartoum, had been excited when 'the Father of the Sudanese' had telegraphed to him from Berber, but he had written home: 'I hope Gordon will be a nice fellow. We will be living together etc. I hope I will get on with him.'[4] Power had been lodging at the Palace with Colonel de Coëtlogan, a British soldier in the Egyptian service who was acting Governor-General but longing to escape to safety.

Four days after Gordon and Stewart had taken up residence Power wrote home glowingly: 'Gordon is a most lovable character, quiet mild gentle and strong. We live together, his room is next mine, all eat together, and the way he pats you on the shoulder when he says "Look here dear fellow now what do you advise" would make you love him.' Gordon was specially pleased that Frank ('He calls me Frank') went among the people: de Coëtlogan 'never mixed with them, that was a mortal sin in Gordon's eyes.'

Frank Power was a Roman Catholic from Dublin but Gordon found him rather ignorant of 'Thomas à Kempis which he reads every day and has given me an "Imitation of Christ" to read. He says he loves Catholics. He is indeed I believe the greatest man of this century.'[5]

Gordon also gave Power another book, a gift which would have a wide influence when both were dead. He had received it himself from Edward Maund, who was expecting to join him in the Congo. During their chats in Southampton Gordon's account of his Christian re-dedication at his father's death-bed in 1865 had reminded Maund of Newman's great poem *The Dream of Gerontius*, published that same year and dedicated by coincidence to a priest named John Joseph Gordon. He obtained a copy, unbound to save postage, which the General received before leaving Berber and read on the river boat. He delighted in Newman's treatment of his theme, the Christian's preparation for heaven through the cleansing of fiery pain. He marked many passages in pencil, mostly at the side but underlining the lines, *I have no fear – In His dear might prepared for weal or woe.*

On his first day in Khartoum Gordon gave the copy to Power, who bound it in red velvet backed by a war correspondent's authority to draw rations, and sticking a gilt cross, made from a can or a cartridge case, on the front.

He sent it home inscribed: 'Dearest Mother, I send you this little book which General Gordon has given me. The pencil marking through the book is his.'

Power's mother and sister Mary lent it to Cardinal Newman, who was 'deeply moved,' and to Augusta, who copied the markings into another copy which she gave to a friend. In 1888 this friend secured permission for a small edition reproducing Gordon's pencil markings in red; and in 1889 the parish priest of the young composer Edward Elgar gave him a copy as a wedding present. This was the germ of his inspiration to compose, after long gestation, his immortal oratorio *The Dream of Gerontius*.[*6]

The evacuation of Egyptian widows, wives and children down river was already under way, organized by Stewart. The first steamer left on 22 February with de Coëtlogan 'who was delighted to get away and asked Power to come with him.'[7] Power refused.

Gordon had telegraphed to Cuzzi at Berber to receive the refugees and help them on their way. Evelyn Wood in Cairo sent a Gunner in the Egyptian service, Colonel F. Duncan, to Korosko, to arrange for them to go wherever they wished in Egypt. Gordon asked 'that some motherly European woman might also be sent, as many of the female refugees ... might feel strange on reaching Egypt,' so Geigler Pasha and his wife were placed at Duncan's disposal. As each steamer left Khartoum, the names, ages and occupations of all on board were telegraphed ahead.

*The copies which Gordon gave Power, and Augusta gave to Lawrence Dillon, were presented to the Gordon Boys' Home. Elgar once contemplated writing a symphony on Gordon.

When the refugees arrived at Korosko, 'Their references to Gordon were invariably couched in language of affection and gratitude,' Duncan wrote afterwards, 'and the adjective most frequently applied to him was "just."' Old soldiers arrived with their documents made out, and Duncan was touched 'to see the perfect confidence they had that the promises of "Gordon Pasha" would be fulfilled and his requests complied with.'[8]

Baring had told Gordon that he would need to evacuate at least 15,000 men, women and children, civil and military. Some 2,500 had got through before the Mahdi's forces cut the river route, and 200 afterwards; many would probably have lost their lives in Khartoum. Gordon also sent down several officers and officials whose loyalty he suspected or who were useless.

While the refugees were leaving, Gordon was rebuilding what he described as 'the ruin of govenment'[9] after his four years' absence, and reorganizing the troops: he planned to send away first the Egyptians ('whites') although many merchants and officials begged him not to, and then the Bashi-Bazouks or Turkish irregulars ('browns'), and to entrust the defence of Khartoum to the Sudanese ('blacks'). He knew that some would desert to the Mahdi.

In late February Gordon ordered Stewart with a force of Bashi-Bazouks 'to scour the river White Nile.' Power went with Stewart 'so I am left alone,' Gordon wrote to Augusta, 'in the vast palace of which you have a photo, but not alone, for I feel great confidence in my Saviour's presence. The primitive pain which comes from the excessive anxiety one cannot help being in for this people, comes back to me at times. I think that our Lord sitting over Jerusalem is ruling all things to the glory of His Kingdom, and cannot wish things even different than they are, for if I did do so, then I wish *my will* not *His* be done.

'The Sudan is a ruin, and humanly speaking there is no hope. Either I must believe He does all things in mercy and love, or else I disbelieve His existence, there is no half way in the matter. What holes do I not put myself in! and for what. So mixed are my ideas. I believe ambition put me here, in this ruin.

'However I trust, and stay myself on the fact that not one sparrow falls to the ground without our Lord's permission, also that enough for the day is its evil. "God provideth for the way, strength sufficient for the day."'

He added to the letter two days later, on 1 March, after Stewart and Power had returned: 'We are all right at present, and I have hope, but certainly things are not in a good way humanly speaking. Baker's defeat at Suakin has been a great disaster, and now it has its effects up here. It is nothing to our God to help with many or with few and I now take my worries more quietly than before. All things are ruled by Him, for His glory, and it is rebellion to murmur against His will.'[10]

In the next door room Frank Power was writing to his mother on that 1 March. He had received a letter from his sister Mary, assuring him of her prayers. 'Gordon says he hopes sincerely you will all pray for his success and have his name joined with mine when she gets a Mass said.'

Power added: 'I like Gordon more and more every day; he has a most lovable manner and disposition and is so kind to me. He is glad if you show the smallest desire to help him in his great trouble. How one man could have dared to attempt his task, I wonder. One day of his work and bother would kill another man, yet he is so cheerful at breakfast, lunch and dinner, but I know he suffers fearfully from low spirits. I hear him walking up and down his room all night. It is only his great piety carries him through. He is quite a Catholic in his views and believes in the real presence in our Holy Communion.'[11]

Power had slightly confused Gordon's emphasis on 'the indwelling of God' with the Roman doctrine of Transubstantiation, the bread and wine of the Sacrament becoming the body and blood of Christ. No Catholic or Orthodox priest or Protestant missionary remained. The Austrian mission had withdrawn, and their stone church near the Palace stood empty. Gordon had told Barnes there would be 'no eating in Khartoum.' He decided without scruple to conduct his own daily Communion in his room. He prayed over bread and whatever wine was at hand. Whether Power's phrase, 'our Holy Communion,' means that he joined Gordon on Sundays, against the rule of his Church, cannot be known.

Gordon had good cause to pace up and down at night for he was being refused the man he wanted: Zubair.

Gordon had become all the more certain, the nearer he had approached Khartoum, that Zubair could secure the evacuation and create a stable government. On the Nile, Stewart had been doubtful, even warning Baring to prevent Zubair's departure, for Stewart had been told to act as Gordon's 'wet nurse,' communicating direct if they disagreed: a situation which created tensions but not disaster, thanks to the generosity of both, who ended firm friends.

When they had landed at Khartoum, Stewart was neutral. A pasha who had come up river to meet them had advised against, but he was later revealed as a secret adherent of the Mahdi. During the night after landing, Gordon telegraphed Baring his firm conviction that Zubair 'alone has the ability to rule the Sudan and would be universally accepted by the Sudan.'[12] He suggested he should rule under a British Protectorate, accepting strict conditions. Next day Stewart agreed: 'I think policy which Gordon urges would greatly facilitate our retirement from the country.'[13] Baring forwarded the telegrams to Granville in London, only stipulating that Zubair and Gordon should not be in Khartoum together,[14] an attitude which Gordon dismissed: 'Zubair is my great hope,' he wrote to Henry on 6 March. 'I would much wish him to come here at once. It is all nonsense about his blood feud.'[15]

Hope of Zubair's coming led Gordon to write: 'Things look, thank God, better here,' and to say he expected to be in Brussels on the way to the Congo in six months.

But his asking for Zubair led to uproar in England. With tragic irony, the British public, flocking into the churches to pray for Gordon, rejected Zubair because Gordon had called him the worst slaver of all.

The Anti-Slavery Society had been shocked by Gordon's proclamation promising not to interfere with slaves. Its secretary, Gordon's friend, C. H. Allen, forgetting all he knew of his character, supposed that Gordon had been 'compelled by the machinations of his enemies to issue his proclamation'[16]; nor did the Society remember that in the context of the proclamation 'slave trading' meant changes of ownership, not 'slave hunting,' to which Gordon remained implacably opposed and hoped to stop for ever when he reached the Congo.

A strong Government would have ignored public opinion but Gladstone's Cabinet wavered. Wolseley might telegraph Gordon: 'My private advice. Do not answer telegrams about your doings. Ask to be let alone. Results speak for themselves'[17] Wolseley might write to King Leopold: 'The Government have wisely given him carte blanche ... and his name is on every one's mouth as a hero, the like of whom the world seldom sees'[18]; Sir Charles Dilke might tell the House of Commons that Gordon 'knew more of the conditions, and was better able to form a judgement on the subject than any one else ... we showed that he had the highest confidence which could be placed in any man. General Gordon has had all the support for which he asked.'[19]

Yet when he asked for Zubair he was refused. 'He hammered at Baring to send him Zubair,' wrote Wingate, 'and Baring hammered at London. The series of telegrams between Gordon, Baring and London is painful to read. For the British Cabinet not only categorically refused to permit the despatch of Zubair, but refused, in spite of urgent and almost desperate explanations by Baring, to recognize that Gordon was in danger.'[20]

Gladstone was inclined to agree to Zubair but Lord Granville claimed that 'the public opinion of this country would not tolerate the appointment.'[21] Gladstone fell ill before the Cabinet which should make the decision. The Queen thought 'from what Mr.Gladstone said that Gen Gordon must be *listened to*,'[22] but Dilke recorded in his Diary: 'Zubair not to be put up by us in spite of Gordon and Baring'; and a few days later: 'Mr. G. at last unwillingly gave up his Zubair.'[23]

Thus the Anti-Slavery Society helped to kill its own hero, for as Wingate wrote after exhaustive study of events: 'If anyone knew what the Slave Trade was, and was sincerely devoted to its suppression, that one was Gordon ... Baring and Gordon together could have evacuated the Sudan, prevented Gordon's death and prevented the costly expedition which failed to relieve Khartoum. But an anti-slavery society baulked all their plans.'[24] And Zubair told Watson, who told Augusta, that he 'could never forget how when everyone was against him, your brother said: "I can trust you, come and help me."'[25]

The Queen wrote in her Journal ten months later, when all was still not lost: 'Poor, poor Gordon, whom the Govt. would not listen to!'[26]

CHAPTER THIRTY-TWO
Hemmed In

On 11 March, writing in his room in the Palace overlooking the Blue Nile and the opposite bank some eight hundred yards away, Gordon answered a kind letter from Lord Dufferin, the ambassador in Constantinople who had been Special Commissioner in Egypt and was soon to be Viceroy of India after Ripon. 'We are in a pickle here,' he wrote, 'and I almost doubt if this letter will get through, for the tribes around here, owing to our weakness, have gone over to the Mahdi, and are about to hem us in. We have lots of provisions, but there does not seem to be any likelihood of our affairs improving. As for the Mahdi he is in reality nothing, and cannot move from Obeid; it is his emissaries which raise the tribes, who see by our sending down the sick that we do not mean to keep the country. Of course one cannot expect them to be faithful to me, when they know I only want to get the Cairo employees and white troops down.'

Stewart's recent reconnaissances up the Blue and White Niles had encouraged Gordon's belief that the Mahdi's revolt 'was nothing had it been taken in hand at once,' but the tribes would worship the rising sun. 'I could only do my best but things are too far gone to remedy.'[1]

Gordon had already told Baring that without Zubair 'I can see no use in holding Khartoum' since he could not save the other garrisons. In a series of telegrams he first suggested removing the seat of government, with all the Egyptian civilians and troops down river to Berber; next, to send Stewart to Berber while he took the black troops up the river to the equatorial provinces which he would hold for King Leopold, whose approval he had secured.[2] He had also pointed out that 'my duty is evacuation, and the best I can for establishing a quiet government. The first I hope to accomplish. The second is a more difficult task, and concerns Egypt more than me. If Egypt is to be quiet, Mahdi must be smashed up. Mahdi is most unpopular, and with care and time could be smashed.'[3] He then suggested what Egypt must do to 'smash the Mahdi.' This telegram was much misunderstood when forwarded to London, worrying Gladstone that Gordon wanted to turn a mission of peace into an expedition of war, whereas he had only pointed out consequences which came to pass.

Baring, on instructions from the Cabinet, refused Gordon's request to retire up the Nile: he must stay in Khartoum. Gordon obeyed; yet many years later Baring (by then Lord Cromer) would assert: 'The real truth is, that it did not in the least matter *what* instructions Gordon received, as he never paid the smallest attention to them.'[4]

Baring never understood Gordon. On the very day that Gordon was writing to Dufferin, Baring was writing to his cousin Lord Northbrook: 'I wish to goodness that Gordon, like Dickens's young lady, could be made to count twenty before he writes and telegraphs. He is certainly a queer fellow. There is a very feminine side to his character. he is impulsive and a good hater'[5] – but this he was not. Evelyn Wood was nearer the truth when he said that for Gordon a man's repentance was all; he would forgive and trust a ruffian if he showed repentance. And Gordon's telegrams were the expression of a fertile mind wrestling with the grave problems of the hour. Like Churchill sixty years later he was always thinking of ways to win. Baring, perhaps, was almost relieved when the line was cut by the rebels on 12 March and the flow of telegrams ceased.

The siege had begun, at first not pressed close to Khartoum itself, especially as Gordon had his armed steamers on the Nile. He encouraged the people to believe that a British force would soon be at Berber to secure their line of retreat, for he knew that his dear friend Sir Gerald Graham had been sent with two brigades of British and Indian troops to protect Suakin and had inflicted a defeat on Osman Digna at the very place where Osman had smashed Valentine Baker. Then, on the day after the wires to Khartoum were cut, Graham won the battle of Tamai, turning a near disaster, when the enemy broke a brigade square, into a decisive victory. Although fighting continued, the route across 280 miles of desert to Berber was found to be open and peaceful and the wells full.

The British Government refused Graham leave to advance, despite Baring's urgent support. Graham afterwards bitterly regretted not advancing without orders, telegraphing for approval when too far to recall.[6]

Graham's force was withdrawn to Egypt except for a small screen to protect Suakin. The tribes took the hint. They had no wish to be devastated with fire and sword; they declared for the Mahdi. Berber fell the next month.

Gordon wrote on 4 April: 'No human power can deliver us now, we are surrounded, and unless God causes the savage Arab tribes to disperse no English troops will do so until they have racked Khartoum and massacred the inhabitants.'[7] He was cut off from the outside world except for the coming and going of spies and the presence of his thirteen small paddle steamers if he risked sending one or more through hostile territory and through the cataracts.

He could not know that the eyes of the world were on him, nor of the 'long, loud and universal' execrations of public opinion against the Cabinet (as Waller wrote)[8]; nor that Granville had summoned Sir Henry and told him, with unconscious irony or conscious deceit, that 'the Government were fully satisfied with what Charley had done, and would support Charley through everything he did. He told me *confidentially* that the Government would not let Zubair go up since this bad information that he would hang Charley if he got up . . .' 'The Government will do all they can to assist him and I am sure they are sincere,' Henry told Augusta, adding that Charley must not know of the interview.[9] Augusta was more anxious than Henry and they were inclined to bicker by post, but Augusta was heartened by letters like Lady Wolseley's of 21 April: 'All England is praying for your brother.'[10] Lady Wolseley wanted Augusta to appeal to the Queen but the Queen was alert already: 'Most unsatisfactory accounts from Egypt,' she wrote in her Journal on 26 April. 'Gen Gordon, thanks to the deplorable conduct of the Govt., in considerable danger.'[11]

From Power – Khartoum to Moberly Bell – Cairo. Easter Monday. 'Since we heard that we had been abandoned by the British government, General Gordon has been indefatigable in carrying out this unequal war against the Arabs. He is putting down mines in all directions and the steamers are almost daily engaged with the Arabs. In a brush with the Arabs yesterday at Omdurman the latter lost 125 men. The Commandant of Omdurman sent over the heads of two Khartoum men found amongst the rebel slain. On Good Friday the Arabs had a parade on the plain opposite the palace. Their cavalry seemed to number between 4 and 500 horsemen. We have besides the line of fortifications 4 fortified posts . . . A screen of mines entirely masks the lines and mines will today be put down on the other side of Blue Nile. Omdurman is protected by mines.'[12]

Gordon was in his element, his skills and experience as commander, engineer and administrator at full stretch. The townsfolk and garrison included many who favoured the Mahdi, and the first major action of the siege was a defeat throught the treachery of two black Sudanese pashas, who volunteered to join a force to recapture a village below the junction of the two Niles, but organized a rout which cost many lives: one pasha even sliced off the head of a bugler as he sounded the advance. The two pashas were tried by court martial and being found guilty were shot, though Gordon would have liked to have spared them, and later believed they had been innocent.

Soon afterwards the Mahdi's emissaries brought his lengthy rejection of Gordon's letter and a demand that Gordon surrender the town to the Expected One and become a Moslem, or suffer tortures in this world and the next. Gordon showed the letter to the Moslem Ulemas who drew up a reply rejecting the claims of 'the pretended Mahdi' and pronouncing him a religious fraud.

The siege pressed more heavily. Gordon leased the empty Austrian church and mission, the strong stone building next to the Palace, and made it the arsenal. When the Nile waters sank with the coming of summer he extended the fortified ditch to the White Nile and placed a chain across the Blue Nile, linked to mined barges, and garrisoned the uncovered sandbanks. He had already fortified his little 'penny' steamers and sent them up and down the river to bombard rebel positions.

The *Bordein* had been down at Berber when the siege began. As she neared Khartoum on her return the crew fought their way past an Arab (Ansar or Dervish) post, then ran aground in sight of the town. Gordon rescued her by arranging a diversion to draw off the Arab fire, but when the *Bordein* tied up at the quay he was most disappointed that the gold and silver specie which he was expecting was not on board.

He had found the Khartoum treasury almost empty and the pay of the troops fifteen months in arrear. Baring had promised to send £100,000: it was learned much later that £40,000 had been looted by tribes on the route from Cairo to Berber; the remaining £60,000 was held back by the governor, without authority, and thus went into the Mahdi's coffers after Berber fell.

With nothing for his treasury, Gordon designed his own paper money and had it printed by lithograph, with an impression of his Arabic seal. As clerks numbered the notes, Gordon signed them, scores and scores at a time: in addition to all his other duties he is reckoned to have signed nearly 50,000 notes of various denominations before ordering the head printer to find a

way to reproduce his signature. The notes, which technically were debts on
Gordon himself, became the currency of Khartoum throughout the siege.[13]

Gordon next found that merchants were hiding their grain, hoping for
inflated prices as the siege dragged on. He formed a commission to search all
houses and shops, and then sold the grain at a fixed price, leaving only three
months' supply to each owner. Then some of the poorest inhabitants, 'such
as wood-gatherers, beggars, etc., became very clamorous, bitterly complain-
ing that they had no means of subsistence. Gordon Pasha therefore,
assembling a meeting of all the sheikhs of the various quarters, and a number
of the townspeople, asked them to obtain the exact number of persons who
were destitute.'[14] They found about three thousand. He ordered them a
daily ration of biscuit.

The hospital had become cramped with wounded and sick. He enlisted
the Greek civilian doctor, Nicolo, at a good salary, who established a proper
system. 'Fresh bread, butter and meat were supplied daily to the hospital,'
runs the contemporary report, 'and Gordon Pasha himself instituted games,
such as backgammon and dominoes, to interest the poor patients.'

Gordon put much ingenuity into keeping up morale. Bands played on
Fridays and Sundays; he had metal stars made, to reward good service; and
Gordon would regularly pretend that he had 'received letters, saying that
30,000 English soldiers are now at Dongola on their way to relieve us; a force
of 30,000 is also coming *via* Kassala ... Turkish troops are also coming from
Suakin to Berber, and 30,000 men, under the guidance of Sheikh
Mohammed Osman El Morghani, are advancing *via* Rufa'a. Gordon Pasha
used also to draw pictures of all sorts of different soldiers on tissue paper, and
tell the people that they had come by the post. In this way he succeeded in
keeping up hope and allaying fear and anxiety.

'But all this time the dervishes were getting more and more troublesome.
They seemed to take no account of their losses.'[15]

The dervish strategy was to starve out the garrison, making frequent minor
attacks but no assault. Gordon retaliated by skilful use of his fire power. On
24 June the fasting month of Ramadan began. Gordon obtained a ruling
from the *ulemas* that fasting could be waived in time of war, and he ordered
the month to be announced by a salute of guns the moment the new moon
rose. 'The dervishes, however,' runs the official (Nushi) report of the siege,
'continued to harass the garrison during the whole of the month of

Ramadan, and Gordon Pasha appeared greatly surprised that these fanatics should call themselves Moslems and yet fail to observe the usual religious formalities of this holy month.'

They sent a force across to the east bank of the White Nile above the town. Gordon sent the *Telahwieh* with 300 volunteers to drive them back but these were defeated and Gordon's senior steamer captain killed. The dervishes paraded his head in sight of the chief line of fortification, which ran about 1200 yards south of the town. Six days later on 9 July Gordon sent out a strong force which defeated the dervishes with great slaughter for the loss of only two men of their own. After the troops returned 'there were great rejoicings in the city on account of this victory. The bands played, women cried for joy, and all the city was glad. The devishes, however, were overwhelmed with sorrow; they did not appear for many days, not a flag was to be seen, nor a "naggarra" heard.'[16]

At the end of July Gordon's forces won an even greater victory on the Blue Nile, relieving the pressure and capturing stocks of food. By late August they had virtually lifted the siege themselves and had recaptured a great trade centre on the White Nile, with much grain and oil, while two steamers were sent to encourage the garrison at Sennar up the Blue Nile. Another victory was won on 31 August.

Gordon knew that this was merely remission. Although he laid plans for Stewart to recapture Berber, only a strong relief force could enable him to evacuate and leave a firm government. On 23 August he had sent off a firm message which eventually reached Cairo and was cabled to England. As summarized for the Queen on 18 September it ran: 'Following from Gordon without date: "On arrival at Khartoum found it impossible to withdraw soldiers etc. I therefore asked for reinforcements. They have not come, hence the events at Berber. Is it right that I should have been sent here with only seven followers and no attention paid to me? Hope you will telegraph intentions as regards Sudan in Arabic: telegrams in English only ask for information and waste time. Having often promised people of Khartoum that assistance will come we appear as liars. Cannot hold Soudan with only Soudanese troops. Better send Turkish troops. Here I am as hostage and guardian. Impossible to leave Khartoum without a regular Govt. ..."'[17]

Unknown to Gordon, relief was at last on its way. About the time he wrote the telegram a messenger got through from Major Herbert Kitchener, who was living at Debbeh on the Nile disguised as the Arab merchant Abd el Kader el Soubri. The batch of letters, for Gordon, Stewart and Power, included one from Augusta, discreetly anonymous, which told how she had been invited to Osborne by the Queen.

Another, also anonymous, came from Wolseley, dated 13 June, and was abusive of Gladstone: '... Your going out to Egypt saved him from "going out of office" at the time and he was then very grateful, but now because you are too noble to run away and desert your soldiers and followers, in his heart he wishes you were in Abraham's bosom. However although he is a craven politician, cares nothing for your honor or for your safety only as it affects his political influence and believe me that the heart of what was once a great proud and still powerful people beats for you, and will do all that its despot will permit to relieve you from your present horrible position. – To you and Stewart I need scarcely say, "Hold out to the last". – "Be of good courage". I have no fear for you: the God in whom you trust will not desert you even though you be deserted by an infamous Minister ..."[18]

On 9 September Wolseley landed in Cairo to lead the Gordon Relief Expedition, Gladstone having been forced at last. (Gordon was most displeased when he learned its name: 'I altogether *decline* the imputation that the projected expedition has come to relieve me. It has come to *save our national* honour in extricating the garrisons ... As for myself I could make good my retreat at any moment ... I am not the *rescued lamb*, and I will not be.')[19]

As Wolseley left home he had written to Sir Henry Gordon: 'Please remember me most affectionately to your brother who is the only man I have ever known who comes up to my notions of what a real hero is and should be.'[20]

A few days before Wolseley took command, disaster struck Khartoum. The pasha who had won the notable victory up the Blue Nile disobeyed Gordon's orders to return, advanced into a trap, and was killed with most of his men. When the steamers returned with the survivors and the news spread over the city 'the inhabitants fell into despair and distress,' wrote a rich merchant, Bordeini, 'and wept for their state. Gordon Pasha, seeing them in such distress, wept with them too. This was the first and last time I ever saw Gordon Pasha in tears, but he tried to strengthen them and calm them by all means in his power.'[21]

The disaster reversed the balance of strength. From that day Gordon was on the defensive and the Mahdi's men in the ascendant. The Mahdi himself now moved towards Khartoum with a large army, reinforced as it marched by tribes whose lands he threatened to lay waste unless they joined him.

Gordon and Stewart were agreed that they must communicate urgently with Egypt. The Nile was now high. Gordon decided to send Stewart north down river through the hostile tribes to friendly territory, where he could telegraph precise details and meet any relieving forces. Stewart declined to desert Gordon unless ordered. Gordon replied that he would not order Stewart into a risk he was not taking himself but invited him to carry a letter exonerating Stewart from any imputation of desertion.

Stewart would take the cipher books so that he could telegraph freely. Power would go too so that he could send full despatches to *The Times*; the French consul also, and one or two Egyptian officials to whom Gordon gave glowing testimonials and recommendations for honours though secretly he wished to be rid of them.

The expedition was planned carefully. The *Abbas* would carry them, escorted by two armed steamers towing small sailing vessels. They steamed away north on 12 September, carrying the mail and Stewart's journal.

When the escorting steamers returned, reporting that Stewart and Power were safely past Berber, Gordon was alarmed that Stewart had not kept them. For week upon week he heard no more.

Shortly before the village of Abu Hammed, where Gordon and Stewart had reached the Nile in January after their desert dash, The *Abbas* ran on a rock through the misjudgement or treachery of the pilot. Stewart accepted the help of a local sheikh who appeared to be loyal and promised camels. The sheikh invited the party to come, unarmed, to a meal. They went, relying on the rules of Arab hospitality.

At a given signal they were set upon and murdered, both Stewart and Power putting up a fight.

CHAPTER THIRTY-THREE

'I Have *Tried* To Do My Duty'

On 21 October the Mahdi arrived in the neighbourhood of Khartoum, setting up his camp to the south-west of Omdurman. His army had been greatly enlarged and armed from the captured garrisons. Slatin Pasha and Lupton Bey were with him as prisoners in chains while many of their men had become his soldiers. He had forced tribes to join him, yet tribesmen from all over the Sudan were hastening voluntarily to serve under his banner in a Holy War. He now controlled guns and ammunition for a powerful offensive, but until he took Khartoum he could not conquer the Sudan.

Khartoum could still have been relieved with ease. General William Earle was at Wady Halfa by 22 September with two battalions of British infantry. He had intended to proceed at once with this small force. As his chief of staff wrote: 'Gordon had said that all he wanted was a few Red-coats to give confidence to his troops. But, even if a much larger force had been required, when once we had shaken hands with him in Khartoum, time would not have been of such absolute importance. We could at first have acted on the defensive, until a sufficient force had been collected to cover the retreat from Khartoum, or, if wished, to conquer the Mahdi.'[1]

Instead, Wolseley was slowly forming a larger force, including troops from England. Gordon expected its arrival by late November. He knew nothing of earlier and somewhat fantastic plans of rescue, including one by the celebrated Colonel Fred Burnaby of the Blues, and his friend Lieutenant-Colonel John Sterling of the Coldstream Guards, who proposed to raise a camel corps at their own expense, dash to Khartoum and kidnap Gordon if he refused to desert his garrison. As serving officers they had to seek official sanction. The assistant adjutant-general, Sir Redvers Buller, refused it with a remark out of tune with the times: 'The man is not worth the camels.'[2]

Gordon would not 'bolt.' 'I don't believe the Christian lunatic has the slightest intention of coming back again,'[3] wrote the Queen's Private secretary, Ponsonby, to one of Gladstone's secretaries. Meanwhile Lord Northbrook, now briefly in Egypt, advocated the course which Gordon had suggested earlier and the Cabinet had rejected: to retire to the equator with the garrison. Northbrook suggested that the Queen should give Gordon the Grand Cross of the Bath and her personal congratulations 'for his gallant defence'. She was willing, but the opportunity had passed and he would have refused an honour recommended by Gladstone's cabinet.[4]

He would never, he wrote in the daily Journal he had begun after Stewart's departure, leave men who 'though they may not come up to our idea of heroes have stuck to me, though a Christian dog in their eyes, through great difficulties, and thus force them to surrender to those who have not conquered them, and to do that, at the bidding of a foreign Power, to save one's skin! Why the black sluts would stone me if they thought I meditated such action. Stewart knows all this, and used to groan over perversity.'[5]

Nor would he deny his faith. He deplored the apostasy of Rudolf Slatin (who had converted to Islam before surrender, thinking to encourage his troops) and of Lupton and Cuzzi. He faced his own future frankly. Although he had once told Baring that he would not be taken alive, and although he expected the Relief Force in time, he tossed up in his mind whether 'to blow up the palace and all in it, or else to be taken, and, with God's help, to maintain the faith, and if necessary suffer for it (which is most probable). The blowing up of the palace is the simplest, while the other means long and weary suffering and humiliation of all sorts. I think I shall elect the last, not from fear of death, but because the former has more or less the taint of suicide, as it can do no good to anyone, and is, in a way, taking things out of God's hands.'[6]

Every day and part of the night he was out among the defences, which stretched in a six-mile line about three miles south of the town, with forts on both sides of the Blue and the White Nile, and outlying defences round Omdurman, and Tuti island at the junction of the rivers and as far down the Nile as Halfeyeh. The main fortifications were protected by mines, some more terrifying than lethal: a donkey trod on one and walked away looking angry.

Gordon rode a bay horse with black legs, and as he always wore the red rimless tarbush or fez, the symbol of authority in the Turkish Empire, he carried an umbrella for shade against the sun. He wore an ordinary short black English coat with a black waistcoat, or sometimes a white one, except on Fridays and Sundays when he took out his red Royal Engineers waistcoat with its narrow gold braid and gilt buttons. His trousers and regulation boots were black. Occasionally he put on the undress blue frock coat of an English general, over blue trousers with a red stripe edged with gold lace, but he very seldom wore the red sash and gold sword belt and his ivory handled sword.[7]

Gordon was not only military commander. He was the civil Governor-General, although his empire had contracted to the three isolated garrisons of Khartoum, Senaar and Kassala, and the equatorial province under Emin Pasha, who was cut off from Khartoum. He kept such contact as he could by water or by spies but Khartoum alone needed much administration, with leading men coming for audiences. 'How astonished and edified I always was by his conversation,' said a Sherif (Prince) of Mecca, resident in Khartoum, who survived the siege and left the Sudan. 'How humble he was for so great a Pasha! The rich and the poor, the free and the slaves, were alike his children. He was one of those men to whom the verse of the Koran applies: "The servants of the Merciful are those who walk meekly in the earth, and when the ignorant speak unto them answer Peace! and who pass the night adoring their Lord and standing up to pray unto Him." Before I knew him I hated the Christians, but Gordon has taught me to love them, and I see more clearly every day that a religion which makes such heroic, faithful, and disinterested men can only be a religion coming from the true God.'*[8]

Back at the Palace Gordon treated the flat roof as his command post, where he often sat or stood to use his telescope. Down below was the *divan* or reception room where he conferred with his Egyptian and Sudanese staff or interviewed the stream of messengers with news, or locals with petitions, complaints or information. He had telegraph lines laid to all his outlying military posts and the dockyard; the arsenal in the former Roman Catholic mission was near enough for runners.

As both sides had plenty of ammunition the daylight hours were noisy. 'You can scarcely imagine,' he wrote one evening in his Journal, 'the state one gets in when one is constantly hearing explosions; what with the guns, mines, and musketry, one's nerves get strained, and nothing can drop without one thinking it is an explosion ... It has slackened off now, but still

---

*One of Gordon's cavasses (armed bodyguards) who also survived, though badly wounded, wanted to be baptized after peace had returned in 1898. Rigid rules against proselytizing obliged the chaplain to refuse.[9] John Ward, *The Living Age*, Vol. XVII, p. 412.

any loud noise, in this clear air, makes me jump (ie be, for a moment, afraid.)'[10]

Gordon's *Journal of Events* became his safety valve and amusement as well as the military record of the siege. He used it as he had used his letters to Augusta, to record and comment and reflect, to joke, sometimes to explode, but never pausing to consider how it would read. ('To be pruned down if published' he wrote on the flyleaf.) He put a thin diagonal line across the private sections, which took up most of each volume: the whole, from 24 September to 14 December, ran to over 300 printed pages when published, almost complete, some six months after his death, plus nearly 200 pages of documents which he had pasted in.

He would move from subject to subject as he did in conversation: thus after remarking that he intended 'to let out all the political prisoners (which will shock the townspeople) but will be a true joy and delight to me,' he reflects on freedom and free will and then adds, 'I must say that I feel it a great compliment, when my counsellors say to *me*, "*Do what you think right, irrespective of our advice*," *when they know I am ignorant of all that goes on, ignorant of the Arabic language, except in my style, ignorant of the Arab customs, etc. etc.* "*You will do better than we do*,"is what they say, and *I, poor Devil, do not know where to turn*. Oh! our Government, our Government! what has it not to answer for? Not to *me*, but to these poor people. I declare if I thought the town wished the Mahdi, I would give it up: so much do I respect free will.'[11]

Again and again he deplores the loss of life which the Government has caused by indecision. On 2 November he had reckoned they had only six weeks' food 'and then the sponge must be thrown up. I could write volumes of pent-up wrath on this subject if I did not believe things are ordained and all work for the best . . . I should be an angel (which I am not, needless to say) if I was not rabid with H. M. G. . . . but to lose all my beautiful black soldiers is enough to make me angry with those who have the direction of our future.'

Humour breaks in, despite the pressures which were turning his hair and whiskers white. 'I own to having been very insubordinate to Her Majesty's Government and its officials, but it is my nature, and I cannot help it. I fear I have not even tried to play battledore and shuttlecock with them. I know if *I* was chief I would never employ myself, for I am incorrigible.' He then wondered how much the telegrams about the Sudan has cost, with all the confusion of similar names of towns and people; and had a happy moment imagining two Foreign Office officials puzzling them out. '"Eureka, I have found it out; there is a *man* called *El Obeid* and a *town* called *El Obeid*. When a movement occurs, it is the *man*, not the *town*, which has moved!"' He much enjoyed the thought of Baring bumping up on a camel, and he loved the antics of the Palace turkey cock and his harem.

Sometimes he inserted brief meditations, for at night, alone in his room, he could read his Bible and remember his friends in the prayers which had been squeezed out of the mornings: 'Paul said, "*I have learned*" (as in a school) "*in whatsoever state I am to be content.*" I can only say, "*I am learning*" but have "not learned."'[12]

His Moslem servants also had their prayers, genuflecting towards Mecca five times a day. This sometimes caused difficulties. 'If these Arabs (one's servants) are not *eating*, they are *saying* their *prayers*; if not *saying their prayers*, they are *sleeping*; if not *sleeping*, they are *sick*. One snatches at them at intervals. Now figure to yourself the position; you cannot do anything with them while in these fortresses *eating*, *saying prayers*, *sleeping*, or *sick*, and they know it. You would be a brute if you did (which I fear I often am). You want to send an immediate order, and there is your servant bobbing up and down, and you cannot disturb him. It is a beautiful country for trying experiments with your patience.

'It is very curious, but if I am in a bad temper, which I fear is often the case, my servants will be always at their prayers, and thus religious practices follow the scale of my temper; they are pagans if all goes well.'[13]

His servants loved him even when he boxed their ears. Two of them, Hassan and Mohammed el Amin, mere boys, were spared at the massacre after the fall and survived to take service again in the Palace. About 1908 the assistant military secretary to Wingate, now Governor-General and Sirdar, 'heard a yarn that Gordon was addicted to drink, and used to lock himself up in his room at Khartoum and give way to drinking bouts.' Harry Lewin* put this to the two servants separately.

'Each one when he heard this imputation, raised his hands in horror. "Drink? Who said so?" "The Liars." "It is a lie" "Gordon Pasha locked himself in his room and prayed at the open window to his God." "He was a Holy man (Fiki)" "He never drank" "It is a lie."'[14]

Twenty years later the elderly Hassan was still serving in the Palace, his sole duty to hoist and lower the correct flags. The Governor-General, Sir

---

*H. F. E. Lewin (later Brigadier General) a Gunner; he married Lord Roberts's younger daughter who became Countess Roberts.

John Maffey (Lord Rugby) made 'occasional discreet enquiries and his account,' Maffey told King George V's Private Secretary, 'does not in any way confirm the commonly accepted story that Gordon was a heavy drinker.'[15]

On 5 November The *Bordein* was to sail at dawn downriver with letters and the fifth volume of the Journal, to await the Relieving Force at Metemmeh, since Gordon supposed it nearer than many hundreds of miles away. The steamer did not sail until evening, and as the Arabs were quiet Gordon seized the opportunity to write more letters.

To Augusta he grieved and puzzled over the loss of Stewart and Power, for a message had got through from Kitchener which left him in no doubt. He added: 'I expect Her Majesty's Government are in a precious rage with me for holding out and forcing their hand.'[16]

Then he wrote to Barnes in Exeter, to send 'kind love' to all the family and ask after friends. 'I am learning to be content in whatsoever state I am,' he went on. 'Thoughts have deepened in me but nothing new. Killing people or devising means to do so, has been my lot ... We have had nothing but disaster on disaster, yet in general we are successful. God will not let this solution give any glory to man. I always felt that if we got through, it would be a scramble, there would be no glory to man. Our deliverance (if it happens) is due to prayer of others.

'He is not unfaithful if we fall, for it may be for His greater glory and he does not promise everything we ask, if it is not good for us to have it. I am content. He will enable me to keep my faith and not deny Him, for I have news that all the Europeans have apostatized , even the nuns, who are ostensibly married to the Greeks to avoid a worse fate (Union Latin and Greek Church)'.[17]

He wrote also to Longley Hall, the missionary at Jaffa, mentioning the constant hidden threat of the gates being opened by a traitor. 'It is a sort of position where one may say one has no hope but in our Lord. This ought to suffice to us, but till one knows his position one cannot realise what it is to say, "We know not what to do, but our eyes are upon Thee" (2 Chron. xx.12) The revolt would be nothing if we had any forces at all, but these we lack, and I am (it is odd to write it) obliged to trust to God alone, as if He was not enough. Yet my human nature is so weak that I do worry myself about these things, not always but at times.

'What a strange set of inconsistent things we are, half flesh, half spirit, yet God works at us, and shapes us like stones for His temple. What is the object and design of our existence? You can scarcely tell how torn I am between the two. "Is my hand shortened?" and "you have no possible way of escape" and continually contending one with another ... Do not think I forget you, for when Job (xlii,10) prayed for his friends God turned his captivity. Make your little girl ask our Lord to help me, for vain indeed is the help of man. How wonderful the shaping of the stones! how we hate being chipped! Yet I have dared to ask that the sins of these may fall on me, hid in Christ. Good-bye. Many thanks to you both for your prayers.'[18]

The next day a mass of hoarded biscuit was discovered, putting off the day of starvation. Four days later the dervishes made a great attack on Omdurman. Gordon was caught unprepared through the disobedience of his telegraph clerk who had failed to send up a wire during the night which reported three escaped slaves' warning, so that the two steamers had no steam up and could not bombard the attackers until nearly too late.

Gordon had tumbled at 3 a.m. 'into a troubled sleep; a drum beats – tup! tup! tup! It comes into a dream, but after a few moments one becomes more awake, and it is revealed to the brain that *one is in Khartoum*. The next query is, where is this tup, tupping going on? A hope arises it will die away. No, it goes on, and increases in intensity. The thought strikes one, "Have they enough ammunition?" (The excuse of bad soldiers.) One exerts oneself. At last, it is no use, up one must get, and go on the roof of the palace; then telegrams, orders swearing and cursing goes on till about 9 am. Men may say what they like about glorious war, but to me it is a horrid nuisance (if it is permitted to say anything is a nuisance which comes to us).'

Gordon watched and commanded the battle by telescope and telegraph ('I have lived *years* in these last *hours*') knowing that if the steamers were sunk he would lose Omdurman and the North Fort. 'I saw that poor little beast, The *Husseinieh* (a Thames launch) fall back, stern foremost, under a terrific fire of breach loaders. I saw a shell strike the water at her bows; I saw her stop and puff off steam, and I gave my glass to my boy, *sickened unto death*, and I will say my thoughts turned on Baring more than any one, and they are not beneficient towards him.'[19] He was being unfair to Baring, as Baring later was to him.

The attack was beaten off but *Husseinieh* remained grounded and abandoned, a useful decoy for Dervish ammunition, and Omdurman was cut off except by semaphore. The noose tightened. Fifty-four days of mutual bombardment began, by guns, rockets and rifles. The Palace itself was under fire. Some of the principal men asked the merchant Bordeini to beg Gordon not to have lights in the rooms at night. 'Gordon Pasha was very angry. "Who has said Gordon was ever afraid?"'

A few nights later Bordeini urged him put sand boxes in front of the lighted window where he sat, 'to stop the bullets. Gordon Pasha was then more enraged than ever. He called up the guard, and gave them orders to shoot me if I moved; he then brought a very large lantern which would hold twenty-four candles. He and I then put the candles into the sockets, placed the lantern on the table. The pasha then said, "When God was portioning out fear to all the people in the world, at last it came to my turn, and there was no fear left to give me; go, tell all the people in Khartoum that Gordon fears nothing, for God has created him without fear."'[20]

Some forty years later a young British doctor serving in the Anglo-Egyptian Sudan met an old watchman in Khartoum who had been a young soldier of the Mahdi's most famous regiment, trained sharpshooters armed with Remington rifles.

'He pointed across the river to Tuti Island: "Every night one of us was posted there to snipe at Ghordoun Bashi. We would lie at the river's edge and fire at him as he sat in the yellow rays of his reading-lamp."

'Mentally I measured the distance. It was perhaps five hundred yards. "But the strange thing about it was," he continued, "that no matter how clear the target, no matter how certain the aim, none of the bullets ever reached its mark! The most expert shots in the regiment tried and failed. Ghordoun Bashi went on writing night after night and the shutters were never closed. The Mahdi was furious. He ordered us to be flogged with whips of green hippo-hide. But that made no difference.

'"One dark night I pushed out into mid-stream in a *surtug* (small boat like a coracle). *It was then that I saw the reason why the bullets had failed.*" He looked me straight in the eyes and spoke in slow and measured tones. When I got near to the Palace, I saw the figure of an angel standing outside the window. When I fired he caught the bullets and threw them back at me. I heard them go 'plop!' 'plop!' just like that, into the water, not a yard away from my *surtug*." There was no more sniping after that. And Ghordoun

Bashi still went on writing, writing – always writing, his figure black against the yellow glare. The shutters were never closed.'[21]

In the Journal Gordon had declared '*positively* and *once for all, that I will not leave the Sudan until everyone who wants to go down is given the chance to do so*, unless a government is established that relieves me of the charge; therefore if any emissary or letter comes up here ordering me to come down, I WILL NOT OBEY IT, BUT WILL STAY HERE, AND FALL WITH THE TOWN, AND RUN ALL RISKS.'[22]

He still had no clear news of the Relief except through rumours brought across from the dervish camp. He had failed to relieve Omdurman and his steamers had been heavily shelled (he always had 'gnawing anxiety for my penny steamers.')[23] *The Bordein* had returned from down river and he now decided to send it back with letters and the latest volume of the Journal to await the Relief column at Metemmeh, where it would regain the Nile after crossing the desert from Korti.

On 14 December he wrote to Watson: 'I think the game is up, and send Mrs. Watson, you and Graham my adieux. We may expect a catastrophe in the town on or after ten days' time . . .'[24] To Augusta he wrote: 'This may be the last letter you will receive from me, for we are on our last legs, owing to the delay of the expedition. However, God rules all, and, as He will rule to His glory and our welfare, His will be done.' He added a few lines about money matters, now missing from the manuscript, and ended as he always had: 'Believe me, my dear Augusta, your affectionate brother, C. G. Gordon.' He signed the letter. His thoughts must have strayed to the Siege of Lucknow in the Indian Mutiny and the famous last words of the fatally wounded Sir Henry Lawrence, for Gordon added: 'P. S. I am quite happy, thank God, and like Lawrence, I have "*tried* to do my duty".'[25]

In the last pages of the Journal he stressed again his need of Zubair to establish a lasting government, and for a small number of troops, swiftly: 'all that is absolutely necessary is for fifty of the Expeditionary Force to get on board a steamer and come up to Halfaya, and thus let their presence be felt; this is not asking much, but it must happen *at once* or it will, as usual, be too late.'[26]

He foresaw the town falling 'under the nose of the Expeditionary Force,' and could not understand the delay. 'Now MARK THIS,' he wrote on the last page (he had been using the back of quarto telegraph forms), 'if the

Expeditionary Force, and I ask for no more than two hundred men, does not come in ten days, *the town may fall*; and I have done my best for the honour of our country. Good-bye. C. G. Gordon.' He then added at an angle on the corner of the page: 'You send me no information, though you have lots of money, C. G. G.'[27]

CHAPTER THIRTY-FOUR
'Strike Hard!'

That same day, 14 December 1884, the two hundred and seventy seventh of the siege, a messenger from Wolseley smuggled himself through the enemy lines and was brought to Gordon. Gordon gave him a cigarette. (Wolseley was delighted when he heard that 'Gordon, who is one of the very greatest smokers I have ever known, still has cigarettes.'[1] Wolseley was bringing him a box of 500.)

The messenger had left Wolseley more than six weeks before but Gordon could not decipher the letter he brought (Wolseley thought Gordon had been 'idiotic' to send away the cipher book, which he could have burned). Then Gordon signed and sealed a message the size of a postage stamp: 'Khartoum, all right – 14–12–84. C. G. Gordon.' This optimistic message could have been intended to deceive the Mahdi if the man was caught, for Gordon gave as well a long oral message.

Now comes a fatal mystery. The message as reported by the man verbally to Wolseley at Korti, seventeen days later, conflicts with the whole tone of Gordon's Journal. Instead of urging supreme haste by a small force because the town might fall in ten days the 'long rambling message,' as given by the man, mentioned the shortage of supplies and the need for speed; but it also said: 'Bring plenty of troops,' and: 'Do not leave Berber in your rear' – advice which must undoubtedly slow up the column.[2]

The messenger may have misunderstood Gordon, or misheard him and his interpreter because of rifle fire from the Palace roof, where Gordon's bugler boys standing on boxes, were happily taunting the dervishes across the Blue Nile with rifle fire and cheeky bugle calls. Or, more likely, the four days the messenger is known to have spent in the Mahdi's camp had turned him into a double agent deliberately misleading Wolseley.

Wolseley on reflection accepted the message as genuine if difficult to understand, and his cautious strategy became more cautious although 'our relief of Gordon will be thus greatly postponed.'[3] He sent one column up the Nile to take Berber and another including the Guards' Camel Corps to cross the desert, leaving Korti on 8 January 1885, nine days after Gordon's messenger had arrived.

Back at Khartoum, the fort of Omdurman had already fallen: Gordon had been unable to reinforce it, and he sorely missed the guns of *Bordein*, which strategists believe he should never have sent downriver. In the town, starvation was near. Troops and townspeople killed dogs and donkeys; townspeople died in the streets and Gordon would walk among them, promising that the English were almost here.

To save food for the troops he arranged for a steamer and boats to take off any inhabitants who wished to go to the dervish lines, and wrote a letter to the Mahdi asking him to treat them mercifully: but many were stripped and their goods seized as they stepped ashore. They spread the news of the famine in Khartoum, where those who remained would beg Gordon pitifully for food. By 20 January every animal had been eaten. All, including Gordon, were existing on the gum and core of palm trees, and this tended to bring on diarrhoea. Yet a number of black troops, who had served under Gordon in the south, deserted the Mahdi at this late stage to join the starving garrison.

The Mahdi had already written urging Gordon to 'enter into our security and guarantee – that is what we wish. If, however, you would rather rejoin the English we will send you to them.'[4] Gordon ignored the letter.

On 21 January the Mahdists fired a salute of 101 guns – their signal of victory. But Gordon saw by his telescope a large number of women weeping and guessed that the Expeditionary Force column had defeated the Arabs. That night his woman spy came across the Nile with firm news: a great battle had been fought at the Wells of Abu Klea. Babikr Bedri, then a young Ansar soldier, wrote in his memoirs: 'The Mahdi's army was destroyed and their general killed and very few of them escaped alive.'[5]

The Force must already have reached the steamers. Gordon at once made ostentatious preparations to receive them, and gave his own troops more pay. But unknown to him Sir Herbert Stewart had been fatally wounded two days after Abu Klea, and Fred Burnaby, who would have succeeded him, had been killed in the battle. The command had devolved on Sir Charles Wilson, a Sapper and a personal friend of the Gordon family who had never commanded troops in a campaign: he was an expert in Intelligence and in

Survey. He rose to the occasion yet he lacked decisiveness (the cavalrymen called him derisively 'the secretary' and his staff 'the committee.')[6] On reaching the Nile he and the Naval Brigade commander spent two fatal days in reconnaissance and strengthening the steamers, while Gordon, on the roof of the Palace when not going round the posts or the streets, looked in vain through his telescope for their puffs of smoke.

In the town, 'We began again to despair,' recorded Bordeini, 'Gordon Pasha used to say every day "They must come to-morrow"; but they never came, and we began to think that they must have been defeated by the rebels after all. We all became heartbroken, and concluded that no army was coming to relieve Khartoum. If a steamer had come and we had known the truth, and that help was so near, we should have taken fresh courage; and though we were starving, still we should have made a good resistance, as we all knew we should be badly treated by the rebels if we fell into their hands.'[7] In the streets men were saying that Gordon had deceived them.

Yet with the triumphant English so near, the Mahdi was about to raise the siege and withdraw, despite evidence that the defenders were weak from starvation. Then he learned – no traitor was positively identified – that at the south-west corner of the main defence line, about 150 yards of the ditch had not been fully repaired where the Nile waters had receded; Gordon had ordered repairs but the troops had been too weakened for the work, and he may have too readily accepted the assurance of the local commander, Farag Pasha, who may have turned traitor, that the flood plain was soggy and could not be crossed in an assault.

On the morning of Sunday 25 January, the 319th day of the siege, Gordon detected from the Palace roof the signs of a big enemy movement, with camels, in the south; to the north, he had looked in vain for the smoke of his steamers. He summoned a council but as he was unwell he sent a staff officer, Giriagis Bey, to order them to collect every man and boy to help man the defences and resist the attack, for in twenty-four hours the English would arrive.

Bordeini Bey the merchant asked to see Gordon. Bordeini claimed that Gordon, sitting on a divan, threw his fez across the room and exclaimed in despair that his promises had all proved false: help had not arrived. 'If this, my last promise, fails, I can do nothing more. Go and collect all the people you can on the lines and make a good stand. Now leave me to smoke these cigarettes.'[8]

Bordeini was not a reliable witness: Wingate thought him too much of a liar and Hassan the body servant was sure he was not in the Palace that day; yet if Gordon had a moment of despair he would have recalled that Christ had known despair on the Cross. In Palestine Gordon had loved to meditate on the lowliness of Christ, how He was hurt and despised and lonely, crucified and forsaken. Thanks to His death and resurrection Gordon had long been ready for death. As he had written some years before to a friend: 'I would look on death as a cheerful friend who takes us from a world of trial to our true home.'⁹ He had been ready for a swift death in battle, or from disease in Central Africa; he was being allowed, in effect, to suffer the prolonged agony of a crucifixion.

When, exactly one month later, Wolseley finished reading Gordon's Journals he put him not far behind the authors of the Bible. 'He was not an inspired writer. He was a mortal,' Wolseley wrote in his own Journal, 'And yet if God ever granted the gift of inspiration in our day to men, I know of no one more suited from the purity of his life, his intense faith in God and in Christ, and from what I may call his close communion at all hours of his daily life with his God, to have received such a commission from the Almighty. He trusted in God and yet God allowed him to be murdered, and all his labour and pain, all his self-sacrifice and devotion to duty to go for nought.'¹⁰

Gordon would have disagreed: somehow this agony must bring glory to God and good to the Sudan.

It certainly brought unsought honour to Gordon. For when the legends and the interpretations fall away, this fiery, lovable man, so human, yet striving for truth and perfection, stands untarnished among the immortals.

At dusk that Sunday evening Gordon probably went on his usual rounds, urging all to make a good stand, then back on the roof, or perhaps to write up the seventh volume of his Journal, soon to be lost. The night wore on, ominously quiet. Gordon apparently 'tumbled into sleep' at last.

He was woken shortly before dawn on 26 January by intense firing and loud yells. A great horde of up to 40,000 Ansar had broken in at the weak place near the White Nile; the mines were damp and failed to explode. Once inside the perimeter they brushed aside the starving defenders, killing all who would not join them, and raced the three miles into the city. The slaughter and pillage began, to continue for four days, not interrupted when Sir Charles Wilson's steamers appeared in the river on Gordon's birthday, and retreated under fire. They were two days too late. Khartoum had fallen. Gordon was dead.

Before the assault the Mahdi had proclaimed loudly from his camel that Gordon was not to be killed; yet Kitchener and others believed this a ruse, that the killers acted under orders, like the marksmen who had fired at the lighted window. Gordon was too respected as a holy man to be allowed in the Mahdi's camp, even as a prisoner.

His severed head was brought to Slatin Pasha in his chains: 'Is this the head of your uncle, the unbeliever?'

Precisely how Gordon died was never established. Contradictory reports came in, one after another: that he had been shot or cut down as he walked with his cavasses from the Palace to the arsenal in the former Austrian Catholic mission, whether to make a last stand or to blow it up; that he and his cavasses fought with sword and revolver in the Palace until overwhelmed; that he was shot from below and rolled down the Palace stairs; that he died as in G. W. Joy's famous picture calmly waiting at the top.

Forty-three years later a young Englishman in the Sudan Political Service was with a circle of villagers on the east bank of the Blue Nile when they were chatting about Slatin Pasha, who had converted to Islam, temporarily, to hearten his troops. The villagers condemned this and one exclaimed: '"What about the troops in Khartoum? *They* fought bravely enough under the command of an infidel. Gordon didn't have to deny his faith."

'There were murmurs of assent to this, and an elderly man at the back of the circle suddenly said, "I saw him die."

'He went on to describe the break-through on the river bank, the slaughter of 'the Copts' and the final arrival at the Palace, where they found Gordon standing unarmed at the top of the steps.

'"We looked at him and he looked at us. Then he tore open his tunic and said "Strike! Strike hard!" and somebody flung a spear, and it was over."

'There was a brief pause and he, or it may have been another, added the words, "*Kan shadeed fi deenu*. He was strong in his Faith."'[11]

Appendix: Gordon's Ancestry

General Gordon's branch derived from a soldier in the service of George II named David Gordon, whose ancestry is mysterious. David possessed a pedigree chart, which was lost in the early nineteenth century, to show his descent from the Gordons of Park in Banffshire, themselves descended from an illegitimate cousin of Elizabeth, the chief of Clan Gordon (died 1439) she was ancestress of the Marquesses of Huntly and the Dukes of Gordon, who in the seventeenth century were the leading Roman Catholic laymen in Scotland, whereas the Gordons of Park were Episcopalian.

David Gordon cannot be found in the pedigree of the Gordons of Park by modern research. Perhaps, as a family tradition suggests, he or his father had been disinherited for deserting the Jacobite cause, and his name expunged; or the father may have been illegitimate: his Christian name remains unknown but he seems to have come down from Scotland to serve in the regular army of William III or Queen Anne.

According to his own son, David was 'upwards of forty years' in the service, and had been severely wounded; so he may have fought as a youth in the last years of the wars of Marlborough, or against the Jacobites in the Rising of 1715. When George II's second surviving son, William Augustus, was created Duke of Cumberland at the age of nine and given his own household, David Gordon, already married, may have been a bodyguard; for when his own son was born in 1739 he was christened William Augustus at St. George's, Hanover Square. The eighteen-year-old royal duke stood sponsor, probably by proxy.

In 1741, after twenty-nine years service or more, David Gordon received a commission as an ensign on the formation of Lascelles Regiment (47th Foot) and in September 1745 was captured by the victorious Jacobites at the battle of Preston Pans. With the three other captured officers, and two doctors, Ensign Gordon was released on parole by the Young Pretender before he marched south to invade England; but Gordon's patron, the Duke of Cumberland, reaching Scotland three months later on the heels of the retreating Highlanders, told him that he was not bound by a parole given to a rebel. Family tradition believes that Gordon fought at the battle of Culloden which ended the Rising.

In 1750, now a lieutenant, Gordon went with his regiment to Nova Scotia, taking his eleven-year-old son; but in 1752 he 'broke his neck tumbling downstairs' at Halifax, and died, not knowing he had been promoted captain. William Augustus returned to his mother and two sisters in London. After schooling he received a commission in the infantry. He served at the long siege of Louisbourg and 'in the battle of Quebec, where with tears I lamented the fall of Wolfe.'

This Gordon went no higher than captain. He made a good match with a Miss Anna Maria Starke whose father had a substantial wholesale business in London, 'dealing largely in whalebone,' but he sold his commission at a bad time and could not get back into the service: he rented Bowhill, a fine old house on the outskirts of Exeter, which had been built in 1422 and had a great hall with a beamed roof, and a large garden, but he missed an opportunity to buy it. He tried to bring up a large family, who all adored him, on slender means, and suffered many griefs. In 1796 his wife died; his eldest son, who had purchased a captaincy in the 95th at the age of nineteen, thanks to a rich uncle, was killed by a fall from his horse at the Cape. Five years later Gordon's next son, a lieutenant in the Royal Engineers, died of lung disease at the age of twenty-one, 'esteemed by all ... a pattern of excellence and a devout Christian.'

Only the youngest remained, Henry William, who was to be General Gordon's father and was twenty-three when his father died in 1809.

References and Notes

A Augusta Gordon
G Charles Gordon
H Sir Henry Gordon
M Their Mother, Mrs H.W. Gordon

BL British Library
CA *Colonel Gordon in Central Africa*
CUL Cambridge University Library
DNB Dictionary of National Biography
Events: Events in the Life of Charles George Gordon by Henry Gordon.
FO Foreign Office Papers in Public Record Office
HP Harvey Papers
MHR Mary Hammond Raitt
PRO Public Record Office
PRONI Public Record Office of Northern Ireland
QVJ Journal of Queen Victoria
RA Royal Archives
RCS Royal Commonwealth Society Archives in Cambridge University Library
RE Archives of the Institution of Royal Engineers
Sister: Letters of General C.G. Gordon to His Sister

A number standing alone refers to *Additional Manuscripts*, British Library, eg 51291 f. 17

Note These Gordon Papers were in packets during the main research for this book. When they were bound into volumes afterwards some *folio* numbers were slightly changed. Letters may be easily located by date and the old number is generally still visible.

Prologue – TOO LATE

1 Wilson, Sir C., *Korti to Khartoum* pp. 170–75.
2 Wilson to H., 11 March 85. 50401 f. 74.
3 Waller to A., quoting E. Stuart-Wortley, 27 June 85. 51300 f. 138; and E. Stuart-Wortley to A., 11 Dec 85, *ibid* ff. 173–76.
4 Preston, p. 134.
5 Wolseley to H., 11 March 85. 50401 f. 76.
6 *ibid*. 5 March 85. *ibid*. f. 35.
7 Hamilton Diary, 5 Feb 85. 48639.
8 Gladstone Diaries XI, p. 289.
9 RA. QVJ, 5 Feb 85.
10 *ibid*. (copy pasted in.)
11 Telegrams, 51300 f. 68.
12 Telegram, 51299 f. 147
13 Duke of Cambridge's Journal, 5 Feb 85. FitzGeorge-Balfour Papers (Cambridge Journal).
14 G. to General Eyre, 6 March 84, Spiro Collection. A copy is in RA.
15 RA Lady Geraldine Somerset's Journal, 5 Feb 85.
16 Cambridge Journal, 6 Feb 85.
17 *ibid*.
18 Sir Gerald Graham to H., 52399 f. 10.
19 Townshend Wilson to H., 5 Feb 85. 52399 f. 12.
20 Hamilton Diary, 11 Feb 85. 48639 f. 49.
21 Speech by George Arnold, Mayor, at unveiling of Gravesend Statue, 4 Oct 1893, Report, p. 10.
22 Kitchener to A., 16 Oct 85. 51300 f. 156.
23 General Sir J. Stokes to H., 16 Feb 85. 52399 f. 162.
24 Col. Thomas Owen Jones to H., 7 Feb 85. 52399 ff. 44–45.
25 W. T. Stead to A., 31 Dec 85. 51300 f. 178.
26 Lord Cromer, typescript of draft Memoirs, 44904 f.147. See *Modern Egypt*, p. 430.
27 Randolph S. Churchill, *Churchill*, I, p. 426.
28 Cromer to Viscount Knutsford in 1912, sold at Sotherbys 4 Oct 1977. Quoted *Sunday Telegraph*, 25 Sept 77.
29 Margaret Gordon to H., 16 Feb [85] 52399 ff. 164–65.

Chapter 1 – THE POWDER KEG

1 G. to Augusta Louisa G. ('Tiny') afterwards Mrs G. H. Blunt, 22 April 79. Blunt Papers.

2 Hake p. 6.

3 For the Enderbys see: C. H. Gordon, *The Vigorous Enderbys*, New Zealand Railways Magazine, December 1938, January 1939; infm from A. G. E. Jones to MHR; Wills of Enderbys; notes by George Enderby, circa 1874; research by MHR.

4 *Gordon Memoirs*, p. 71.

5 The manuscript letters of G's family and friends show no consistency in the spelling of Charley or Charlie. His eldest brother, Sir Henry, could write to his sister about Charl*ey* and then immediately address G in a letter as 'My dear Charl*ie*.' G always signed *C. G. Gordon* even to his mother and his sister, but once refers to himself when quoting someone, as Charley.

6 G. to G. W. Rusden, 14 Sept 83 Rusden Papers.

7 *Gordon Memoirs*, pp. 82–3.

8 The anonymous narrative, 'Gordon's Travels' dated 3 May 1847 in a schoolboy hand, in RE Archives (Gordon School MSS) is not by Gordon but his younger brother Frederick. Internal evidence is conclusive: The writer says he was born in 1835, Frederick's year of birth; the narrative includes a family journey home from Corfu via Venice, Switzerland, Belgium etc to England which follows exactly the itinerary 3 Sept–4 Oct 1845 given by the boys' father, General H. W. Gordon, printed in *Gordon Memoirs* pp. 131–2. He also states (p. 84) that Charles, Emily and Mrs Gordon had already returned, in July 1843, by sea (HMS *Acheron* to Malta, S.S. *Oriental* to England.).

Thus at the date of 'Gordon's Travels' Charles Gordon had never seen Venice, Switzerland etc. J. H. Waller, *Gordon of Khartoum*, New York, 1988 is therefore misled in ascribing it to Charles, and the quotes and deductions are not valid to a life of General Gordon.

9 Hake, p. 6.

10 Memories of Helen Moffitt, née Gordon, recorded by her son, Colonel F. Moffitt in a letter to his cousin Brigadier Gordon Blunt (T/S copy) Blunt Papers.

11 Duke of Cambridge to H., 19 Feb 85, copy in Blunt Papers, RA; Lady Geraldine Somerset's Diary, 7 Apr 84; *Morning Post*, 19 July 1902 (Cambridge's speech at unveiling of Gordon Memorial).

12 G. to A., 25 Feb 64. 51291 f. 27.

13 *Gordon Memoirs*, p. 84.

14 "The Story of Follands", T/S by Robin Bush, Somerset R.O. 1985. Folland's school closed in 1887 and was sold as a private house. Many years later, in 1946, the house and grounds were bought by King's College, Taunton and Follands became part of a school again until sold off in 1990 for redesign into private retirement flats.

15 G to Barnes, 13 Oct 83, Barnes Papers, Boston, Mass, City Library MS Eng 450/33, Waller, p. 20 misreads G's words 'writing in haste' to read 'writing in hurt.'

The MS has nothing about Rogers' prophesying a bad end for G, as Waller claims.

16 Wilbraham Taylor to Sir Henry Ponsonby 28 May 85. RA Add MSS 1733.

17 Infm Robin Bush, Somerset County Archivist, 9 Oct 89.

18 Memories of D. J. Pring, Somerset Notes and Queries Vol 21, 1933–35, p. 150.

19 RE, Gordon School MSS.

20 *ibid*.

21 Helen's Memories.

22 HWG (*Gordon Memoirs*, p. 137) gives the date as 1 Jan 47. The printed register in RA Archives (p. 170) gives it as 16 Nov 44 – probably a misprint or miscopy for 46.

23 Helen's Memories. Mrs Blunt (née 'Tiny' Gordon) used to tell her children that Charlie and Helen took after the Enderbys, full of fun and practical jokes, while Henry and Augusta, 'rather pompous,' were typical of the Gordon side of the family.

24 Helen's Memories.

25 *ibid*. Molyneaux later went to London, first as minister of a well known Evangelical chapel and then for twelve years as the first vicar of a new church, St. Paul's in Onslow Square, which had been laid out twenty years earlier with handsome stuccoed houses, replacing the market gardens of South Kensington.

26 G to Barnes, 26 Sept 83, Boston 21.

Chapter 2 – YOUNG SAPPER

1 Major General (Sir) John Browne, Governor RMA, to H. 7 Sept 85. 52402 f. 154.

2 T. Bland Strange, *Gunner Jingo's Jubilee* p. 26.

3 F. G. Ravenhill to J. Ruck Keene 24 Sept 85 52402 ff. 172/3.

4 Strange, *op. cit* p. 26.

5 G to Mrs Charles Harvey 31 Dec 69, HP, 62.

6 Strange *op. cit* p. 26.

7 G. to Enderby G. 2 Oct 75 Blunt Papers.

8 Ravenhill to Ruck Keene, as above.

9 R.E. Veitch: Major General Edward Renouard James Pt I. RE Journal. Oct 1910 p. 272 (Subsequent references: *James Memoir*).

10 In the Army List Jenkins was listed as a major 1851–8 but as G. invariably addressed him as Colonel he may have had an honorary local rank before being promoted Brevet Lieutenant Colonel on 15 Jan 58.

11 G. to Jenkins 1 Sept 74 Jenkins Papers.

12 *ibid*. 14 Nov 81.

13 G. to Jenkins 14 Nov 80 Jenkins Papers.

14 G. to Mother 18 Aug 54 Blunt Papers.
15 Note by G. in Freese Papers (4), quoted Elton, pp. 97–8.
16 *Sister* p. 1. The Ms is lost.
17 *ibid.* pp. 1, 3.
18 *ibid.* p. 1 and G. to M. 30 Nov 54, Blunt Papers.
19 G. to Jenkins 12 Dec 78 Jenkins Papers.
20 G. to M. 30 Nov 54 Blunt Papers.
21 *ibid.*

Chapter 3 – THE CRIMEA

1 G. to M. 8 Jan 55 52389 ff. 8 and 10. Young British gentry addressed their letters home, intended to be read by both parents, to the mother. (Note: In G's letters I have supplied capitals, which he used seldom, and have expanded abbreviations).
2 G. to H. 12 Feb 55 *ibid* f. 11.
3 G. to H. 17 Feb 55 *ibid* ff. 13, 14.
4 G. to H. 28 Feb 55, Nat. Army Museum 6246.
5 Crimea Diary 27 Feb 55 Freese Papers (4).
6 General Sir C. Staveley to H. 10 Oct 85. 57403 ff. 14–15.
7 Wolseley, *A Soldier's Life*, I, pp. 147–8.
8 G. to Barnes 26 April 83. Boston 21.
9 G. to A. 11 Nov 80 51296 f. 63.
10 Wolseley *op cit* pp. 147–8.
11 Quoted in Viner *Sir Henry William Gordon KCB*, 1953 pp. 14–15.
12 G. to M. 20 Nov 56 5289 f. 4.
13 G. to A. 4 May 55 51291 f. 3.
14 G. to M. 8 June 55. 33222 ff. 1–4.
15 G. to M. 12 June 55 52389 f. 29.
16 G. to H. 17 June 55 56105 D.
17 Kinglake, *The War in the Crimea* vol 9. 1888 ed. pp. 184–5.
18 E. R. James, *Memoir*, *op. cit.* p. 272.
19 C. G. Chesney, *Fraser's Magazine*, Feb 1869, p. 144.
20 G. to M. 16 Sept 55 33222 ff. 6–7.
21 G. to M. 10 Sept 55 Boston, 35.
22 Wheeler was living as a pensioner in Gravesend when G served there 1865–71 and the story grew in the telling. In 1885 he told it to a journalist of the *Pall Mall Gazette* (Macaulay, *Gordon Anecdotes* p. 66) but by 1911 (*Kent Messenger*, 11 Aug) Gordon was said to have asked who in the ward wanted to send money home; he took £5 from several men and they all found that their wives received £10 each..

23 Graham, G, *Last Words with General Gordon*, (*Fortnightly Review*), Jan 1887 p. 84.

24 G. to Graham, 11 Dec 77 Nat. Army Museum 7312–4–7; G. to Major Lloyd, RE, 1 Dec 77 57772 BB.

25 G. to M. 9 March 56 Bell Papers. Ms not in the BL collection..

26 G. to M. 25 April 56 52389 f. 59.

Chapter 4 – RIVER AND MOUNTAINS

1 G. to M., (and when only the date is shown in this chapter's refs:) 23 May 56. 52389 f. 62.

2 Major General Edward Renouard James, Memoir ed. R. H. Veitch. R. E. Mag. 1910, p. 272..

3 29 Dec 56, Bell Mss; 10, 18 Nov 56 52389 ff. 78–9.

4 29 June 56 pp. 3–4. Bell Mss.

5 10 Nov 56. 52389 f. 78.

6 10 April 57. *ibid* f. 93.

7 James, p. 276.

8 No contemporary printed or Ms evidence supports the unlikely story in R. MacGregor-Hastie, *Never to be Taken Alive*, 1985, of G. living in Bucharest at Gessi's home while on the Danube Commission. This also conflicts with the standard *Vita di Romolo Gessi* by C. Zaghi (1939), pp. 24, 338..

9 25 May 57 52389 f. 102.

10 R. E. Journal 1 Sep 1903: obit. of F. M. Sir Lintorn Simmons.

11 7 May and 17 June 57, 52389 ff. 99, 105; James p. 279.

12 James, p. 277.

13 21 June 57 *ibid* f. 106.

14 22 July 57 33222 ff. 16–21.

15 James, p. 357.

16 8 July 52389 ff. 115–16.

17 28 Sept 57 *ibid* f. 131.

18 General Williams 'is not much of a hero here.' 25 May 57 *ibid* f. 102.

19 7 Oct 57 f. 195.

20 G. to Helen 20 June 58 *ibid* f. 151.

21 Deduced from dating of letters in January and March 1858. He would have been working on a report..

22 James, p. 360.

23 G. to Lt Col M. A. S. Biddulph ND (Nov 1858) 56366.

24 3 June 58 52389 ff. 142–3.

25 5 June 56 *ibid* f. 142; 29 June 56 f. 148; 17 Aug, 10 Sept 58 f. 158.

26 G. to Helen 29 June 56 *ibid* ff. 148, 150.

27 James, p. 363.
28 10 Sept 58 p. 6 Bell Mss, and James p. 364. G.'s copious notes and abstract of his journal in Armenia are in 51302.
29 17 Nov 58 52389 f. 163.
30 Col. (later Lt. Gen. Sir) J. W. Gordon to Lt. Gen. W. H. Gordon, 13 Dec (58) 51305 f. 183.
31 G. to Biddulph 'Thursday evening'; 'Wednesday'; 'Monday' 56366.

Chapter 5 – CHINA PRELUDE

1 Redmayne, R. *Men, Mines and Memories*, p. 84.
2 G. to Harvey 11 Sep 59. H.P. 2.
3 *ibid* 29 Dec 59. *ibid*, 6.
4 *ibid* 27 May 60. *ibid*, 9.
5 G. to M. 25 July 60 (G. wrote *February*. A later hand corrects it.) Blunt Papers.
6 G. to Harvey, 10 Sept 60. H.P., 13.
7 Veitch, *Graham* pp. 185–86.
8 G. to M. 8 Oct 60. 52386 ff. 192–93, 195.
9 G. to Harvey, 5 Feb 61, 13 Dec 60, 25 Oct 60, H.P., 21, 18, 15.
10 G. to Col. J. W. Gordon, C.B., 10 March 61, 8 July 61, 10 Feb 62. 59652M f. 54, 59, 70.
11 G. to A. 11 Oct 61 51291 f. 21.
12 Boulger, *Gordon*, p. 72.
13 G. to Harvey 11 March 61, H.P. 19, and to A. 13 March 61. 51291, f. 17.
14 G. to A. 15 March 62. 51291 f. 23.
15 G. to Barnes, 26 Sept 83. Boston 21.

Chapter 6 – TAIPING

1 A vast literature on every aspect of the Taiping rebellion is easily accessible. For reasons of space I give only a brief note to provide background for Gordon's involvement.
2 G. B. Endicott and D. E. She, *The Diocese of Victoria, Hong Kong 1849–1949*. Hong Kong, 1949. p. 24.
3 Quoted p. 239, J. S. Gregory, *Great Britain and the Taipings*, 1967.
4 See Caleb Carr, *The Devil Soldier*, New York 1992.
5 Staveley to Viceroy Tsang, April 1863. PRO FO 405/10/237 p. 148.
6 G. to Harvey, 2 Aug 62 HP 21a.
7 Staveley to H. 10 Oct 85. 52403 ff. 16–19..
8 *ibid*.

9 Lyster, p. 192.

10 G. to Harvey 2 Aug 62 HP 21a.

11 *ibid*.

12 Lyster, pp. 84, 88, 284.

13 *ibid*, p. 86.

14 G. to M. 21 Dec 62. 52389 f. 305.

15 Li to Vice-Consul Markham 24 April 63 FO 405/10.

16 FO 405/10 inclosure to No 9.

17 Wade to G. 25 Jan 63 52386 f. 5.

18 G. to M. 16 Jan 63 52389.

19 *ibid*, 23 Feb 63.

20 Staveley to H. 9 Nov [85] 52403 f. 41. For a detailed account of events leading to G's appointment and for much light on every aspect of the Ever Victorious Army see R. J. Smith, *Mercenaries and Mandarins*. His account of 1862–64 is invaluable, though some of his comments on G. should be contested..

21 Lyster, p. 136.

22 G's Ms "Notes for Mr Mossman." RE 8907–11, Note in Margin, and p. 1.

23 Lyster, p. 137; Veitch, *Gordon's Campaign*, p. 36.

Chapter 7 – THE EVER VICTORIOUS

1 Wade to H. 14 Jan 86. CUL Add Mss 8.28.4.

2 Memorandum 6 June 64 FO 17/410.

3 Veitch, p. 38.

4 G. to Florence Nightingale April 80, 45806 ff. 21–26.

5 G. to M. 18 April 62 52389 f. 330.

6 Li to Vice-Consul J. Markham 24 April 63 FO 405/10, 103 inclosure 3.

7 Major-General W. R. Brown to Sir F. Bruce 17 April 63 FO 405/10, 104 inclosure 2, and 27 April, *ibid*, 103 inclosure 1..

8 Li to G., translated by W. S. F. Mayers, 10 May 63. BL Or Ms. 12914.

9 Veitch, p. 42.

10 G. to Barnes 26 Sept 83 Boston, 21.

11 G. to M. 2 May 63 52389 f. 334.

12 Lyster, p. 144 and G. to Brown. 52393. f. 50.

13 R. Sillars to Rev. J. Scarth 5 March 85 Univ. of Texas at Austin Mss.

14 G. to M. 18 April 63 52393 f. 330.

15 G.'s "Notes for Mossman" Ms..

16 G. to M. 10 May 63 52393 f. 337.

17 *Events*, p. 60.

18 G.'s despatch. FO 17/392 p. 185; printed version FO 405/10/237 p. 221.

Chapter 8 – BETRAYED AT SOOCHOW

1 G.'s "Notes for Mossman" *Ms* p. 4.

2 G. to M. 3 June 63 52389 f. 325.

3 G.'s "Notes", *Ms cit.*, p. 4 margin.

4 G. to M. 23 June 63 52389 f. 334.

5 G. to Li 25 July 63 FO 405/10/237 p. 18.

6 25 July is the date G. gives in his "Notes for Mossman". In his 1876 article in RE *Professional Papers* he gives 26 July. There are other discrepancies. I follow his earlier account..

7 Burgevine to G. 25 July 63 52386 f. 58.

8 Markham to Bruce 4 Aug 63 FO 405/10/237. p. 14 and enclosing G.'s report..

9 *ibid* p. 21.

10 *ibid* p. 17.

11 G. to Earl de Grey and Ripon (S. of S. for War) 11 Sept 63 Ripon Papers, Duke.

12 BL Or. Ms 12914(3).

13 Burgevine to G. 30 Oct 63 5238 ff. 85–6.

14 Copied in FO 405/10/237 p. 63.

15 *ibid* p. 68.

16 'Major General Li Heng Sung to Major-General Gordon' 13 Oct 63 BL Or Ms 12914 f.12 (Chinese original f. 13).

17 FO 405/10/237 p. 64.

18 Michael, Franz, *The Taiping Rebellion*, p. 1195.

19 Burgevine to G. 12 Dec 64 52387 f. 130.

20 [F. L. Storey] in Hake, *Taeping*, pp. 484–5, 525. The anon. author can be no other.

21 Michael, Franz, *op. cit* pp. 1195–7.

22 G.'s Memorandum [9] Dec 63 FO 405/10/237 p. 85.

23 *Ms cit* p. 86.

24 Storey (pp. 490–1) has conflated the events of 5 and 6 Dec.

25 70 *Ms cit* p. 87. An undated memo. quoted in the Shanghai press, 11 Dec 63.

26 *ibid*.

27 *ibid* p. 97.

28 *ibid* p. 87.

29 Storey, *op. cit*, pp. 497.

30 G. to M. 12 Dec 63 52389 f. 387.

31 G. to M. 7 Dec 63 52389 f. 379.

32 Macartney to Sir Harry Parkes 28 June 64 Parkes Papers, Jardine Matheson Archives, CUL.

33 12 Dec 63 FO 405/10/237 p. 97, and (14 Dec 63) pp. 89.

34 *ibid* p. 90.

35 Storey, in Hake, p. 498.
36 G. to M. 15 Dec 63 (added to note of 7 Dec) 52389 f. 400.
37 G. to de Grey and Ripon 24 Dec 63 (copied extract) Ripon Papers, Duke.

Chapter 9 – 'THE ADMIRATION OF ALL'

1 *Events* pp 73–4.
2 BL Or 35348 ff. 7–19; Mayers' translation, Or 12914 f. 39.
3 S. F. Mayers to Sir Hesketh Bell, Bell Papers, RCS Papers in CUL. See also Elton, pp 209–10.
4 See, *eg*, Veitch, *Graham*, p. 196, where Graham refers to 'Charlie with his usual candour.'
5 Stanley Diary, 20 May 88 (Microfilm copy) BL RP 2435.
6 Hart's Journal Vol 5. 18 Jan 64 Queen's Univ. of Belfast, Special Collections.
7 *ibid*.
8 *ibid* 22 Jan 64.
9 *ibid* 31 Jan 64.
10 *ibid* 1 Feb 64.
11 *ibid* 4 Feb 64.
12 Li to G. BL Or 12914 ff. 18–19.
13 Hart's Journal Vol 26. 2 Aug 80.
14 *ibid* 2, 19 Feb 64.
15 G. to Bruce. 6 Feb 64 FO 17/407/ pp. 294–5.
16 Hart's Journal 22 Feb 64; and Bruce to G. 12 March 64. Copy in Blunt Papers.
17 G. to A. 25 Feb 64 51291 f. 28.
18 G. to Markham 3 March 64. Parkes Papers, Jardine Matheson Archives, CUL.
19 Storey, in Hake, pp. 512–13.
20 G. to Col. Hough 22 March 64. Copy in Layard Papers, 39109 ff. 194–5.
21 Storey in Hake, p. 500.
22 "Notes for Mossman" Ms p. 15 (wrongly dating it 21 March).
23 G. to Col Hough, as above, f. 195.
24 Hart to G. [1 April 64] 52387 f. 80.
25 G. to Col. Hough 31 March 64, copy in Layard Papers 39109 ff. 196–7.
26 G. to Parkes 4 April 64 Layard Papers 39109 ff. 198–202.
27 Hart to H. 22 April 64. 52398 f. 1.
28 G. to Bruce 9 April 64 FO 17/408.x.1.2105.
29 G. to Parkes 4 April 64 39109 f. 200.
30 G. to M. 10 May 64 52389 f. 391.
31 Palmerston to the Queen 23 April 64 FA Add. A32/53.
32 G. to M. 2 June 64 (copy in Blunt Papers).
33 *ibid*.

34 G. Memorandum 10 May 80 RE GR70; and G. to Lady Cardwell 17 Feb 80 57772E.

35 Hart to G. 17 June 84 52387 f. 110.

36 Li to G. [1866] copy in Blunt Papers.

37 Hake. *Chinese Gordon* I p. 207.

38 Lane Poole, *Parkes* I p. 500.

39 G. to Harvey "13 March" (prob. Aug) 64 HP 23.

40 H. to Marquis Toseng, Chinese envoy in London, 6 March 85 (draft) 52401 f. 37.

41 G. to Harvey *Ms cit* HP 23.

42 Lane Poole, *op. cit*, p. 501.

43 Storey in Hake pp. 520, 523–4.

44 52389 f. 439.

45 *ibid*.

46 34480 printed in *Events* pp. 95–6.

47 Lane Poole, *op. cit*, p. 502.

48 Ponsonby to his wife 28 Dec 72 RA Add.A/36–483.

49 *Times, The*

50 Beauvois, *Journey*, p. 78.

Chapter 10 – WHERE NEXT FOR CHINESE GORDON?

1 Bruce to Earl Russell 12 July 64 copy in Blunt Papers.

2 G. to Harvey 10 Jan 65 HP 25.

3 'A Student of History' (Col. C. C. Chesney) in letter to *The Times* 19 Aug 73.

4 Lane Poole, *op. cit*, p. 502.

5 G. to Harvey, 16, 31 March 65 HP 31, 33.

6 *ibid* 24 Feb 65 HP 29.

7 *ibid* 10 March 65 HP 30.

8 Harrison, *A Life*, p. 118. Unfortunately, the speeches were not noted down..

9 G. to Harvey 24 Feb 65 HP.

10 Noted in 52389 f. 249.

11 G. to Harvey 19 May 65 HP 34.

12 *ibid* 28 April 65 HP 35.

13 *ibid* 10 March 65 HP 30.

14 *ibid* 28 June, 8 July. HP 42, 43.

15 Veitch, *Clarke*, p. 90.

16 G. to Harvey 30 July 65 H 46.

17 *ibid* 13 [Aug] 64 HP 23.

Chapter 11 – THE GRAVESEND COLONEL

1 G. to Harvey 1 Sept 65 HP 47.
2 *ibid* 12 Feb 83. Printed copy in 58070. *Ms* missing from HP.
3 Freese Papers (4), quoted Elton, p. 98.
4 G. to Harvey 7 Dec 65 HP 50.
5 Harrison, *op. cit*, pp. 118–19.
6 Stannard, *Gordon at Gravesend*, pp. 714–5.
7 *ibid* p. 716.
8 The Rev. Frederick Freese, *Gordon* T/S pp. 7–9. Freese Papers (3).
9 Freese Papers (4) quoted Elton p. 98.
10 G. to Barnes 26 Sept 83 Boston.
11 G. to A 26 Oct 65 51291 f. 31.
12 *ibid* 12 June 66 *ibid* f. 34–5.
13 Freese Papers (4), quoted Elton p. 98.
14 G. to Harvey 14 Dec 65 HP 50a.
15 RA Add Mss A/15 918.
16 M. H. McClintock, *The Queen Thanks Sir Howard 1945* p. 96.
17 G. to Barnes 26 Sept 83 Boston.
18 [O. Freese,] *More about Gordon*, p. 44.
19 H. Carruthers Wilson, *The Theology of General Gordon*, p. 37.
20 From a version of G's tract in RE Archives. A slightly shorter version is in BL.
21 G. to Harvey 19 July 67 HP 56.
22 From G's tract.

Chapter 12 – SCUTTLERS AND WANGS

1 G. to Mrs Hutchinson [1870] *Cornhill Magazine*, April 1917 p. 236.
2 *Ragged School Magazine* April 1885 p. 7.
3 Stannard, *op. cit* p. 714.
4 W. H. Lilley, *General Gordon at Gravesend*, [1885] p. 21.
5 Stannard, *op. cit* p. 719.
6 *More About Gordon*, p. 3 and F. Freese, T/S, p. 2.
7 Lilley, *op. cit* p. 44.
8 Veitch, *Clarke*, p. 97.
9 G. to Rev. J. Scarth 2 July 69. Univ of Texas at Austin.
10 Harold Begbie, *The Little that is Good*, 1917, pp. 153–69.
11 *Gravesend and Dartford Reporter* 20 Nov 69.
12 *ibid* 20 March 69.
13 *Ragged School Magazine* April 1885 pp. 68–9.
14 L. J. Johnson to 1st Lord Elton 24 Aug 1951.
15 John Robson T/S Gravesend Central Library Papers, p. 12.

16 Horace Hutchinson, *Cornhill Magazine* Feb 1917, p. 231.

17 Stanley Diary 20 May 88 *Ms cit*.

18 Quoted Elton p. 151.

Chapter 13 – A SCHEME OF MERCY

1 G. to Harvey 3 May 66 HP 52.

2 Wilson's *The Ever Victorious Army* was not published until 1878.

3 G. to Anson Burlinghame 26 Nov 68, Library of Congress Mss Division.

4 G. to J. Hudson Taylor 28 Dec 65 China Inland Mission/Overseas Missionary Fellowship Archives.

5 G. to A. 28 May 67. 51291 f. 54.

6 G. to Harvey 16 July 70. HP 61 A (Sir William Gordon had died in February) see also 51294 ff. 110–11 for the events leading to his suicide.

7 G. to Mrs Hutchinson, *Cornhill* Feb 1917 p. 236.

8 *ibid*.

9 *Gravesend and Dartford Reporter*, 6 March 69.

10 Robson T/S pp. 14–15.

11 *Reporter*, 22 Oct 70.

Chapter 14 – DANUBE BACKWATER

1 G. to Jenkins 26 Sept 71 Jenkins Papers.

2 G. to Mrs Hutchinson 2 Nov 71 59652 M f. 77.

3 G. to W. G. Penman 5 March 72 appendix to Gravesend Mayor's address 1893, printed copy in Shaftesbury Society's Papers.

4 G. to Mrs Hutchinson *MS cit*.

5 G. to (Sir) William Goodenough 8 Jan 73, Sudan Archives, Durham.

6 G. to Sir H. Elliot 20 May 72, National Library of Scotland Ms 21206 f. 26.

7 G. to Harvey 3 Oct 71 HP 63.

8 G. to Sir H. Elliot 3 July Nat. Lib. Scotland Ms 21206 f. 29. For much description and discussion of the Commission see HP 63 and 64. Letters to Sir Charles Hartley, civil engineer, are in private hands. Photostats at St Antony's College, Oxford.

9 G. to Goodenough, *Ms cit*.

10 G. to Harvey 15 Jan 72 HP 65.

11 G. to Jenkins 24 Nov 72 Jenkins Papers.

12 G. to Harvey 26 July 72 HP 66.

13 G. to Penman 5 March 72, *op. cit*.

14 G. to Miss Broom, 12 May [72], misdated 1871. Ms framed, in possession of Mr G. J. Stewart, of Wayne, N. J. in 1972. Raitt Papers.

15 G. to O'Hara Steward 31 Dec 71 RE CR 170.

16 G. to Harvey 6 Dec 71 HP 64.

17 *ibid* 18 Sept 72 RE 4811/113 (HP 67).

18 Adye, Sir John, *Recollections*, pp. 237.

19 G. to (Sir) J. Stokes 2 June 85 52402 f. 72.

20 G. to Harvey 15 Nov 73 HP 69.

21 *Memories de Nubar Pasha*, Beirut 1983 p. 440.

22 Ponsonby to his wife 28 Dec, 30 Dec 72 RA Add.A/36/483, 485. (the passage shown by dots was quoted in Ch. 9 p. 96.

23 Freese *op. cit.*, p. 95.

24 F. Freese *Recollections, Ms cit* p. 4.

25 Freese, *op. cit* pp. 98–9.

26 G. to Harvey 26 April 73 HP 68.

27 Ponsonby to his wife, 23 Sep 73 RA Add 36/647.

28 *The Times*, 14 July, 19 Aug 73.

29 G. to Amy Enderby, 18 Nov 73 Spiro Collection.

30 Copy in RA E20/150.

31 G. to Elliot 5 Sept 73 Nat. Lib. Scotland 21206 f. 39.

32 Ponsonby to the Queen, Memos, 21, 22 Sept 73 RA E 20/160, 162; to his wife *MS cit*; Cowell to Ponsonby n.d., E20/159.

33 G. to H. 5 Oct 73 Blunt Papers.

34 G. to Elliot 16 Oct 73 Nat. Lib. Scotland 21206 f. 48.

35 Atkins, *W. H. Russell* II., p. 246.

Chapter 15 – SUDAN PRELUDE

1 [Moberly Bell] *Khedives and Pashas* pp. 5–6.

2 Adye, *op. cit* p. 274.

3 G. to A. 16 Feb 74 5192 f. 4.

4 *ibid*.

5 G to A, 17 March 74 51293 f. 16.

6 Long, *Central Africa*, pp. 8–19, *My Life* p. 83. For his muddled dating, see Shukry, pp. 44–5.

7 G to A, 28 March 74, *ib* f. 24.

8 see G to A, *ib* f. 23.

9 G. to A. 8 Sept 75. See also to Harvey 25 July 74 HP 71.

10 G. to Cooper and Sturge, Anti-Slavery Society 18 May 74 47609.

11 *ibid*.

12 CA p. 116.

13 Hook, *Home from the Hill.* 1987. The incident took place at Lafone village, 60 miles north of Torit in January 1950.

14 G. to Jenkins 1 Sept 74 Jenkins Papers.

15 G. to Enderby 17 Oct 74 Blunt Papers.

16 G. to Waller 22 Oct 74 Waller Papers f. 22.

17 Quoted by Leonard Huxley, *The Times*, 7 Feb 1933.

18 W. H. Martinadale and W. W. Westcote, *Extra Pharmacopæia*. 1906 p. 599.

19 G. to A. '5 Oct' (i.e. Nov) 75 51293 f. 74.

20 G. to Harvey 24 Nov 74. RE 4801–113 (HP 86).

21 Lane Poole, *Watson*, pp. 54–5.

22 Watson to James Grant 21 Nov 74 Nat. Lib. Scotland 17909 f. 109.

23 W. H. Chippindall,'Experiences with Colonel Gordon on the White Nile.' T/S,
    p. 12 RE GR 39.

24 Lane Poole, *Watson, op. cit.*, p. 73.

25 G. to A. 29 June 74 5129 f. 175.

26 Chippindall, *Ms cit* p. 12.

27 Chaillé-Long, 'The Key to the Tragedy of Gordon's Death,' unpublished T/S
    [1908] Mss Dept, Library of Congress, Chaillé-Long Papers.

28 Chippindall, *Ms cit.*, p. 8.

29 Chippindall to General Sir Bindon Blood, 15 Jan 1932 RE GR 39.

30 Redmayne, *op. cit* p. 300.

31 G. to A. 3 Aug 75 CA 95.

32 *ibid*.

33 Chippindall, *Ms cit* p. 18.

34 G. to A. 15 July 75 CA 93.

35 *ibid*.

36 G. to Edward White.

37 G. to A. Sept 75 51293 f. 15, 30.

38 G. to A. 51293 f. 30

39 Licurgo Alois Santoni, Journal, 1 April 78 in Santi and Hill, p. 221.

40 16 of G's autographed maps of the Nile below Ouffli and Magungo, with *Ms*
    notes are at John H. Jenkins College, Austin, Texas.

41 P. Eyre to H. ND [1876] 51300 f. 2.

42 G. to A. Sept 75 51293 ff. 21, 24.

43 *ibid* 4 Nov 76 *ibid* f. 263.

44 *ibid* 23 Aug 76 *ibid* ff. 223–4 and 4 Nov 76 f. 265.

45 *ibid* 27 Aug 76 *ibid* f. 225.

46 G. to Rev J. Stevenson 1 Jan 77 49597H.

47 G. to A. 24 Dec 76 51293 f. 271.

48 Butler, *Autobiography*, 1911 p. 191.

49 Quoted in J. K. Galbraith, *Mackinnon*, p. 54.

50 G. to Waller 17 Jan 76 Waller Papers ff. 55–6.

51 Diary of 15th Earl of Derby 11 Jan 76.

52 G. to Waller 19 Jan 77 Waller Papers f. 64.

53 *ibid* f. 62.
54 Derby's Diary 1 Feb 77.
55 G. to A. 21 Jan 77 51294 f. 1.
56 *ibid*
57 *ibid*

Chapter 16 – THE GOVERNOR-GENERAL

1 G. to Gerald Graham 9 Feb 77 RE 670703 GR 189.
2 Quoted RE Journal 1 April 77 p. 82.
3 CA p. 213.
4 G. to Graham 26 March 67 (copy in Graham's hand in HP).
5 G. to Mrs Freese 18 May 77 Freece Papers (1).
6 G. to A. 20 April 77 51294 f. 55.
7 Wolseley Journal 4 Oct 84 in Preston, p. 29.
8 G. to A. 7 June 77 51294 f. 74.
9 G. to (Sir) William Goodenough 22 June 77 Durham, Sudan Archive G//S68 SAD 723/1/8.
10 G. to A. 7 Aug 77 51294 f. 147.
11 G. to Colonel Nugent 18 July 77 Nat. Army Museum. 7312–4–6.
12 G. to A. 17 July 77 51294 f. 112.
13 G. to Rose G. 1 June 77. Copy by E. S. Jones in 1912. 52390 f. 6 and G. to A. 51294 f. 75.
14 G. to Nugent 18 July 77 *Ms cit*.
15 See Zubair's Autobiography 61856.
16 CA 271 (missing from *Mss*).
17 Sir John Cowell to Queen Victoria 28 Feb 84 RA O20/149.
18 G. to A. 2 Sept 77 51294.
19 *ibid*.
20 *ibid*.
21 *ibid*.
22 *ibid*.
23 Caption in G's hand to photo of Berzati in G's Photograph Album (owned by John Hillelson Agency).
24 Licurgo Santoni's Journal in Santi and Hill, pp. 212–13.
25 G. to Harvey 25 Feb 78 HP 81 (RE D.T 107.3)
26 Elton p. 251.
27 Santoni in Santi and Hill, p. 220.
28 *ibid*
29 "The Egyptian Embroglio," Memo by G. printed *Events* pp. 109–125 (*Ms* is in 52395).

30 Baring to Goschen 8 March 78 PRO Cromer Papers FO/638/2/p. 217 (T/S).
31 G. to Mrs Freese 10 March 78 Freese Papers (1).
32 G. to Graham 31 March 78 Nat. Army Museum 7312–4–8.
33 *ibid*.

Chapter 17 – BUILDING A NATION

 1 G. to Jenkins 15 Sept 78 Jenkins Papers.
 2 Ronald Wingate, *Wingate*, p. 24.
 3 A. B. Wylde, *'83–'87 in the Sudan*, 1888.
 4 G. to A. 23 Sept 78 51295 f. 96.
 5 *ibid* 31 Oct 73 51291 f. 144.
 6 Camboni biography (T/S) p. 307.
 7 Letter in *Explorate* (Milan) 4 Aug 78.
 8 Camboni, p. 339.
 9 Rivers Wilson, *My Official Life*, p. 199.
10 Letter of Sir Shane Leslie in *Morning Post* (cutting, N.D but probably 1932 in RE GR 39(c).
11 G. to 3 missionaries 28 May 78. *Ms* copy in CMS Papers CA/019/6A f. 40.
12 G. to Henry Wright (CMS Secretary).
13 *Church Missionary Gleaner*, 1 Nov 98 p. 169.
14 C. W. Pearson to G. CMS Papers CA/6/0/11.
15 G. to Graham 17 Sept 78. Nat. Army Museum 7312–4–8.
16 G. to Jenkins 1 Sept 78 Jenkins Papers.
17 G. to A. 51295 ff. 297–9.
18 G. to Graham 21 April 79 quoted in catalogue when letters sold at London Stamp Auction, 1973. Present whereabouts unknown.
19 Miss R. Felkin's account. 51299 ff. 86–92, and see G. T. Wilson and R. W. Felkin, *Uganda and the Egyptian Sudan* Vol II.
20 *Anti-Slavery Reporter* Dec 96, p. 97.
21 G's Memo to Anti-Slavery Society 16 Feb 80 47609.
22 CA p. 324.
23 R. Slatin, *Fire and Sword in the Sudan*, p. 6.
24 Allen's Memo of Conversation with G, 16 Feb 80 47609.
25 G. to A. 15 Feb 79 51295 f. 324.
26 *ibid* 31 Aug 79 *ibid* f. 39.
27 U.S. Consul to Secretary of State 6 Sept 79. Mss Dept, Library of Congress.

Chapter 18 – CAST ASIDE

 1 G. to Harvey 5 Oct 79 HP 89.
 2 *ibid* 15 Dec 79 HP 90.

3 52402 ff. 18–19.

4 G.'s Report 51304 f. 91.

5 G. to Harvey 15 Dec 79 RE Box 402/5/4 HP 90.

6 *Ibid* 5 Oct 79 HP 89.

7 G.'s Report 51304 f. 81.

8 G.'s Memo printed in *Events*, especially p. 135 Ms is in 51304.

9 Note in Sir Hesketh Bell's hand. Bell Papers RCS Papers in CUL.

10 C. M. Watson, "Justice to General Gordon" in *National Review* 1908, p. 555.

11 Edward Malet to 3rd Marquess of Salisbury 14 Jan 80 Hatfield Papers 3M/A6/60.

12 G. to A. 8 Jan 80 51296 f. 1.

Chapter 19 – CONGO OR ZANZIBAR?

1 Joseph Reinach, 'Gordon Pacha' *Revue Politique et Littéraire*. Paris. 16 Feb 84 (translated).

2 Rivers Wilson, *op. cit*, pp. 197–8.

3 G. to Olagnier 16 Jan 80. Brinton Papers.

4 Reinach, *op. cit* and to Cromer 28 July 1909 (typed copy) Cromer Papers PRO/ FO/633./12/p. 189/3.

5 *Sister*, p. 204.

6 *The Times*, 12 Nov 1929.

7 G. to H. ND [1880] 52390 ff. 17–18.

8 G. to Mrs Freese. Freese Papers (4) Elton p. 269.

9 G. to Jenkins 6 Feb 80, Jenkins Papers and G. to Harvey 12 Feb 80, HP 92.

10 J. Martineau, *Sir Barbtle Frere*, Vol. 2 p. 443.

11 P. Ceulemans, 'Les Tentatives de Leopold II pour Engager Le Colonel Charles Gordon au Service de l'Association International Africaine (1880)' in Zaire: *Revue Congolaise*, Belgian African Review, Vol 12 No 3, 1958 pp. 251–274. Tr. MHR. p. 254.

12 G. to Mackinnon 5 Feb 80. Nat. Lib. Scotland.

13 *ibid* 12 Feb 80.

14 G. to Waller Feb 80, Waller Papers f. 113.

15 *Zaire, op. cit*, p. 257.

16 G. to A. 1 March 80 51295 f. 2.

17 G. to Mackinnon 3 March (misdated Feb) and 4 March 80 Nat. Lib. Scotland.

18 G. to Waller 25 Feb and 12 March 80 Waller Papers ff. 109, 119.

19 John Bonar to H. 24 March 85. 51300 f. 97.

20 Barnes and Brown, *Gordon*, pp. 1, 2, 4.

21 Irene Vanbrugh, *To Tell My Story* pp. 10–11.

22 G. to Mrs Enderby Gordon, with P.S by Charlie 16 March 80 Blunt Papers.

23 Barnes and Brown, *op. cit*, p. 8.
24 *Contemporary Review*, Feb 1890, p. 278.
25 G. to Waller 23 March 80 Waller Papers f. 124.
26 G. to H. 18 March 80 52390 f. 15, and ND, f. 19.
27 G. to Mrs Enderby G. 1 April 80 and G. to Charlie, same date. Blunt Papers.
28 Ceulemans, *Zaire*, pp. 269–70.
29 A postscript, upside down below Charlie's signature in their joint letter of 15 March 80 Blunt Papers.
30 G. to Mary Anne ('Coco') Lyster (née Granet, then Burnaby) 30 April 80 Blunt Papers.

Chapter 20 – PASSAGE TO INDIA

1 G. to H. ND [1880] 52390 f. 17.
2 G. to A. 1 May 80 51296 f. 14.
3 G. to A. 7 Aug 65 51291 f. 36.
4 Spencer Childers, *H. C. E. Childers*, p. 169.
5 G. to Waller. Waller Papers f. 132.
6 G. to A. 4 May 80 51296 *Sister*, p. 207.
7 Lucius Wolf, *Lord Ripon* Vol. II p. 2 footnote.
8 *Daily News* 1 June 80.
9 Quoted in the *Standard* 5 July 80.
10 J. F. D. Donnelly, Memo of conversation with G. 30 Oct 80 Blunt Papers.
11 Cowell to Ponsonby 4 June 80 RA Add./14.
12 G. to Charles Allen 47609 f. 6.
13 *Ms* of letter to the *Times of India* 3 June 80. RE (Gordon School Papers).
14 G. to Rose G. 13 May 80.
15 Boulger (p. 297) places the interview with the Prince on a Sunday afternoon. Reading the military paper is mentioned by G. to Major-General Dillon, 6 June 80. (Bernard Quaritch Catalogue 931, 1973.) Wolf (*Ripon* II, p. 6) places the dinner at Carlton Gardens. The family story was given by Col. Moffitt to 1st Lord Elton 1951.
16 G. to A. 5126 f. 17.
17 Ripon to Lady Ripon 16 May 80 Ripon Papers 43620 f. 2.
18 *ibid* 18 May. *ibid* f. 7.
19 Veitch, *Clarke*, p. 217.
20 Ripon Papers 43620 f. 10.
21 G. to A. 20 May 80 51296 f. 19.
22 Childers, *op. cit*, p. 176.
23 G. to A. 20 May 60 51296 f. 21.
24 G. to C. M. Allen 23 May 80 47609.

25 Childers, *op. cit*, p. 36.
26 Sinker, *Keith-Falconer*, p. 177.
27 Donnelly memo, *Ms cit*.
28 G. to A. 24 May 80 51296 f. 21.
29 *ibid* 28 May *ibid* f. 23.
30 *ibid* ff. 23–4.
31 Childers, *op. cit* II p. 37.
32 Donnelly memo, *Ms cit* pp. 1–3.
33 Arthur Bigge to Sir Henry Ponsonby 12 Sept 84 RA Add.A/34/7 pp. 3, 4.
34 G. to unnamed correspondent, 22 June 80, quoted in *The Times* 2 Feb 1931 when letter about to be sold by Puttick and Simpson.
35 G. to Florence Nightingale 25 March 81 45806 ff. 155–6.
36 Wilfrid Blunt, *India Under Ripon* p. 83n.
37 Ripon to Lady Ripon 43620 ff. 39–40.
38 Veitch, *Clarke* p. 218–19.
39 *Ms* of Gordon's letter, RE (Gordon School Papers).
40 42390 f. 28.
41 Childers, *op. cit* II p. 36.
42 G. to Dillon 6 June 80 *Ms cit*, note 16 above.
43 G. to Ripon 6 June 80 43626 f. 105.

Chapter 21 – RETURN TO CHINA

1 G. to G. Bates (Secretary RGS) requesting maps. Penang 21 June 80 Royal Geographical Society Papers.
2 Wade to Salisbury 5 Jan 80. F.O 17/829/4, quoted in Immanuel C.Y Hsu, *Gordon in China 1880*, Pacific Historical Review Vol. 33, 1964, p. 150. Hsu's (pp. 147–166) is the best general account of the episode, though without benefit of the Gordon *Mss*. Boulger's account is unreliable and must be rejected.
3 Hsu p. 151.
4 Local Telegram No. 2543. 52388, and for the following telegrams.
5 G. to Henry G. 16 June 80 52390 f. 32.
6 Quoted, *Events*, p. 146.
7 Hart's Journal, *Ms* Vol. 26, 24 and 23 June 80, Queen's Univ. of Belfast, special collections.
8 G. to A. headed 3 July 80 51296 ff. 36–7.
9 *ibid*.
10 *ibid* and Hsu, *op. cit*, p. 159.
11 G. to McKean 7 July 80 PRONI T/2581 45–56.
12 *ibid*.
13 *ibid* 24 July 80.

14 G. to Sir John Pope-Hennessy. Rhodes House Mss and G. to A. 13 July 51296 f. 41.

15 Hart's Journal Vol. 26 13, 17 July 80 *Ms cit.*

16 Hsu, p. 155 quoting FO 17/832/123. The original is not in the Gordon Papers.

17 G. to McKean, 22 July 80 *Mss cit.*

18 Wade to H. 14 Jan 86 CUL *Add.Mss* 8128.3 ff. 1–6.

19 Hsu, p. 156 quoting FO 418/1/152.

20 G. to McKean, 22 July 80 *Ms cit.*

21 Hsu, p. 156 quoting FO 418/1/145.

22 Hart Journal 22 July 80.

23 Quoted Hsu, p. 158.

24 Donnelly memo, *Ms cit* p. 8.

25 G. to McKean 24 July 80.

26 Wade to H. CUL *Add. Mss* 8/28.4(3).

27 Hsu, p. 157.

28 Hart Journal, 26 July.

29 Hsu, p. 158 quoting FO 418/II/26.

30 Hart Journal, 27, 28 July.

31 Elton, misled by Boulger, is wrong to say G. never entered the Legation.

32 Mrs Albert Gray (widow of Grosvenor, d.1886) to Lady Wade [November 1896] copy by Wade's son to Elton. Raitt Papers.

33 Lady Wade, letter in *The Times* 29 Oct 96.

34 Wade to H., *Ms cit.*

35 *Events* p. 153.

36 Donnelly memo.

37 Mrs Albert Gray's letter.

38 Donnelly memo.

39 H. to Wade 21 Oct [85] CUL *Add.Mss* 8128.2.1 and Wade to H. 14 Jan 86 *Mss cit* 3/4.

40 Donnelly memo.

41 Hart's Journal, 30 July 80.

42 Donnelly memo.

43 Hart's Journal, 5 Aug 80.

44 Donnelly memo.

45 Hsu, pp. 150 and 160 quoting FO 418/1/272 and /11/26.

46 Wade to H. 14 Jan 86 *Ms cit*, and Hart to G. 23 Aug 80 CU *Add.Mss* 8128.9.2.

47 *ibid*

48 G. to C. H. Allen 4 Aug 80 47609 f. 46.

49 Hart's Journal 6, 10 Aug and to Campbell, quoted Wright, *Hart* p. 486.

50 Hsu, p. 161 quoting FO 418/11/26 Encl. 6.

51 G. to Sir Samuel Baker 4 Aug 80, Spiro Collection.

52 Wright, p. 487.
53 Hsu, p. 165 quoting FO 418/1/276 Encl. 5.
54 Hart to G. 23 Aug (received Nov) 80 CUL Add.Mss 8128.9.2.
55 Wade to H. 14 Jan 86 *Ms cit.*
56 *ibid*

Chapter 22 – ISLAND OF DISTRESS

1 Gladstone Papers 44467 f. 43.
2 Sir J. Pope-Hennessy to J. Henniker Heaton 8 May 85 Rhodes House Mss Brit. Emp. s. 409 Box 3/4 ff. 1–28.
3 Anon quote in *China Mail* obit. 7 March 85, written out and encl. in letter from Governor of Hong Kong (Sir G. F. Bower) to Foreign Secretary (Lord Derby) 52402 f. 18.
4 Quoted by G. to Waller 8 Sept 80 Waller Papers f. 138.
5 see Ceulemans, *Zaire, op. cit*, pp. 271–3.
6 G. to A. XX 80 51296 ff. 56–8. Mrs Kathryn Johnson, curator of Mss at BL, tried by every means to read the words beneath the scratching out, here and in other G. letters, but as similar ink had been used at a date near the original writing, modern technology cannot yet penetrate it.
7 G. to Jenkins 22 Oct 80 Jenkins Papers.
8 G. to Harvey 15 Nov 80 HP 95.
9 G. to Waller 1 Nov 80 Waller Papers f. 142.
10 G. to Harvey 30 Nov 80 HP 96.
11 G. to Jenkins 28 Dec 80 Jenkins Papers.
12 G. to A. postcard 15 Nov 80 given by Elton to MHR Raitt Papers.
13 G. to A. 17 Nov 80 51296 f. 72.
14 Northbrook to G. 30 Nov 80 52388 pkt 5.
15 G.'s 6 page memo is in Gladstone Papers, 44467 ff. 43–47.
16 *ibid*.
17 *ibid*.
18 Comments summarized by Elton, p. 288.
19 G. to Edward White 24 Dec 80, 26 Dec 82, 8 Jan 84 52428 ff. 1, 4, 7.

Chapter 23 – 'TAKE, EAT'

1 G. to A. 6 Dec 80 51296 f. 74.
2 W. H. Bernard Saunders, 'A Great Soldier's Holidays,' *Chambers Magazine* Vol. 6 No. 293, 8 July 1916, pp. 494–6.
3 Albert Bolton to Brigadier Gordon Blunt, 24 Feb 1955 Blunt Papers.

4 G. to A. 16 Dec 80 51296 f. 77.

5 Waller to H. 5 Oct 85 52403 ff. 1–5.

6 See St John's Gospel chapter 6 verses 51–8.

7 Waller to H. *Ms cit*.

8 *Chambers Magazine, op. cit.*

9 G. to A. [16 Dec 80] 51296 f. 76.

10 *ibid* 18 May 81 *ibid* f. 177.

11 1 Samuel ch. 15 verse 32.

12 G. to Waller 15 April 81 Waller Papers ff. 195, 168, 172.

13 Freese Papers (4) quoted Elton pp. 290–1.

14 G. to A. March 81 51296 f. 149.

15 G. to R. Brett (2nd Viscount Esher) 29 March 81 and ND Esher Papers 13/7.

16 G. to A. 28, 29 March 81 51296 ff. 141, 143.

17 G. to Bowles 28 Oct 80 Taylor, *Irrepressible Victorian*, p. 69.

18 G. to A. Feb 81 51296 f. 6.

19 Tennyson, *Lord Tennyson* Vol. 2 p. 224.

20 Lord Tennyson to A. 30 April 85 Spiro Collection.

21 G. to Florence Nightingale 22 April 80 45806 ff. 18–19.

22 *ibid* 25 Jan 81 *ibid* f. 138.

23 Taylor, *op. cit*, pp. 73–4.

24 *ibid* p. 69.

25 *ibid* p. 73.

26 *Vanity Fair*, No. 141, 19 Feb 81. Reprinted in Taylor, *op. cit* pp. 74–7.

27 *Army and Navy Gazette*, 26 Feb 81.

28 Boulger, *Pall Mall Magazine*, May 1896, pp. 143–4.

29 Note by Curzon quoted Lord Ronaldshay, *Lord Curzon* Vol. I pp. 97–8.

30 *The Nineteenth Century*, June 1908 p. 927. See also Lord Esher's *To-day and To-morrow*, 1910 pp. 162–83.

31 Brett to H. 7 Dec 85 52403 f. 53.

32 *The Nineteenth Century op. cit*, p. 926.

33 James Lees-Milne, *The Enigmatic Victorian*, p. 56.

34 G. to Esher [1881] Esher Papers 13/7.

35 *Morning Advertiser*, 21 March 81.

36 G. to Brett 1 March 81 Esher Papers 13/7.

37 Brett to G. 6 March 81 *ibid* 2/6.

38 E. to Sir Philip Sassoon 23 June 1918, Cholmondeley Papers at Houghton, quoted Lees-Milne, p. 56.

39 appended to Mayor's Address at unveiling of Gravesend statue 1893 p. 20.

40 Colonel F. Somerset to H. 9 Feb 85 52399 f. 43.

41 General (Sir) J. F. M. Browne to H. 7 Sept 85 52402 ff. 154–5.

42 G. to H. 18 Sept 80 52390 f. 31.

43 Memo by G. Birkbeck Hill 11 March 95, Birkbeck Hill Papers, Williams College Williamstown, Mass., USA and G. to H. 25 Sept 80 52390.

44 Robert Sinker, *Memorials of Ion Keith-Falconer* 88 p. 114.

45 G. to Florence Nightingale 25 April 81 45806 ff. 131–9.

46 R. K. Douglas to G. 28 April [81] Blunt Papers.

Chapter 24 – GORDON'S EDEN

1 Sir Howard Elphinstone to G. 1 May 81 51302 f. 41.

2 *ibid* f. 53.

3 Ponsonby to the Queen 3 May 81 RA Add.A/15/3418.

4 G. to J. Robson 30 April 81 Catalogue of sale at Francis Edwards 1973.

5 G. to A. May 81 51296 f. 160.

6 Count Permazzery to G. 30 April 81 copy in H.'s hand. Blunt Papers.

7 G. to A. 10 May 81 51296 f. 157 *Sister* p. 220.

8 *ibid* 6 May 81 *ibid* f. 144.

9 *ibid* 18 May *ibid* f. 177.

10 C. M. O'Donel to B. M. Allen T/S 19 Aug 1929 Bell Papers RCS CUL.

11 G. to Mrs Murray 25 June 81 RE (Gordon Sch. Mss).

12 Infm. from C. McIrvine (a boy in 1881) to Sir Hesketh Bell c.1922–24. Bell Papers RCS/CUL.

13 O'Donel to Allen *Ms cit.*

14 Admiral Sir Herbert Purey-Cust, letter to *Sunday Times* 6 Dec 1931.

15 G. to Sir Howard Elphinstone misdated May 81 (prob. July) copy in RE GR 150.

16 G. to H. 6 July 81 Blunt Papers; Sir Hesketh Bell's notes from Book of Confidential Despatches 1880–81 RCS/CUL.

17 Memo by Miss L. E. Clarke (Bp Royston's step dau) Bell Papers RCS/CUL .

18 Memo by John Ackroyd *ibid.*

19 Memo by F. E. O'Connor *ibid.*

20 Bell's notes *ibid.*

21 Leonard Huxley, *Thomas Huxley* 1900 Vol. 2 p. 94. G. was introduced to Huxley by (Sir) J. F. D. Donnelly, RE, Secretary of the South Kensington Museum, a great friend of both.

22 See Waller Papers ff. 178–80.

23 Frank Brodie's account (c.1920) in Bell Papers RCS/CUL.

24 G. to (Sir) William Thiselton-Dyer 9 Dec 82 Royal Botanical Gardens Archives Kew.

25 Brodie, *Ms cit.*

26 G. to Jenkins 3 March 82 Jenkins Papers.

27 Napier Broome to Lord Kimberley (S. of S. for the Colonies) 22 Dec 81. Copy at Kew.

28 Bell's Notes. RCS/CUL.

29 Bell to *Sunday Times* 29 Nov 1931.

30 G. to A. 29 Nov 81 51296 f. 238.

31 *ibid* 25 Dec 81 *ibid* f. 249.

32 Ackroyd memo, *Ms cit*.

33 Bell to *Sunday Times* 29 Nov 1931.

34 G. R. Grier to *Sunday Times* 6 Dec 1931.

35 T. R. D. O'Connor to Bell 7 Jan 1932 Bell Papers RCS/CUL.

36 Ms copy (extract) in Bell Papers RCS/CUL; G. to Brocklehurst 3 Feb 82 Durham, Sudan Archive 630/5/20.

37 The telegrams are in 51302 ff. 55, 56.

38 Quoted W. H. Spence 'Recollections of A Voyage with General Gordon.' *Contemporary Review* Feb. 1890 p. 273.

39 Ackroyd memo. Bell Papers RCS/CUL.

40 Spence, Voyage, *op. cit.*

41 G. to A. 3 April 82. Lady Musgrave Scrapbook, Duke Mss and E. J. S. Boyce to A. April 82 51300 ff. 1, 3, 4.

Chapter 25 – COMMANDANT-GENERAL

1 The quotes from Mrs Duncan and Captain Duncan are from Spence, Voyage, *Contemporary Review* Feb 90 *op. cit.*

2 *Sister*, p. 254.

3 Undated fragment (probably Oct 81) 51292 ff. 221–2.

4 G. to A. 4 May 82 51296 ff. 276, 280.

5 Joseph M. Orpen: *Mayor-General Charles George Gordons' Visit to Basutoland in 1882* .... T/S of over 125 pp. ND (post 1901). Cape Archives Acc. 302, p. 22.

6 Spence, Voyage, *op. cit*, p. 280.

7 Orpen, p. 27.

8 *ibid*

9 G. to Waller 13 May 80 Waller Papers f. 207.

10 G. to Mackinnon 13 May 80. Nat. Lib. of Scotland.

11 Orpen, p. 28.

12 *ibid* p. 25.

13 *ibid* p. 25.

14 G. to A. 20 May 82 51296 f. 363.

15 Orpen, p. 31.

16 *ibid* pp. 31–2.

17 *ibid* p. 34.

18 *Correspondence between Major-General Gordon and Mr Scanlen 1882*, privately printed 1905 Cape Archives A.968.7038 GOR, p. 5.
19 *Life of Sir E. Y. Brabant*, unpublished autobiography, T/S pp. 119–124 Cape Archives Acc. 459.
20 Van Riebeck Society Vol. 41, p. 960.
21 G. to A. Garcia 27 June 82 Garcia Papers Cape Archives Acc. 250 II.
22 *National Review* 1936 p. 65.

Chapter 26 – MOUNTAIN OF NIGHT

1 G. to Mackinnon [12 Aug 82] Nat. Lib. Scotland.
2 G. to Sauer 30 Aug 82 Cape Archives Acc. 6.
3 Orpen, p. 51.
4 G. to Sir Samuel Baker 2 Oct 82 Spiro Coll.
5 Orpen, p. 52.
6 *ibid* p. 57.
7 Garcia *Recollections* T/S Cape Archives 250w.
8 E. R. Maund, *Cecil Rhodes Reminiscences: Rhodes and General Gordon* Ms dated 18 Dec 1924 Rhodes House 2183.1. (21 pp.) p. 7.
9 *ibid* p. 14.
10 *ibid* p. 13.
11 John Widdicombe, *Fourteen Years in Basutoland* [1891] pp. 204–06.
12 *ibid* p. 206.
13 Edna Bradlow, 'General Gordon in Basutoland, *Historia* 15 (1970), p. 234.
14 *ibid* p. 235.
15 510302 f. quoted, Orpen, p. 30.
16 Orpen, p. 73.
17 Garcia Recollections, Cape Archives, Acc.250w.
18 Arthur Pattison to *The Times* 20 Aug 85, quoted *Events* p. 237.
19 Cape Blue Book G.61883; quoted *Events* p. 231 but garbled.
20 Brabant, p. 123.
21 Scanlen Correspondence. Letter 19.
22 G. to Mackinnon 22 Oct 82. Nat. Lib. Scotland.

Chapter 27 – GORDON'S CALVARY

1 G. to Jenkins 25 Nov 82 Jenkins Papers.
2 Memo of 17 Nov 82 Esher Papers ESHR 13/6.
3 Orpen, p. 27.
4 Lady Anne Blunt's Diary 8 Dec 82 53918/274A; W. Blunt, *Gordon at Khartoum* p. 135.

5 American Consul's Reports, Library of Congress.

6 G. to A. 16 Jan 83 51297 f. 20.

7 *ibid* 17 Jan 83 *ibid* ff. 20, 22.

8 Bertha Spafford Vester *Our Jerusalem* pp. 103–4 and following quotes.

9 Elton mentioned 300 letters as extant in 1954 but did not quote nor specify location, which remains unknown.

10 Barnes and Brown, *op. cit*, p. 30.

11 G. to Sir Samuel Baker 24 Sept 83 RGS.

12 G. to Edward White 5 Feb 82 (*sic* i.e. 83) 52428 f. 2.

13 G. to Harvey 12 Feb 83. Missing from HP but printed as a pamphlet.

14 51297 ff. 1–12.

15 G. to A. 8 Feb 83 *ibid* f. 47.

16 G. to Harvey 12 Feb 83 as above.

17 G. to Sir John Cowell 8 March 83 Garden Tomb Papers.

18 *Reflections in Palestine* pp. 88–9.

19 Blackwood's Magazine, June 1884.

20 *Reflections*, p. 45.

21 G. to Cowell 8 March 83 Garden Tomb Papers.

22 G. to H. 8 March 83 52390 f. 67.

23 *Zechariah* chapter 14 verse 8.

24 G. to Rusden 3 July 83 Trinity Coll. Parkville, Victoria Mss.

25 *ibid*.

26 Philip Henderson, *Life of Laurence Oliphant* 1956, p. 283.

27 Oliphant to A. 15 July 85 Spiro Collection.

28 W. Greene to H. 3 Nov 85 51300 ff. 162–3; *Church Missionary Gleaner*, June 85 p. 65.

29 Greene, *Ms cit*.

30 G. to Harvey 6 Oct 83 HP 100.

Chapter 28 – 'GORDON FOR THE SUDAN'

1 Mackinnon to H. 52398 f. 33.

2 G. to Mackinnon 4 Oct 82 Nat. Lib. Scotland.

3 *ibid* 17 Nov 82.

4 G. to H. Nov 52390 ff. 128–9.

5 Granville to Ponsonby 15 Jan 84 RA O20/21.

6 G. to H. 17 Nov 83 52390 f. 134.

7 G. to Mackinnon 17 Nov 83 Nat. Lib. Scotland.

8 G. to A. 1 Jan 84 51298 f. 142.

9 G. to Cowell Feb 83 Garden Tomb Papers.

10 G. to Watson ND (c.1878) Fitzwilliam Museum, Cambridge.

11 Wolseley to G. 4 Jan 84 52388 f. 138.

12 Oliphant, *Haifa*, p. 275.

13 Childers, *Childers*, pp. 176–7.

14 *ibid.*

15 'for 2½ months.' Sir Evelyn Wood to Ponsonby 1 Feb 84, quoted Wood, *Winnowed Memories*, p. 345.

16 Wood to the Queen 11 Dec 83 RAO 19/104.

17 G. to Miss Felkin 3 Jan 84 RE: Gordon Sch. Mss.

18 G. to Baker 8 Jan 84 Spiro Collection.

19 Frederick Whyte, *W. T. Stead* Vol. 1, p. 122.

20 The interview is reprinted in *Events* pp. 296–308.

21 Preface to 2nd edition of CA, p. xi.

22 Wood to Ponsonby 1 Feb 84 *Winnowed Memories*, p. 346.

23 Sir Kenneth Barnes, *Welcome Good Friends*, p. 3.

24 Violet Vanbrugh, *Dare to be Wise*, p. 17.

25 Sir Kenneth Barnes to Lord Elton, Easter Saturday 1951 Raitt Papers.

26 E. G. Sandford (ed.), *Archbishop Temple* 1906 Vol. 2, p. 154.

27 B. F. Cresswell, *Exeter Churches* 1908 p. 174.

28 Barnes and Brown, *op. cit*, p. 72.

29 Baker to (Viscount) Knollys RA T.8.105 pp. 6–7.

30 Quoted by Wilberforce at a temperance meeting at Canterbury. *Gravesend Argus* 2 Feb 84.

31 Wolseley to H. 6 Sept 85 52402 ff. 152–3.

32 B. Holland. *Life of 8th Duke of Devonshire* 1911 Vol. 1, p. 419 for a detailed discussion see Chenevix-Trench, pp. 199–201.

33 G. to Donnelly 21 Jan 84. Sold at Sothebys 24 Feb 1953. *Ms* not at Boston; present whereabouts unknown.

34 G. to Wolseley 16 Jan 84. Wolseley Papers. E. Sussex R.O.

35 The originals of the telegrams are in the Brocklehurst Papers, Sudan Archive, Durham 630/6/6.

36 G. to Mrs Jenkins 17 Jan 84. Jenkins Papers.

37 *Letters of Queen Victoria* Second Series, Vol. 2. p. 472.

38 Granville to Gladstone 11 March 88 56451 ff. 73–82.

39 Granville to the Queen 18 Jan 84 RA O.20/27.

40 RA QVJ 23 Jan 84.

41 G. to A. 19 Jan 84 copy in Blunt Papers. Printed in Wilfrid Blunt, *Gordon at Khartoum*, appendix A.

42 Granville to the Queen 18 Jan 84 O.20/28; and see Granville to Gladstone 11 March 88 56451 f. 75.

43 Quoted *Gravesend Argus* 2 Feb 84.

44 Duke of Cambridge Journal 18 Jan 84, (Vol. 1, 1 Jan 84–19 Oct 85) FitzGeorge-Balfour Papers.

45 Lady Geraldine Somerset's Diary 18 Jan 84 RA. As for the tickets it was said at the time that the banks being shut, Hartington borrowed from friends found at the Athenaeum and the Reform clubs to pay for the railway and steamer!: (S. Gwynne, *Letters and Friendships of Sir Cecil Spring-Rice*, 1929.

Chapter 29 – CAIRO

1 G. to Lord Northbrook 20 Jan 84 (copy) Ripon Papers 4373.

2 Stewart to Haddie Stewart 24 Jan 84 Stewart Papers, Sudan Archive Durham SAD D/S.1.

3 Memo by Charles Watson 10 Feb 84 5130 f. 190 (Memo is printed in W. Blunt, *Gordon at Khartoum* pp. 512–19).

4 Baring to G. 22 Jan 84 52388 f.

5 Graham to G., *Events*, p. 326.

6 *The Carthusian*, June 1885.

7 See FO 407/60 pp. 136–7.

8 G. to Northbrook, *Ms cit*.

9 Baron Malorte, *Here, There and Everywhere*, p. 196.

10 Memo by E. W. Hamilton 12 May 84 Gladstone Papers 56451 f. 44.

11 Stewart to E. Hudson 25 Jan 84 (copy) Stewart Papers, Sudan Archive Durham SAD D//S.1.

12 General Sir F. Stephenson, *At Home and on the Battlefield*, p. 214.

13 See *Events*, pp. 327–331 and Boulger, *Life*, p. 416; Mss in 52395.

14 Graham, *Last Words*, p. 22.

15 Boulger, *op. cit*, pp. 417–18.

16 Summary, transcribed by Samuel Davies the Shorthand writer present. Sudan Archive, Durham.

17 Baron de Kusel, *An Englishman's Recollections of Egypt*, p. 262.

18 G. to A. 26 Jan 84 51298 f. 170.

19 Wingate, in an unpublished *Ms* written after 1919 at earliest, which is quoted by Chenevix-Trench, says that G. angrily refused to attend the dinner and had soup in his room. This conflicts with the memory of Graham, Stewart, Grenfell and Wood himself. This Wingate *Ms* is inaccurate at other points too.

Chapter 30 – NILE JOURNEY

1 Stewart Journal pp. 4–5. 27 Jan. (Journal is in Sudan Archive, Durham).

2 Graham, *Last Words*, p. 37.

3 Veitch, *Graham*, p. 257 (Graham's Diary 29 Jan 84).

4 *Last Words*, p. 6.

5 Stewart's Journal, p. 9.

6 Quoted by A. to Miss Power 58070.

7 Watson to A. 22 Sept 85 51300 f. 145.

8 Lieut-Col. Angel Scott to General Sir Bindon Blood, 10 Jan 1932 RE GR 165.

9 In 1935 the shorthand writer at the Cairo Council *re* Zubair remembered Gordon as a total abstainer; possibly the other officers sipped whisky during the meetings and Gordon sipped lime juice. T/S, dated 1935, in National Library of Wales Ms 12676C, p. 4.

10 Granville to Baring 8 Feb 84 FO/633/7 Letter 26.

11 Wood to the Queen 11 Feb 84 RA O.20/65 pp. 7, 8.

12 A. H. Sayce, *Reminiscences*, p. 230.

13 *Last Words*, p. 41.

14 *ibid* pp. 35–6.

15 Graham to H. 4 Feb 84 52398 ff. 68–9.

16 Stewart Diary 5 Feb 84.

17 G. to Brocklehurst 8 Feb 84 Brocklehurst Papers Sudan Archive, Durham.

18 Barnes and Brown, p. 78.

19 Stewart to his Mother 15 Feb [84] Sudan Archive, Durham SAD D//S.

20 Guisippi Cuzzi, *Fifteen Years A Prisoner*, p. 51.

21 E. A. Floyer in *The Carthusian* June 1885.

22 The Queen to Ponsonby n.d. (8 or 9 Feb 84) RA O.20/52.

23 Stewart Diary 13 Feb 84.

24 Stewart Diary 29 Jan 84.

25 Cuzzi, *Ms cit* p. 53.

Chapter 31 – RETURN TO KHARTOUM

1 Stewart Diary 18 Feb 84.

2 Paraphrasing two accounts: Stewart's Diary 18 Feb 84 and Nushi Report p. 2 (tv. and ed. Wingate: see *intro* Ch 32 note 13).

3 C. Moberly Bell to Cromer 23 Feb 1908 Cromer Papers FO/633/12 p. 87.

4 Power to his Mother n.d. [16 Feb] 84 58069.

5 *ibid* 22 Feb 84 *ibid*.

6 Article by W. E. A. Axon in *Longman's Magazine*, Oct 1890 pp. 632–9; Percy Young, *Elgar*, 1955, p. 239; Basil Maine, *Elgar*, 1933, Vol. 1.56, 156.

7 Stewart Diary 22 Feb 84. For details, see Chenevix-Trench, pp. 227 ff.

8 Col. F. Duncan to A. 29 Nov 86 51300 ff. 196–210.

9 G. to Harvey 28 Feb 84 HP 101.

10 G. to A. 27 Feb, 1 March 84. 33222 f. 51 (this is in the selection of G. letters presented to the British Museum by Sir Henry and Augusta.).

11 Power to his Mother, 1 March 84 58069.

12 G. to Baring 18 Feb 84 FO 407/60:710. p. 198.

13 Stewart to Baring 19 Feb 84 *ibid* p. 197.

14 *ibid* p. 200.

15 G. to H. 6 March 84 52390 ff. 158–9.

16 C. H. Allen to H. 26 Feb 84 52398 f. 85.

17 Wolseley to G. 21 Feb 84 Spiro Collection.

18 Wolseley to King Leopold 20 Feb 84 (copy) Wolseley Papers West Sussex R.O W/PLB/1/12.

19 Debate of 14 Feb 84 quoted by 'Videx' (i.e. G. W. Rusden) *The Great Refusal*, 1890, p. 8. For the political moves in detail see Marlowe, *Mission to Khartoum*, 1969, except that he is over inclined to see conspiracy everywhere.

20 Wingate Mss Sudan Archive. Durham, 245/6/7 p. 13.

21 Note by E. W. Hamilton 3 April 84, Gladstone Papers 56452 f. 39 and Dilke Diary 15 March 84 43926.

22 Note by the Queen n.d. [?4 March] 84 RA O. 21/28.

23 Dilke Diary 5, 15 March 84 43926.

24 From 'Portions expunged as being too political' from Wingate's *Mahdiism*, T/S, Sudan Archive, Durham SAD/1/14.15.

25 Watson to Augusta 22 Feb 85 51300 f. 80.

26 RA QVJ 2 Jan 85.

Chapter 32 – HEMMED IN

1 Lyall, *Dufferin* Vol. 2 pp. 57–8.

2 see also G. to A. 11 March 84 51298 f. 195.

3 FO 78/3667 26 Feb 84.

4 Cromer to R. W. Snelling 15 Nov 1905 Snelling Papers, Duke University Mss.

5 Baring to Northbrook 11 March 84 FO/633/4 Letter 46.

6 G. to Mr Hall at Jaffa, quoted by Waller to A. 30 April 84 51300 f. 29. Gordon and Stewart always called the Mahdi's followers 'Arabs' or 'rebels'. The Mahdi had originally called them *darwish*, hence British newspapers referred to them as 'dervishes'; but as *darwish* means 'madman' in colloquial Sudanese the Mahdi forbade its use in April 1884 and called them *Ansar* ('Helpers of the Prophet') See P. M. Holt, *The Mahdist State in the Sudan 1881–1895*, 2nd Ed. 1970, p. 121.

7 G. to Mr Hall at Jaffa 4 April, quoted Waller to A. 30 April 84 51300 f. 29

8 Waller to A. *ibid*.

9 H. to A. 30 March [84] 51300 ff. 5, 6.

10 Lady Wolseley to A. [21 April 84] 51300 f. 21.

11 RA QVJ 26 April 8.

12 Copy in Evelyn Wood Papers, Duke University Mss.
13 See Martin W. Parr, *A Rough Outline of the History of the Gordon Notes*, unpublished T/S n.d. [1933] 9 pp. in RE. After the Fall most of the notes were burned by order of the Mahdi. Some were smuggled to Egypt and handed in but the Govt. refused to honour them as 'unofficial.' They lay forgotten in a Cairo vault until 1931 when 3,486 were auctioned for the Gordon Memorial Fund. A signed note was offered for sale in U.S.A for $975 in December 1992.
14 Nushi Report, *The Siege and Fall of Khartoum*, tr. and ed. F. R. Wingate, p. 15. *Sudan Notes and Records*.
15 *ibid* p. 23.
16 *ibid* pp. 25, 27.
17 RA O.23/19/20.
18 Typed copy in Brocklehurst Papers, Sudan Archive, Durham.
19 *Journal*, p. 93. 24 Sept 84. The *Mss* are 34474–83 but for convenience I give the page numbers of the 1885 edition.
20 Wolseley to H. 52398 f. 27.
21 Wingate, *Mahdiism*, p. 164.

Chapter 33 – 'I HAVE *TRIED* TO DO MY DUTY'

1 Harrison, *A Life in the British Army*, p. 285.
2 *Sunday Times* 25 Jan 1931. Burnaby was killed at Abu Klea; Sterling died a Major-General aged 86.
3 Ponsonby to H. Seymour 27 Aug 84 RA Add.A12/2217.
4 Granville to the Queen RA O.23/46/47.
5 *Journal*, p. 115 29 Sept 84.
6 *ibid* p. 31 13 Sept 84.
7 Watson to H. 20 Aug 85 52402 ff. 58–9 and 3 May 86 52403 f. 99.
8 *Jewish Intelligencer* 1890.
9 John Ward, *The Living Age* Vol. XVII, p. 412.
10 *Journal*, p. 97 25 Sept 84.
11 *ibid* pp. 197–8 15 Oct 84.
12 *ibid* p. 194 14 Oct 84.
13 *ibid* p. 223 23 Oct 84.
14 Brigadier-General H. F. E. Lewin to Major-General Sir Louis Jackson 24 Jan 1932 RE Archives. Lewin married Field Marshal Lord Roberts's younger daughter who became Countess Roberts.
15 Sir John Maffey to Lord Stamfordham, 2 April 1933 RA GV P2116/89.
16 G. to A. 5 Nov 84 51298 f. 190.
17 *ibid*
18 *Church Missionary Gleaner*, June 85 p. 65.

19 *Journal* pp. 316–18. 12 Nov 84.

20 Bordeini Diary in Wingate, *op. cit*, p. 164.

21 Allen Worsley, *Land of the Blue Veil* 1940, pp. 56–8 slightly abbreviated.

22 *Journal*, p. 307–8 4 Nov 84.

23 *ibid* p. 387 8 Dec 84.

24 G. to Watson 14 Dec 84 RE 5001 41/8(E.S.4).

25 G. to A. 14 Dec 84 51298 f. 193.

26 *Journal* p. 394 13 Dec 84.

27 *ibid* p. 395 14 Dec 84.

Chapter 34 – 'STRIKE HARD!'

1 Wolseley's Journal 1 Jan 85, Preston, *op. cit*, p. 104.

2 *ibid* 31 Dec 84, Preston p. 102. The Queen inserted a copy of W.'s précis of the message, received by wire via Baring, in her Journal for 1 Jan 85. RA QVJ.

3 *ibid* 2 Jan 85 Preston, p. 105.

4 *Sudan Notes and Records* Vol. 24 (1941) pp. 229–31.

5 *The Memoirs of Babikr Bedri*, translated from the Arabic 1969 p. 28.

6 *Eagle and Carbine*, (magazine of Scots Dragoon Guards) 1985, p. 185.

7 Bordeini in Wingate, *op. cit*, p. 168.

8 *ibid* p. 169.

9 Copy of a letter from G. to Heneage Smith, n.d., incorporated in letter from Smith to H. 21 March 85 52401 f. 175.

10 Wolseley Journal, 25 Feb 85 Preston, *op. cit*, p. 155.

11 K. D. D ('Bill') Henderson to Headmaster, Gordon Boy's School 23 Feb 1981 RE, Gordon School Archives.

Appendix – GORDON'S ANCESTRY

1 52407 f. 89. In 1834 G.'s father wrote that his eldest son, at Sandhurst, 'is the fifth generation of my family who have served in the Army,' (quoted *Notes and Queries* 11 Feb 1933 p. 45) David's date of birth cannot be determined as the entry in the burial register at St Paul's Church, Halifax, Nova Scotia on 22 September 1752 does not give his age and there is no other contemporary documentary evidence. (Infm fr Public Archives of Nova Scotia).

2 52407 ff. 79, 8, 38.

3 *ibid* f. 8.

4 quoted *Notes and Queries* 11 Feb 1933, p. 93.

5 *Memoirs* p. 8.

6 *ibid* p. 26.

Manuscript Sources

(for Catalogue numbers see References and Notes)

BRITISH LIBRARY

Gordon Papers

Moffitt and Bell Collections: 45 volumes.

Moffitt: 22 volumes, derived from Augusta Gordon, including 8 vols. of letters from
G to her, each vol. about 300ff., 1855–1884.

Also general and family correspondence; official and personal papers; maps,
plans, reports, photographs, relating to each place of G's service; religious
writings; letters and addresses of condolence, etc.

Bell: 23 volumes, derived from Sir Henry Gordon. G's letters to his parents and to
Henry; papers relating to the Ever Victorious Army, the Sudan and other places
of service; Sir Henry's correspondence with public figures 1884–5; letters of
condolence; biographical material collected for *Events*; many miscellaneous
papers. Also papers of their father, Lieut-General H.W. Gordon, and on family
history.

Other Gordon Papers in BL

Chinese documents presented by G. himself, in the Oriental MSS department.

The Khartoum Journals. 9 vols.

Letters selected and presented by Sir Henry and Augusta.

Letters to (Sir) Charles Watson (1 vol.)

    C.H. Allen (1 vol.)

    R. Gessi (1 vol.)

    R.S. Standen, E. White,

Lieutenant Danyell, Viscountess Cardwell,

and others, in various volumes.

Other Papers with Gordon-related material in BL
Lady Anne Blunt's Diary
Cromer Papers
Gladstone Papers
E. W. Hamilton's Diary
Ripon Papers
Zubair Pasha Papers

ROYAL ARCHIVES

Queen Victoria's Journal
Letters to and from the Queen
Letters to and from Sir Henry Ponsonby

OTHER ARCHIVES

Barnes Papers: see Boston
Blunt Papers, owned by G's great-great-niece, Miss Elizabeth Blunt
Boston City Library, Mass. Barnes Papers, 87 items MS Eng 450
   Jenkins Papers 35 items MS Eng 411
   (most of my research done from photostats acquired by MHR when the Jenkins
   Papers were in private hands in Northern Ireland)
   A small number of other G. letters.
Brighton, West Sussex R. O. Wolseley Papers
Cambridge, Churchill College: Esher Papers
   University Library: Parkes Papers in Jardine Matheson Archives; Wade Papers
Cape Town Archives: Brabant T/S
   Orpen T/S
   Gordon-Scanlen Corr: privately printed.
   Blue Books
Church Missionary Society Papers, Birmingham University Library
Comboni Papers (in typescript): Verona Fathers, Bayswater.
Cowell Papers, Garden Tomb Association
Derby Papers, Journal of 15th Earl of Derby, deposited at Liverpool Record Office
Donaldson Papers, 6 letters, G. to Enderby Gordon, owned by Mrs Sonia
   Donaldson, researched by MHR
Duke University, Williams E. Perkins Library, Durham, North Carolina: Ripon
   Papers; Snelling Papers; Evelyn Wood Papers

Durham University Library, Sudan Archive: Brocklehurst Papers; Broadhurst Collection; Goodenough Papers; Journal of D. Hammill Stewart; Wingate Papers; miscellaneous Sudan items.

Fitzgeorge-Balfour Papers. Journal of Field Marshal H.R.H the Duke of Cambridge, owned by his great-grandson, General Sir Victor FitzGeorge-Balfour KCB, CBE, DSO, MC.

Freese Papers, owned by Mrs Edward Macken (1) African letters (2) Crimea Diary (3) Rev. F. Freese's Recollections of G (T/S). All these are also in photostat at St Antony's College, Oxford, Middle East Centre. (4) Letters on religious and social subjects, researched by Lord Elton circa 1951 but cannot now be located by owner.

Gravesend Public Library, J. Robson T/S; press cuttings; Proceedings at unveiling of statue

Hart's Journal: Journal of Sir Robert Hart, Queen's University, Belfast

Harvey Papers: Letters of G. to Colonel Charles Elwyn Harvey. 5 in RE, 103 were researched (photostats) by MHR when in private hands before sale in 1973, since when dispersed. Present locations unknown

Jenkins Papers, see Boston

Larkin Papers, Gordon and related papers collected by Mr Antony Larkin of Milton-next-Gravesend

Library of Congress, Chaillé-Long Papers, *ms* reports of U.S. Consuls in China and Egypt

National Army Museum, letters to Sir Gerald Graham (only 11 out of 34 were bought at sale; rest dispersed, locations unknown); letters to Colonel Nugent.

National Library of Scotland, Sir Henry Elliot Papers (15 G. letters)
James Grant Papers (13 G. letters)
Sir William Mackinnon Papers (38 G. letters)

Olagnier Papers, owned by Mr John Brinton and his daughter Ms Alice Brinton

Oxford, Bodleian Library: a few miscellaneous G. letters; R. Hart letters.
Rhodes House: 241 G. letters to Rev. H. Walker

Palestine Exploration Society

Public Record Office, Cromer Papers
Foreign Office Papers

Public Record Office of Northern Ireland, Dufferin Papers
McKean Papers

Raitt Papers, Miscellaneous G. items collected by Miss Mary Hammond Raitt

Royal Botanic Gardens, Kew

Royal Geographical Society

Royal Engineers, Archives of the Institution of Royal Engineers: numerous miscellaneous Gordon manuscripts and memorabilia. Also the Archives of the Gordon School, Woking

Rusden Papers. Trinity College, Parkville, Victoria, Australia

Spiro Collection, Gordon and related letters collected by Mrs Brigitte Spiro of New
  York

Texas, University of Texas at Austin, Scarth Papers

Waller Papers see Oxford, Rhodes House
    Note: G's official correspondence, once in the Abdin Palace, Cairo, could not be
    located

Bibliography

WRITINGS BY GORDON

Notes on the Operations Round Shanghai in 1862–3–4 by Lt Col. C. G. Gordon, CB, RE, contributed to *The Professional Papers of the Corps of Royal Engineers*, Vol XIX, 1871. Re-issued in Book Form, with Introduction by R. H. Veitch, 1900, as *Gordon's Campaign in China*, by Himself.

This is the only writing by G. not edited by another hand, apart from letters and memoranda in the press, for which see Bulloch, J. M, *A Bibliography of the Gordons*, Aberdeen, 1924, pp. 129–175, a useful guide to all the literature to that date

CHINA: *General Gordon's Letters from the Crimea, the Danube and Armenia*, edited by D. C. Boulger, 1884

General Gordon's Private Diary of his Exploits in China ... edited by Samuel Mossman, 1885 (a garbled version of the *ms* notes written for Mossman, now in RE. *Not* a Diary.)

SUDAN 1874–79

Provinces of the Equator: Summary of letters and Reports of H. E. The Governor-General, Part I: Year 1874. Cairo 1877 (abridged and translated from G's letters in French: see below.)

Equatoria Under Egyptian Rule. G's letters in French, edited with introduction by M. F. Shukry. Cairo 1953

Colonel Gordon in Central Africa, 1874–1879, from Original Letters and Documents, edited by George Birkbeck Hill, 1881

Letters of General C. G. Gordon to His Sister M. A. Gordon [edited by Augusta Gordon] 1888 (selected, pruned, polished and often re-arranged from what is now the Moffitt Collection)

Reflections in Palestine, 1883 [edited by R. H. Barnes.] 1884

SUDAN 1884–85

The Journals of Major-Gen. C. G. Gordon C. B. at Kartoum (sic). Intro. and Notes by A. Egmont Hake [and by Sir Henry Gordon] 1885 (G. headed his *ms* journals: Events in the siege of Kartum, hence Sir Henry's title for his own book). Contrary to rumour, almost nothing was omitted.

LIVES

Like T. E. Lawrence, Gordon has a perennial fascination for biographers and novelists or semi-novelists. This list is confined to books which are wholly or largely based on research in manuscript or contemporary printed sources. Thus Lytton Strachey's *Eminent Victorians*, 1918, does not qualify.

Before 1900, in alphabetical order
[ALLNATT, ELIZABETH SURTEES] *Gordon: A Woman's Memories*, 1885
BARNES, R. H. AND BROWN, C. F. *Charles George Gordon, A Sketch*, 1885
BOULGER, D. C. *The Life of Gordon* ... 1896 (my refs. to 1 volume edition of 1910)
BUTLER, (GENERAL SIR) WILLIAM, *Charles George Gordon*, 1889
[FREESE, OLIVIA], *More About Gordon*. By one who knew him, 1894
GORDON, HENRY WILLIAMS, *Events in the Life of Charles George Gordon*, 1886
[GORDON, H. W., SR. AND JR.] *Gordon Memoirs* 1745–1887. Edinburgh, privately printed, 1895
HAKE, E. A., *The Story of Chinese Gordon* Vol 1. 1884, Vol 2. 1885
— *Events in the Taeping Rebellion*. 1891
LILLEY, W. E., The Life and Work of General Gordon at Gravesend n.d [1885]
MACAULAY, JAMES, *Gordon Anecdotes*, 1887
WILSON, ANDREW, *The 'Ever Victorious Army*,' 1878
WILSON, H. CARRUTHERS, *The Theology of General Gordon*, being introduction to a reprint of Joseph Hall's *Christ Mystical* showing Gordon's markings

After 1900 in chronological order
BLUNT, WILFRID, *Gordon at Khartoum*, 1913
ALLEN, BERNARD, *Gordon in the Sudan*, 1931
— *Gordon in China*, 1933
ELTON, LORD, *General Gordon*, 1954
NUTTING, ANTHONY, *Gordon, Martyr and Misfit*, 1966
MARLOWE, JOHN, *Mission to Khartum: The Apotheosis of General Gordon*, 1969
CHENEVIX-TRENCH, CHARLES, *Charley Gordon: An Eminent Victorian Reassessed*, 1978

OTHER WORKS CITED

Gordon has attracted an extensive literature, together with the political, military and social biographies and histories of the period. This list is confined to works cited in the text or the References and Notes. Place of publication is London unless otherwise stated.

ADYE, SIR JOHN. *Recollections of A Military Life*, 1895

ATKINS, J. B., *Life of Sir William Howard Russell*, 1911

BARNES, SIR KENNETH, *Welcome Good Friends*, 1958

BEAUVOIS, LUDOVIC MARQUIS DE, *The Conclusion of a Journey Round the World*, 1872 (translated from *Voyage Autour de Monde*, 1868.)

[BELL, C. F. MOBERLY] *Khedives and Pashas*, 1884

BLUNT, WILFRID, *The Secret History of the English Occupation of Egypt*, 1907

— *India under Ripon*, 1909

— *Gordon at Khartoum*, 1911

BUTLER, SIR WILLIAM, *An Autobiography*, 1911

CARR, CALEB, *The Devil Soldier*. New York 1992

CHILDERS, SPENCER, *Life and Correspondence of H. C. E. Childers*, 1901

CHURCHILL, RANDOLPH S., *Winston S. Churchill*, I. 1966

CROMER, LORD, *Modern Egypt*, I. 1908

CUZZI, GUISIPPI, *Fifteen Years A Prisoner of the False Prophet*. Sudanese Heritage Series No 3, Khartoum. 1968 (Italian edition published 1900)

ESHER, VISCOUNT (REGINALD BRETT), *Journals and Letters*, 1934

— *Cloud Capp'd Towers*

— *To-day and To-morrow*, 1910

GALBRAITH, J. K., *Mackinnon and East Africa, 1878–95*, 1972

GESSI, ROMOLO, *Seven Years in the Sudan*, 1892

Gladstone Diaries, The Vol XI 1883–1886, ed. by H. C. G. Matthew, Oxford 1990

GRAHAM, SIR GERALD, *Last Words with Gordon*, 1887

GREGORY, J. S., *Great Britain and the Taipings*, 1967

HARRISON, SIR RICHARD, *A Life in the British Army*, 1908

HILL, RICHARD, *A Biographical Dictionary of the Sudan*, 2nd ed. 1967

KINGLAKE, A. W., *The War in the Crimea*, Vol 9. 1888 ed.

KUSEL, BARON DE, *An Englishman's Recollections of Egypt.*

LONG, C. CHAILLÉ, *Naked Truth About Naked People*, 1876

— *The Three Prophets*, 1884

— *My Life in Four Continents*, 1912

LEES-MILNE, JAMES, *The Enigmatic Edwardian.*

LYALL, SIR A., *Life of the Marquis of Dufferin and Ava*, 1905

LYSTER, THOMAS, *With Gordon in China*, 1891

MALORTE, BARON C., *Here, There and Everywhere.* [1894]

NUBAR PASHA, *Memoires.* Beirut (Librarie de Liban) 1983

OLIPHANT, LAWRENCE, *Haifa,* 1887

POOLE, STANLEY LANE, *Sir Harry Parkes,* Vol I. 1894

— *Sir Charles Moore Watson,* 1919

POWER, FRANK, *Letters from Khartoum*

PRESTON, ADRIAN (ed.) *In Relief of Gordon: Lord Wolseley's Campaign Journal*

REDMAYNE, SIR RICHARD, *Men, Mines and Memories,* 1942

SANTI, PAUL AND HILL, RICHARD, *The Europeans in the Sudan 1834–1878.* Oxford 1982

SINKER, R., *Memorials of the Hon Ian Keith-Falconer,* 1888

SLATIN, SIR RUDOLF, *Fire and Sword in the Sudan,* 1896

SMITH, RICHARD J., *Mercenaries and Mandarins,* New York 1978

STEPHENSON, SIR FREDERICK, *At Home and On the Battlefield,* 1915

STRANGE, T. BLAND, *Gunner Jingo's Jubilee*

TAYLOR, L. E., *The Irrepressible Victorian,* 1967

TENNYSON, HALLAM, *Life of Alfred Lord Tennyson,* 1897

VANBRUGH, IRENE, *To Tell My Story,* 1948

VANBRUGH, VIOLET, *Dare To Be Wise,* 1925

VEITCH, R. H., *Sir Andrew Clarke,* 1905

— *Sir Gerald Graham, V.C.,* 1901

VESTER, BERTHA SPAFFORD, *Our Jerusalem*

VICTORIA, *The Letters of Queen Victoria,* Second Series, Vol 3 ed. by G. E. Buckle, 1928

[VINER, G. A.] *Sir Henry William Gordon, KCB.,* 1953

WHYTE, FREDERICK, *The Life of W. T. Stead,* 1927

WILSON, SIR CHARLES, *From Korti to Khartoum,* 1886

WILSON, SIR C. RIVERS, *Chapters From My Official Life,* 1916

WINGATE, SIR REGINALD, *Mahdiism and the Egyptian Sudan,* 1891

WINGATE, SIR RONALD, *Wingate of the Sudan,* 1955

WOLF, LUCIUS, *Life of the First Marquess of Ripon,* 1921

WOLSELEY, VISCOUNT, *The Story of A Soldier's Life,* 1903

WORSLEY, ALAN, *Land of the Blue Veil,* 1940

WRIGHT, S. F., *Hart and the Chinese Customs.* Belfast 1950

Many magazine articles throw light on one aspect or another. Details of those cited are at each reference concerned.

Index